A MORE PERFECT LEGACY

A MORE PERFECT LEGACY

A Portrait of
Brother Ephrem O'Dwyer, C.S.C.
1888–1978

by

BROTHER PHILIP ARMSTRONG, C.S.C.

UNIVERSITY OF NOTRE DAME PRESS

Notre Dame   London

Manufactured in the United States of America

Photos: Archives of Holy Cross Eastern Brothers
Province and Midwest Brothers Province

Library of Congress Cataloging-in-Publication Data

Armstrong, Philip, C.S.C.
    A more perfect legacy : a portrait of Brother Ephrem
O'Dwyer, C.S.C., 1888–1978 / by Philip Armstrong.
        p.   cm.
    Includes bibliographical references and index.
    ISBN 0-268-01414-0 (alk. paper)
    1. O'Dwyer, Ephrem, 1888–1978. 2. Congregation of
Holy Cross—Biography. 3. Congregation of Holy Cross—
History. I. Title.
BX4705.035A76   1994
271'.79—dc20
[B]   94-15933
                                                            CIP

 ♾ *The paper used in this publication meets the minimum requirements*
of the American National Standard for Information Sciences—Permanence of Paper
for Printed Library Materials, ANSI Z39.48-1984.

. . . These pages will have sufficient sequence to connect the past with the present, and to place us in a position to view, in retrospect and in prospect, our mission as Brothers of Holy Cross. With us, as with all men, there is a natural tendency to judge things in the light of what exists today, leaving out of our calculations the fact that *we are heirs to all the ages in the foremost files of time*, and forgetting that in very many cases the faithful departed should be given credit for the success we attribute to ourselves and to our generation. If we are faring well, we might humbly and wisely seek the cause in the vision and sacrifices of a preceding generation. And if, perchance, we find some ills in our inheritance, it is for us, the living, to improve upon the past and thus leave a more perfect legacy.

Brother Ephrem O'Dwyer, C.S.C.
"The First Hundred Years"

Contents

V. REMINISCENCES OF BROTHER EPHREM

Foreword

This portrait of Br. Ephrem O'Dwyer is long overdue. Two or three brief biographical sketches of the first provincial of the brothers' province in the United States have been produced over the years, but circumstances made it impossible to complete a major project until now. As we celebrate the 175th anniversary of the founding of the Brothers of St. Joseph, this book by Br. Philip Armstrong offers us a fine analysis of the life and work of Br. Ephrem.

This view of Br. Ephrem affords us a better understanding of the unusually gifted man and his decisive role in the development of the Congregation of Holy Cross, and helps us appreciate his contribution both to Holy Cross and to the Church.

When the Congregation of Holy Cross was granted papal approval in 1856, the Decree of Approbation described the community as *an institute composed of priests and laymen who mean to be united by a covenant of friendship in such a fashion that each society preserves its own nature, neither one prevailing over the other.* From the outset, Father Basil Moreau, founder of the congregation, proposed a governmental structure that, he hoped, would safeguard this "covenant of friendship" based on equality and mutuality. History, however, would soon show how difficult it was for the congregation to develop so that the priests and brothers would truly live and work as equal partners.

In an unprecedented manner, Fr. Moreau structured the Congregation of Holy Cross as a partnership of lay and clerical religious joined together in unity and equality to serve the Church. The congregation has had to search throughout its history for ways to make this model of religious life truly operative. Always present has been the danger of assimilating Holy Cross to the more prevailing and familiar model of the clerical congregation in which brothers play a significant part, but without a true sense of equality and complementarity between the lay and clerical roles. More accustomed to the clerical paradigm, the authorities in the Church have often found difficulty in understanding the implications of the nature of the religious family proposed by Holy Cross.

Br. Ephrem emerged as a natural leader of the brothers at a time when the originality of the model proposed by Holy Cross was in danger of being lost. To preserve the original intuition of the founder, Holy Cross required a strong leadership figure among the brothers, a man who, by his wisdom and fortitude, would guide them toward the firm establishment of their place in the congregation. Br. Philip shows with remarkable clarity how Br. Ephrem O'Dwyer became the central figure in this effort.

When in the late thirties the congregation discerned the need to develop an alternate organizational structure, Br. Ephrem worked assiduously to represent the perspective and interests of the brothers. Then, as the new structures provided greater autonomy for the brothers through the establishment of a homogeneous and autonomous province, Br. Ephrem became provincial superior of the brothers in the United States and toiled at forming a strong and vibrant group of lay religious. Later, when a general chapter mandated the reorganization of the swiftly developing single brothers' province into three geographical units, he agreed to lead the new vice-province in the eastern part of the United States.

Although Br. Ephrem was not a theologian and did not utilize theology as such to argue the place of the brothers in the Church and in a congregation constituted of both lay and clerical religious, his approach was the expression of his clear understanding of the Church and of the place of brothers in it.

Br. Philip has chosen to focus on a period of twenty-five years, 1931–1956, in the life of Br. Ephrem and to analyze through his actions during these years his contribution to the development of the Brothers of Holy Cross. In 1931 Br. Ephrem was appointed treasurer for both the United States Province of Holy Cross and the University of Notre Dame. This role brought him to the center of the province, where he rapidly recognized his ability and sharpened his determination to defend the rights of the brothers. From then until the reorganization of the one province into two homogeneous units in 1945, he labored to clarify the status of the brothers and played a central role in the process of redefining the needed structures. From 1946 to 1956 Br. Ephrem was provincial of the brothers' province in the United States. In the Preface Br. Philip explains that the man he writes about is not perceived as a saint, and the study surely exhibits no hagiographical overtones. Rather, Br. Ephrem is portrayed as *one of us* with his strengths and weaknesses, with his greatness, but with his very human struggles.

A More Perfect Legacy is an important book for members of the Congregation of Holy Cross as well as for those interested in the history of the congregation. But it should also be valuable to anyone seeking to study the place of religious brothers in the Church. The quest by Holy Cross for its own identity as a congregation built on the basis of equality and mutuality between the lay and clerical members raises important questions today for the Church. Its calls us to continue our reflection on the very nature of religious life.

Br. Ephrem's efforts to clarify the role of brothers in a congregation composed of priests and brothers is important for us today. The Church still grapples with the basic concerns that were voiced by Br. Ephrem more than sixty years ago in his letter to Fr. John F. O'Hara. Because the issues so central to Br. Ephrem remain relevant today, a study of his life and work is particularly important in the present efforts of the Church to come to grips with the reality experienced.

Br. Philip is well placed to understand the significance of Br. Ephrem O'Dwyer. In his early years of formation and as a teacher, Br. Philip was acquainted with Br. Ephrem. Later, as provincial and assistant general, the author was called to pursue in our time what Br. Ephrem had initiated so well. Br. Philip's own sense of the Church, his capacity to understand the complexity of the questions raised by the life and work of Br. Ephrem, have permitted him to reveal a portrait that should be of more than common interest and importance for Holy Cross and those associated with it, as well as for the Church.

Claude Grou, C.S.C.
Superior General

Preface

During 1991 the Congregation of Holy Cross marked the completion of 150 years of apostolic presence in the United States. Upon their arrival in America from Le Mans, France, in 1841, a priest and six brothers immediately began their involvement in education and parochial ministry in the diocese of Vincennes, Indiana. The following year a contingent struck out for the northern part of the state and established what became the University of Notre Dame du Lac just outside South Bend. Thus in 1992 the university celebrated its 150th year. All of Holy Cross joined in noting these significant events.

In 1995 the 175th anniversary of the foundation in 1820 of the Brothers of St. Joseph, later known as the Brothers of Holy Cross, will be celebrated. In 1835, their founder, Fr. James Dujarié of Ruillé in the diocese of Le Mans, for health reasons handed over the administration of some seventy brothers to Fr. Basil Moreau, who had already organized a group of a dozen or so priests into a small community in Le Mans. The two units began to attract further members and develop as the Association of Holy Cross, to be approved by Rome in 1857 as the Congregation of Holy Cross.

Given the sesquicentennial celebrations, it was only fitting that some concrete forms of acknowledgment be arranged. Several events were scheduled throughout the United States among Holy Cross religious, articles and publications were assembled marking different aspects of the occasion, and Holy Cross gathered locally along with their fellow workers in ministry to pay tribute to the memory of their community ancestors and to renew and refocus their vision of mission for both present and future.

In considering what the special contribution of the Midwest Province might be for 1995, Br. Thomas Moser, provincial, together with his council chose among other things to add to the relatively small collection of historical research and writing done on the community's evolution in North America. Several options were discussed, and the choice eventually fell on the unique personality of Br. Ephrem (Dennis) O'Dwyer, first provincial superior of the brothers' autonomous and homogeneous province.

Br. Ephrem, an immigrant Irishman, represents the contribution a single individual can make to the Church through the growth and development of the overall mission of a religious congregation. For a very significant half century in the history of the United States he exerted an impact through teaching, administration, and other forms of influence in the schools of the community as well as by internal ministry to the religious themselves. His temperament suited him to move confidently and aggressively into areas of progress that others, accorded less respect and support, would never have been able to manage. Among the brothers in the United States he was the person most instrumental in forging the particular strength of unity which has carried the relationship between the priests and brothers of the congregation through some long and difficult years of development as a unique community of religious. He led the brothers into a new arena of distinct societal identity and responsibility as lay religious after over a hundred years of fairly limited autonomy within the parameters of the Church's then cleric-dominated hierarchy of authority.

A man with a clear vision of what the brothers ought to be within the overall context of the Congregation of Holy Cross, with a faith and determination nourished by his Irish upbringing and temperament, and with an unflagging perseverance despite personal limitations and external hardships, Br. Ephrem was a logical choice as the first provincial. Both at that time and subsequently the judgment of his peers and of history has recognized that the right man at the right time in the right place was without question Br. Ephrem O'Dwyer.

As I was completing my term as assistant to the superior general and was in dialogue with the provincial about possible ministry in the province, he suggested that I think of writing something fairly substantial about Br. Ephrem, a project never undertaken before. I accepted the challenge enthusiastically despite some misgivings based on lack of experience in formal research, writing, and publishing.

Br. Ephrem was provincial when I joined Holy Cross in 1950 out of a high school conducted and staffed almost exclusively by some very dedicated Holy Cross Brothers. I grew up in South Bend, my father being Alumni Director at Notre Dame from 1926 till his retirement in 1967. His association with the university enabled me as I grew up to become familiar not only with the nature of the congregation in general, but with individuals—priests and brothers—who had influenced its development in the United States. One of these was Br. Ephrem, whom my father remembered as a most understanding officer of the university when he was treasurer and a staunch supporter during the very difficult times of the Depression when the Alumni Office was struggling for relevance, identity and sure footing, indeed for its very existence. The two shared an inclination toward wit and humor, as well as a recognition of the great need for and value of Catholic education on every level.

In Holy Cross my personal association with Br. Ephrem was quite limited. He was the provincial; I was a very young brother, first in formation and then as an inexperienced teacher newly engaged in my first mission assignments. I recall only one occasion, apart from the official visit made by Br. Ephrem to Dujarie Hall, the scholasticate, when I was invited to sit down with him in his office at the Community House to discuss my future. With others, I shared the sentiments of awed respect for Br. Ephrem, as well as a judicious fear of his wit, temper, and dominating personality, housed as these were in a small but intensely compelling physique. I knew this man had done much for the congregation and was universally recognized, even beyond the province, as "the brother in charge." I experienced in him both the determined administrator and the sensitive father figure who, despite his reputation, could make a young brother feel quite at ease in the presence of his unfailing competence.

Over the years I have enjoyed the experience of being a teacher, an administrator, a local superior, a provincial, and an assistant general, all capacities in which Br. Ephrem also served, and from that perspective I appreciated in a special way the monumental challenges he faced with such apparent equanimity but at such great personal cost. Thus the labor of writing something of a portrait of the man has taken on the nature of a personal privilege as well as a useful province project.

Beginning initial research into the archives, I became aware that, given the amount of available documentation on Br. Ephrem, only a full-sized book would do him justice. His own business correspondence, letters and other material written about him by others, a bit of personal intracommunity correspondence which he apparently believed destroyed long since, and his own formal writings served as the foundation on which I was able to recall my experience of the man as well as to learn many interesting and valuable things about him which, if ever directly alluded to in the past at all, had somehow wandered off into that nebulous state between reality and legend or had been altogether forgotten.

At the outset it was my intention to focus only on the ten-year period during which Br. Ephrem served as provincial of the single brothers' province in the United States, that is, 1946–1956. It soon became clear to me, however, that to attempt that task without giving attention to his earlier years in Holy Cross and the multiple events and directions that led to his being the natural choice as first provincial would be a disservice to the readers and a well nigh impossible feat if I intended to portray anything of the reality of Br. Ephrem during his term as provincial.

As a result, the first part of the book is organized as something of a loose chronological development centered around significant events in Br. Ephrem's life. Then it settles on a topical and largely anecdotal treatment of his personality and methodology as provincial from 1946 to 1956. An appendix is added, comprised of reminiscences of religious who were to some degree his contemporaries and who graciously agreed to submit their recollections of him in writing, on tape, or in an interview.

I thought it useful to devote an entire chapter to the significant letter Br. Ephrem directed in 1933 to Father John F. O'Hara, later Cardinal Archbishop of Philadelphia, when Fr. O'Hara was acting president of Notre Dame. The letter summarizes particularly well not only the respectful administrative diplomacy of Br. Ephrem, but the fairly typical circumstances existing in the congregation which Br. Ephrem felt needed to be addressed.

And though chapters 8 to 14 provide a purposeful partitioning of several aspects of Br. Ephrem's role as provincial, I thought it helpful to introduce those portions more generally in chapter 7 by an overview of his ten-year term as provincial.

Chapter 16 is an almost inexcusably brief consideration of Br. Ephrem's life and work beyond 1956, the time at which the one brothers' province subdivided into three units and Br. Ephrem became the first vice provincial in the East. I consciously chose not to flesh out at greater length events between then and his death in 1978. My hope is that this significant period in his life and in the development of the Eastern Brothers' Province will some time soon be given the close attention it deserves, although it would have proved unwieldy in the context of this present volume.

I was also forced to make a choice as to how to work with the rich material which came to me in the form of reminiscences. Eventually I decided that, rather than trying to insert them here and there in the text, I would let them speak for themselves in an appendix. Br. Ephrem, himself writing about an illustrious predecessor of his at Notre Dame, Br. Alexander Smith, utilized this method in his book, remarking that the reminiscences on Br. Alexander submitted by several alumni of the university were such as to suggest their forming on their own a chapter that could easily serve as an epilogue. Following his example, I incorporate the reminiscences at the end, hoping that the unique flavor of direct experience found in most of them might be left undisturbed and so they might serve in their own unimpeded way to highlight the essence of Br. Ephrem.

Several portions of the book offer lengthy quotations from Br. Ephrem's letters or from documents of persons in direct contact with him concerning more or less momentous events or circumstances in the development of the congregation and its apostolates. At the risk of incorporating what might appear to be superfluous material, I have chosen to include certain documentation in its entirety, or nearly so, that the intent of the writer might come through more clearly in the first person and the situation be revealed more thoroughly and accurately by those directly involved.

The anecdotal approach has been generously utilized as well in some chapters to exemplify and confirm by multiple incidents the particular qualities of personality or technique attributed to Br. Ephrem.

In the process of writing about Br. Ephrem I have been brought back repeatedly to the realization that I certainly have not been preparing a brief meant in any way to advance his cause for canonization. Tendencies I might have developed over the years toward idealizing him or softening the rougher fibers of his personality ground quickly to a halt as I immersed myself in the available documentation and found, as will be noted often in the text, an eminently humble but human Br. Ephrem in the midst of the glitter and notoriety normally associated with his highly consequential achievements. No one denies his accomplishments. Some claim that, given the times and circumstances, none other than he could have been as successful in so many ways. Many remember his pastoral and compassionate approach to his religious. But in the same breath these considerations are offset by recollections of the harsher realities of his temperament—his irascibility, his sometimes too stubborn determination, his occasional swift and seemingly inconsiderate shifting of manpower, his impetuously barbed tongue. The fact is that while the manner of his life was heroic, and while he did value and struggle to practice the virtues associated with the religious life, there are few, if any, who will assert that he was ostensibly a man of heroic virtue. He was rather one of us, and it was his participation in the common reality of life among his peers, however much he seemed to stand out, which made it possible for him to lead so effectively and for us to follow.

Where he led—and where we followed—was always forward in the context of a well-calculated vision of mission, always toward openness to the developing future of apostolic ministry in the Church, discerning and responding to the needs of the times as brothers in the Congregation of Holy Cross. His contribution to the overall sense of identity of the congregation and in particular of the brothers as lay religious was significant, and those of us who benefitted from his magnificent leadership enjoy much today for which to be grateful to him.

Acknowledgments

I would like to thank in a special way Br. Thomas Moser, provincial at the time of the inception of this project, for suggesting that I consider undertaking such a work and for organizing and supporting the ambient in which it could be accomplished. I am indebted to those who in any way participated in the retrieval of archival material, especially Br. Wilbert Leveling, Midwest Province archivist, Fr. James Connelly and Mrs. Jacqueline Dougherty of the Indiana Province Archives, Br. Laurian LaForest, archivist of the Eastern Brothers Province, Br. Jeremias Mysliewiec, archivist of the South-West Province, and Fr. Jacques Grisé, archivist for the General Administration in Rome. I am grateful as well to Mr. Peter Lysy of the University of Notre Dame Archives for his assistance. Living and working at the Holy Cross Brothers Center has been a supportive experience, and I owe gratitude to my brothers in Holy Cross whose persistent but discreet curiosity and staunch encouragement have contributed in no small way to my pursuing the project with enthusiasm. And without the unfailingly patient and professional help and advice of my brother Douglas, the mysterious intricacies of the computer would have thwarted me and rendered the timely publication of this work impossible.

Worthy of special mention are the many diocesan ordinaries, Holy Cross provincials, and presidents and principals of Holy Cross institutions who have contributed generously to the completion of this project. They are: Most Rev. Howard Hubbard of Albany, Most Rev. Francis Hurley of Anchorage, Most Rev. Thomas Dailey of Brooklyn, His Eminence Joseph Cardinal Bernardin of Chicago, Most Rev. Daniel Pilarczyk of Cincinnati, Most Rev. Anthony Pilla of Cleveland, Most Rev. Adam Maida of Detroit, Most Rev. John D'Arcy of Fort Wayne–South Bend, Most Rev. Norbert Gaughan of Gary, Most Rev. Daniel Cronin of Hartford, His Eminence Roger Cardinal Mahoney of Los Angeles, Most Rev. Thomas Kelly of Louisville, Most Rev. Edward McCarthy of Miami, His Eminence John Cardinal O'Connor of New York, Most Rev. Patrick Flores of San Antonio, Most Rev. Pierre Dumaine of San Jose, His Eminence James Cardinal Hickey of Washington.

The Holy Cross personnel include Rev. Edward Malloy of the University of Notre Dame; Br. Charles Krupp of LeMans Academy; Br. Charles-Edouard Smith of Collège Notre-Dame; Rev. Robert McInroy, provincial of the English Canadian Province; Rev. Carl Ebey, provincial of the Indiana Province; Br. Richard Gilman of Holy Cross College; Dr. Patricia Hayes of St. Edward's University; Br. Walter Davenport of Holy Cross High School in River Grove, Illinois; Br. John Paige of Bishop McNamara High School; Mr. Joseph Connell of Moreau High School; Br. James Spooner of St. Edward High School; Br. Paul Kelly of Archbishop Hoban High School; Br. William Nick of Notre Dame High School; Fr. Bartley MacPhaidin of Stonehill College; Rev. Pierre Guitton, provincial of the Province of France; Br. Donald Blauvelt, provincial of the South-West Province; and Br. John Gleason, provincial of the Eastern Province of Brothers.

Those who have in any other way advanced the publication of this anniversary volume are deserving not only of my personal sincere thanks, but of that of the entire congregation.

If the spirit of Br. Ephrem comes alive through these pages and serves once again to influence among both brothers and laity the perpetuation of the vision and animation which motivate our evolving Holy Cross apostolates today, the project will have been well worth the effort.

Significant Dates in the Life of Brother Ephrem (Dennis) O'Dwyer, C.S.C.

1888 — May 25, born in Hollyford, Kilkummin, diocese of Cashel, County Tipperary, Ireland

1907 — March 23, entered postulate (now Old College) at Notre Dame, Ind.

1907 — July 6, received habit and entered novitiate

1908 — July, student at Dujarie Hall

1909 — July 6, first profession of vows

1913 — July 9, perpetual profession of vows

1911–1919 — teacher at Central Catholic High School, Fort Wayne, Ind.

1918 — February 5, became naturalized American citizen, Fort Wayne, Ind.

1918 — July 23–September 7 (Sergeant as of Aug. 23), Co. A, 411th Reserve Labor Battalion, Quartermaster Corps, U.S. Army, Fort Zachary Taylor, Ky.

1919 — August, first principal of Boys' Catholic High School, Evansville, Ind.

1923–1924 — sabbatical year, completed studies at Notre Dame, Ph.B. in education, July 1923, and M.A., July 1924; determined current scholastic/degree status of all brothers

1924–1925 — returned to Evansville to complete term as superior/principal at new Reitz Memorial High School

1925–1928 — superior and principal at Cathedral High School, Indianapolis

1928–1931 — superior and principal at Holy Cross High School, New Orleans

1931 — assigned to Holy Trinity High School, Chicago. Assignment rescinded after several weeks

1931–1933 — Treasurer at the University of Notre Dame, Notre Dame, Ind.

1932–1938 — Provincial councilor on the administration of Rev. James Burns, C.S.C.

1933–1938 — instructor at Notre Dame during summer school; Holy Cross Seminary, Dujarie Hall

1938–1945 — assistant General during the administration of Rev. Albert Cousineau, C.S.C.: Community House, Notre Dame, Ind.; Rhode Island Ave., Washington, D.C.; 4 E. 80th Ave., New York City. While resident in New York City, spent significant time teaching at the juniorate in Valatie, N.Y.

1945–1946 — member of interim provincial council of Rev. Thomas Steiner, C.S.C.

1946–1956 — first provincial of the autonomous homogeneous brothers' province of the United States

1956–1962 — vice provincial, then provincial of the newly established Eastern Brothers' Vice Province, then Province. Residences at Flushing, N.Y., and then West Haven, Conn.

1957 — May 30, received honorary LL.D., St. Edward's University, Austin, Tex.

1960 — June 5, received honorary Doctor of Laws degree, Stonehill College, North Easton, Mass.

1962–1963 — teacher and accountant, Moreau Hall, North Easton

1963–1964 — teacher and steward, St. Edmond's Academy, Wilmington, Del.

1964–1965 — teacher, Holy Cross High School, Flushing, N.Y.

1965–1967 — teacher, Bishop Hendricken High School, Warwick, R.I.

1967–1970 — assistant to treasurer, Holy Cross High School, Flushing

1970–1971 — retired, Holy Cross High School, Waterbury, Conn.

1971–1972 — retired, Holy Cross High School, Flushing

1972–1978 — retired, Dujarie House, Holy Cross Brothers Center, Notre Dame

1976 — May 16, honorary Doctor of Laws degree conferred by the University of Notre Dame

1978 — August 21, died at Dujarie House, Holy Cross Brothers Center, Notre Dame; buried at St. Joseph Cemetery, Valatie, N.Y., August 26

I

Early Years and
Emergence in Holy Cross

1

The Early Years (1888–1931)

Dennis Patrick O'Dwyer, later to be known as Br. Ephrem, was born on May 25, 1888, at Gurth, Hollyford, in the diocese of Cashel, County Tipperary, Ireland, and baptized two days later. He was the seventh of eleven children born to Dennis O'Dwyer and Margaret Ryan O'Dwyer. His parents, with the help of the children and a few hired hands, farmed a hundred acres of land some three miles from Hollyford. Of Dennis's ten siblings—Josie, James, Marion, Matthew, Bridget, Patrick, Thomas, Nora, Michael, and John—seven eventually emigrated to the United States. Marion became Sr. Columbina, C.S.C. She died in 1958 at St. Mary's College, Notre Dame, Indiana, after serving for over forty years in many roles, particularly education.

It is related that one of his brothers, probably Michael, became engaged to a girl in Ireland and gave her the ring just before emigrating, unwed, to the United States. While in America he lived in Roosevelt, Long Island, New York, with his sister Josie, who had married Peter Quinn. Michael stayed in the States for thirty-five years or more, only then returning to Ireland. From stories told, the girl to whom he had been engaged was still waiting. He married her and returned almost at once to the United States—alone. It is said his brother Dennis thought him somewhat unbalanced.[1]

Br. Ephrem remained as close to his family over the years as his religious profession and geographical imperatives permitted, and it is clear from reminiscences submitted to Br. Franciscus (Robert) Willett in 1964 by several nieces that there was a bond between Br. Ephrem and his family which no barrier could affect or impair. Sr. M. Alexis (Margaret Mary O'Dwyer), a niece in Swansea, Wales, wrote: *I would like to say that Br. Ephrem means far more to me than an Uncle. He is in a sense a second Father. I have corresponded with him for over thirty years and he with me. I think we (all nieces and nephews) have sensed in him a very deep affection for us all, without partiality, which has endeared him to all of us. Whenever he could he made visits, however short, to all the families and we all felt that his love and affection were all embracing.*[2]

Sr. Mary Patrick, C.S.J., a niece in North Valley Stream, N.Y., commented: *As a child growing up I remember my dear father*

3

(R.I.P.) saying how Br. Ephrem thought about his community ahead of his family. His community was everything to him. As I grew older and entered religion I knew just what my father meant.[3] From Nora Keegan, a niece, came this testimony: *My mother (Br. Ephrem's sister) often said that as a young man he was very determined and not easily baffled by disappointment.*[4] And Mrs. Mary M. Langhans, also a niece, wrote: *When I think of my uncle—I think of him as a humble man—a kind man—a just man—a man young in spirit—and above all a spiritual man.*[5]

SCHOOLING

Regarding his early years and schooling, Br. Ephrem submitted some notes to Br. Franciscus for a biographical project the latter was undertaking at the request of the provincial but which was eventually abandoned. The notes provide the substance of the following paragraphs.

The parish of Kilcommon (or Kilcummin) had two associated or subordinated parishes, those of Hollyford and Rear Cross. The pastor lived in Kilcommon but had a resident assistant in each of the other dependent parishes. These three parishes, being in the northwest part of County Tipperary, were somewhat hilly, and though they boasted good farm and dairy land, they did not compare with the "golden vale" that constituted most of Tipperary.

The O'Dwyer farm of about a hundred acres was in the townsland of Gurth, nearly three miles north of the village of Hollyford. The land was reasonably good for agriculture and dairy purposes, and a few acres provided excellent peat or turf, which, when cut into brick-sized sods and sun dried, made a much more pleasant and effective fire than coal or wood.

Hollyford school was about half a mile south of the village. It was a one-story stone building of some six rooms, three for boys and three for girls, with somewhat fewer than a hundred students in each department. The boys were taught by Mr. James Lamb and the girls by Mrs. Lamb. Each had an assistant.

From the crossroads of Gurth a small stream, called the Multeen, paralleled the road to the village. The group of boys and girls who traversed this road back and forth to school consisted of O'Dwyers, Ryans, Greens, Butlers, Touhys, Quigleys, and Kennedys, the Ryans being the most numerous. The little river afforded the local schoolboys much pleasure and some inconveniences. It was a challenge to jump across the stream at certain places, and on many an occasion those who followed the dare did not quite make the jump. There were a few places where there was good swimming. Treading the river in shallow areas, it became quite a sport to catch the mountain trout by hand. In the spring of the year an occasional salmon branched off the River Suir and came up the Multeen. This going after trout or salmon was not difficult, because in summer nearly all the boys went barefoot to school and wore pants that ended well above the knees.

The summer vacation from school was limited to the month of August. The school day began about nine and ended at three, with about an hour out for lunch and play. All students brought their lunches. Every day a half hour was devoted to religion, that is, to the catechism. The children of the only non-Catholic family in the area were excused from the class.

There was no local provision for education beyond what might be considered the equivalent of junior high school. About half the program consisted of English and mathematics, the latter including the elements of algebra and geometry. Those who sought more education and could afford it had to cycle to or board in such nearby towns as Tipperary, Thurles, or Doon, where religious sisters and brothers conducted secondary schools.

Hollyford had a post office and telegraph service, but electric light and power did not make an entrance into this rural area until about the second decade of the twentieth century. Houses depended on kerosene lamps and candles for light.

Tipperary town published a newspaper, but most people got Cork or Dublin papers by mail. Dancing and card parties were common in the long winter evenings, gatherings being held at convenient farmhouses here and there.[6]

At about fifteen Dennis sensed a vocation to the lay religious life and left for Dublin to become a postulant with the Irish Christian Brothers at Baldoyle. He remained only about six months with the brothers. Nothing is known with certainty of his reason for leaving, but one former Holy Cross missionary to Bengal remembers having spoken with an old Irish Christian Brother in Assam, India, in 1938 who told him that indeed he remembered Dennis O'Dwyer, the youth "sent away because of his ungovernable temper" from the postulate in Baldoyle.

At this point Dennis made his way to Belfast in Northern Ireland, where he took up clerical work for three years. It is reported that, perhaps part time or sporadically, he also functioned in the role of bartender during this time. However, he had not given up the notion of a vocation to the religious life.

THE CALL TO HOLY CROSS

It was while he was engaged in the north that, at the age of eighteen, he met Fr. Patrick Carroll and Br. Aidan O'Reilly, native Irish religious of Holy Cross who had returned from America to their homeland to recruit new members for the congregation. Whatever Dennis O'Dwyer saw in these two gifted and congenial men was enough to stir once again his interest in the religious life and to convince him he had a vocation to Holy Cross. When the two recruiters returned to the United States in early 1907, he accompanied them, having first made a quick trip back to Tipperary to say goodbye to his family before embarking.

The threesome arrived at Notre Dame, Indiana, the United States Province headquarters of the Congregation of Holy Cross. Established in France in 1837 by Fr. Basil Anthony Moreau, a priest of the diocese of Le Mans, the infant community had almost immediately sent missionary priests, brothers, and sisters to North America to labor among the Native Americans and to help bishops—mostly French in origin themselves—in the education and pastoral care of the Catholic families in their dioceses. Holy Cross religious found themselves in the diocese of Vincennes in Indiana and a year later they were given a parcel of land in the northern part of the state where they were to found an educational institution and were free to minister to the nearby residents. The fledgling school had subsequently grown into what was even in 1907 the prestigious University of Notre Dame, and dozens of ministries by both priests and brothers had fanned out into numerous towns of the Midwest as well as areas much farther afield. By the time Dennis O'Dwyer arrived at Notre Dame, it was a well-established institution of learning, catering to students on the elementary, preparatory, and higher levels.

Immediately upon his arrival, Dennis entered the postulate of the Brothers of Holy Cross, located in what is known as the Old College building near the ancient log chapel next to St. Mary's Lake. The date of the beginning of his postulancy is noted as March 23, 1907.

A little more than three months later, on July 6, he received the habit of the brothers of the Congregation of Holy Cross and began his two-year novitiate program in the building north of St. Joseph's Lake. It was customary after the first, or canonical, year of the novitiate, for the novices to begin or continue their studies prior to taking vows at the end of the second year, so in 1908 Dennis, having taken the religious name Br. Ephrem, moved to the western edge of the Notre Dame campus to the newly erected Dujarié Institute, a large house of studies built exclusively for the brothers. The building was named for Fr. James Dujarié, like Fr. Moreau a priest of the diocese of Le Mans in France. Fr. Dujarié had founded the Brothers of St. Joseph, a group of educators, in 1820. Fifteen years later, when Fr. Dujarié became too ill to care for them himself, the group merged with Fr. Moreau's Auxiliary Priests to form the Association of Holy Cross in Le Mans.

At Dujarié Institute, Br. Ephrem finished whatever remained of his secondary education at the Notre Dame Preparatory School. On July 6, 1909, he made his first profession of vows as a Holy Cross Brother and immediately began his undergraduate studies at the University of Notre Dame. He spent the next two years full time in this pursuit as a temporarily professed religious.

YEARS OF ACTIVE MINISTRY

In 1911 Br. Ephrem was assigned by his provincial superior to teach at Central Catholic High School in Fort Wayne, Indiana, a secondary school begun by the brothers only two years earlier as part of a congregational plan of expansion for that society into the field of secondary education.[7] From then until 1923 he spent every summer except one in study at Notre Dame.

It was during the summer of 1913, on July 6, six years after leaving Ireland and four years after his initial profession of the evangelical counsels, that Br. Ephrem committed himself perpetually to God through the vows of poverty, chastity, and obedience in the Congregation of Holy Cross.

The single summer he did not return to South Bend to continue his university studies was an unusual one. That was the summer of 1918. In February of that year Br. Ephrem had received his papers in Fort Wayne confirming him as a naturalized United States citizen. During the previous year the country had entered the Great War on the side of the Allies, and young men were in 1918 still being called up for service to their country in the military. Br. Maurus O'Malley, in a paper entitled "Portrait of a Builder," written for the Holy Cross History Conference in 1987, claims that, as a result of *a protest by the Lutherans in the city who could not understand these young men at Central Catholic not having to serve their country*, and a misunderstanding by the local draft board of the laws regarding exemption from military service, Br. Ephrem and three other brothers— Edmund Gaynor, Gregory Rozczynialski, and Anthony von Bersum— were conscripted into the army. The four brothers were obliged to report to Camp Zachary Taylor, Louisville, Kentucky, for induction into the 411th Reserve Labor Batallion. This they did on July 23.

Meanwhile, the wheels were turning at Notre Dame to secure their exemption *ex post facto* and release from military service. Finally, after formal appeals to the draft board and to the Selective Service Department in Washington, the four were declared divinity students and were honorably discharged from the service. Br. Ephrem's discharge is dated September 7, 1918, two months before the end of the war. Interestingly, within a month of his induction into service, Br. Ephrem had been promoted to sergeant, perhaps an indication that his leadership and administrative capacities, which later would be exhibited so clearly in Holy Cross, were evident even to the army.

The person principally responsible for securing the discharge of the four brothers was Col. William Hoynes of the Law School at the University of Notre Dame. In the "Brief Treating [the] Case of the Notre Dame University Teaching Brothers at Fort Wayne," which eventually resulted in the release of the brothers from the Army, Col. Hoynes described the brothers as *Brothers of the Congregation of Holy Cross and the University of Notre Dame* who were *regular ministers of religion serving in the Central Catholic High School, Fort Wayne, Indiana.* The identification with the university was not without its advantages. The colonel concluded his brief by saying: *Finally, it is hardly to be supposed that the honorable District Board will insist upon taking by force for the army these four teaching Brothers from an Institution which has so greatly exceeded its share of patriotic service—men who are undoubtedly exempt in the light both of the facts and the law. Thus to take them would be a source of unmerited humiliation and embarrassment to the University, a challenge to its enviable record of patriotism and faithful support of the Government, an exasperating hindrance to its eager purpose to serve the country efficiently in the present crisis, a deplorable invasion of the legal rights of men protected by the canons of religion and the principles of law, and a mockery of the sense of justice which we fondly attribute to free government.*

I feel assured, gentlemen of the Board, that you will unhesitatingly correct the unfortunate error casually made in this case, undo the menaced wrong to these teaching Brothers, respect their undoubted status as regular ministers of religion and restore them to Class V, as provided by law and in furtherance of justice.[8]

The colonel unabashedly relied on the prestige of the university to insinuate that membership in Holy Cross and integral association with Notre Dame were inseparable. Perhaps at the time and given the circumstances, this approach seemed appropriate to superiors, who must have been shaken by the implications of the whole situation.

An amusing incident is recounted about Br. Ephrem's time in the military by a niece or cousin, Noreen Raleigh of Nyack, New York, who wrote to Br. Franciscus Willett on February 1, 1964, that a shy young soldier in love, unable to write appropriately and convincingly to his girlfriend at home, asked Br. Ephrem to pen such a letter for him, which he did. The response was so encouraging that the young man asked Br. Ephrem to continue being his ghostwriter. However, after several such letters had been written, Br. Ephrem was rather suddenly mustered out of the military. Regrettably no record remains of the fortunes of the young man and his very effectively wooed girlfriend.[9]

After receiving their discharge papers early in September, the four religious made their way quickly back to Fort Wayne to take up their teaching duties once again at the outset of the new academic year. No doubt there were some absorbing tales recounted in the recreation room of the brothers' house by Sergeant O'Dwyer and the others.

The following year, Br. Ephrem was assigned to open the Boys' Catholic High School in Evansville, Indiana, as first superior and principal of the diocesan institution. The school was housed in temporary quarters and plans were made at once for a new building. Br. Ephrem was assisted the first year by Br. Benedict Gervais.

A 1920 incident prompted Br. Ephrem to speak out on an issue which created some confusion in the congregation and among observers. An article appeared on October 30 in the *Scholastic*, the student magazine at the University of Notre Dame, reporting that *at the* instance *of Rev. James Burns, President of the University of Notre Dame, the Xaverian Brothers would establish a new Notre Dame Prep School at Interlaken, Rolling Prairie, Indiana. The protests and denials came in large numbers and caused a correction in a following issue of the* Scholastic.

Br. Ephrem was not the type of person to let a slight get by and so he did take positive action in this regard. He wrote a letter to Rev. Charles O'Donnell, the Provincial at that time, inquiring about the project, and asking why our Brothers were passed over, and informing him of the opinion of the clergy in Evansville, Indiana, who wondered about the qualification of the Brothers in their local Catholic High when they were not chosen by their own Community to conduct such a prep school. Father

O'Donnell answered in a very kind manner, explaining carefully this misunderstanding about the entire affair. The matter seemed to die at this point.[10] In the end, no school was opened in this rural location twenty miles west of Notre Dame, but nearly fifteen years later the novitiate of the U.S. Province of priests and brothers was built and conducted across the lake from this Interlaken site.

A STUDENT ONCE MORE

In 1923, after four years at the school in Evansville, Br. Ephrem was asked to take a year away from his teaching and administrative work to return to Notre Dame to complete his undergraduate study in philosophy and earn a master of arts degree in education. Thus, during the 1923–1924 academic year he was occupied with his classes, no doubt welcoming both the relief from administrative work and the opportunity to gain a solid foundation for his accreditation in the state of Indiana's institutes of secondary education. His record shows that, out of some thirty-five university courses taken over the years, he received marks well above 90 percent (even a couple of 100s) in all but three of them, and those three were in the high 80s. He was clearly a superior student. During this year he lived at Dujarie Hall and is listed in the Notre Dame Bulletin as its director.[11] Already at this early stage of his life and career in Holy Cross, Br. Ephrem was very conscious of the discrepancies which existed between the need for qualified teaching brothers and the attention that had up to that time been paid by the congregation to their training and accreditation despite legislation passed in previous general chapters mandating the upgrading of the brothers' credentials for teaching and despite the goodwill of many, brothers and priests alike, in improving the professional competency of the teaching brothers. This continued to be a problem. Two or three years later in an undated letter Br. Ephrem wrote to Fr. William Cunningham, a noted educator in the congregation at Notre Dame: *You will pardon me for saying that in Communities it seems that one can get very little done until all the members are convinced of what is needed; and there are always some traditionalists who won't be convinced.*[12] His point was that courses available at Notre Dame were not providing for an educational training of the brothers that would bring them up to the requirements of the state of Indiana. In the memo, among other details, he said, *Personally I think the State plan is the better one because it is more practical. Besides, Notre Dame cannot stand* high in educational circles if graduates are classed only as second raters.

During his sabbatical year of 1923–1924 Br. Ephrem made use of whatever spare time he could find—with the blessing and collaboration of the university authorities and the assistance of some brother scholastics—searching the files of the Office of Studies to clarify and summarize the academic status of all of the brothers of the U.S. Province. As Br. Maurus points out, *The University generously allowed Brother to assist in straightening out the academic records of the Brothers who attended summer sessions for a period of years, working in one field or another. Consequently with Brother Ephrem working on their files it was found that during the summer of 1924, a large number of Brothers received their degrees. The timing for this was perfect because licensing of teachers was now required by the States and the brothers were prepared because of this work by Brother Ephrem.*[13] Br. Ephrem himself, in a letter written to Br. Maurus O'Malley in April, 1963, admitted: *As a result that summer 1924 17 old-timers got degrees: Bernard* [Gervais], *Aidan* [O'Reilly], *Daniel* [Schott] *and many others who had been plugging for years.*[14]

Br. Ephrem is listed for 1924 in the Notre Dame Bulletin as a "Special Instructor in Summer Session, Education."[15] Somehow between all his other duties and interests, Br. Ephrem put together a forty-eight-page vocation booklet for use in recruiting brothers for the province. The publication was revised in the thirties and remained the basic vocation promotion literature into the forties.

BACK TO THE SCHOOLS

Br. Ephrem returned to Evansville in the fall of 1924 to resume his position as superior and principal at what was to become, in January of 1925, the new Reitz Memorial High School on Lincoln Ave. No doubt supervising the move to the graciously modern and expansive new facilities was both a fitting challenge and something of a reward to a man who had accomplished so much during a single sabbatical year. At the end of the year he returned to Notre Dame to teach education classes once again in the summer school session.[16]

Br. Ephrem's talents and capabilities were by this time no secret to the congregation, and they were very much appreciated by his superiors. Now that Evansville was settled into its new quarters and running smoothly, the provincial asked Br. Ephrem to move north to the capital city of Indianapolis to take over the administration of

Cathedral High School as superior and principal, a post he held until 1928.

One task for Br. Ephrem at Cathedral was negotiating with the bishop concerning an increase in salary for the brothers. The principal had no problem getting an impromptu oral agreement from the bishop when he met him by chance one day, but after that was unable to secure the written assent without which the increase could not take effect. Br. Ephrem wrote to his provincial, Fr. Burns, that he was willing to contact the bishop directly and settle the matter once for all, but wanted to check with Notre Dame first to be sure he was not overstepping his authority. He said, *I have not spoken with the Bishop, as I do not know how much pressure you want me to use. I do not know whether you want to go as far as to insist on $700, beginning from last September. In my letter to the Board I gave reasons sufficient for the increase. I shall follow whatever instructions you give me, but I am anxious to know how far I should go. I naturally wish to act under the full approval of the community administration.*

Fr. Burns told Br. Ephrem to act at once by means of a personal visit to the bishop, and to remind the prelate that even $700 was not up to the $800 mandated by the chapter, but it would be adequate for the year.[17]

In 1927 Br. Ephrem was appointed by Fr. James A. Burns to chair a special committee concerning studies for the brothers. Brothers Agatho Heiser and Bernard Gervais were the other members. The minutes of the provincial council meeting state: *Hereafter no one will take classes in Summer school without permission from the committee.*

DEVELOPING ROLE IN HOLY CROSS

The role of Br. Ephrem in the Congregation of Holy Cross continued to emerge. Since its founding by Fr. Moreau as a congregation of priests and brothers, neither society of which was intended in any way to dominate over the other, there had been difficulties of greater or lesser magnitude between the two societies regarding the equality of their rights and privileges. Successive superiors general and provincials had dealt with issues as they arose, and in the early part of the century chapter legislation had attempted to preserve the overall unity of the congregation while simultaneously assuring the protection of the rights peculiar to each of the two societies—lay and clerical.

When the general chapter of 1926 was called, Br. Ephrem was elected a delegate from among the brothers, whose numbers at the chapter, by constitution, had to be equal to those of the priests of the congregation. Although he had been professed only seventeen years and had been in roles of authority only seven years, his astuteness and honest frankness were already widely known in Holy Cross. His research in 1923–24 on the academic status of the brothers, his administrative roles in two schools, his teaching in Fort Wayne, and his becoming something of an unofficial spokesman for the interests of the brothers' society gained him the backing required for election to the chapter. Though the youngest member of the chapter in community rank and precedence, he nevertheless exerted some influence during the meetings. Br. Edward Sniatecki, former archivist for the Midwest Province, wrote a brief monograph on Br. Ephrem in 1983, and in relation to this time in Br. Ephrem's life states that, *During the General Chapter of 1926, of which he was a member, when the early consideration of Autonomy for the Societes was made, Brother Ephrem presented an impressive view of the Brothers' Position on the subject. Religious of both Societies realized then the stature of this person and esteem for him grew.*[18]

In 1928, after teaching education courses again during summer school at Notre Dame, Br. Ephrem was once more transferred, this time to Holy Cross High School in New Orleans, another of the community schools whose administration had earlier in the century been turned over to the brothers. Br. Ephrem remained in New Orleans for three years, making an impact on the school program and expanding its facilities. The provincial council minutes for July 27, 1928, note the following: *Brother Ephrem submitted in writing an itemized statement of expenses for improvements at Holy Cross College, New Orleans. It totaled $15,000. This would necessitate application to Rome to make the loan. After some discussion it was agreed that Brother Ephrem would make necessary repairs up to the amount of $6,000.00 which he will borrow and then take up the matter with the Provincial Council.* And the minutes of the council meeting held October 30 note: *Brother Ephrem asked to borrow an additional $18,000.00. He had exceeded the amount of his budget, because, he said, of rotten beams, rusted pipe, weak cores found when repairs were begun. Expense to date $20,000.00 additional. Council agreed to ask for permission from Rome for $20,000.00 to validate this expenditure.* Though there is no specific mention of it in available documentation, there can be no doubt that the Great Depression beginning in October of 1929 adversely affected Br. Ephrem's administration of Holy Cross College. It seems likely some of the practices and attitudes of frugality he both exemplified and demanded later as principal and provincial resulted not only from his origins on a small farm in Ireland but from this experience as well.

In 1929 the State of Indiana issued to Br. Ephrem a teacher's license covering the following subjects: English, Commercial, Mathematics, French, Latin, History, Social Studies, and All Science. In 1933 he was granted a principal's license by Indiana as well. These licenses were, he noted, valid also in Louisiana.[19]

As a local superior, Br. Ephrem was an ex-officio member of the 1931 provincial chapter and served as a member of the chapter committee on finance. It was during this chapter that he was nominated for a second term as superior/principal at Holy Cross High School in New Orleans, but because of certain circumstances he declined re-election. At the time it was the practice that superiors were chosen during provincial chapters. Men whose names were under consideration had by protocol to absent themselves from the chapter room during the discussion. Br. Ephrem objected to this method, believing that the person being considered ought to have a chance to clarify issues for his electors or defend himself from prejudicial criticism if necessary.

Shortly after the chapter, on July 9, Br. Ephrem was assigned to Holy Trinity High School, Chicago, a short-lived move for him as events were to prove.

2

At Notre Dame (1931–1938)

Br. Ephrem had almost no time to settle into Holy Trinity High School in Chicago, for within six weeks he was summoned to Notre Dame. The provincial council minutes of September 11, 1931, remark: *At a special meeting of the Provincial Council Brother Florence was removed from the office of Provincial [Treasurer] and University Treasurer, Brother Ephrem was appointed Provincial [Treasurer] and University Treasurer temporarily.*[1] For whatever reason, the change was deemed necessary, and Br. Ephrem stood out in his superiors' minds as the best replacement.

It is clear that from the outset Br. Ephrem did not find everything to his liking as university treasurer. For one thing, the congregation and the university, not to mention the entire country, were enveloped by the debilitating and discouraging effects of the Great Depression. There appeared to be no amelioration likely in the foreseeable future. And now Br. Ephrem had been asked to supervise the administration of the financial assets of not only the U.S. Province of Holy Cross but of the constantly growing University of Notre Dame. Br. Agatho Heiser, superior of Dujarie Hall at Notre Dame, where Br. Ephrem had taken up residence, wrote to Fr. James Burns, provincial, saying: *Br. Ephrem will again become* red-headed *instead of auburn-headed if he stays on the Treasurer's job. Too bad you couldn't have been listening to what he was telling me last night as to what's wrong with the system in the Treasurer's Office. It was as good as a show, but I don't think he shares my opinon that it's funny.*[2]

After less than a year on the job as treasurer, Br. Ephrem felt constrained to tender a letter of resignation to his provincial on the grounds that he wished to pursue his proper vocation, that of a teaching brother. In the letter he cited several sources—legislation from a general chapter, the words read at the conferring of the religious habit, and a portion of a circular letter from the superior general in 1912—to support his assertion that as a teacher he was misplaced in the treasurer's office. He complained that for him life at Notre Dame was *very disagreeable, lonesome, lacking in companionship,*

15

*foreign to the community fellowship I have been accustomed to.
I have spent most weekends dumbly smoking in my room, dis-
tracted only by the Sunday paper.* He had recently gone on business
into two of the high schools and found himself rejuvenated in the
academic atmosphere.

But it was the job itself that was his primary concern. *It is true
that the work I have had is not difficult. It requires some attention
and responsibility, and I might add that the position is honorable
and has been so recognized. But the work is terribly mechanical
and monotonous. It is a penance to remain day after day chained
to a desk, doing things that scarcely ever call for a constructive
idea. Such work is far removed from my training and inclination.
Counting nickels may keep the hands busy, but it galls the mind
that is thinking of something else. Medallion buffaloes have not
the same interest as youthful faces.* He concluded deferentially, *It is
not pleasant to write in this strain to one who has been more than
kind to me, but the fear of the buffalo is upon me.*[3] In addition,
Br. Ephrem felt the job to be depressing and the accommodations
productive of loneliness. He lived at the time in the Administration
Building in a corner of the Students' Infirmary near the treasurer's
office. At times he was obliged to transfer cash and securities, mostly
negotiable, from banks in South Bend to institutions in Chicago. For
this task he was professionally bonded against loss or robbery, but he
had to presume that, should it come to it, he himself was personally
expendable. Feeling the burden of the job, he went to the Holy Cross
Sisters' hospital in Columbus for a checkup and was advised to get
out of his present position.[4]

Whatever his estimation of the task and its impact upon him,
Br. Ephrem's term as treasurer was effective. One lay employee
charged with the administration of a significant office at the university
during those years recalled the sympathetic and fair treatment he
was unfailingly accorded by Br. Ephrem relative to fiscal difficulties
resulting from the Depression and its effects. Twenty years later, when
Br. Ephrem was provincial, this same university official was quick to
respond to the request that he help organize and implement a fund
drive for a new consolidated Catholic high school in South Bend.[5]

PROVINCIAL COUNCILOR

While treasurer at the University of Notre Dame, Br. Ephrem was
at the same time a member of the provincial council under Fr. James
Burns. In reply to a request he had received from Fr. Burns to give

some thought to the governmental structure of the university vis-à-vis the religious there, Br. Ephrem penned a suggestion or two. No doubt the perennial question had arisen concerning the president's being at the same time local superior, and Fr. Burns was apparently searching for some method of dealing with the difficulties inherent in having the local authority structured in this way. Br. Ephrem detailed a two-page outline of the relationship between the two offices—superior and president—and indicated how he believed they could be separated without doing damage to either and how in that way both could be of greater service to the religious on the campus.

Dear Father Provincial,

No doubt there was some humor and a grain of seriousness in your suggestion yesterday that I put on paper a few ideas about "running or ruining" Notre Dame. Well, you at least gave me something to do for a couple of hours, and if I have succeeded in bringing an idea to the surface somebody might be able to develop it. I have made no effort to cover details in the dual administration of Notre Dame.

What I have tried to do is outline a dignified position for the president and necessary freedom for his council in academic matters and in certain business matters bound up with the academic.

The second idea is to place the spiritual and temporal control of the members under a local superior, and also to place the material control of the institution under a local council functioning independently of the academic council.

It seems to me we can find a practical demarcation between the functions of a president and the functions of a superior. The former is to deal with the public, with students, with professors. The latter is to look after community men and community property.

I have made no attempt to go into detail about our present system—about such big things as one man announcing a several million expansion program in the morning and defending the loss of a football game in the evening.

Several solutions may be possible. At present I have a hazy idea of two: 1. A president and a superior; 2. A president-superior with much of his authority delegated and defined.

The second plan seems to present the greater difficulties, for if certain authority is delegated (in such a way as to be effective) the holder of such delegated authority is practically a local superior, but by our rules and constitutions he cannot have such authority without being a superior. Moreover, the only one who could delegate such authority would be the superior himself, and he could take it all back again at will. Moreover, whether he delegated or not he could not refuse an appeal from the members.

I believe "the president and the superior" division of labor is within the freedom of our rules and constitutions, for the president would not be outside obedience to the local superior.[6] This farsighted approach to institutional administration eventually found adoption not only at the university but in most Holy Cross apostolic works.

It is not certain how temporary Br. Ephrem's appointment as treasurer was originally meant to have been, but, probably as a result of his earlier letter of resignation, along with other considerations, the obedience list published on July 13, 1933, shows Br. Ephrem assigned to teach at Notre Dame and to be replaced as treasurer by Br. Engelbert Leisse.[7] He taught classes at the university, at least during the summers, from 1933 to 1938.

THE GENERAL CHAPTER OF 1932

During his term as treasurer, the 1932 general chapter of the Congregation of Holy Cross took place. This chapter assumed rather notable proportions because of the ongoing issue of equality between the priests and brothers in the community. After the 1906 chapter had failed in the eyes of some brothers to address adequately what they felt to be flagrant instances of inequality, a move was made by several in the lay society to request of Rome the separation of the priests and brothers. Rome refused the request out of hand, but insisted that any underlying causes of discontent be dealt with immediately. Steps were taken in this direction and a level of satisfaction was eventually achieved, yet when Br. Ephrem came as a young religious to the 1926 general chapter, there still remained elements of feeling that provoked his making a significant intervention concerning societal relationships. Even this early, he was perceived by confreres of both societies in the congregation as a diplomatic and effective proponent of the rights of the brothers.

Then between the 1926 chapter and that of 1932 a serious attempt had been made by a handful of priests to foment feeling toward total separation between the priests and brothers and the formation of something of a federation which would allow each society its own authority structure, including the general level. Several religious, mostly priests, had written position papers on the topic. Fr. Cornelius Hagerty, later an ardent advocate for the brothers, and their chaplain for many years at Dujarie Hall, Notre Dame, undertook to present a lengthy paper on the relationship between the priests and the brothers. In the concluding sentences, Fr. Hagerty wrote: *In the past, the two societies under one administration have been almost merged into one and under another administration they have reappeared as quite distinct. From now on the two societies ought to be distinct and remain distinct unless by a decisive act they are merged or fused or amalgamated, for good and all, into one society. We ought to be done forever with sleight of hand and ambiguity.*[8]

The membership of the congregation was looking forward to a definitive settlement of the unrest which seemed always to lurk beneath the normally cordial relations between the brothers and priests. Those who believed the problem lay in the very nature of the congregation and who counseled total separation were quickly silenced by the action of the chapter. The fact was that, as confirmed by the visit of the superior general a few years later, the vast majority of priests and brothers everywhere favored the preservation at all costs of the fundamental unity between the two societies; and Rome, in its approval of the legislation which emerged from the chapter, affirmed the nature of the congregation and again counseled forceful dealing with the concrete issues that had given rise to proposals for separation.

Fr. James A. Burns, provincial, was a leading proponent of unity within the congregation, as can be seen from his formal intervention on July 7 on the floor of the 1932 general chapter. Br. Maurus O'Malley, in an appendix to his "Portrait of a Builder," quotes the entire intervention. This impassioned speech reveals that Fr. Burns believed there was no solid argument against "equal franchise" for priests and brothers. He dismissed claims that priestly dignity was being undermined by equality between lay and clerical religious, arguing that it was rather more a question of legal qualifications which affected joint interests. He cited exemption from military service for both priests and brothers as a sign that the Church approved equality. To counter the Church was unthinkable. On a practical level, Fr. Burns insisted he had not seen any signs of equal franchise working to the detriment of the interests of the priests. If there were claims that brother councilors experienced conflict when dealing with matters proper to priests, Fr. Burns rejected them, saying that in all his years as a councilor he had never seen any such conflict. He said he could not recall a single instance in which the brothers blocked a move in which the priests were concerned. For example, the brothers did not object to the setting up of Moreau or Holy Cross Seminaries or to the expansion of the university.

One of the capitulants, Fr. Matthew Schumacher, had raised the question whether he himself and others really knew what they were about at the time of their profession. Fr. Burns emphasized, *I knew what I was about when I made my vows in this Congregation, nor can I say that there has been a substantial change in the Congregation since then. The founder of the Congregation was a holy man. The trouble has been that Father Moreau has not been well known; it is only recently that he is becoming better known. He was a man of God, a man of tremendous zeal for God's glory. He had the specific gift of spiritual intuition.* And he referred to the practical consequences of collaboration: *What about the good that has been done by the priests and brothers working together, much of which would not otherwise have been done? Notre Dame is the fruit of the union of priests and brothers. Were it not for that union there would be no Notre Dame today; it would never have been founded. Father Sorin came here with one priest and five brothers. Notre Dame University was founded, continued and developed; it could not even have existed, were it not for the union of the two societies.*

Fr. Burns recalled the sacrifices the brothers had made, both for the congregation and for the university. *What a debt this Congregation owes to them! . . . This present difficulty is not a heredity trouble between priests and brothers. I know its whole story. It is only twenty-five years old. It is a modern move.* When he had been rector of Sorin Hall, Fr. Burns continued, *there was no such trouble as this. We worked in harmony. This is not a hereditary problem, as it has been called here. It doesn't come from equal franchise. It comes from circumstances that could and should be avoided.*

He concluded, *There is grave unrest in this Province, but I do not agree with Father Schumacher that the unrest is in the nature of the Congregation. A plan has been devised to eliminate difficulties. Let us consider that plan. We will never be entirely free from difficulties. With good will on the part of all, we will be able to work our way out of most of these difficulties.*

It can be seen, then, that even as early as 1932 the type of compromise eventually to be settled upon at the 1945 general chapter was being investigated, that is, separation of the priests and brothers into homogeneous and autonomous provinces, yet still united at the level of the general administration. Br. Ephrem was to play an important role in the emergence of this compromise, as will be seen.

At the general chapter of 1932, Br. Ephrem continued to solidify the image he was creating in the congregation. A proven teacher and administrator, a man at home with calculations and projections, and a shrewd but entirely frank community diplomat, he was becoming one of the best known lay religious in Holy Cross. Traditional thinking and practice that placed all authority automatically in the hands of the clerics was changing, due largely to the increasingly extensive education the brothers were receiving and the organized efforts being exerted to situate brothers in positions of authority and responsibility in institutions operated and governed by them. Br. Ephrem's impact was such that he was appointed to the council of the provincial, Fr. James A. Burns, along with Br. Engelbert Leisse and Frs. Matthew Walsh and John O'Hara.[9]

ELEMENTS OF GREATER RESPONSIBILITY

It was while on Fr. Burns's council at Notre Dame that Br. Ephrem was given significant responsibilities in the congregation. In November of 1932, Br. Ephrem, along with Br. Agatho Heiser, was commissioned to draw up a precise definition of a teaching brother. The object of the task was to clarify expectations regarding recruitment and formation of teaching brothers as differentiated from the coadjutor, or non-teaching, brothers. Later in the month Br. Ephrem submitted a preliminary report. In it he made some recommendations, proposing that the new criteria not be made retroactive but be allowed simply to accomplish their purpose over time. He wrote: *The intention of the classification is not to create a social distinction or to claim rights or privileges for either group. There is but one society of brothers, but the Constitution says that these are divided into TEACHERS and COADJUTORS. There is therefore an obligation on the administration to make this classification and in some practical way to define the limits of each group.* He then drew up some specific elements proper to each group, suggesting that by classifying the brothers clearly as teaching or coadjutor, each group would be protected, motivated and encouraged appropriately toward the accomplishment of its goals. On November 29th the provincial read to the council the report of Brs. Ephrem and Agatho—and Br. Engelbert Leisse, who had also been drawn into working on the project.

On September 26, 1933, the council adopted a resolution referring to the manner of determining the status of teaching and working brothers. A copy of the resolution was inserted into the minutes of that meeting. While it is not directly attributed to Br. Ephrem or to either of the other two brothers, it is obvious that Br. Ephrem had a major role in its writing. The recommendation produced by the committee had five points, each covering an aspect of recruitment and formation policy as applicable to teaching brothers or working brothers, as well as the characteristics necessary in each case to retain membership in a given classification. Point 5 was no doubt a clarification of a previously ambiguous situation: *Perpetually professed members who have completed the course of studies for teaching, or who after teaching for some time are obliged to forsake the classroom, or those who for exceptional reasons may have to fill important positions, shall still be regarded as teaching brothers.*[10] The "important positions" referred to were likely school administration and some forms of internal service to the congregation itself.

While the focus of this study was on the nature of the teaching brothers, Br. Ephrem was sensitive to the needs of the coadjutor brothers. In a memo dated April 7, 1933, to Fr. James Burns, provincial, he suggested: *Some system should be worked out for giving professional training to our coadjutor brothers. Most of them are fitted for nothing.*[11]

Earlier in 1933 the provincial council approved the establishment of a summer school at Cathedral High School in Indianapolis *in order to afford opportunity to Brothers to fulfill requirements for teaching experience. The school is to last from six to eight weeks. Br. Ephrem was to visit Indianapolis and make arrangements.*[12] The approval stemmed from a request Br. Ephrem had made to Fr. Burns to consider the following in council: *At present no graduate of Dujarie is qualified to teach in Indiana. Those who go to Indiana schools cannot be listed as teachers the first year. Those who go elsewhere are not eligible to come back to Indiana as teachers until they first qualify. I would suggest that we have a high school summer school at Indianapolis for this practice teaching. Many of our students there pay $15 for summer courses at the public high schools. A $10 fee would cover our expenses.*[13]

An important legal step was taken in the history of the congregation in the United States in November of 1933 when the council met to discuss *in a preliminary way the proposed incorporation of the Congregation in the United States. Fr. Walsh and Br. Ephrem were appointed to report on the proposed articles of incorporation as drawn up by Mr. Farabaugh.* Gallitzin Farabaugh was the head of the South Bend law firm retained by the congregation. Br. Ephrem's role in the council was to learn the intricacies of the proposed articles of incorporation and, along with Fr. Matthew Walsh, interpret their appropriateness to the rest of the council.[14]

In 1934 the triennial provincial chapter was held at Notre Dame. As a provincial councilor, Br. Ephrem appeared on the list of ex-officio capitulants. He participated as a member of the Committee on Foundations and Foreign Missions during this chapter.[15] A special committee was also set up, apparently by the provincial, to function during the chapter. Its nature is not specified in the minutes of the July 4 meeting of the council. Besides Br. Ephrem, the other members of the committee were Frs. John O'Hara and Thomas Crumley, and Br. Agatho Heiser. And then on July 12 the council minutes recorded obediences for the members of the province. Br. Ephrem was listed as Business Manager of the *Ave Maria*, the community-owned magazine, and a member of both the provincial and local councils.[16]

VOCATION PROMOTER

The year 1935 found Br. Ephrem burdened with the additional position of recruiter of vocations for the brothers' society, a duty to which he was appointed in July. The council minutes for the meeting of August 26 remark that the expenses of Br. Ephrem in connection with vocational work were to be charged to the house account of Sacred Heart Juniorate, Watertown, Wisconsin, the institution to which the vocations office was attached.[17]

At the end of July 1936 Br. Ephrem wrote to Fr. Burns from Waveland, Mississippi, saying that he was enjoying the month-long vacation he had been permitted and was about to spend the month between August 15 and September 15 recruiting vocations in the South.[18] In 1924 Br. Ephrem had written an informative and interesting 48-page vocation recruitment pamphlet for prospective candidates. In 1937 he revised the pamphlet into a forty-page edition with attractive pictures. This booklet, a comprehensive description of the life of a brother in Holy Cross, became the basic text for vocation promotion among the brothers for many years.

In October 1938 Br. Ephrem wrote to the provincial, Fr. Burns, giving an unsolicited but very revealing account of his work as vocation recruiter over the previous fifteen months. Among other details included he stated: *When I was recently in Albany, N.Y., Brother*

John Baptist took me to task for not getting more boys for Water-town. It is possible that some others think as he does. Normally, I might be worried about his comments or about what others think in this respect, but I cannot say that I am. However, since you asked me last evening how the recruiting is coming, I believe I should give you a partial report. I do not think it is necessary, un-less you so wish, that I should go back over several years and check all admissions, defections, average length of time at Watertown— and final products.

When I was assigned this work I found I had some definite convictions regarding quantity and mass production and the effect of these things on FINAL PRODUCTS.

While I believe that neither I nor anyone else can actually make vocations, I do believe that most of the vocations we receive will be what we are satisfied they should be. Quantity is easier to get than quality. No inquiry which came to me has been neglected. Cor-respondence has been continued with every correspondent who seems to be worthwhile, and all letters are kept on file. There are a great many who seem to get pleasure out of writing us weekly letters, getting all our literature and then doing nothing. Such are the soft, scrupulous, timid; also those who have good intentions and bad conduct. I doubt if there is a vocation among fifty such. I have preferred to keep in touch with those who want to give something, young fellows who have positive natures and are capable of doing hard things in the fulfillment of their vocation. I have turned down no good coadjutor prospect. I have worked for teacher candidates who are in the fourth year of high school or have high school finished; and not so very many below this level have applied, and those who looked good have been accepted.

Since I took over the work in July 1935, 86 candidates have been accepted at Watertown. 50 of these had high school com-pleted. Of the total of 86, 25 have left to date, 17 having left from Watertown and 8 from the Novitiate.

After giving further statistical information and analyzing factors impinging on the vocation picture, he concluded: *I have not given these statistics and the enclosures for any justification of the course I have pursued. I am doing all I can according to my own convictions, and as yet I have received no order or even an offi-cial hint to change them. Anyway, I feel pretty sure that God is not conditioning Holy Cross vocations on me or my ideas. It is desirable that others should also aid by prayers and by a personal interest in recruiting. The more numerous the applications the greater the possibility in selections.*[19]

It is clear from this report that Br. Ephrem, whatever his other duties, took the work seriously and pursued it with energy and enthusiasm. In subsequent years he was many times to remark that the future of Holy Cross was in its young people, and he spared no effort or attention in looking after them, even personally when possible. His philosophy of operation was forward looking and sound, and not too far removed from more recent strategies of vocation promotion.

In connection with his work on vocations but also because of his expertise in building and administration, Br. Ephrem was asked by the provincial to spend some time at Valatie, New York, at the eastern postulate there. Br. Donard Proskovec, the superior, died suddenly at the age of thirty-one of a heart attack due to asthma, and a degree of uneasiness and confusion resulted among both faculty and postulants. Also, the postulate was in the process of finalizing plans to construct another house on the property to enlarge the capacity of the program. Br. Ephrem wrote to Fr. Burns from Valatie in April 1936, during his first visit there, and then again in November of that year, both instances having to do with construction and his supervision of it in lieu of any other brother knowledgeable along those lines.[20] Later, after he had become assistant general, he was to spend considerable time at Valatie assisting in the program by teaching courses in various subjects to the postulants.

A VALUABLE ADVISER

1937 found the province again preparing for a provincial chapter at Notre Dame. In June the delegates to the chapter were noted in the minutes of the provincial council. Br. Ephrem was duly listed as a capitulant ex-officio and a member of the Finance Committee. After the chapter the community obediences were formalized on July 20, with Br. Ephrem assigned to continue vocational work and to be a member of the provincial council.[21]

During his years on the provincial administration of Fr. Burns, Br. Ephrem was several times sent to visit schools operated by the Brothers of Holy Cross or to investigate possible openings in various parts of the country. Given his experience as teacher and administrator, his insight and practical suggestions were invaluable. In the years 1934–1935 Br. Ephrem made provincial visits to Gibault Home for Boys in Terre Haute, Indiana; Cathedral High School in Indianapolis; and Central Catholic High School in South Bend, which had just opened in the fall of 1934.[22] During the academic year 1935–1936 Br. Ephrem made the provincial visits to Cathedral High School, Indianapolis; Central Catholic High School, Fort Wayne, Indiana; Holy Trinity High School, Chicago; and Reitz Memorial High School, Evansville, Indiana. He wrote up reports of the visits for Fr. Burns. Fr. Thomas Steiner, assistant provincial, handled most of the other regular visits for Fr. Burns.[23] Br. Ephrem wrote to Fr. Burns from New Orleans on August 20, 1937, saying he had enjoyed his vacation and that he was leaving for Los Angeles to talk with the bishop there about land for a school. He discussed personnel problems that Fr. Burns referred to in a letter, and even offered to substitute for someone in the South Bend high school in the fall if a man needed to be changed from there at the last minute.[24] In May of 1938 the provincial council minutes note: *After Br. Ephrem's report on his inspection of Father Flanagan's Boys Home at Omaha council agreed that it could not now consider the question of taking over the home.*[25]

In the years to come Br. Ephrem was to experience serious health problems. The only hint of this impending situation during the years he spent at Notre Dame in the thirties was in March of 1938 when he was in Watertown, Wisconsin, recuperating from an operation, the nature of which is not indicated. Br. Ephrem wrote to Fr. Burns to report on the operation, and the provincial responded: *I was very sorry to learn that you had to have the operation without delay. On the whole, however, it will no doubt turn out all for the best. I am glad to know that the operation was completely successful, and that with a good long rest you will again be in first class condition. Do not try to hasten the process of recuperation, but rest there as long as the doctor thinks it advisable. I know you are in good hands.*[26] It is possible this operation was an appendectomy, the scar from which is noted years later on a medical report.

At the general chapter of 1938 Br. Ephrem was appointed to the general council as an assistant to the newly elected superior general, Fr. Albert Cousineau. His role at the general level of government was extremely important as well as influential, particularly in the light of the pressing business of bettering relations between the priests and brothers, an issue that, despite efforts and intentions, had not been wholly laid to rest at the 1932 chapter. It would become the principal agenda item at the general chapter held immediately after the Second World War.

II

Promoter of the Brothers

The O'Hara Letter (1933)

When he assumed the office of treasurer of the University of Notre Dame in August of 1931, Br. Ephrem became, ex officio, the secretary for the Board of Lay Trustees of the university and is listed as such in the bulletin of the university for the years 1931–32 and 1932–33.[1] Relieved of the job of treasurer in 1933, Br. Ephrem was succeeded by Br. Engelbert Leisse. Br. Engelbert was duly noted as both treasurer and secretary of the board until his own replacement in 1940. For some reason Br. Ephrem continued to function at least as recording secretary for the board, for it is his signature which is to be found on the minutes of their meetings from 1931 to 1940. At the end of that time, because of "community commitments," as he called them, he submitted his letter of resignation to the then president, Rev. J. Hugh O'Donnell. The commitments to which Br. Ephrem referred included his position as assistant to the superior general. In 1940 he moved to Washington, D.C., to live and work at the generalate.

THE PRESIDENT'S REPORT

Not long after Br. Ephrem had left the office of treasurer, on November 24, 1933, a meeting of the Board of Lay Trustees was held at Notre Dame. Fr. John F. O'Hara, acting president, prepared and delivered the President's Report, an annual statement of the current situation of the university. Fr. O'Hara was substituting for Fr. Charles O'Donnell, the poet-president, who was ill and who eventually passed away on June 4, 1934, at the age of forty-nine. Fr. O'Hara remained acting president from July 1933 until his own official appointment to that position in July 1934.

As part of the President's Report Fr. O'Hara related statistics regarding the education of young men in Holy Cross. This training, at the direction of the general chapter of the congregation, was partially funded by the university with a view toward the preparation of teachers and administrators for the institution. The eventual employment of such religious was meant to decrease significantly the amount expended on salaries for lay faculty and staff. The Board of Lay Trustees administered the fund and expected a regular accounting as to its status. As the acting president spoke, Br. Ephrem heard Fr. O'Hara describe how a substantial number of seminarians in the novitiate were being educated through this fund, and how many more in Moreau Seminary and Holy Cross College benefitted, as well as several young ordained priests engaged in higher studies. Nowhere was there a mention of even one brother's profiting from the available funds.

The omission, clearly not inadvertent, was a serious matter for Br. Ephrem. It alerted him to an existing condition, but, even more, it confirmed the experience of many brothers. The desired and expected equality meant to exist between the two societies in Holy Cross did not in fact exist always and everywhere, and the thorny problem of the relationship between priests and brothers was far from resolved, directives from Rome and chapter decrees to the contrary notwithstanding. Br. Ephrem felt that the brothers were being treated unfairly in this situation, even unjustly, by being excluded from participating in the funds available to the Congregation of Holy Cross for the ongoing education and training of its members.

From his earliest years in Holy Cross Br. Ephrem had spoken up for the rights of the lay religious in the congregation. He had gained the respect of both brothers and priests because of his capabilities as teacher and administrator, as well as his involvement in community matters. His being a delegate to the general chapters of 1926 and 1932 and his appointment to the provincial council of Fr. James Burns in 1932 were tangible signs of the deference he was accorded. He always sought to improve relations between the priests and brothers. He was a true son of Fr. Moreau, and the founder's intuition foresaw a tangible unity of purpose in life and mission between the two societies. Br. Ephrem would do whatever it took to foster and secure that unity despite obstacles erected and maintained along the way by the human reality of both societies.

And he was not one to run away from a confrontation. On the contrary, he saw here an opportunity to surface not only what had embarrassed and pained him personally in this instance, but also the more fundamental issues that gnawed away continuously at the delicate relationship between the lay and clerical members of the United States Province of Holy Cross.

Br. Ephrem harbored a vision for the brothers in the congregation, a vision based on fraternal equality, on professional leadership and competence, and on apostolic effectiveness whether in education or in other ministries both within and outside the congregation. Whatever impeded the momentum toward these goals was inimical to the image and concept of the brother in Holy Cross, of whom Br. Ephrem was an outspoken champion. Though prudently diplomatic in his approach to the resolution of sensitive issues, he was fearless, forthright, and persevering. More importantly, in the long run he was almost unerringly right.

Shaken by the implications of the report, Br. Ephrem agonized for some days over an appropriate response to the situation. If he said nothing beyond a few comments whispered to Fr. O'Hara during the meeting, the situation would most likely go entirely unnoticed and unaltered by both Fr. O'Hara and the board members and would serve only to exacerbate the ongoing frustrations of the brothers. In fact, the matter was of such a nature, Br. Ephrem felt, as to warrant the attention of the highest authorities in the Congregation of Holy Cross.

A RESPONSE FROM THE HEART

Accordingly, on December 3 Br. Ephrem drafted a lengthy letter to Fr. O'Hara, with copies and brief covering notices to Fr. James A. Burns, provincial, and Fr. James W. Donahue, superior general. A masterpiece of diplomacy, the letter nevertheless portrayed frankly and forcefully the status of the brothers in the United States Province and at the University of Notre Dame as perceived and experienced by perhaps the most astute and knowledgeable one among them.[2] It would be doing an injustice both to Br. Ephrem and to the significance of his letter to Fr. O'Hara not to include it in its entirety.

Dear Father O'Hara:

I know that you are a busy man and that you have little time to read a rather long letter. Still I believe that you would borrow from the night, if needs be, to peruse a letter dealing with the welfare of Holy Cross. I write in the hope that what I say may be received in the spirit in which it is written. If my words say other than my thoughts, I hope no offense will be taken. If they reflect my thoughts, which I try to keep charitable, they should not offend.

For you I have had the highest esteem; and it has been a plea- sure to associate with you in the Provincial Council, where each member is treated as a man. It is with sincere regret, therefore, that I have to record the keen disappointment that came to me upon hearing the Report of the President of the University which was recently presented at the meeting of the Board of Lay Trustees.

Before commenting on the immediate reasons for my disappointment, I must ask your patience until I try to put in writing the things that appear to me to be the bases of our different viewpoints; at least I shall endeavor to state briefly the influences that have been responsible for the viewpoint I hold.

The group relationship that has existed, especially during summer school, between priests and brothers at Notre Dame has not been ideal. The Brothers believe the fault does not lie with them; and I must frankly and honestly say that I share their opinion. The recollection of my two years' service at the University, which ended last summer, is not extremely pleasant. In general, the priests were polite but not friendly; and only a small number acknowledged me to be of the family of Notre Dame. I got little consideration and not much social courtesy from many of the officials. Though an officer of the University, I was never invited to the non-sacerdotal functions to which the other officers, clerical and lay, were invited. I was on the University Council, but my province was to agree with what was announced.

But I am not so much concerned about how I fared personally. The general state of mind existing among the brothers is of more importance. It is not necessary for me now to go into detail about the things that have made them regard Notre Dame as a stepmother. In general, they have been neglected in the University publications; they have been humiliated in the dining halls; they have been made aware that they should regard Notre Dame as for the priests and consider themselves as boarders. Mission brothers, especially, who have experienced the cordiality of the secular clergy and the clergy of other religious societies, are all the more conscious of the unwelcome atmosphere of Notre Dame.

Though influenced by those things, my object in speaking of Notre Dame is to touch on conditions rather than to place blame. Doubtless many of the priests at Notre Dame see other causes for the Notre Dame atmosphere I have referred to. Causes and conditions were discussed at the General Chapter. Things having been decided according to decrees that have been announced, the business ahead is to face the future with a view of eliminating the conditions that are causing or could cause friction.

This is now the second year since the General Chapter. The objective of that Chapter, after reviewing the past, was to plan for the future. Certain principles, based on the will of the Founder, the Constitutions, and experience, were held to be necessary for the welfare of our composite Congregation. It was hoped that the

Community's troublesome problems would disappear under the leadership of higher superiors who in theory and in practice have accepted the 50-50 plan of our Constitutions. Among the things admitted which the brothers have a right to consider basic are: (a) equal facilities for priests and brothers in secular education; (b) equality of rights in considering the non-sacerdotal problems of the Community; (c) treatment of the brothers in public and in private in accordance with their status as religious co-workers, not as laymen, much less as servants; (d) admission of the brother's viewpoint that he should not be regarded as an inferior human being because he is a brother.

The brothers have placed full confidence in the General and Provincial Administrations, on whom in particular rest the obligations of the Constitutions and Decrees made to direct the Community. These Administrations are by virtue of the Chapter committed to the task of carrying out the "new deal" we all hope is at hand. The next factor in importance in the rebirth of the Congregation will be the attitude of the local superiors selected to carry out the determinations of the General Chapter.

The final factor in determining the future success of our Community must be the unselfish efforts of the priests and brothers, everywhere, to establish and to recognize common bases for cooperation and harmony. Neither element can get anywhere by ignoring the rights or prerogatives of the other. In the nature of things the priests must always excel the brothers; and from this it follows that the higher the level of the brothers the greater the excellence of the priests. Since Holy Cross Brothers share in the prestige of Holy Cross priests, the brothers cannot but desire to see great leaders and great scholars among the priests. The Congregation is composed of _monks_ rather than of priests and brothers, and it is with the viewpoint of _monks_, or Religious of Holy Cross, that we are to vision the objectives of the Congregation.

Having expressed my conception of the new and better Holy Cross which I look for, I shall now take the liberty of making a few remarks about Section XXV of the Report of the President [Notre Dame University] read at the meeting of the Board of Lay Trustees, November 24, 1933.

XXV. In accordance with the decree of the last General Chapter of the Congregation of Holy Cross, one-third of the annual surplus of the University was given to the Provincial Administration to defray the expenses of training future members of the religious faculty. Only one-seventh of the cost of faculty salaries is met by the present endowment.

The Provincial reports that there are at present in training the following numbers of young men: in the Novitiate, 55 seminarians; in Moreau Seminary, 79; in Holy Cross College, 69—a total of 203. In addition, sixteen young priests are doing advanced work in various universities. When these young men are available for work at Notre Dame, the salary-burden, which is so very heavy at present, will be lightened very materially. Further it is hoped that a notable enlargement of the scope of graduate work, for which there is at present no endowment, will be made possible by the present policy of teacher-training.

The composition and scope of our Congregation, as conceived and comprehended by this Report, struck me on hearing it as being narrow and unfair towards the brothers of the Congregation, who by right and by number are a constituent half of that same Congregation. I did not believe the Report reflected your viewpoint. Therefore, I somewhat tensely asked the question that opened the following dialog, which was carried on between us as we sat together at the meeting table, conversing in low tones:

"Who wrote this Report, you or the President?"

"I wrote it."

"Why did you ignore the brothers?"

"I had to put it that way, for the members of the Board would go up in arms if they knew that their money was being used to educate high school teachers."

"I do not think you have authority to determine the status of the brothers. That is a Community problem."

"Yes, it is a Community problem. We need not talk about it here."

My feelings in regard to this Report, and my disappointment in learning that you had written it, undoubtedly gave a curt tone to my questions. If my manner, rather than my purpose, was at fault or gave offense, though you have not so indicated, I hereby express my regrets. After hearing such a Report I felt like an intruder at the meeting, and I left immediately after adjournment.

Some time has elapsed since this meeting, and I feel more than ever the lack of recognition evinced towards the brothers of the Congregation. I must of necessity place the problem before the higher superiors; and I think it only fair that you should know why and how I present it, why and how I regret the presence of

Section XXV, at least as worded, in the Report. It is not for me to determine either Community or University policies, but I think it is admitted that in a matter which concerns the brothers at least, I may with respectful freedom and frankness place my views before those priests whose office as higher superiors necessitates a broader view of the position and mission of the brothers.

Knowing you as I do, I feel certain you had no intention of slighting the brothers. You merely acted in harmony with the accepted Notre Dame treatment of brothers. The harshest thing I could say is that you have been unconsciously influenced by association, by environment, and by modern tradition in regard to the position of the brothers in our Congregation. The Report shows that you have looked at the Congregation through Notre Dame eyes; that you regard the Congregation as composed of priests and seminarians; that the Congregation exists for Notre Dame. Your omission of reference to the brothers in the composition of the Congregation forces this choice upon the public: There are no brothers in Holy Cross; or, if there are brothers, they don't count. I, a brother, the secretary of the meeting, sat there thinking— thinking of the forgotten dead whose holy crosses on "Seminary Hill" in goodly numbers mutely testify to the part played by the brothers in Holy Cross and . . . Notre Dame. Their endowment of Notre Dame was not restricted to half the Congregation. They went up in sacrifice—not in arms, as you said would go the Board of Lay Trustees if they heard they were aiding brothers whose status, fixed by what authority I know not, they were supposed to know by some form of intuition.

For the first time, brothers are not included among the Province's young men in training; for the first time, brothers are excluded from the young men training to teach at the University of Notre Dame; for the first time, the Province share of a school's surplus is totally assigned for the education of priests. Such declarations and implications are not considerate towards the fifteen brothers now aiding the University, nor to the quota of brothers that since the founding have been on the University staff. I have always been of the opinion that the disposition of Province money, and the selection of a religious faculty for a house, are the business of higher superiors.

Elsewhere I have referred to a certain traditional Notre Dame spirit towards the brothers. I might call it a Notre Dame attitude, one of those intangible things whose presence is evinced by looks, frowns, aloofness, etc. Sometimes it is manifested in a *more positive manner. I shall give an example. For years the Notre Dame catalog as a matter of history made mention of Father Sorin and five brothers in the founding of Notre Dame. A few years ago Notre Dame, or more correctly some officials though I know not who (and I don't want to), omitted mention of the brothers in order to give prestige to the University and the Sorinites. Not all Holy Cross priests, not all Notre Dame priests, have the attitude of which I speak. Still it is present at Notre Dame, and it even finds a reflex in the hired help.*

I shall not weary myself or trouble you further by dwelling on these traditional and contagious things. It will be more in order to make a few remarks about the <u>high school status</u> of the brothers.

In the early years of this century, a policy, aimed at the extinction of the teaching brothers in this Community, was put into operation. This is what started the modern priest-brother problem. Some priests have suffered unjustly on account of the blundering policy which they actually, though not openly, opposed. And since that time many brothers have suffered unjustly because they have, in good conscience, labored constitutionally to restore the homestead of their vows. What I am writing may be news to you, and I write it because I believe you can judge a problem without bias when you know the facts. When you came to Notre Dame the brothers did not have a single high school, and not for many years after was there a graduate brother in Holy Cross. In order to preserve the brotherhood, the Holy See, familiar with the whole situation, urged or ordered that the brothers, according to the limited education the few remaining teachers had, be given control of separate schools, such as commercial schools and high schools. The Holy See did not limit the scope of the brothers' teaching. Neither is it limited by any Constitution, Rule, or Decree.

There is an admission on the part of higher superiors and of Chapters, as well as a universal belief among the brothers, that high schools are necessary for the brothers in order to further recruiting, organization, and leadership. There is also the fact, recognized in Catholic education and supported by the bishops of the country, that the high school is more necessary than the college. Even with the high schools, the Holy Cross Brothers are not in the same advantageous position as the brothers of other teaching institutes from the viewpoint of public appeal. Without doubt we have many compensating privileges and conveniences which they do not possess, but the appeal of the Congregation must of necessity be the appeal of a clerical institute, and the problems of the brothers must be decided by clerical superiors, who must be familiar with the brothers' viewpoint in order to decide judiciously.

So much for the high school status and the substantial conformity with the objective of the Holy See. Today practically all the brothers are college graduates, thanks to the cooperation of higher superiors. Many brothers have the Master's degree. As a group, they lack neither talent nor energy nor zeal nor devotion in the objectives of the religious life God has called them to. Many of them could, with little or no additional preparation, do some mighty fine teaching at the University of Notre Dame or at any other college of the Community. With the high school ideal not neglected, there is no unwillingness on the part of the brothers—as you officially know—to cooperate with the priests in college work. It is for the higher superiors to make such assignments; and I do not think they would wish to cast a reflection on the character and intelligence of the brothers as a group by excluding them from the faculty of Notre Dame University while considering them qualified for the other colleges.

There may be problems in mixed houses, but there are also problems in houses that are not mixed. As far as the teaching goes there should be no problem. Teachers are usually considered according to their qualifications. The badge of excellence is not peculiar to the sacerdotal dignity in the classroom or in the recreation room. Agreeableness, character, ability, aptitude, judgment, scholarship, and a host of other virtues and accomplishments, may reside either in priests or brothers. Common interests provided by an educational level, and coupled with religious charity, form the basis of companionship and recreation in community life. This ideal also embraces the coadjutor brother, for, because of universal and higher education standards in the world, the new coadjutor is well fitted not only to be a sincere religious, like the older type, but to take an active interest in Community affairs. They are coadjutors by choice; and many of them have a practical acumen exceeding that of the cloister-trained.

As a matter of fact, outside Notre Dame there appears to be no real problem due to association of priests and brothers. In most of these houses there is the family struggle for existence that there was at Notre Dame years ago before sacrifices brought prosperity, before prosperity brought pride. Notre Dame as a family enjoyed the benefits of the savings and the labors of the Province—and other provinces. There was no question about who was supporting the brothers or if they paid their dining hall bills. The brothers closed their schools to come to the help of Notre Dame; and now Notre Dame, wealthy Notre Dame, is ashamed of the brothers. We are far from the day when Our Lady's Home would not be sold for a million dollars.

It is just as well to recognize the fact that the brotherhood, re-established in 1906 and reconsecrated in 1932, is an integral part of Notre Dame and of the Community, pledged to cooperation and to Community spirit on the only possible basis—the Constitutions and Rules approved for our guidance by the Holy See.

You may reasonably wonder why all this writing to express a displeasure I already expressed immediately after the presentation of the Report. Well, I did not intend to write; I did not expect it would be necessary for me to write. I had hoped that though you might now have my viewpoint of the problem, you would nevertheless not consider it to be _infra dig._ for you or the University to defer towards the brothers of the Community by instructing me to return the Report for further consideration. I have had to abandon such hopes, because a couple of days ago your office favored me with a copy of the Report of the President in mimeographed circulation. I might interpret this courtesy as the _standum est_ of you or the University towards the brothers of the Congregation or at least towards me. I don't so choose to interpret it. The fact that my first objection did not influence you does not make me believe that it is your purpose to be an exponent of the Notre Dame attitude I have spoken of elsewhere. I consider the objectionable mention of your Report as an accidental result of the Notre Dame atmosphere, not an evidence of your being animated by the attitude. It is rather my opinion that my verbal protest did not influence you because I failed to give reasons for my objection. Though my reasons are too late for that purpose now, I offer them in the hope that they may be of value in similar situations. My feelings towards you are not the same as they are towards that Report, which is so foreign to what I have seen in you as a member of the Provincial Administration. It has been your privilege to enjoy the confidence and esteem of a large number of priests and brothers; and many of us hoped that under your influence the family spirit would again prevail at Notre Dame. That hope I still entertain. It is not inconsistent with my desire to have certain

issues raised by your Report settled by the higher superiors, to whom I have presumed the freedom of presenting them.
   With kindest personal regards, I remain

> *Yours devotedly in and for Holy Cross,*
> */s/ Brother Ephrem, C.S.C.*

CONSEQUENCES

Matters alluded to in the letter were effectively dealt with over time to the extent to which they were acknowledged by the involved religious as an accurate interpretation of the reality existing within the university's academic community. Few denied at least some concrete substance to the assertions. If any written reply was made to Br. Ephrem's letter, it is unfortunately not extant. It seems likely that, because all the principals involved in this scenario—Br. Ephrem, Fr. O'Hara, the provincial, and the superior general—were clustered on the campus of the University of Notre Dame, any overt resolution of issues occurred face to face among those involved. Despite the fact that even after Br. Ephrem's objection to Section XXV the president's report was submitted and approved as written, his continuing respect for Fr. O'Hara, a fellow councilor for the province, was not damaged by the circumstances. In fact, his relationship with the priests, especially those in authority, remained virtually always cordial and free throughout his life. His personal sense of identity and worth was never threatened by the then presumed superiority of the clerical state—which, by the way, Br. Ephrem never contested—and he could deal fairly, determinedly, and openly with anyone, bishop, priest, or lay person. All learned quickly to accept him for who and what he was and to negotiate accordingly.

If any negative consequence was generated by the letter, it did not affect Br. Ephrem's relationship with either the Congregation of Holy Cross or the University of Notre Dame. As seen, he continued as *de facto* secretary for the board and remained as a teacher for several more years on the campus. In 1938 he was elected to the general council of the congregation. His position in Holy Cross seems rather to have been strengthened as a result of this carefully crafted communication and the honest feelings it represented. The letter is symbolic as a point of departure for Br. Ephrem as he moved confidently and more securely toward the future as a significant leader in Holy Cross. Monumental issues were surfacing that required these qualities and more of the feisty little Irish immigrant.

4

Toward Autonomy (1938–1945)

At the general chapter of 1938 Br. Ephrem was elected to the general council of the Congregation of Holy Cross to assist the new superior general, Rev. Albert F. Cousineau of Canada, in the government of the congregation for the ensuing six years. He thus became one of two brothers, along with two priests, to serve the entire community as assistant general in this position of supervisory authority.

At the time, a new general headquarters building in Rome was contemplated, but the shadows of threatening war on the continent cautioned a prudent delay in pursuing construction. Meanwhile, the official residence of the general administration was set up in Washington, D.C., on Rhode Island Ave., not far from the Catholic University site of the congregation's theologate. However, Br. Ephrem remained at Notre Dame from 1938 to 1940 to continue his teaching and vocation work and traveled to Washington for meetings of the council. In 1940, however, he moved full time to the nation's capital, where he remained for two years before accompanying the general administration and staff to 4 E. 80th St., New York City, the location of the generalate until after the war when the new seminary and general offices were transferred to Italy and constructed in Rome at Via Aurelia Antica 319. What ordinarily would have been a six-year term was stretched into seven because of the postponement of the 1944 general chapter until the end of the European phase of the war in 1945.

Br. Maurus O'Malley in his paper "The Portrait of a Builder" relates of Br. Ephrem: *During his time in New York City the Generalate work did not keep him sufficiently occupied and so he often went up to Valatie, New York, near Albany, to help out in the programs there* [the community's eastern postulate], *often for extended periods. He was not an individual who spent long periods meditating. He preferred action, and the action was due to come.*[1] The action due to come was of course the preparation for and implementation of the concept of autonomous provinces for the priests and brothers. The role of Br. Ephrem in the general administration in helping to bring about the reality of homogeneous provinces was significant and deserves attention.

40

Though indications were clear enough as to what needed to be addressed eventually at the general chapter of 1945, the early years of Br. Ephrem's term as assistant general were relatively quiet. The Depression was drawing to an end with the social programs of President Franklin D. Roosevelt and the economic resurgence resulting from the production of wartime goods for the Allies. While war first threatened and then began in Europe and the Far East, there was no assurance that the United States would become involved. The country's internal recovery and development was a priority, and Holy Cross in the United States pursued its own programs of apostolic expansion.

SIGNIFICANT SIDELINES

As was customary in general administrations until the 1960s when Vatican II challenged religious congregations to reassess their nature and purpose and to respond accordingly, there was little traveling within the community by general council members. Meetings dealing with the canonical and constitutional aspects of congregational government were regularly scheduled, but, apart from relatively infrequent planning sessions, much of the decision-making process was technical and required the application of specific criteria more than creative discernment and on-site implementation. Topics were fairly straightforward and set within the parameters of the constitutionally structured and regulated style of life and mission in the congregation.

As a result, general assistants found it advisable to seek some occupation besides that of councilor. Part-time work on other ministries or projects was encouraged and even expected. Br. Ephrem found an outlet in two particular projects.

The first was his joining the faculty of the postulancy program at Valatie, New York, near Albany. He could travel with ease by train either from Washington or New York City to Valatie, and eventually he spent more time in the northern part of the state than at the generalate itself, returning to the city only when necessary. One reason for his decision was a personality conflict with the superior of the generalate community, Rev. William Doheny, a straightlaced canon lawyer who eventually went to Rome and served until his death as a judge of the Roman Rota. These two strong individuals found it difficult to associate companionably, and Br. Ephrem discovered in Valatie a healthy and useful outlet for his energy by teaching mathematics and other courses to the young candidates, many of whom came to Holy Cross before completing their high school education.

As already seen from Br. Ephrem's unsuccessful attempt to resign from the office of treasurer of Notre Dame in favor of a return to teaching—which he considered his primary vocation within the religious life—he felt at ease in the classroom, not to mention far more productive. No doubt the opportunity to teach once more, even as a general assistant, contributed to his psychological well-being and offered him a mental challenge not readily available in the pedestrian day-to-day work of the general council.

The second project was writing. As a general assistant knowledgeable in French, he was asked to translate from French to English the various circular letters of the superior general to the membership, but that was business-related writing. On the more creative side, in 1939 Br. Ephrem found time to depict in a brief biography the life of a greatly admired predecessor, Br. Alexander Smith, who for years had taught and prefected youngsters in the preparatory school at Notre Dame. The book was published with the approval of the provincial council, which, on November 10, voted unanimously to allow $500 for the printing and binding of 800 copies of the book on Br. Alexander.

Other writing that Br. Ephrem had been contemplating for some time and had received encouragement to pursue was the fashioning of a history of the brothers in the United States from their arrival in America in 1841, a project meant to mark the centenary of the congregation's presence in the United States. As it turned out, the history was not written in time for that celebration. His original idea was to update the small volume, *Holy Cross Brothers*, written in 1906 by Fr. James Trahey. Instead, for 1941 he first fulfilled the requirement of a 1938 general chapter decree and wrote a biography of Fr. James Francis Dujarié, founder of the Brothers of St. Joseph, entitled *The Curé of Ruillé*. This work was published in July of 1941 by the Ave Maria Press at Notre Dame. Utilizing the archives of the generalate and aided by suggestions from Br. Bernard Gervais, Br. Ephrem wrote the biography, as he noted in the Foreword, in order *to bring into relief the work and ideals of the Founder of the Brothers of St. Joseph—a Community that some years after its inception became associated with a group of priests to constitute the Congregation of Holy Cross.* He also hoped *to make the apostolic zeal of Fr. Dujarié better known.* The book was well received throughout the congregation, and this biography, along with that of Br. Alexander, added to Br. Ephrem's stature as a significant figure in Holy Cross, now not only as teacher, administrator, and councilor, but also as author. The work on Fr. Dujarié remains a resource volume in formation houses and serves as general community reading for the membership of Holy Cross.

A HISTORY OF THE BROTHERS IN THE U.S.

Br. Ephrem was particularly intent on advancing the image and identity of the brothers during the occasion of the centenary of the arrival of Holy Cross in the United States. His specific role was in authoring the book on Fr. Dujarié and beginning work on the history of the brothers in America. In the meantime, a committee had been formed to plan the celebration of the 100th anniversary of the university in 1942. Its makeup was problematic for some, Br. Ephrem among them. At one point Br. Justin Dwyer, a teacher at Notre Dame, dropped a note to Br. Ephrem in May 1941, saying he had been asked by the Centennial Committee of the university to prepare a monograph on the "Working Brothers." Br. Justin was soliciting suggestions from Br. Ephrem. The response he received, however, was probably not what he anticipated.

I am in receipt of your note saying you have been deputed to write a Monograph on the Working Brothers for the University Centennial. To such a Monograph I could have no reasonable objection, for the Working Brothers did much for the University. But if the idea is to play up the Working Brothers to the neglect of the Teaching Brothers who labored for the University, then I think the scheme is downright mean and unjust. Consequently I shall have no information or suggestions to offer until I know what the complete plan is.

The whole affair so far has been a terrible disappointment to me. The University was established by the Community. Father Sorin came to America with six Brothers, but during his first year at Notre Dame he was the only priest of the Congregation, and instead of six Brothers he had eighteen helping him. From the very first day the school was opened the Brothers taught at Notre Dame, and the property at Notre Dame was bought jointly by Father Sorin and Brother Vincent, and the first prospectus published in the South Bend newspaper said that the faculty consisted of the priests and the most capable of the Brothers. I need not go into detail about the two charters and the fact that more than half of the Notre Dame property is still in the legal name of the Brothers of St. Joseph. That is not the important question. Father Burns (of happy memory) and others said many a time that the Brothers closed their schools to come back to Notre Dame to help the University. Every penny they earned went to the University. Not until 1912 or so did the University have any account separate from the Congregation or rather the Province. Even when the Levee Property was sold at New Orleans the money was sent to Notre Dame to help pay its debts.

Now comes a Centennial, and the authorities do not want a Brother on the Executive Committee, for they do not want to recognize a fact that cannot be denied that the Brothers have any claim on the University both as to ownership and development. I wrote to Father O'Donnell and to Father Cavanaugh to protest against this attitude and I got no satisfactory reply. At that time only half the Executive Committee had been announced, and I suggested that representative Brothers could be selected from Brothers William, Justin, Columba, Chrysostom, Patrick, Albinus, etc. Later on I saw your name and Brother Patrick's on some minor committees, just as the laymen got similar positions. Personally I should prefer to see no recognition than such recognition as that for the Brothers. The fact remains that the Brothers have been shut out from the Community Committee—the Executive Committee. The whole situation is a denial of history and fact and a thing that cannot bring any blessing to the University. I am at a loss to understand the principles governing such a procedure, for I see neither justice nor charity in it. I need not say more. God took care of the Teaching Brothers when Father Zahm said they were not wanted, and I have trust and faith enough to believe He will do it again. The Centennial was a chance to work for a more charitable Community. I fear the chance is lost, and that while the ignorant world is lauding the material growth of Notre Dame what internal charity there is will grow less. God grant this may not be so!

I have openly and frankly given you my opinion and also expressed my convictions, a thing I shall always feel free to do. I believe an injustice has been done and that it should be remedied. Principles are more important than personal comfort.[2]

Br. Ephrem's reference to Fr. John A. Zahm had a point. Zahm, down through the years, has been considered by some as opposed to the advancement of the brothers, or at best apathetic toward their welfare. Whatever its justification, perhaps this accusation is harsher than he deserves. Admittedly, during his tenure as provincial of the United States Province of Priests and Brothers much of his attention was centered on the needs of the priests' society (e.g., building Holy Cross theologate in Washington, D.C.) and to the University of Notre Dame as such. As Ralph E. Weber notes in his *Notre Dame's John Zahm*, Fr. Zahm had problems. *In the midst of the extensive projects for developing Notre Dame and the Congregation in America generally, there arose a serious problem of morale within the ranks of the Brothers.*[3] In August 1901 eleven brothers signed a letter of grievance to Fr. Zahm complaining of injustices and Zahm's role in them. But as Weber notes, *The Brothers' objections began long before Zahm's term as Provincial. While it is true that some of the problems were accentuated during his administration, it is equally important to emphasize that this was largely because of conditions over which he had no control. These same problems continued after his Provincialship and were solved finally by the development of new high schools.*[4] Still, Fr. Gilbert Français, superior general, wrote to Fr. Zahm on September 1, 1901, saying that he felt the brothers had some grounds for their complaints, based on what he had himself observed while on a visit to the Notre Dame campus in 1897. The brothers cited various forms of prejudicial and unequal treatment. A commission was set up by Fr. Français to look into the matter, and Fr. Zahm was a member of the commission. The commission found no substance in the complaints and individually the brothers retracted their accusations.[5]

The problems referred to were largely based in the lack of adequate professional training given the brothers and their not having opportunities to found, staff, and operate institutions of their own. Weber saw Zahm's dilemma: *A major problem facing Zahm was to reorganize and rehabilitate the teaching brotherhood which was slowly disintegrating because the Brothers' schools were closing one by one. Only about six were left. Burns* [Fr. James A. Burns, a leading professor at Notre Dame and later provincial] *believed one of the main causes for this depletion was that the Brothers were not qualified to teach since they were only one-half educated. Thus, he recommended to the new Provincial a four-year course for the Brothers and Zahm was highly pleased.*[6] Weber, in his doctoral dissertation—from which his book emerged—quotes Burns as stating: *An even more important consideration was that the teaching Sisters replaced the Brothers because of the great savings involved. One estimate is that one Brother taught for one-half the cost of a male public school teacher, and that a Sister taught for one-half the Brother's salary.*[7] The brothers were losing their primary schools but were at the same time being offered high schools. The problem was that there were not enough brothers sufficiently trained to engage in secondary education. Fr. Zahm was perceived as being more inclined towards the education of the priests than the brothers. *It seems certain that Fr. Zahm sought to improve the priests' education before he improved the training of the Brothers.*[8]

Zahm had been appointed provincial in early January 1898 by the superior general, Fr. Gilbert Français, to fill out the term of Fr. William Corby of Civil War Gettysburg fame, who had died on December 28, 1897. But the general chapter scheduled for the summer of 1898 had to confirm Zahm by election or choose another man. While Zahm did not want the job of provincial, preferring to remain in Rome, where he had been sent in 1896 as procurator general for the congregation, and to immerse himself in his scientific studies, for which he was internationally renowned, he accepted the position obediently. As Weber puts it, *A few days after his arrival, when told of the gossip regarding the coming election, Zahm replied that he would be conciliatory but* _he_ *would be Provincial, and he would use no gifts to assure reelection—that he would "do his duty fearlessly and prudently, and leave the rest to God."*[9] As Weber quotes Fr. James Burns's diary, *Even before his return, some members quietly speculated whether he could be elected at the General Chapter in August, 1898. It appeared highly probable, however, the Brothers generally were unfavorable to him since some believed he had discriminated against them when he was President during Fr. Thomas Walsh's trip to Europe in 1888.*[10]

Zahm ended up having the support of Br. Engelbert Leisse, who had previously opposed his candidacy, and by April of 1898 it appeared to Fr. Français as if the brothers were turning to favor him.[11] Zahm was in fact elected at the chapter. The following years were not by any means entirely harmonious, but on March 19, 1906, Fr. Zahm extended a peace offering to the brothers by erecting a statue of St. Joseph next to the brothers' house of studies on campus.[12] He had earlier that year responded to the superior general's inquiry about the lack of lay religious vocations under Zahm's administration: *We have done everything that human ingenuity could suggest to increase the number of subjects for the Brotherhood, but the results achieved in no wise respond to the efforts put forth.*[13]

Nevertheless, down through the subsequent years nuances of feeling remained operative among the brothers, and Zahm's name was never entirely cleared of negative overtones in that society. Nor did the general chapter of 1906 and the election of Fr. Andrew Morrissey to replace Fr. Zahm sufficiently resolve the issues, and in 1910 the brothers appealed to Rome for total separation from the priests. The appeal was rejected by Rome because, as they noted, Holy Cross was a voluntary organization from which members were free to withdraw at any time.[14]

It seems likely that, in the end, the centenary celebrations came off well as far as Br. Ephrem was concerned, and, as the opportunity remained and his original intent had not flagged in the meantime, he eventually completed work on a short history entitled "The Brothers of Holy Cross in the United States," divided into two parts. From the generalate in Washington, D.C., Br. Ephrem wrote his provincial, Father Thomas Steiner, on May 23, 1944, concerning the publication of the manuscript he had recently prepared. The letter, quoted here nearly in its entirety, is self-explanatory.

Five or six years ago Father Burns suggested on more than one occasion that I revise Father Trahey's Brothers of Holy Cross, *which appeared in 1906, and bring it up to date. I considered the problem, reread Father Trahey's book, and came to the conclusion that because of the lapse of time and the reorientation of everything since 1906 a new book rather than a revision of an old one was what was needed. I made some notes, but I couldn't seem to find topics that would make appropriate chapters. I postponed the idea and wrote about Father Dujarié in order to meet the Decree of the General Chapter.*

The outcome of the University Centennial revived my notion to bring out something concerning the Brothers, for, as you know, some recognition of a century's work at Notre Dame and elsewhere is assuredly in order.

In trying to put something together that would take the place of Father Trahey's book I thought it best to consider the Brothers in the United States for the past hundred years and not merely Brothers at Notre Dame University. In following this plan even the chapters having to do with Notre Dame are about Notre Dame *rather than about the* University of Notre Dame; *that is, they are about the whole of Notre Dame and not just about a part.*

Historically, Notre Dame, considered in its widest sense, has played an important part in the Centenary of the Brothers, and the Priests too, for that matter (but I am not writing about the Congregation as such). Though much of the Brothers' history is concerned with Notre Dame I believe I have given sufficient consideration to this in the chapters. Most of the chapters, however, deal with activities outside Notre Dame and with men who were not much associated with Notre Dame. The aim has been to give a cross-section of the Brothers' activities during the past hundred years, taking into account every field and place in which they labored, whether alone or with the Priests.

I am sending you copy A (original) of the manuscript, and copy B (carbon) to Brother William. I hope you will be able to find time, though I can imagine how busy you are, to read the copy completely. You have more personal knowledge about the men and matters mentioned than anyone else I can think of at Notre Dame, and I believe you have a better appreciation of the characters mentioned too. I think there are three things to consider in the reading: the historical fact, the propriety or manner of its telling, and the diction in which it is told. As to the fact, I do not think I have over-stated anything, for I have been more inclined to understate; and I have either documentary evidence or personal knowledge of the facts related. Naturally I didn't say everything I could. As regards the propriety of saying certain things I have said, I am of course open to counsel. And with regard to diction, I know it can be improved even by myself. But for comments here I would suggest Father McElhone, and I think he would be willing. He spoke to me a few times about doing some more writing, particularly along the line of this manuscript. He is apparently interested in this type of work, and he is a good English critic too. . . . I have tried to plan the copy to help unity in ideals among the Brothers and also to improve morale, and perhaps the undertaking may aid in orientating those who may be thinking of entering the Postulate. You are fully aware that the priestly calling is admiringly and clearly recognized. But many people, even some Brothers, have doubts about anything worthwhile in the Brotherhood calling, and it is only by showing them that Brothers lead useful and holy lives that this concept can be corrected. I believe that the vast majority of our Priests subscribe to this need of making the activities of the Brothers known. Though the doctrine of the Church is clear, the odds against Brothers in any Institute are great. Those already in might get on tolerably well without recognition, but some public recognition is necessary if vocations are to be procured. I heard all the opposition arguments towards entering Brotherhoods during my years of vocational correspondence. In the modern world it seems that an ideal of activity as well as an ideal of holiness is necessary. It is a philosophy of "being somebody for God's sake." Later on, some may become so perfect as to be <u>willing</u> "to be nobody for God's sake."

As for my own years in the Community, nothing has made more of an impression on me than the memory of the ancients who have passed away in my time. Even the simplest had a story and an ideal. It is true of both Priests and Brothers, and I hope that some day a kindly pen will bring them to life to be a meditation for the youngsters who know not the cost of the glory they have inherited. I hope the pen will not so much tell of the big and important things they did—on account of merely holding high offices—but of the finer touches that made them the men they were, their simple and holy human-ness, so to say, the things that didn't get into the newspapers but which made the recreation room a family circle.

I am aware that Brother Aidan is doing some research or archivist work about the Brothers, or perhaps about the Congregation in general, but the matters he will cover (or uncover) will probably not be the things that I have tried to cover in this manuscript. No doubt a medium for his findings will be found when the time comes to add a little more detail to Community history, to add a little more to sacred traditional directives. But if he has something more to the point at the present time than I have written I shall be happy to have consideration of the present manuscript passed up and shall gladly turn it over for any good purpose it may serve in promoting the end I have in view. My interest is not in getting out a book but in furthering a cause that is a concern not only of Brothers but of the whole Church.[15]

On the same day, Br. Ephrem wrote to Br. William Mang about the manuscript. He indicated he had given the work to the superior general to read. Fr. Cousineau responded favorably and hoped the same type of book could be prepared in Canada. Br. Ephrem also enclosed a copy of his letter to Fr. Steiner and asked Br. William not to mention that to the provincial. In his letter to Br. William the author states, *Now, about this whole thing, I do not feel that you are opposed to the idea, but I fear you are afraid it will in some way interfere with Brother Aidan's work; and that's something I would wish to avoid myself. The first thing I would like you to do is to read the copy completely. I am in no rush about anything. My only desire is to try to do something that will help the Brothers. I have tried to show their integrity as a Society, an autonomous Society, and any new developments that may come at the next Chapter will fit in with this idea. In any case, I have tried to set the ideal of unity and government within ourselves. Little lines here and there bring out that, for example at the end of the first page in Chapter 15.*

A real history would be much larger, and I have merely touched on things relating to parochial schools, for these and a lot of other things must wait details from Brother Aidan's work. I had no room anywhere for detail, as I was not concerned with too much research. There is much more that I know from documents or experience that I could have put in, but I didn't think it the place to do so. The aim was to present unit views rather than bring in details that might weaken the impression of each chapter. Besides, I was anxious that we get something at this time of Notre Dame Anniversaries. *I may have a grammar school or two omitted, and may need correction from Brother Aidan. For the rest I probably had more facts here than I needed. If you have a doubt about the whole thing I can talk it over with you when I get to N.D., and if you see a better thing to do I shall be glad to cooperate. A complete reading will settle your mind.*[16] The manuscript in fact was never published, and is preserved in the Midwest Archives under the title "The Brothers of Holy Cross in the U.S." An edited form of the manuscript was prepared but not published in 1980 by Br. Laurian LaForest, archivist of the Eastern Province of Brothers.

A reply to Br. Ephrem's letter came nearly a month later from Fr. Thomas A. Steiner, provincial. It was written June 18, 1944, and acknowledged receipt of the manuscript. Fr. Steiner indicated that he had begun reading it, and, as suggested, was about to give it to Fr. McElhone to read. He clearly expected it to be published.

I have been negligent about answering your letter about the opus you sent on. . . . I have started reading the manuscript, doing a little at a time. I have read about one-half of the first book, and I find it very interesting. I hope to have a little more time evenings to get through with it.

Father General has written to me about the book, and asked me to read it, telling me that it was a pleasure to him to read it, and that I would likewise enjoy its perusal. As soon as I finish the reading, I will ask Father McElhone to go over it.[17]

Why the volume was never published remains something of a mystery, perhaps partially explained by the times. World War II was still very much in progress, and there were government restrictions covering the use of paper, which included the printing of books. There is no indication that any effort was ever made by anyone to prevent the publication of the book.

As he noted in his book, Br. Ephrem intended to highlight the role played by the society of brothers in the first hundred years of the congregation in the United States. He wrote: *We have the more difficult task of singling out the less prominent of the two branches that constitute Holy Cross and of showing how the members of this branch contributed to Notre Dame. However autonomous may be the position of the Brothers in the Congregation, the lead in the larger movements naturally fell to the Society of Priests. This, nevertheless, in no way diminishes the admittedly important part played by the less prominent partners who gave themselves whole-heartedly to the building of Notre Dame.*[18]

Br. Ephrem acknowledged that for many years after the arrival of Holy Cross in the U.S. the brothers, though more numerous than the priests, consecrated their talents and muscles to the advancement of Notre Dame and other schools under the direction of the priests.[19] Recent years, Br. Ephrem noted, had produced policies in the congregation favoring the advancement of the brothers, especially in their academic training. He devoted several chapters to brothers who played vital roles in the firm establishment of the lay society in the United States. He remarked that *the Brothers of Holy Cross were the first teaching Community of Brothers to be permanently established in the United States. They came to teach in whatever type of institution needed their services, and they desired to have American teachers for American boys as soon as possible.*[20]

Br. Ephrem pointed out how, as noted eloquently by Fr. James Burns in the chapter of 1932, the brothers had sacrificed themselves for the greater good of larger institutions, largely boarding, such as Notre Dame, St. Edward's University, and Holy Cross College in New Orleans. Many small apostolates, mostly in primary education, had to be abandoned because of the needs of the province institutions. Yet he asserted that *the Brothers of Holy Cross must have policies that will further their interests as a Society and at the same time further the interests of the Congregation as such. Their contribution towards the common goal is made through their Society as a whole and not directly through the particular services of this or that Brother.*[21] He went on, *The Brothers were founded and exist as a teaching Society, and it is to this purpose that all their activities are directed. All efforts are to further the established objectives of the Society of Brothers—considered as a component of a Congregation which consists of two integral parts so oriented as to produce the most effective resultant.*[22] And he continued, *The first ideal of Holy Cross, however, is to produce religious men, and the second is to place each in the position for which nature and training and grace appear to have best fitted him, a not very difficult task in a Congregation whose activities in education and related works are practically without limit in affording fields for every worthwhile kind of talent, scholarship, and professional skill.*[23]

It is easy to see not only how Br. Ephrem kept himself very profitably occupied during his years on the general administration, but also how he made a significant contribution both to the wider membership of the community by his research and writing, and to the current crop of young candidates entering the congregation through the postulancy program at Valatie.

PREPARATION FOR THE 1945 CHAPTER AND AUTONOMY

However important these contributions were, they tend to pale in significance when measured against the role Br. Ephrem played during these years in the preparation for the sensitive yet monumental issues to be dealt with at the 1945 general chapter.

In 1976, at the request of Br. Elmo Bransby, then an assistant general, Br. Ephrem, in retirement, wrote a very brief reflection on what, in his opinion, had led to the need for autonomous priests' and brothers' provinces in 1945. He said: *As you know, I was on the General Council for seven years ending in 1945. From various brothers in all provinces remarks came in that the Brothers should have more to say in their own affairs. As a ground basis, it was stated that from the beginning we were two distinct Societies—a society of priests and a society of Brothers—both constituting the CONGREGATION of Holy Cross.*

From many places, U.S., etc., remarks came to the Generalate during the years I was with Father General that the priests dominated almost everywhere. In New Orleans, for example, for years there was a priest boss though almost all the faculty consisted of Brothers. No matter how many Brothers in any house, the priests had majority in the Councils. Provincial Chapters made decisions on what the priests wanted, sometimes with the aid of a couple of brothers.

Father Cousineau considered the matter serious. He consulted other communities and even Rome. He figured that autonomy might be a solution. He brought this idea to the General Chapter in 1945. Even the priests were much in favor of it as it would do away with the Brothers on the local councils with priests. The Brothers used to vote even on clerical matters of various kinds, and I had many such experiences on Provincial Council matters— having at times voted to expel two priests for misconduct.[24]

Some years earlier, at the request of Br. Maurus O'Malley, Br. Ephrem had written a similar account. After giving a brief historical sketch concerning the problems leading up to 1945, he wrote: *When*

Father Cousineau was elected in 1938, he set about working out a plan that would make Priests and Brothers rather independent of each other. He noted that before autonomy *we had two competitive societies instead of cooperating ones.* As superior general, Father Donahue failed to satisfy the priests who desired total separation in 1932. Neither did his successor Fr. Cousineau see complete separation as an option. He preferred a compromise. And, as Br. Ephrem related, *the plan was all his own with the assistance I and others on the Council could give him.*[25]

Br. Bonaventure Foley, who played a vital role in the pre-chapter negotiations and preparation for autonomy, recalled what had led up to that point, responding to the request of Br. Elmo Bransby, assistant general. On October 19, 1976, he wrote, *In the 1938 general chapter Fr. Donahue, the superior general, brought up the question of separation of the two Societies, and it was voted down by a large percentage of the delegates. . . . The question did not rest as finished.*

Immediately after Fr. Cousineau was elected general, he was again approached by [priests] *who insisted that the general resurrect the issue and settle it.*

As I remember, the Apostolic Delegate to the U.S., Msgr. Cicognani, advised Fr. Cousineau to reintroduce the issue and settle it. Fr. Cousineau contacted the procurator general, Fr. Sauvage, on the issue, and he in turn contacted a Fr. Joseph Rousseau, procurator general of the Oblate Fathers, who proposed that the chapter consider autonomous provinces rather than separation of the two Societies.

Br. Bonaventure went on to insist that, in discussing autonomous provinces, it must be kept in mind that such a move was agitated for by priests and not brothers. The brothers had not been interested in any form of separation since 1910, when they petitioned Rome on the basis of their belief they were being absorbed into the priests' activities and had no control over their own work.

Br. Bonaventure's involvement in the preparation for the 1945 chapter began on the day of Fr. James W. Donahue's funeral, when Br. Ephrem, who had come to the services with the superior general, Fr. Cousineau, approached Br. Bonaventure and told him of the proposal to move toward autonomous provinces.[26] The following fall, Fr. Cousineau appointed a commission to study the issue of homogeneous provinces, specifically the matter of the division of assets. Br. Bonaventure was asked to be a member of the commission. It was he who recalled that it was at Fr. Donahue's funeral that

Br. Ephrem suggested a commission and that Br. Bonaventure be a member of it.[27]

Br. William Mang was also a member of the commission, and on May 15, 1945, Br. Ephrem wrote him: *The Committee is supposed to be a Committee for Father General. Chapter Committees must be proposed by the General Council and approved by the Chapter in session. I shall be interested in the permanent Committees, and my interest now is to keep the road open and in good condition. Closed action now would not be binding, but it would naturally carry weight. The Special Chapter Committee will have representatives from more than one Province, and they would take it for granted that what each Province sent in was O.K. That is why, unless the thing is perfect, the road should be kept open for reconsideration. Naturally we can all get behind our representatives on that Special Committee. It will not be on the spot as you two are now. You might mention that what you agree to now is personal and you may modify it later on after consultation with the other Brother Delegates.[28]*

The emergence of the issue of autonomy and the organized and practical planning for its presentation to the chapter of 1945 were preceded by several years of data gathering. Opinion was solicited and welcomed from members throughout the congregation, as noted in Br. Ephrem's earlier remarks. Between 1938 and 1944, however, except for a congregation-wide visit by the superior general, little by way of concrete preparation was done outside the general council on the presentation of the matter as an agenda item at the chapter.

THREE IMPORTANT CORRESPONDENTS

As 1945 dawned, however, the waters which had been steadily but quietly rising were ruffled by the winds of imminent change. Br. Ephrem's correspondence during this period with three notable figures among the brothers in the congregation is typical of the sensitive communications touching the vital issue of possible division into autonomous and homogeneous provinces.

The first correspondent was Br. Léopold Taillon of the Canadian Province, a man who had been chosen as a delegate to the general chapter but who had serious reservations about accepting his election. Br. Ephrem sided with Br. Léopold's province confreres and encouraged him to join forces with the other delegates at the chapter to present and defend his viewpoint. Stationed at the University of St. Joseph in New Brunswick, Br. Léopold confessed to some confusion: *Around here, everybody wonders what kind of <u>greater autonomy</u> for the two elements of Holy Cross is being hinted at. And I am in the dark! I wish at least the capitulants may eventually be told what is looming up.*[29]

Br. Ephrem wrote back to insist that Br. Léopold, known for his frankness and respected by the superior general for it, not resign as a capitulant. While Fr. Cousineau did not share Br. Léopold's views on some matters, he appreciated them and knew that Br. Léopold would stand up for his position. Br. Ephrem went on to hope that the circular letter of the superior general had clarified the issues at hand but then explained in some depth what was being proposed to the chapter. He added, *I personally think it will be the means of giving us a real united Community, and that it will give the Brothers a positive position before the public, since they will be standing on their own feet and backed up by the General Council.*

All, of course, will be up to the Chapter; and I think all the delegates will go into this Chapter in a charitable and cooperative spirit. Relations in the Province are very cordial, the best I can remember. With God's help, I feel sure that some plan for the benefit of all will result.

Again, do not think of resigning. We need experienced and honest men. There are many things we can talk over ahead of time. When we follow conscience we can expect Divine guidance.[30]

Br. Léopold replied, thanking Br. Ephrem for his support. However, his interpretation of what was afoot was that it was but an intermediate step toward eventual total separation, and he protested: *Personally, I strongly resent the perspective of becoming the member of <u>another</u> community, as I feel the new order would likely assume such face for me.* Br. Léopold suggested that there were other ways to resolve the issues that had led to the consideration of autonomy. He was convinced union was essential, but feared the present move was rather towards division. *Now of course we talk of GREATER UNION to be achieved through some sort of loosening the bonds that thus far tended to make our two bodies just ONE. Is really the action of PUTTING FARTHER APART the ideal means of achieving a greater unity? I must admit the solution leaves me nonplussed.*[31]

Br. Ephrem responded saying that Fr. Cousineau's proposed solution would emphasize friendly relations rather than additional uniting by decree. Because capitular decrees had not solved the problem in the past, it was not likely they would at this time either, and a "plan of union through cooperation" was being proposed with sufficient "legal union" retained to provide any necessary sanctions.

Br. Ephrem went on to say, *I am not so familiar with the situation in Canada, but from the winds that blow this way and the copies of "anonymous" letters that have come my way, I would judge that things are far from satisfactory.* He alluded then to occasional conversations he had had with both priest and brother capitulants from Canada who suggested that their societal interests would best be served by autonomy. He summarized, *I believe the Community wants and is ready for a rather radical change in our plan of union, but that union is still desired. I believe that the plan now being offered is more in conformity with the original ideals of both Societies than anything we have had for the past eighty years. I think it is an application of what Rome approved. I am supporting it because I believe it will make for* better *union, even more* actual *union.*

It is not easy for one of my age to vision such a change, nor do I fail to see that there must be many others who probably do not relish change in what may be the last decade of their lives. It is the welfare of the coming generation that is important, and in the hope and belief that the proposed legislation will be for their benefit I feel that it should be tried. Time may call for modifications. From the beginning we have been modifying our constitutions, and Rome has been approving the modifications in ours as in other communities.

How the Chapter will take the plan I don't know, and though I am in favor of the plan I do not think I shall be any bit upset if the Chapter turns it down. After all, I am still old-fashioned enough to believe that the Holy Ghost does have a hand in Chapters even though we put so much faith in votes. Votes may pass something but only the Holy Ghost can make it operative.

He concluded by saying, *If we all thought alike there would be no reason for Chapters. And often times Chapter discussions make us change our minds, and while I have opinions now they may undergo much modification this summer.*[32] He was trying to allay the reservations of Br. Léopold by acknowledging his own, but at the same time he emphasized his openness to the action of the Spirit through the canonical process of the chapter.

The second individual with whom Br. Ephrem was in frequent contact during the months prior to the chapter was Br. William Mang, at that time a member of the provincial council and one of the appointees to the commission set up by Fr. Cousineau to study the equitable division of properties between the two societies to be effected should the decision on autonomous provinces be approved by the chapter. Recognizing his lack of background in financial matters, Br. William sought Br. Ephrem's advice on how to proceed in the commission meetings, what to suggest, what to demand. As early as 1942 Br. Ephrem had written Br. William stating his belief about the basic equal rights of the brothers saying, *Whether I satisfy any authorities or not, I have no idea of changing my attitude on working for the consideration that we ought to get, and of letting people know we can expect that consideration.*[33] Then a year later he had written, *In both provinces there is a strong feeling for greater autonomy, and things have not been as quiet as they look in either place for the past few years. But a broader and more charitable view is prevailing.*[34] And in February of 1945 he wrote, *As you probably know, a Committee has been appointed to do preliminary work about assets and the property in the U.S. Province. The job will not be easy, but some ground may be cleared. I rather favor present values than long term promises, except for continued scholarships and the like.*[35] All Br. Ephrem's counsels to both Br. William and Br. Bonaventure were to be colored by his principle of "present values" over "long term promises."

The present values he envisioned, even many months earlier, were expressed in another letter to Br. William. *The more I have time to think things over the more convinced I am that we should have revenue schools, at least a good boarding prep and a good high-priced property* [province owned] *day school in a large town. If proposals for managing our own affairs work out these things would be easy, and then we would need many men for these and other things. I think we ought to conserve and educate during the delay, for I see the biggest difficulty in the financial angle in the future. If we could get into a position to produce income we could then spread out. All the world would be open to our zeal and initiative and we wouldn't have to worry which branch was going where.*[36]

He elaborated on this theme in January of 1945 when he wrote Br. William: *Our well founded desire is to have property schools for the sake of morale and security, and your last Provincial Chapter passed a decree or resolution to that effect. The Provincial Council should not try to over-rule that Chapter Decree. Decrees should be looked upon as Decrees. At present we administer no more* than _Five_ percent of the U.S. Province property, and we should be administering _Fifty_.

It is true that our scattered day schools are fulfilling a real need in the country and are worthwhile, but they do not produce the needed stability and revenue. I feel sure that God is blessing our work, but I think it is in harmony with His will that we use our influence and constitutional authority to benefit our position. That is why we have Councils and Chapters. There is some criticism among our men because we have taken small places like Spokane, Monroe, Biloxi. With you I favored each of these and still believe we did right. I also see that we should conserve men for some hoped-for property schools and not pinch ourselves too much in the next couple of years while we are waiting for the break we hope to get. I shall also be in favor of some kind of school in Los Angeles to keep company with Long Beach, and I see some advantages in Tucson. Then there is Cleveland. And since the Sacred Heart Brothers and the Christian Brothers are getting schools in New Orleans, it may be that we shall be offered the Boys' Home there. However, I see a very great need of building up in the East, and somewhat with a view to a future Eastern Province. We need some Eastern properties for a nucleus. Boston and Brooklyn are rich in first-class vocations even after seminaries are taken care of, and we ought to get established in both dioceses as soon as possible.

In some ways I wish we were not being pushed until we see what policies next summer will bring. We shall need so many men if we get a chance to decide policies that look good to us. In the meantime I hate to have us let anything worthwhile pass us up. I think that a prep school should finish the Mid-west for some time (allowing for Cleveland), then we should add some things in the East and the far West. At the present time obediences and other travel expenses are running us all over the country, and we may have to cut that down when, as I hope, we shall be assigned our own resources. We should have in mind local centers of development.

Let the priests take a day high school if they want an outlet. It should be our turn to get property schools. Only in such schools can we escape the tendency to have secular priests head our institutions. Should the priests take a high school they probably would not have this trouble. A day school would serve them just as well for the "vocational influence" they are looking for.

I can fully realize that you find yourself on the spot once in a while, but I have full confidence in your tact and ability, and I

know that all the other members feel the same too. So if you stick
to your principles you will have done all you can, and if things go
otherwise all we can do is trust in God and await better times. If
we are honest we can feel sure of doing God's will.

. . . Nothing more to add. I appreciate your keeping me in
touch with affairs. Don't lose hope. You can see that we are making
progress anyway and that our work is being blessed. I write you
each time as I feel, and my letters are not for archives.[37]

In December of 1944 Br. Ephrem had written to Br. William on
the same matter. I think our Brothers have a mission and I trust
God to take care of them. But since in human justice they are
responsible for at least half the wealth of the American Province,
I believe they are entitled to manage their share of the property or
assets—if there is going to be a division of management. I believe
this should consist of assignment of properties without debts, the
building of a prep school, a fund for a college, a fund to take care
of formation houses and old age provisions, an educational fund,
compensation for continued work. . . .

With regard to the Los Angeles proposal, I believe that if the
Brothers decide they want such an institution they should get it.
Money should be no object, since if we are to manage half the material interests the principle might be just as well recognized—that
we want money and property, not as a concession but as justice.

. . . My last talks with Fr. Steiner make me believe he will
be willing, but I haven't much faith in some others being willing
to spend anything on us. Property schools are real homes and
are our own in summer and winter. And they are good morale
builders. A couple of places in the East would insure future stability and eventually make the East stand on its own feet. But we
can stand a place in the West too. The Prep School would be our
Mid-west home. This three-division plan would give us sectional
homes during summer, and all the better if each could be near a
university. . . .

But I have said enough. You know most of my ideals already.
There will be no dearth of vocations if we have the right kind
of life and work for them. Education is making the brotherhoods
respected.[38]

Early in February 1944 Br. William had returned from a trip he
took with Fr. John J. Cavanaugh to California to investigate property
in the San Fernando Valley for a community school. During the trip
Fr. Cavanaugh and Br. William discussed the upcoming general chapter and the implications of dividing into provinces, if, as anticipated,

that were to be decided. Br. William wrote to Br. Ephrem and mentioned several points about California and about Fr. Cavanaugh's feelings on the division of the province. Br. Ephrem replied on February 9: *I wrote all the enclosed pages yesterday after school, and I didn't have much time to think things through or even say many prayers for light—which is probably the most important thing. But I enclose a copy for you so that all I think and do in this matter is for your use.*

Br. Ephrem enclosed a four-page set of "Considerations" he felt ought to be kept in mind when discussing the eventual division of the provinces and the equitable allocation of assets. The entirety of the first half of Br. Ephrem's document is produced here because it illustrates so clearly the logical functioning of his mind in this matter.

COMMUNITY PROPERTY

(1) Our institutions have developed, God favoring them, because of free labor and the re-investment of profits. Present assets are the natural fruit of earlier sowing. All development is due to the use of what previously existed, even though at the beginning there was only faith and willing hands. All we possess belongs to the Community as a whole. Each profit arose from a previous profit.

(2) In our history, Rule and Constitutions the material assets of the Congregation have been held in common by Priests and Brothers since 1837. For civil reasons it was sometimes necessary that an institution or even one of the Societies hold property in its own name.

(3) In principle, it must be held, as a basis for discussion, that all the assets, of whatever nature, in the Province are subject to division or assignment in the formation of two new Provinces from an old one.

DIVISION OF ASSETS

(1) The formation of two new Provinces does not mean that the trunk of the tree remains with one Society and that a branch is cut off to form a tree for another Society. The Priests do not retain the old Province and set up a new one for the Brothers. The concept must be like that of dividing a farm among two sons— twin sons at that. If one is given certain buildings already existing the other must get equivalent value in cash or other assets.

(2) Since functioning institutions cannot be materially divided they should be retained in their integrity. After separate buildings or institutions are assigned to one or other Society, the Society having the smaller share of real estate should receive compensation in cash, credit, or other forms of assets. This balancing compensation should be paid in immediate cash, but if there is not sufficient cash to make this balance a system of annual payments from revenues should be arranged. There should be no thought of "charity" or "subsidy" but a clear understanding of paying a debt based on equity.

PRESENT PROVINCE ASSETS

(1) All property and assets in the Province are carried on the books at a value between 20 and 24 millions of dollars. About three-fourths of the total value is listed in the name of the University of Notre Dame.

(2) From this it is evident that most of the assets for the Brothers' Province must come from the present assets and future revenues of the University, which naturally should be assigned to the Priests' Province.

(3) All angles considered, the Brothers should in equity be entitled to a third or so of the total assets of the present Province. Without impairing the efficiency of the Priests' Province, the land and buildings and enterprises that could now be assigned to the Brothers' Province would not exceed 2,500,000. The balance of the settlement would have to be in a large cash payment, annual payments over a number of years, and certain contributed services having a monetary value.

NEEDS IN A BROTHERS' PROVINCE

(1) Postulates, consideration of those already existing.

(2) Novitiate—one Society should have ownership of present novitiates, even if for a time at least common novitiates are used. A new novitiate or else continued facilities should be assured.

(3) Property schools capable of producing considerable income for the support of formation houses and for expansion. These should include the immediate erection of a Notre Dame Prep School for 500 boys, the erection of a couple of prep schools or day schools in suitable localities, the acquisition of a small college in the near future.

(4) Limited expansion in the high school field and in homes for delinquent boys.

(5) Provision for the education of Brothers in training, provisions for higher education.

(6) Reserve and facilities for old age.

ASSIGNMENT TO THE BROTHERS

(1) A total assignment of 6,000,000 might meet the demands of equity. If the property assignment amounts to 2,500,000 there would remain a cash-credit-service balance of 3,500,000.

(2) The present cash reserves of the Province now existing could not meet this all at once. [Br. Ephrem itemized how this $3,500,000 might come to the Brothers' Province: the priests would build the prep school for the brothers and finance it; the priests would give a million in cash; scholarships would be assigned to Dujarie Hall; a credit would be assigned for chaplain services; a credit would be assigned for infirmary living; and, if the last two points are not desired, the priests would pay $50,000 annually for twenty years.]

(3) All these things would not provide the small college for the Brothers, and it would have to be procured from annual earnings. Formation houses too would have to be supported from annual earnings.

A further subdivision of his "Considerations" covered the situation of brothers in priests' establishments. Basically, Br. Ephrem felt that *Priests should get all the help possible, particularly coadjutors* [brothers engaged in working with the priests]; *about half the total of the coadjutors should be guaranteed to them.* He then went into some detail about salaries, including those of chaplains working for the brothers. Parenthetically he noted that *we have been losing money in high schools in which the Brothers cannot bring home over $300 to the Community.*

He then listed the properties that were currently controlled by the brothers, the total value of which he calculates to be $1,054,000. He speculated on how the balance of the estimated $2,500,000 would be taken from various other properties: land; Notre Dame Farm; the summer camp at Lawton, Michigan; the Ave Maria Press at Notre Dame; the novitiate at Rolling Prairie, Indiana; St. Edward's University in Texas; Stonehill College in Massachusetts; the novitiate at North Dartmouth, Massachusetts; the University of Portland in Oregon; and the Community Infirmary at Notre Dame. The estimated value of these combined properties was $2,354,000. He suggested that $1,446,000 should be selected from this amount.

Br. Ephrem then remarked at the foot of the page: *It will not be easy to get enough real estate to make 2,500,000.*

The Ave Maria, Portland, and the Community Infirmary are more desirable assets for the Priests.

As part allotment of the cash settlement, Brothers could be cared for at the Community Infirmary.

All Brothers at the Ave Maria would be paid salaries. The University and Priests' Province would need that plant.

Brothers working at the Post Office would draw full government salary.

On the last page of his "Considerations," Br. Ephrem itemized how he arrived at the nearly $24,000,000 estimated value of the assets of the province. Eighteen million of it was entailed in the property, cash, investments, etc., of the University of Notre Dame. Texas, Portland, and New Orleans were valued at $1,500,000 net. The rest of the holdings of the community together were estimated to be worth $4,175,000, less $300,000 in debts, for a total of $3,875,000, making an exact total of $23,375,000.

Br. William in return confided to Br. Ephrem in a letter dated February 28, 1945: *Having never served on any finance group, my knowledge of financial arrangements or property arrangements that might be proposed is meager. All I can say is what you have said or implied: we have to approach problems of property or finance with the points of view that Justice demands a 50-50 division unless we are willing to waive the fifty-fifty arrangement; and that we shouldn't expect any priests' establishment (one conducted by them) to be handed over to us unless they are willing to give it up and we are willing to accept it. The only other point in your outline which I'd question is the amount set aside for the education of the Brothers. At full tuition rates, $500,000 would last about twenty years for seventy-five Brothers, not counting summer school work. I'd prefer double that amount set aside for education purposes.*

At some later time that spring, Br. Ephrem had a chance to visit with Br. William, and on April 11 he wrote Br. William: *I have nothing to add since I saw you. Father General returned, well satisfied with his visit, finding most in favor of the movement. Father Steiner (told some important person, not me) that he thinks it will not be hard to deal with the Brothers, and they want a deal badly. I doubt if he knows all the demands yet. I am definitely convinced that $6,000,000 should be minimum in common justice. I have again outlined according to values and things we talked about. It* *should be definitely understood that building work should begin as soon as possible—before the U. starts its own expansion program. A mere promise of an N.D. Prep would not be worth much. In the discussion it should be made clear that the scholarships really cost them nothing. They can actually afford our program without injury to themselves. We should accept no debts, as we shall have to incur our own to complete the program, for the TWO MILLION would not complete the schools (the four) we are thinking about.*

Steps should be taken right away to put the Brothers of Saint Joseph charter in order and convert it to the Brothers of Holy Cross, so that from the very beginning there will be a legal entity to deal with assignments and bargains.

On May 11, Br. William wrote to Br. Ephrem about the progress of special committee discussions relative to the division of properties. Br. William was a member, along with Brs. Chrysostom Schaefer, and Bonaventure Foley, and the priest members were Frs. Thomas Steiner (chairman), J. Hugh O'Donnell, and John J. Cavanaugh. Br. William said: *I think it is unfortunate that two of the Brothers on this special General Chapter committee have had no experience in financial matters. Maybe, as you say, what has been done so far is unfortunate. We have insisted, and there was no opposition, that the various houses of the Province belong to the Congregation and that in dealing with this problem we must consider two distinct societies with equal rights in so far as goods of the Congregation is concerned.*

I don't know what Monday will bring when meetings are resumed, but I rather think we won't come to any agreement. If the priest representatives insist that the Province hasn't control and ownership over the earnings and assets of houses, then of course our demands and rights could never be met by the Province. So the whole problem will be thrown in the lap of the Chapter. If the General Chapter should be as agreeable as the General Council has always been and approve things agreed to or passed by Provincial meetings, then I can see great danger in our signing anything, unless it were absolutely and without doubt for our best interests. I believe I can withstand pressure that might be brought to bear and Brother Bonaventure will too.[39]

On May 17 he continued: *Our meetings concluded yesterday without coming to any agreement. We are going to send in separate reports, and the way we are drawing ours up, it will be almost minutes of our meetings. In the meeting yesterday, we handed in a typewritten sheet embodying principles such as you drew up and stating that anything less than a fifty-fifty division was a concession on our part. In equity and justice we felt we should have control over the properties that Brother Bonaventure mentioned in his letter to you, plus one million dollars for educational purposes and three million in cash for building schools.*

Because the strip across from the golf course and between the railroad tracks is so narrow, we thought it best to put in a claim for two pieces of property along the Dixie Highway north of the Douglas Road and south of it. The piece south of the Douglas Road is the land west of Moreau and along the walk that goes past the cemetery. We think that is the best site and Professor Kervick agrees that it is a better site for a school than the spot across from the golf course.

I mentioned that, personally, I had no desire for North Easton or St. Edward's University but that if we didn't get some property, the cash and credit allowances would have to be higher. I also mentioned that if we received St. Edward's, the Priests would be relieved of a headache. But it is quite evident that they don't want to give up any of their establishments for reasons easy enough to see. However, in the case of North Easton, they evidently want it as a base for operations in the New England states, and since recently a high school for Brothers in Boston has not been mentioned, I suspect that covetous eyes are being cast on it. We are mentioning in our report that the cash settlement is for schools at Notre Dame, Los Angeles, and Boston.

Our meetings have been pleasant enough, but our points of view differ. The priests think that since this isn't a question of separation, there isn't question of equitable distribution in the same sense there would be if separation were the issue. They believe that with a Prep School at Notre Dame and another school in Los Angeles we would be in a very favorable condition for expansion. They don't see our problem. I still think we'd be making a mistake if we assume that they are trying to get rid of us at the cheapest figure possible. Although it may be hard to justify the view, I still give them credit for acting in good faith.[40]

Then on May 20 Br. William wrote again: *As I mentioned in my last letter, our meetings broke up and each group will send in separate reports through Father Steiner. In the last meeting we presented the principles on which our thinking and suggestions had been based (the principles the final day were the ones you had sent along). Whether it was something in the principles or not, I don't know, but the day after the meetings were over, Mr. Dwyer, the auditor, was on hand to dig up all old financial records for as far back as such records go to find out the contribution of the University to the Province. Anyway, I'd suggest that you have on hand full support of the principles on which you are working and thinking. The priests think that since this is not a question of separation but since the goods are still going to be in the Congregation of Holy Cross, there is no need for anything like equitable distribution. I presented this case: Suppose now the Brothers were making enough on their schools to pay for their expenses, would it mean that we shouldn't receive a dime of cash or property?*

We have drawn up our suggestions and when they are in final form, I'll send you a duplicate copy. We asked for the property B.B. [Br. Bonaventure] outlined to you, plus a million in credit for education and three in cash.

In the course of our meetings I had occasion to mention at length that the Brothers wanted more to say in managing their own affairs, and I pointed out that as things stand, we can't even make a decision about anything when it comes to a new school, spending money, etc. It is because of that, I think, that the Provincial Council passed favorably on both Cleveland schools. It looks as though the Lakewood school will have to be accepted since the Brothers have been promised when the Bishop of Cleveland calls for them. The other site is exceptional for a boarding school and has small communities surrounding it. Brothers Seraphim, Dominic, and Theophane are strong for it. I couldn't say no since it is the first chance that is materializing for a property school.[41]

On May 21 Br. Ephrem wrote to Br. William: *I won't write you much today, as I shall wait for developments after your report comes in. Nothing has been lost by letting the matter hang in the air. You can always get the same as offered now and probably more, if it looks like a bargain should be made.*

There are many angles to things that I cannot talk about now. I too believe that good faith exists all around, but that their concept of good faith is very different from ours I realize in more ways than one. There are some additional things I can mention to you when Chapter opens. . . .

I still see nothing but property schools, and if we don't follow that policy, regardless of what happens this summer, we shall be in the same position twenty years from now as we are now—still have nothing. Regardless of the autonomy, the least we should get *out of the action of this summer is property schools. That is more important than autonomy, as it would be <u>practical</u> autonomy.*[42]

Two days later Br. Ephrem again wrote to Br. William, continuing on the theme of property schools. In the division of assets, he wanted to be certain that whatever else emerged, the brothers would have the capacity to acquire and govern property schools. Apparently not everyone was thinking similarly about equitable distribution: *So somebody said: "There is no need for anything like equitable distribution since this is not a question of separation." If this is the case why should they worry about giving us properties now? Why not give us more than 50-50 since "it would be in the Community anyway." Why not give us a share in N.D. since "it would be in the Community anyway." Why not give us the Brother Trustees of N.D. called for by the last General Chapter? Some comments are really funny! It is well known that Province Assets are separate and independent and once fixed are fixed. What control has Canada now over the U.S. Province? What control would a Brothers' Province have after a Province was established by another party? Do you remember what was said about this by Fathers O'Donnell and Sauvage in a former Chapter? If not, I'll tell you sometime. It wasn't meant for the floor but it got there.*

No need to write you more. I know you are busy with summer students, etc. Be assured that I have absolute confidence in your ability and sincerity in all things, and because we have a just cause I am confident the good Lord will not neglect us. We need greater help than logical arguments. I am still optimistic that we shall have a chance to fare reasonably well.[43]

The third individual with whom Br. Ephrem shared substantial information and advice during the pre-chapter preparation period was Br. Bonaventure Foley, at that time superior of Sacred Heart Juniorate, Watertown, Wisconsin.

Br. Bonaventure was nominated by the provincial to be one of the three brothers and three priests to constitute a special commission to consider the apportionment of properties if and when the province were divided. In January, before the naming of the members, Br. Ephrem, from his position on the general council, wrote to Br. Bonaventure alerting him to his imminent nomination and asking him to keep it quiet until he got official word on it. In the same letter of January 21 Br. Ephrem wrote: *I have some knowledge of the sentiment in various quarters, and perhaps some slants on various things. I might mention now that when the time comes for you to discuss, it would be well to look for all the tangible things you can now: property, money, etc. What you get now will be sure. What you might be promised annually for so many years doesn't seem so safe in my eyes, as future Chapters and Councils may modify things. So as far as possible, let it be a "bird in the hand." This applies only to actual cash, not to such deals for example as free tuition for men at Dujarie for 50 or more years, and things like that where no cash actually would have to be paid. Naturally there will have to be some annual payments, since there would not be enough property or cash at the present time to make a full adjustment. But all the "tangibles" should be a couple of millions in cash for an immediate prep school and a couple of property high schools. The time payments could be applied to formation houses, etc. It may be that Novitiates would have to continue jointly for a time until things are worked out. But that shouldn't interfere with taking ownership, etc., now.*

If you give us a good plan it will probably go as given us to the Chapter. Of course there may be some kicks here, and no doubt there will be more when the Chapter opens. Father Hugh [J. Hugh O'Donnell, president of Notre Dame] *was here a couple of days ago. I think he will be fairly reasonable, but I feel he leans to long time settlements. If we can get proper resources now we can get institutions of our own which will earn for us and they could be free from future Chapter influence. I have confidence that you and B.W.* [Br. William Mang] *understand our needs. He knows most of my sentiments already. I am feeling rather optimistic. Our policy should be no charity or donations, just equity. We are not splitting off from a Province: two new Provinces are arising out of an old one. So it is not a case of a father giving some of his holdings to his son. It is not a case of one keeping and another getting. Both get.*[44]

On February 6 Br. Bonaventure, sharing with Br. William a lack of a fiscal background, responded to Br. Ephrem's letter of January 21. He mused: *I have been wondering just what course of action we should follow at the coming proposed meeting. True, we have thought of autonomy but the question of making two provinces out of one will necessarily call for some sort of a division of temporalities and this division must be worked out on the bases of equity and justice to the men who labored in America during the past 100 years as well as to the labors of the present members and a right of security for their future development.* Then Br. Bonaventure revealed his initial thoughts on the division of temporalities and on a plan of operation by which the work of Holy Cross would be continued. At the end of his proposal he stated: *I must admit that I do not know much about the financial set-up of the Community and I may seem radical. If so, be patient with me and take out the time to tell me what you would consider a safer and more prudent course to follow.*[45]

Br. Ephrem answered Br. Bonaventure's letter at once on February 9. *I hasten to reply to your letter of February 6. I have written my ideas as rapidly as I could, and I am enclosing a copy for you and at the same time sending a duplicate to Brother William. Frankly I have no set idea of what material settlement we should claim. The problem is very complicated. I do not wish to impose my idea on anyone, and I feel that you and Brother William can work out something. Because I am somewhat familiar with the business interests of the Province and Congregation, I believe that what I am enclosing may help you in some way, at least give you a starting point in the consideration. I had not intended to be so specific in my analysis, but since you appear to want my ideas I have frankly given them. After you both see what the Priests wish to claim you will see better. In the early meetings at least, I think you both should ask for plenty; for it is easy to cut down later. The theory of 50-50 should be maintained, and anything below that is a goodwill concession on the part of the Brothers. So a drop from 50% (12,000,000) to 6,000,000 is a big concession. Honestly I think we should get 6,000,000 as a simple matter of equity, and it would not hurt the Priests' Province.* Br. Ephrem was a realist and knew there was no way the brothers could be allotted 50 percent of the province assets without jeopardizing the very existence of the University of Notre Dame, in which the lion's share of the province assets was invested. He was willing to settle for approximately 25 percent of the value of the total congregational assets in the United States.

He went on: *As I see it, I don't know how we can get more than $2,500,000 of the present property. This means all the loose property except Texas, the Ave Maria, and the Community Infirmary, and the University. and the Priests' formation houses. I am not so stuck on counting Texas and North Easton in on the total, but I can't see how you can get a total of 2,500,000 otherwise. I can't see how we can ask for Portland. I think it would be to our gain to have the Priests keep the Infirmary. I think a salary from all men at the Ave would be best. Most of the profits come from printing for the University and from the printing of books—both* *of which interests belong to the Priests. They also edit the Ave, but the Ave as a magazine does not make very much. Annual profits on the whole plant over $40,000, but without University printing, Priests novels, and salary allowance to priest-editors, the present apparent profit would soon disappear. Anyway you may want to keep the Ave included in the Brothers' share. So try if you wish. The Community Infirmary would be but $12,000 or so a year expense, and it would be much cheaper to pay for our patients there and charge for our helpers.*

Why $2,500,000 in property wanted? Because if we get less property we would have to ask for more cash, and I do not think it would be easy to give us more than the $3,500,000 I have listed. At present the U.N.D. must have about 2,000,000 in actual free cash outside all board of trustee funds. It wouldn't hurt to give a million of that right away. It could spend another million on the prep school and pay for it all in one sum or annually as the Univ sees fit. The point would be to put up the school now in our name with the debt on the Univ. Then we should have so many scholarships at N.D. to be checked off annually against a fixed amount of 500,000. The same for chaplains, etc., if need be. The credit in our favor would save us certain annual payments and not put any actual burden on the Priests' Province, since for these two latter things they would be putting out no cash. I think it important that we should get a reasonable salary for all Brothers, as this should be our normal income for formation houses upkeep. If we "ask" too little we shall have an annual deficit for our workers instead of an annual gain. The C.S.C. Sisters at N.Y. get $500 a year besides board and room, etc. The plan I have outlined saves us against long time payments which are inclined to die with the years. It would insure us income houses, give us free tuition for Dujarie, etc.[46]

On March 7 Br. Bonaventure replied to Br. Ephrem, thanking him for his suggestions a month earlier. He felt it would be difficult to secure more than six million in the ways suggested. *But that and their good will and proper compensation for our services would be a good deal in furthering the work of Holy Cross.*

Then Br. Bonaventure advanced the theory that, if there were to be a division of the one province into two, the brothers should begin thinking at once of splitting their own newborn province into three sections—Midwest, East, and South—and he enclosed his proposal for how that might be done. He explained: *In each section there is enough property, activity and possibilities for expansion to keep a man [provincial] occupied. At the same time I think that such a set-up would help towards coordination, strengthening and developing the present and future foundations of that area as well as lend itself to a greater religious spirit of sacrifice and Community spirit. And in a short time these areas would be able to take care of their own expansion and necessary replacements and certainly the Fourth Vow men can always be moved around when an emergency arises. (I think Fourth Vow men were intended by the Founder as much for that purpose as for the Missions.)*

He continued along another line: *There has always been a great deal of talk about that strip of property on the Niles Road across from Dujarie as a location for a Prep School. As the present picture seems to indicate that the Bishop is going to build a Day School in South Bend, I would conclude that a Prep School at Notre Dame would be primarily a Boarding School. Therefore in place of asking for the property across from Dujarie why not ask for that block of land between the Moreau Property and the Niles Road. There you would have a road on two sides and not a railroad so close nor in your backyard and yet a switch on your property. And too you would be on the east side of the main road. You would also be as close, if not closer, to the University than you would be if across from Dujarié.*

At this point Br. Bonaventure brought up an issue which was also destined to become a source of controversy following the 1945 chapter. *Since the question of the Coadjutor has become a question in the Community, I think that after the Chapter there should be a letter issued on the status of the Coadjutor Brother. As it now is, I think the Coadjutor feels that his state is an end in itself rather than a means to further the work of the Priests and Brothers. And there are Coadjutors right here in this house who feel that when one is once classified as a Coadjutor he should not be allowed to change to that of the teacher anymore than that a Brother could move up to Orders. Their ideas are very inconsistent for in one breath they complain because we are trying to give all a decent education here and in the next they are moaning over the fact that none of the young men in the Ave Maria and the various maintenance departments are sent away to school to become more efficient in their various fields. I think it would be well if the Chapter would rule out the distinction and insist that we are religious first and then that men will be placed where talents and aptitudes best fit them. I know it is a difficult matter and that there is a danger of something rising up as it did in the days of*

Father Sorin when he tried to establish a lay order branch of the Holy Cross Sisters at Notre Dame.

I . . . noticed in the letter that you were translating a new Circular Letter which is to come out March 19th. I suppose it will be well on in April when the Ave gets it out to us. However I sure hope it explains or defines some of the ideas stated in the last letter for there are many Brothers who do want to know just what is this all about. They think that it is open Separation. There are others who are afraid to talk about the matter in any way till they hear more on the subject from the General. But the more I think of the problem the more I feel that it has to come. But with it I hope that Union can be maintained. Do you think that Union could be helped by a common Novitiate? There are many advantages from that form of a set-up and I hope it can be worked out. It certainly would be a definite link and means for maintaining traditions and ideals as that has been the one house where some form of equality existed. To avoid confusion it seems that the General could reserve the right to appoint the Novice Masters.[47]

On May 8, 1945—coincidentally V-E Day in Europe, marking the end of World War II hostilities there—Br. Bonaventure wrote to Br. Ephrem about the progress of the meetings of the committee set up to address issues surrounding the apportionment of goods should the province divide into two. He outlined the proposal presented by the brothers at the last meeting concerning the settlement of property and the cash settlement counterproposed by the priests. Other replies to the proposals of the brothers (which were in essence those of Br. Ephrem) were discussed. Br. Bonaventure concluded: *Believe me this is a job but I sure hope that we are on the right path and that if some such arrangement is worked out that we who proposed it will never be termed a "Judas" by our own men. . . . If I have erred in any way by passing on any of this information please destroy it and forgive me.* And as a second paragraph to a postscript, Br. Bonaventure notes about Fr. John J. Cavanaugh, *My observations are that when you are dealing with the Vice Pres. of N.D. you are dealing with a pretty shrewd business man.*[48]

A day later, May 9, Br. Ephrem wrote to Br. Bonaventure. It is not clear whether he had yet received the letter written the day before, though the closing remark might indicate that he had. Br. Ephrem wrote: *I am enclosing some comments for you and Brother William. While they are for the two of you in the present work in which you are engaged, a work preparatory to the Chapter and confidential, I am making no comment now that I shall not make in Chapter if the occasion requires it. I am honestly saying what I say and I have no hesitation in repeating it. We are facing serious problems, and we must face them in an honest businesslike way, being sincere before God.*

According to my mind our plan for the future should be to have institutions that will produce income. We have every right to expect that in dividing the present Province we shall have the necessary income institutions in the future Province of Brothers. We should be given enough now to establish those institutions. That is neither charity nor subsidy. It is justice. We have a group of almost financially useless day schools on which we cannot depend. Nor can we depend much on salaries from Brothers who will work in Priests' houses. In figuring income, these two items don't appear of much worth to me. Had we the four property schools: Notre Dame, Los Angeles, Boston, Brooklyn, (along with New Orleans) we would have good geographical centers. The two Eastern schools will provide vocations and income for an Eastern Province eventually. I have gone over these things with Owen, Harold, Venard, Baptist and others; and you and Br. William seem to agree with the idea. All consider this plan advantageous. If there are other plans they should get consideration too. If these ideas are accepted, I see all our men tied up for the next five years manning such institutions.

Br. Ephrem recognized the importance of the Canadian confreres in arriving at any determination regarding the division of properties and assets in the United States. *I have nothing in the line of news to send you at this time. A plan may be arrived at in Canada. I can't say yet. The problems may come to the Chapter floor—not the theory, but the division of assets. They know, as I do, that the idea did not originate with Brothers, and that if we are to agree with it we should get a fair deal. If they are not satisfied, anything done at N.D. will probably be worth nothing. While the work of your Committee will not be binding on the Chapter, it would not be easy to raise the bid agreed on when the matter comes before the Chapter Committee. Rather than get too little, it might be better to let some things hang. I don't know how many of our Brothers will think as I do, but I can't see any deal in which we shall not have enough cash to build property schools. We couldn't borrow and pay interest on such schools. We should have about $2,500,000 plus the 35-year scholarships, and more if we are not offered $2,500,000 in present property.*

My only reason for being interested in the work of both of you now is to try to keep together in our ideas in the future Chapter. A weak bargain would kill the morale of our Brothers, and it may be shaken anyway. I would not be worried about any personal odium if the future can be made bright.[49]

A small note inserted in the archives file along with the May 9 letter was probably written by Br. Ephrem. To whom is not entirely clear, but another such note in the same location, while not signed by Br. Ephrem, seems to be directed to Br. Bonaventure and mentions Br. William as well. The anonymous note says: *I am sorry I suggested such a low minimum in the beginning. It wasn't enough. Work for more. Make the point that what you are asking may not satisfy the Brothers in Chapter. Don't put the rest of us in a position of having to support anything less than a good deal. You are in danger of being cut down item by item now—first in cash, then in property, etc. If a cut in property is suggested, then go back and increase the cash equivalent demand. I think I suggested $6,500,000 minimum. It should be this first and then Income and Expenses. The Brothers expect us to represent them. I'm going to do it to the limit of friends or enemies. Only justice is asked.*

CONTRIBUTION TO THE COMMISSION STUDY

However forcefully and practically Br. Ephrem counseled Brs. William and Bonaventure, he had no direct role in the several sessions held by the commission on the distribution of assets. The group met twelve times at Notre Dame. On several points immediate agreement was reached between the priest and brother members; on others, even after extensive dialogue, there was no consensus. The brothers requested that both Stonehill College in North Easton, Massachusetts, and St. Edward's University in Austin, Texas, should be part of their patrimony. To this they added the suggestion that the brothers also receive property at Notre Dame north of Douglas Road and adjacent to the east side of the Niles Road (now U.S. highway 31/33), as well as property just south of Douglas Road and west of Moreau Seminary. As for cash, the brothers suggested that three million dollars would be equitable. The priest members of the committee countered that ceding both institutions of higher education would be too much. Also there was a problem with the Notre Dame property and the cash settlement.[50] The priests had in mind the negotiable or saleable value of assets and property, and the brothers, it seemed to them, were requesting the lion's share of these. In the end the commission decided to submit its report to the superior general in two parts, one written and signed by the priest members, the other by the brother members, each party stating reasons for its conclusions. Even at that, Fr. Steiner, the chairman, had to request a two-week extension of the time originally suggested by Fr. Cousineau. The matter was a decidedly thorny one, not amenable to facile resolution. But the men had done their job well.

However, before the final reports were submitted and after being updated by Brs. William and Bonaventure on the progress of negotiations, Br. Ephrem had opportunities to respond. Fearing that the university might try to manipulate matters to its own advantage, he was watchful as the commission work unfolded. Remarking on a document submitted to him, probably by Br. Bonaventure, Br. Ephrem said: *My first reaction to the initial agreements is not favorable. . . . I feared from the beginning that the University would want to pull a fast one, and it evidently is on the track. It appears it wants to remain as it is, without assuming any obligations and even to squawk about the one-third. As I see the proposal it is giving nothing as an institution. What does it want to do for all the Brothers' contribution for the past 100 years? All it offers from its $20,000,000 assets (at least half of which is due to the Brothers) is $1,000,000 in scholarships, a thing we have been getting all the time.*

He admitted he was sorry to see the consideration based on present income instead of present assets. *The procedure on consideration of income instead of assets is based on a mere accident of what the Priests and Brothers are administering now. I think that is false, since all the present goods are Community goods: a position I have taken from the beginning. The University has tried to get out of this way of looking at things and has thrown the discussion into income.* The income plan would leave the brothers with a deficit, while assuring both the priests and the university of a significant amount annually for expansion. The assets plan, though, would allow the brothers to start out on a positive footing.

In brief, I am still of my original estimate—better than $6,000,000 in property or cash.

In justice to our Brothers I would not like to be a party to anything less. I would prefer to let the matter go to the Chapter floor, for I think it could be shown there that the University is not playing fair. We were entitled to 50% of the present assets of the Province. We were ready to concede a part of this, getting only 25% or a little better. It should have been readily conceded to us, as it could be done without injury. I think any Church tribunal would do us this justice after we had stated our case, and showed our historical stake in Notre Dame and all other property. Notice that the present Income Plan *is so unjust that it leaves the Priests with $100,000 annual net for expansion, plus $300,000 more net for the University for expansion. And we get $28,000 deficit for living and expansion.*

If you agree along these lines and it passes the Chapter I must abide by it, but I cannot support it at the Chapter. Needless to say, Brothers William and Bonaventure did not agree "along these lines."

Arguing canonically as well as from the congregation's constitutions, Br. Ephrem pointed out that the brothers were entitled to far more than they were claiming, and the protests of the university were legally unfounded as well as constitutionally unsound. He believed that in Church law the congregation had the right to take from the university, as one of its institutions, what it needed. But Br. Ephrem conceded that in practice *no more burden than is necessary should be placed upon an institution.* Those canonists who argued for "house independence" misinterpreted the nature of Holy Cross, considering it more like the Benedictine federation of virtually independent houses. Having been treasurer at Notre Dame and therefore acquainted with its fiscal status, Br. Ephrem realized the institution was strained by varieties of constant needs, and he said, *We all believe that houses should have some rights to grow and develop, and that Notre Dame should not be hampered more than is necessary for Community needs.* Still, he reminded Br. Bonaventure, *The argument that the University is independent in its property and earnings is the plain bunk. It would be laughed at in Chapter. . . . The two points are: the Brothers have 50% ownership in the University. The University is a house of the Province. Trustees funds are not being spent outside the University, nor are the earnings of these funds. They are not a drop in the bucket of Community earnings. After a settlement with the Brothers is made, the University can fight out its future donations problem with the Priest's Province. Consider now what actually belongs to the Congregation of Holy Cross.*[51]

On May 11 Br. Ephrem wrote again to Br. Bonaventure reiterating his insistence that anything less than a settlement of $6,000,000 for the brothers was unacceptable and unjust. He continued to offer suggestions as to how this could be managed without major upset to either the priests or the university. He repeated some original considerations in the form of principles and suggestions as to how a practical division of assets and sources of revenue could be developed.

In one paragraph he explained, *The aim would be to start off each of the two new Provinces with equal fixed assets and equal revenue producing facilities, consideration being given to the ratio in each Province between the total earning capacity and the total maintenance expenses.*

Later in the month he wrote a few miscellaneous considerations, the second of which concerned the proposed apportionment of goods between the societies, and it argued that the priests and the University of Notre Dame were getting by far the better of it all. *It seems a lot to keep 75% of the assets and to have a net income of $500,000 a year, giving the other party 25% of the assets and no provision to meet an estimated annual deficit of $26,000 per year.*

The question of deficit is on the assumption that N.D. belongs to the priests. Without this assumption the deficit would be on the side of the priests.

The total assets of the Province (total houses) are increasing, and the longer a division is delayed the more the Brothers will be entitled to.

For 100 years 50 or more Brothers gave their services to N.D. free. See Father Burns' talk: they made Notre Dame. What does N.D. owe the Brothers? Reference to the Board of Lay Trustees: forgetting their limited authority and minimum of funds, do they object to laymen getting $4000 a year salary? Should they object to Brothers getting compensation for 100 years?[52]

Clearly the issue was one close to Br. Ephrem's heart, not to mention his field of expertise. Here was a man, a Holy Cross man, who knew from thirty-four years' experience the ins and outs of the difficulties which faced each society in its agreeing to an equitable distribution of assets at the time of the division into autonomous provinces. He was not seeking anything more than was just. He was not pointing fingers in blame for past inequities or for skewed attitudes on the part of either group. He simply wanted, when the division came, that which was rightly due the brothers, because he was a man with a vision of what the brothers could, and would if he had any role in it, become for the Church and for Holy Cross in apostolic ministry throughout the United States and in missions abroad. To start out on an unequal footing would be improper and wholly unfair for either society. He was willing to concede millions of dollars of assets on that principle; but he would not take one penny less than he believed the brothers' society absolutely required to commence its autonomous role in the mission of Holy Cross and to have its equal chance to succeed. All he asked for was the right to make the attempt. Thus his strongly worded suggestions to the men on the commission studying the distribution of assets. And they were grateful to have his advice. As will be seen, Br. Ephrem's active and integral involvement in the preparation for what happened at the 1945 general chapter paved the way for his facilitating the smooth transition which lay beyond that momentous and potentially disconcerting occasion.

5

The General Chapter of 1945

Br. Ephrem no doubt shared his conviction that, besides himself, there were others among the brothers in the congregation who could handle the responsibility of guiding them into the future. He hoped he would be allowed at the age of fifty-seven and after many years in administration, both of schools and community, to return to full-time teaching. The year before, he had written to Br. William Mang from the generalate, *I am just 56 now, and I have had about enough of the Community policies or politics, whichever you wish to call it, and all I hope to see now is a more positive road for those who come after me. I am going to hold on till the Chapter, though I am tired of this job already, and I want to be in a little quiet place where one can play cards and dream about flowers and trees. All I want to see is our Society handling its own affairs, for I believe that both founding and history intended this. "Two societies" runs through Rule and Constitutions, and a Society is an autonomous thing.*[1]

To no one's surprise, he was not to be let off so easily. Br. William, in a letter to Br. Ephrem on February 28, 1945, wrote: *In our educational conventions and committees, I've noticed that Brother Philip of the Christian Brothers, Brother Benjamin of the Xaverians, and Brother Eugene Paulin of the Brothers of Mary are men well over sixty, and they are influential because of their age and experience. I've often mentioned that in my opinion, one of our great deficiencies (and maybe the cause of some of our difficulties) is that we haven't representative men in the sixties (I mean not enough representative men) to give us direction, stability, and tradition. So I can't repress a smile when I hear those in their fifties talk about retiring, no matter how hard they might have worked. On one or two occasions, someone in his forties notified me that his work is done! Well, that is humorous. Come to think of it, I've been out teaching almost as long as you and have held some responsibility almost as long as you. And like you, I've never wanted anything but a teaching job. In ten years from now there ought to be a good number of Brothers with a broadened outlook, if we get responsibility, and then retiring will be in order for you.*[2]

A few months later, on May 26, practically the eve of the chapter, Br. Ephrem wrote a "personal and private" letter to Br. William at Notre Dame, asking him not to mention the content to the provincial or anyone else, because he considered it "a bit delicate." He explained: *I could not receive better treatment than I have received on the G.A. [General Administration] and I feel I have been of some use. However, in case it is the wish of the Brothers or Father General that I continue in this job, I want to make it clear now that I cannot do so. This resolution is one that has lasted seven years, and often during that time the urge came upon me to ask for another job. I have almost broken my nerves trying to hold on, and only with God's help was I able to hold on. Now I feel no further responsibility, and the thought of continuation would be beyond endurance, for I am not temperamentally fitted for this kind of life. It is not the official business, but the inactivity that kills me. Regardless of how you reply to the second point of my letter* [concerning an alternate obedience], *my resolution on this first point, if the job is offered me, is that on no account will I accept it. As I said I cannot stand the life of inactivity.*

Then Br. Ephrem revealed the reason for secrecy: he had not yet informed Fr. Cousineau, the superior general, and believed it only right that he be the first to notify him. Better yet, he could simply wait for the chapter to choose someone else. That would obviate the need for Br. Ephrem to say anything at all on the matter to his superior. He concluded: *My recent letters probably made it plain to you that I am mentally tired. I think I have acted for the best in telling you honestly how I feel.*[3]

Br. William replied on May 29. He said: *From your letters during the past year I knew your sentiments about another term on the General Council. I thought and hoped that in view of problems that might confront us next year, depending on the decisions of the General Chapter, you would consent to another term since your advice would be essential. Whether or not I were a personal friend of yours, I'd have to admit, knowing some of your work and thoughts, that you are and have been a power in the Congregation because of your intelligence, your power of thought, your knowledge of the Congregation, and your devotion to it. Frankly, I hate to think of the next six years, that may mean so much to us, if your counsel were not always available. It has been a sustaining thought to me to know that any mistakes I made would be rectified by your greater knowledge and intelligence.*[4]

On June 1, Br. Ephrem responded: *He (the Superior General) has no suspicion, I believe, that I want to leave him. But on that I must be positive. I must call it the end of my years on the general administration. I want to leave with the friendship and esteem he has accorded me—and I must do it in the best way possible, so that for the good of the Brothers I can still have his confidence and good will. I hope, with your help, to handle it diplomatically during chapter. I still see a bright future for our Society. The present crack-ups indicate all the more that we need a new and stronger set-up, a means of being closer to check some things in time. Present authority with the Brothers is only indirect, and for that reason not taken as it should be taken.*

Don't let yourself get down. We have honest reasons to hope for the best. We must build from the inside, and loyalty and cooperation must be our ideal.[5]

The eventual decisions taken by the general chapter led almost inevitably to the election of Br. Ephrem as the first provincial of the brothers in the United States. He was in fact prevailed upon to continue to serve the congregation as only he could in this most sensitive, demanding and essential role. He was still many years away from retirement, even from laying down the burdens of administration within the congregation.

The choice of Br. Ephrem as provincial resulted from the action of the 1945 general chapter in creating autonomous and virtually independent provinces of priests and brothers. Though the initiative toward separate provinces had been taken by Fr. Albert Cousineau, superior general, in response to encouragement from the Vatican, Br. Ephrem had from the outset been part of the planning and preparation for this move. He had experienced the tensions between priests and brothers from the earliest part of the century and had been involved in congregational administration long enough to recognize the problems and what realistically could be done to resolve them. He had written Br. William Mang in 1943, *I have much faith in our men and in a future in which the Brothers determine their own policies inside and outside. I see the first step to be trained leaders, for we must become self-powered. I believe this to be our rightful position in the plan of Holy Cross, the one God destined us to have. I see no other way of having the two societies respect each other. Cooperation must be mutually sought and not forced. Each must operate, and in the necessary things co-operate.*

*If we can establish principles in C.S.C. I think much good can
be done. If we see each other as two free and cooperating societies
there will be mutual respect.*

And such a view would mean that the priests should be free
to have any type of school they want and that we should have the
same freedom to have grammar schools, high schools, colleges—or
whatever is necessary for the complete life of a complete society,
associated with another society for mutual and common good. If a
society is to function it must have officers who actually represent
it and are in a position to act in its behalf. Even apart from
our original founding I think we can see clearly why the whole
organization came to be called the Association of Holy Cross and
not the Society of Holy Cross.[6]

Br. Ephrem, along with the other members of the general council,
assisted Fr. Cousineau in the structuring of an equitable and productive plan for dividing the two societies that would nevertheless
preserve on the general level the essential unity between the priests
and brothers intended by the founder, Fr. Moreau. There is value in
looking more closely at Br. Ephrem's role in influencing the outcome
of the legislation at the 1945 chapter.

GENERAL COUNCIL ACTION ON AUTONOMOUS PROVINCES

Despite wartime complications, Fr. Cousineau hoped that the
general chapter could be held as regularly scheduled in 1944. Br.
Ephrem wrote Br. William Mang in late 1943, *If at all possible the
Chapter will be held in summer—if enough of the foreign delegates can get here. This is the latest desire in order to get the
problems over with.*[7] He wrote a month later: *Things are going
along well and quietly here, and some little consideration is being
given to problems that may arise in the next Chapter, though as
yet no prediction can be made for next summer.*[8]

In the spring of 1944, having completed the canonical visitations
urged by Rome (except in war-torn France), Fr. Cousineau felt a
strong need to address the issue that was of such great significance
for the congregation—the nature of the union existing between the
societies of priests and brothers. But wartime conditions dictated the
postponement of the chapter.

Fr. Cousineau continued to address the primary issue, however.
As superior general, he was expected to organize a provisional agenda
for the general chapter and, with his assistants, to prepare whatever
other documentation would heighten the awareness of the chapter members, or "capitulants," and facilitate their involvement. Fr.

Cousineau wrote an important paper addressing the union of the two societies and submitted it to his council for approval before making it available, with modifications, to the chapter members as background material for their discussions and action at the chapter. The document was crucial in introducing the issue and preparing the way for a frank and open dialogue among chapter members. He wrote: *After my canonical visitations, and after making investigations which I believe were somewhat thorough—even though I could not make the canonical visitation in France—I have come to the conclusion that we must look for those ways and means which are most appropriate to help us find for our problem a solution based on peace and charity and enable us to avoid any ill-considered act on the part of our community members.*[9]

In fact, he noted, the eventual decision to hold the general chapter in 1945, even if war continued, was based on certain difficulties present in the congregation, particularly the problem of union. In Fr. Cousineau's estimation, the need to gather the delegates was so imperative that he had determined to move ahead with the chapter. He told them that the question of union was foremost, because it was the union of the two societies that demanded serious consideration, not only with a view to maintaining it, but of reinforcing it by the best possible means.

To safeguard the sometimes fragile unity between the societies of brothers and priests in Holy Cross, an "Oath of Union" had traditionally been taken by capitulants of chapters, by major and local superiors and directors, and by those in charge of novices and postulants. The oath included a promise to God and the congregation never to say or do anything, or to allow anything to be said or done, contrary to the preservation of union between the two societies unless the Holy See judged otherwise. Any violation of the oath could result in the loss of one's office and his vote in chapter.[10]

Because of this oath it had been necessary to obtain from Rome a dispensation for the superior general and his council so they would be entirely at liberty to discuss openly and frankly the concept of union and all the implications involved in the potential for the separation of the two societies. Exemption from the oath also had to be obtained for any other members of the congregation whom the superior general wished to bring into the dialogue at any time, including the capitulants.

Fr. Cousineau felt that "relative peace" was being maintained among the priests in the United States on this issue, and he believed this situation was largely due to his having promised to seek out a solution to the problem of union. He revealed that *the more radical among them want separation. It seems that the Brothers, and with them a great many priests, would be content without going to such extremes.*

Although some tension between the societies did exist in Canada, Fr. Cousineau quoted a confidential memo received from some Canadian members in which they laid down two unambiguous principles: *(1) The principle of union of our two societies must be safeguarded at the cost of whatever sacrifices required; (2) We must return without bias to the spirit of our Founder, who wanted two societies distinct but not separate.* It seems, therefore, that if a problem existed, it was primarily among the clerical members of the United States province.[11]

Fr. Cousineau thought it time to deal concretely with the issues and *to give more administrative autonomy to each of our societies.* He believed that, if there had indeed been a lag in the development of the community, particularly in the society of brothers—as most contended—it was undoubtedly due *to no lack of alertness, but rather to a combination of circumstances and governmental procedures which have hampered development and the spirit of initiative among the Brothers in authority. The sense of responsibility is too often paralyzed, and the development of the society of Brothers as a whole is retarded. If the Brothers had more freedom of action in the machinery of administration the leaders among them would be more apt to take up their own problems, to look into them more carefully, and to solve them more in accordance with their mentality and needs.* As a result, it seemed to Fr. Cousineau that it would be logical to give the brothers greater autonomy regarding the means of assuring the carrying out of projects as well as in the administration of community funds, *even if that necessitated separate financial organizations.*

The superior general then proposed two possible scenarios for addressing the resolution of the problem of union: to retain the status quo, but with a few modifications such as separate novitiates; or to revise the constitutions so that autonomous priest and brother provinces could be established, maintaining, however, union "in and through the general administration." It is curious to note that in a French edition of this memo Fr. Cousineau lists three scenarios, the third being *the separation of the two societies in order that each may move toward the ideal of their respective founders— thus abandoning that of Rev. Fr. Moreau.*[12] This third option was included, in English, in a one-page memo distributed to the general council members in the spring of 1944, but all words following "the separation of the two societies" were penciled out of the copy in the

Midwest Province archives, probably that belonging to Br. Ephrem. From the outset, Fr. Cousineau never saw this third option as viable for Holy Cross.

The seriousness and significance of this council discussion must not be minimized. Fr. Cousineau and his assistants knew full well that any views and proposals for action they brought to the general chapter would be open to grave criticism, even rejection, if they did not clearly embody the vision of the congregational membership and provide a realistic, practical resolution protective of the nature of the congregation and thus acceptable to the majority of the Holy Cross religious as represented by the capitulants. Fr. Cousineau wanted to be certain that the issue was clearly comprehended by his assistants and that the implications of the vote they would be asked to cast secretly in council for or against the proposal would be understood unambiguously. Though from the outset he himself favored one of the three scenarios, he felt his councilors must be free to examine all possible options before a consensus was reached. In this matter, he and his council had to come to the chapter thoroughly united.

The document Fr. Cousineau presented to the general council for discussion in the spring of 1944 was the following:

The General Council will be requested to consider the following proposition concerning union between our two societies, after which a ballot will be taken.

The General Council upon the request of the Superior General has resolved to devote any remaining portion of time left after disposing of routine business to the preparation of the next General Chapter, as required by article 408 of our Rules.

One of the problems most worthy of our attention is that of union between our two societies. The project as presented by the Superior General, concerning union between the two societies in the Congregation of Holy Cross, gives rise to three main solutions:

1) Keep the status quo with a few modifications; such as, separate novitiates, etc.

2) Separation of the two societies [the following words are canceled in pencil, presumably by Br. Ephrem, whose handwriting appears at the foot of the page] *and return to the ideal of each respective founder (this means Father Moreau's ideal would be abandoned).*

3) A revision of our Constitutions with provision for union in the General Administration and separate Provinces.

The first two solutions in the project mentioned above seem unacceptable, and, therefore, rejected a priori, because the first, being only a half-measure, would not give satisfactory results, and the second, which is not imperative de facto, would do more harm than good.

The third solution is submitted to the General Council as a basis for discussion. It might be summarized thus: Distinct Provinces for the Society of Priests and for the Society of Brothers with respective Provincial Superiors, all Provinces being united by the bond of the General Administration.

Two points remain intact: a) Union is preserved, b) the spirit of the Founder is respected as mentioned in our Rules and Constitutions as approved by the Holy See. The Congregation of Holy Cross is composed of two societies, distinct but not separate (Constitution 1, Article 1).

Today the General Council is called upon to decide, by secret ballot, whether or not it is in favor of revising our Constitutions according to Solution No. 3, as expressed above, in its principles, while reserving the right to accept, reject or modify in whole or in part, after further consideration, the whole plan or any part thereof as presented by the Superior General.

A vote in the affirmative means that the Council accepts in principle Solution No. 3: Separate Provinces for Priests and for Brothers, each Province having its own Provincial Superior, and all Provinces united in the supreme authority of the Congregation. A negative vote means that the majority is in favor of considering either of the first two solutions.[13]

Br. Ephrem, as a member of the general council, engaged conscientiously in the preparation of this issue for the general chapter, and he cast his vote for the third option of Fr. Cousineau rather than for the status quo or for complete separation. Once he had the unanimous backing of his council members, Fr. Cousineau was able to move ahead in formulating the background as well as the plan of action to be followed in bringing the matter of autonomous provinces to the general chapter.[14]

Any discussion among religious prior to the chapter was, according to the Cousineau document, to be held *in the spirit of justice and charity, and if possible, in conformity with our Constitutions; that is, we must abide by the principle of union of our two societies. This I think is feasible.* Rome insisted on dialogue in this spirit, Cousineau warned. According to the instructions of the Sacred Congregation of Religious there was to be no further talk of complete separation. Any resolution would be sought and eventually found under the umbrella of union. Two points had to be strictly adhered to: *maintain union, and respect the mind of our Founder in his concept of two societies distinct but not separate.* Fr. Cousineau felt that this dual principle called for maximum initiative and freedom in the provincial administration under the unity of the general administration.

Then Fr. Cousineau carefully outlined the plan for autonomous provinces, should the general chapter choose to ratify this direction. After detailing some areas, he wrote: *The Congregation is to be composed, in principle, of autonomous Provinces of Fathers and of Brothers, with a Provincial Superior at the head of each: a priest Provincial for the priests and a Brother Provincial for the Brothers.*

There will be union in persona and in operibus. (1) In persona: Fathers and Brothers will be united in the moral person of the General Chapter, the General Council, and the Superior General. This union will not be merely nominal but effectively efficacious according to the terms of the Constitutions. (2) In operibus: Fathers and Brothers can and should help each other in common works according to a well defined plan of coordination.

In addition, union will be made more perfect, because the main causes of friction will be removed—questions of inequality in treatment, real or imaginary, suspicions and the like. There should also result greater initiative among both Societies.[15]

The superior general noted further points about the proposed functioning of general authority, including the general council and the provincial chapter and councils, emphasizing the need for co-operation among the provinces. It has to be borne in mind that the question of autonomous provinces affected not only the United States Province of priests and brothers, but governmental units in Canada, France, and Bengal. Still, as alluded to in an earlier chapter, the approach to some aspects of the question of union and autonomy was sometimes different in Canada. For both areas, however, the question of financial rights necessarily had to be raised, and Fr. Cousineau gave some attention to that aspect of the proposal, revealing that *each autonomous Province will administer its property independently of other Provinces, being obliged, however, to refer to the General Council in all cases prescribed by Canon Law and the Constitutions. Independent ownership of property will entail the dividing of Community real estate and other assets between the Provinces of Priests and Brothers concerned. . . . I realize that the financial question is particularly delicate. . . . Difficult as is the problem, there must be a solution that will not impede the apportionment of finances for the greater good of all.*

How would brothers engaged in manual labor fit into the new structure? Sensitivity was required in addressing this question. Fr. Cousineau appended a separate section on "Brothers for Manual Work." He said: *Before bringing these suggestions to a close I must needs refer to the question of Brothers engaged in manual labor. According to our Constitutions and Rules we have but one society of Brothers, and I therefore contemplate the coadjutor Brothers as continuing in their historical position.*

They can, as is the case now, continue to be of great service in the houses of the priests, and whenever possible, live in a house conducted by the Brothers. It is assumed that the cooperation in the works of the priests, so evident in the past, will continue to exist. However, should the future bring cause for complaint in this respect, the question of the coadjutor Brothers aiding in the common interests of the Congregation will be open for discussion and ruling in any subsequent Chapter. This last sentence was prescient, to say the least.

The superior general concluded: *I must admit, as you see, that my exposition of the problem is still incomplete. Our preliminary work as members of the General Council was to prepare a plan as clear, precise and religiously inspired as possible in order to avoid the weariness that might be attached to it in Chapter. The work is now up to the Chapter, and it is hoped that the plan elaborated by the General Council will serve as a basis for discussion and decision, even though amendments may be needed now or in the future.*

Let us not then leave much to chance unless we wish to see the work of Holy Cross proceed haphazardly without leadership or direction.[16]

It is evident that Fr. Cousineau anticipated the development of some thorny problems in relation to the coadjutor question, and, while subsequently in the chapter the problem was, as everyone thought, dealt with in an unambiguous manner, the clear distinction did not emerge as decreed there but—as will be seen—evolved otherwise in the eventual decision emanating from Rome.

The superior general appended a separate page to his memorandum, one which he entitled "Considerations in Favor of Autonomous Provinces of Fathers and Brothers." He noted two main points: *The Common Good is Fundamental* and *Advantages of this Project from the Point of View of the End Pursued.* He focused primarily on the spiritual advantages of the proposed change, perhaps realizing that discussion at the chapter would almost of necessity have to be directed to the practical implications involved. It is interesting to note Fr. Cousineau's reasons for preferring the autonomous province proposal to that of either complete separation or maintaining the status quo.

In our present position we have not been able to avoid serious crises. Our history has been a record of such trials, which because of our increasing membership and greater facility in communication are in danger of augmenting.

Separation would be disastrous to our morale and reputation.

Autonomous Provinces, in view of the reasons given, should not only conserve but strengthen union, and in addition (a) the general influence of the Congregation will be maintained and augmented by the mutual aid sincerely accorded; (b) the ideal of Fathers Moreau and Dujarie will be conserved; (c) the Brothers will retain the advantages of a clerical society; *and (d) an autonomous society means greater initiative and disinclination to separate. Finally we must bear in mind that before all else we must be the instruments of God.*[17]

As a result, then, of congregational unrest surfaced during the visits paid by the superior general to the membership, the general chapter of 1945 dealt with the problem of union in a direct and sincere manner. It would be fair to say that both societies came to the table with their proper agendas and accurate to presume that even within societies there were individuals who defended particular perspectives and harbored certain hopes. Br. Ephrem, a man of principle and vision in his own right, approached the task with eagerness, anticipating that his personal proposals might form at least a part of the foundation for whatever would be decided. Yet he knew also that he represented a large majority of the brothers who acknowledged their inexperience, if not inability, in dealing with matters of such scope and import, and he wanted to be faithful to that charge. Through it all, however, for him there was something of the "holy indifference" which was open to the inspiration of the Holy Spirit moving within the capitulants and the workings of the chapter. The enthusiasm with which Br. Ephrem subsequently entered into his role as the first brother provincial is indicative of his belief that what emerged from the chapter of 1945 was indeed inspired by God and was the best possible solution not only for the brothers in the United States but for the entire congregation.

THE REPORT OF THE SUPERIOR GENERAL

At the opening of a general chapter it is customary for the superior general to present a report to the delegates on the status of the congregation. At least implicitly he also intends to stir up the enthusiasm of the capitulants for the task before them and to shape in their consciousness something of his own agenda, to whose broader perspective the capitulants respond in dealing with the various points for consideration.

Fr. Cousineau knew that the manner in which he presented the proposal for autonomous provinces was crucial. He had to be a salesman. No matter how convinced of the appropriateness of the plan he and the councilors were, the delegates brought with them their own biases and those of the wider membership who sent them to represent the totality of Holy Cross throughout the world. There was no reason to believe there would be serious opposition to the plan; but to be effective it had to be accepted with enthusiasm and conviction by the capitulants. Thus the superior general worded his report to the chapter with conscious diplomacy and persuasiveness.

After presenting a brief review of developments in the congregation since the 1938 chapter and posing a few of the less urgent issues facing the delegates, he concluded his report with an honest appraisal of the union between the two societies. Because the question so deeply concerned the future of the congregation, and because Br. Ephrem had played such a vital role in the development of the proposal and was to be given a mandate to see to its implementation among the brothers, the text of Fr. Cousineau's concluding remarks in English—sometimes rhetorically affected by his French Canadian background—is included here.

> . . . *Finally, I want to broach the subject of the union of our two societies together, of the priests and the brothers together. The matter is not novel. It was taken up many times at different Chapters. In 1932 the Capitulants reasserted their love for unity, whilst yielding more and more concessions in favor of the autonomy of our two societies.*
>
> *Today, treading along the same path, I propose to you a plan of autonomy for our two societies already studied by the General Council and various committees assigned to this task. All the details will be carried to your attention in the course of the Chapter.*
>
> *The reason for this proposal? During my visitation throughout the American Province, a large number of priests freely spoke to me of their wish to improve the situation. I invited them to prayer and to submission in regard to the present state of things; in return I promised them I would deservedly study the problem.*

On the 22nd of May 1941, His Excellency the Apostolic Delegate in Washington called upon me to forward him a report in connection with the union of our two societies. This report was made to him. June the 4th of the same year, the Delegate, having read the memorandum, thanked me and granted me an audience. June 12th I met him at his home. He advised me to consult under secrecy each one of our religious during my canonical visitation, to fully sound the opinion. The dispensation from the oath of union was conceded by the Holy See to the Superior General and to all the members of his Council, that they might speak of and discuss at liberty among themselves the measures which they should believe most appropriate to meet the situation and to prepare for the future in a spirit of charity and, if possible, in keeping with our Constitutions. Furthermore, the Superior General had the right to question on this matter, whomsoever he deemed fit, especially in the course of his regular visitations, with the faculty to relieve of the oath, during the inquiry, the subject queried.

What is the result of this inquiry carried out with a fair amount of difficulties, on account of the danger to be avoided at all cost, of troubling certain souls more timorous than straightforward?

Here it is: a) The older and the younger religious, most of them at least, love the Congregation just as it is; they intend to spend their life and die within its fold.

b) Those who range between thirty and fifty years of age, and who have never had anything to do with the administration, respond differently. No one, aside from a very few individuals, wants the separation. All wish for peace in a fair settlement of the question. They own up that the formula is not easy to find. Among those, and not of the less reliable, some avowed having noticed an ill influence borne on the spiritual life, of too great an intimacy of life between priests and brothers. The priest does not always set a good example, they say and certain brothers are surprised at first, then saddened at the sight and finally prevail themselves of it to justify their lax conduct.

On the other hand, a number of priests grow bitter from what they designate as breaches against their dignity—and they no longer behave toward the brothers with the respect due to them.

c) Those who have had a hand in the administration mention other widely-known reasons. Priests and brothers claim it is necessary to constantly look after the rights of each society, because there is always a tendency of the one prevailing over the other.

The priests complain of the broad influence of the brothers in the choice of the superiors; they claim that the Constitutions or the Rules in specifying what works belong to the one or the other society, have barred them from expansion.

In counterpart, certain brothers complain of the little interest the cleric superiors (major or others) show in the development of their society. They speak of the neglect in which they are held in affairs with the ecclesiastical authority, in financial dealings, and especially in the foundings, in the demonstrations, in the external representations and in the public manifestations put on by our mixed establishments.

I can declare that, with the exception of the scholastics and novices, I must have directly or indirectly questioned, in relation with the matter, 90% of our religious. I believe there is not one who, either in one way or another, has not related one or several facts corroborative of the general reasons of the above-mentioned complaints.

Following my last circular letter in which I clearly spoke of the broader autonomy of our societies, I hardly received five letters of disappoval to a like measure. I met most of our religious, priests and brothers, in our American and Canadian Provinces; I questioned more intimately at least thirty of those who bear a radiating influence on their confreres. I chatted at ease with them on the problem, going into the main details. There were not five who opposed the principle of the autonomy of homogeneous Provinces of priests and brothers.

Of those who did oppose this project, I inquired what they wished for. Peace and an end to these campaigns for or against the union, as each new Chapter draws close, answered certain fathers. More initiative for the brothers, replied a number of brothers, by endowing a brother with increased authority that will allow, more directly, for closer relations with the ecclesiastical authorities in behalf of the expansion of our society.

This precisely, I replied to both groups, is the aim sought in the foundation of these autonomous, homogeneous Provinces. That which you propose, a provincial power independent of the Superior Provincial, would quickly lead us to anarchy. The Provincial is the one who is and must remain the chief executive in the whole Province.

Such, dear Capitulants, is the situation as it has appeared to me. I have laid it before you in as objective a manner as possible, with the intention of helping you to find the answer that will permit us not only to maintain, but also to strengthen our unity.

Consider the proposition of autonomous Provinces of priests and brothers in the light of your reason and faith. Your reason will help you to understand that the story of these whirlpools of discontent sometimes so crudely expressed in the past, is fatally leading us to disaster, according as in both societies the number of priests and brothers increases and according as this innate need of liberty of action in both our societies stands out more prominently.

Your faith will convince you that we must maintain the union of both our societies. This is the plain and precise idea of the Very Rev. Father Moreau, our Founder. Was it not also the Very Rev. Father Dujarie's, who himself witnessed the functioning in unity of our two societies? And this decision of the Founder was formally approved by the Holy See in many instances. Rome even went to the extent of granting its approval to a special oath to maintain union in the Congregation.

The plan that I propose to you aims at nothing else, either immediately or distantly, directly or indirectly. It is thoroughly inspired with the maintaining of unity. It will provide for unity by dispelling the remote causes of friction and misunderstanding. After taking advice of canonists and even of outsiders, after chatting oftentimes with men unconcerned in the matter and deeply pious, I have found among them a unanimousness which prompts me to believe that God asks that we should stop and consider the proposition. The project is not perfect. It is up to you to carry it to completion through your work. Needless to say, you always remain at liberty to propose another plan which you would judge more appropriate for the development of the Congregation.

Whatever the results, I beg of you, with all my soul, dear Capitulants, to retain for Holy Cross its quite definite character in the Church of Christ. According to circumstances, and for the best, in keeping with our present views, let us allow for certain modifications in operation, but may we preserve in its integrity the ideal of the Founder; the union of our two societies, in a spirit of justice and charity.

Let us finally recall that our decisions, whatever they may be, will be carried to Rome, and if they obtain the necessary ratification our Founder himself cannot help but approve any evolution in unity, apt to aid us in loving one another all the better.

May the Holy Ghost shed his light upon us and preside over these deliberations.[18]

THE REPORT OF THE COMMITTEE
ON THE DIVISION OF ASSETS

Following the general council's consideration of the question of union and autonomy, and the promulgation of the topic as the key issue of concern to capitulants at the chapter to be held in Washington, D.C., in the summer of 1945, serious deliberation had begun throughout Canada and the United States on precisely what the concrete reality of autonomy, of homogeneous provinces, would mean.

As discussed at length earlier, Fr. Cousineau, superior general, had commissioned a group of religious—three brothers and three priests—to ascertain the practical and equitable distribution of the assets of the United States Province between the brothers and the priests should the chapter accede to the proposed settlement. He wrote to Fr. Thomas Steiner, provincial of the U.S. Province, on March 6, 1945, setting up the committee to discuss the matter for the American religious. He said, *As I am of the opinion that much of the discussion ground can be prepared ahead of time, I am appointing Province Committees to consider the ways and means by which this plan can be made operative in the new type of Provinces contemplated. For the United States I hereby name as a preparative Committee: Fathers Thomas Steiner (Chairman), Hugh O'Donnell, John Cavanaugh, Brothers William, Chrysostom, Bonaventure.* As its mandate, the group was informed: *This Committee is named to aid me personally by furnishing information, proposals and plans which I hope to be able to embody in the program which I am to present for the consideration of the Chapter.* The deadline proposed for submitting *a rather definitive and constructive report, signed by all the members of the Committee* was May 1. Because of the sensitivity of the issue, at the first meeting of the group each member was to pledge himself not to discuss with anyone outside the committee the problems being looked into or the agreements being reached. In Canada a similar committee was set up to settle the question as it applied there.

Fr. Cousineau proceeded to give Fr. Steiner some guidance by way of principles for the committee. *Actually you are to take an old Province and make two new ones out of it. In the new and ensuing Provinces each Society should have an equitable proportion of the establishments or houses, the real estate, the present current and liquid assets of whatever nature. If it is seen that this procedure gives too large a share to one of the Societies, then the wealthier in goods or income should make annual contributions in cash or services until the goal set according to equity has been reached. I believe the basic idea of justice should be to provide each Society with the means for reasonable support and development, while at the same time protecting the healthy development of the present establishments.* Fr. Cousineau remarked in a practical vein that even if the chapter were to approve the proposals as presented, it would likely take time and subsequent chapter legislation to adjust arrangements to render them more acceptable to both societies.

The committee began its work almost at once, having a very limited time in which to come up with the expected results, and when they found that even with compromise they were not able to arrive at an agreement each society was willing to sign, Fr. Steiner asked for an extension on the deadline. On May 1, the day on which the report was to have been finished, Fr. Cousineau wrote to Fr. Steiner granting him an extension of two weeks or more to "persecute your work diligently and as rapidly as possible." The matters over which there was disagreement were in the expected areas: the designation of certain houses as belonging either to the priests or to the brothers and the projection of future assets and liabilities and the incomes and expenses of the new provinces. There was full agreement on the principles of division, on what should constitute the new provincial councils, on the composition of the general council, on the affiliation of members of one society working in the other, on the novitiates, and on the assets and liabilities and incomes and expenses of each activity of the province over the last fifteen to twenty years. The committee, noting their inability to concur on all points, alerted the superior general to their plan to submit two reports, one from the brothers and one from the priests on the committee. Both priest and brother committee members appended explanations as to how they would settle the two controversial points of the agenda, allowing the superior general to determine for himself what to present as a final proposal to the chapter.[19]

The proposals submitted by the members of the committee for review and presentation to the chapter by the Committee on Finance eventually emerged in the form of a decree entitled "1945 General Chapter Agreement for Distribution of Property Between Provinces." Br. Ephrem was a member of the chapter committee and fought forcefully for the inclusion of every penny in property, institutions, and cash which he had felt from the outset was due the brothers. Br. Maurus O'Malley in his paper "The Portrait of a Builder" notes, *On the strength of the knowledge that he had of the 100 years of work contributed by Brothers of Holy Cross at Notre Dame and of the statistics the Rev. James Burns presented to the general chapter of 1938, he [Br. Ephrem] felt sure that Notre Dame would be very generous in affording the Brothers sufficient assistance in setting up their Province and getting a start on their own. He was painfully disappointed with the share given the Brothers in the Chapter. But he was not defeated, as the record of new foundations and general development would later indicate.*[20] Nowhere else apart from a personal recollection or two is there any allusion by anyone in Holy Cross to Br. Ephrem's being "painfully disappointed" in the results of the 1945 general chapter as to the division of assets. What seems more clearly documented is his realistic appraisal of what the priests, taking into account the circumstances of the university, would be able to give to the brothers, and his willingness to accept approximately 25 percent of the province assets as opposed to the 50 percent which in justice could have been claimed. Some support may be found for Br. Ephrem's reportedly having later on regretted accepting scholarship assistance from the university in terms of an overall amount rather than in numbers of scholarships, as the agreement began in time to work against the interests of the brothers. Even in this case, however, it is possible to defend Br. Ephrem's rationale in proposing the scheme as he did and as the chapter eventually approved it. He felt that with the acquisition of St. Edward's University or the University of Portland, whichever was to be ceded to them in the division of property, the brothers would have a new center for the training of their own members and would not rely as completely on Notre Dame in the future. He intended transferring the bulk of scholastic training to Texas or Oregon—and eventually other regional sites controlled by the brothers—leaving only sufficient men at Notre Dame to take advantage of the scholarship agreement which would, in that case, be more than adequate. Events did not develop precisely as anticipated, which may by hindsight have cast the decision of the chapter in a less favorable light.[21]

The agreement forged for the brothers at the chapter was in essence the plan proposed by the special committee. In its turn the committee had forwarded to the chapter essentially what Br. Ephrem, consulting with Brs. William and Bonaventure, had suggested. The brothers were to have the following properties, assets and activities assigned to them: Valatie, New York; Dujarie Hall on the campus of Notre Dame; Sacred Heart College in Watertown, Wisconsin; St. Joseph Farm a few miles east of Notre Dame; Holy Cross College in New Orleans; the camp at Bankson Lake in Michigan; St. Joseph Novitiate at Rolling Prairie, Indiana; St. Edward's University in Austin, Texas; a parcel of land for a preparatory school connected with Notre Dame; and some property in San Fernando Valley, California, for a school. The total appraised value of these assets was $2,303,879.35. In addition, the brothers were to have the use, under a ninety-nine-year lease, of the Community House on the campus of Notre Dame, even though its ownership would be retained by the priests, and were to be given scholarships and cash by the university. These particular assets totaled $3,026,643.45. Thus the brothers were awarded a net package of $5,330,522.80. If Br. Ephrem was disappointed, it was because the total value did not more closely reach the originally desired goal of $6,000,000. But he had already indicated long before the chapter his satisfaction with a figure in the neighborhood of $5,500,000. Br. Ephrem himself, as a member of the Finance Committee, wrote up the details of the agreement that went to the chapter floor for approval.

But this financial settlement between societies was only the practical side—important though it was—of the far more crucial alteration in the structure of Holy Cross that had been mandated during the chapter. The capitulants had approved Fr. Cousineau's proposal for the separation of the two societies into autonomous, homogeneous provinces. Henceforth provinces would operate separately under their own administrations. All priests and clerical religious would be members of the priests' society; all brothers, whether teachers or coadjutors, would be members of the brothers' society. On the general level there would be collaboration and parity of representation in the makeup of the general council and the general chapter; and the superior general, though a priest, would continue to represent and guide the interests of the entire congregation, priests and brothers alike.

Writing in 1976, Br. Bonaventure Foley, who had been a member of the commission established to determine the equitable division of assets and a member of the general chapter, wrote: *I did find that Fr. Cousineau's proposal was practical since all previous suggestions were unacceptable by some discontented priests. It was philosophical because it seemed to be a solution to the issue. It was [in effect] charismatic because I don't think it was ever considered [to be so] from this point of view by Fr. Cousineau. [Yet] Fr. Cousineau's solution was endorsed by the entire chapter as a solution to the discontent that existed.*

It might be said that there was no such harmony in the Congregation as there has been since the 1945 general chapter.

The main steering committee during the chapter which dealt with the issue was Fr. John Cavanaugh, Br. Ephrem, who as I recall implemented the study made by the six commission people under the chairmanship of Fr. Steiner.[22]

An interesting item of note was: at the close of the chapter Fr. William Bolger spontaneously arose and gave a homily to the chapter on the courage of Fr. Cousineau to bring up the issue boldly. He referred to Cousineau as an Albert the Great who had the courage to enter the den of fight [arena] and untangle the tails of the warring lions. But I would say the whole chapter was a very pleasant affair—no bitterness manifested by any delegate.

An exception may be made for the Canadians, especially Br. Leopold, who said the issue was better settled by the American religious than the Canadians: for in America it was dividing assets, but in Canada it was dividing debts between the two Societies. At the same time Leopold referred to Winston Churchill, who at a meeting in London said: I'm for preserving the union, and not dissolving the British Empire.

Fr. Joseph Rousseau, the Oblate who made the proposal for autonomous provinces instead of separation of the two CSC societies, is the person I always referred to as the author of the solution adopted by CSC. Very few refer to him as the man responsible for the policy that was adopted by CSC, yet he was the man.[23]

The plan proposed by Fr. Rousseau was prepared by him in the spring of 1945 at the request of Fr. Cousineau through Fr. Georges Sauvage, procurator general of Holy Cross in Rome. The procurator knew the Canadian Fr. Rousseau and of his research in this area of congregational government. In a nine-page paper Fr. Rousseau detailed possible options for the congregation, including total separation even on the general level, but he too rejected at the outset either maintaining the status quo or opting for total separation. He proposed "the erection of homogeneous and distinct provinces" as the answer to the problem. Some of his arguments found their way verbatim into Fr. Cousineau's preparatory document for the capitulants.[24]

In any case, Fr. Cousineau's intuition and insistence, Fr. Rousseau's plan, and the work of the preparatory commissions, the Finance Committee of the general chapter, and the chapter itself resulted at the end of the session at Holy Cross College, Washington, D.C., in the acceptance of the concept of autonomy for the two societies according to the specific plan submitted to the capitulants for their approval. Twenty-six capitulants voted affirmatively for separate province autonomy, six voted rather to retain the status quo, and one submitted a blank ballot.[25]

IMMEDIATE CONSEQUENCES OF THE CHAPTER

The chapter closed under an aura of mutual satisfaction and harmony between the two societies. A new spirit, a new direction, had been breathed into the congregation by the acceptance of the monumental alteration proposed by Fr. Cousineau and his council. With the establishment of autonomous provinces came the immediate need to plan the method by which the single province government at work in both Canada and the United States would shift gears into the creation of two provinces in both countries, each province completely homogeneous—all brothers or all priests—and autonomous.

There was of course need for an interim period between the closing of the chapter and the formal implementation of the new proposals. The Sacred Congregation of Religious required time to review and approve the legislation of the chapter, and, though that Vatican office was anticipating the action taken by the general chapter, it had still to look seriously at the results and their implications before confirming the decrees. Also, each province had to assess the practical steps to be taken to ready itself for autonomous government. Time was needed before the financial arrangements could be completed. Yet both societies were anxious to get on with their individual agendas for the future.

The chapter set up a method by which the brother provincials in Canada and the United States could be chosen and the priest provincials confirmed in office. In his Circular Letter No. 21, written shortly after approval of the legislation had arrived from Rome, Fr. Cousineau notified the congregation of the mode of procedure. Granted were the faculties needed by the superior general and his council to confirm the priest provincials in office as elected by the last general chapter and *to proceed with the brother Assistants General to the election of the first Brother Provincial in each province, after consulting the Brother Capitulants of the last General Chapter, the local brother superiors and, in the existing mixed establishments, the brother councillors.* Fr. Cousineau asked all those brothers who were named as participants in the process to indicate to him in writing on a special ballot from the generalate their choice for the future brother provincial of their respective provinces. Apostolic Delegate Amleto Cicognani executed the handing over of the chapter decrees

to Holy Cross and decided that the effective date for their promulgation was to be February 2, 1946.[26] In the meantime, Br. Ephrem and
Br. William Mang were chosen to represent the brothers' society on
the interim provincial council of Fr. Thomas A. Steiner. This council
was designated to function until the effective date of the separation
into autonomous provinces.

An unanticipated complication accompanied Rome's approval of
the legislation of the general chapter of 1945. While Fr. Cousineau
had no illusions about the tension surrounding the role of the coadjutor brothers, he did not expect problems to scuttle efforts at a mutually
acceptable resolution of the autonomy question, nor had they. Before
the chapter he had alluded to the possible need for a future chapter to
refine the nature and status of the coadjutors, but was not looking so
soon for complications. The reply from the Sacred Congregation of
Religious mandated in each society the creation of coadjutor brothers
separate from the clerics and from the teaching brothers. The decision
caused confusion and strong reactions on the part of many in the
congregation and generated the immediate involvement of several
members of the brothers' society, among them Br. Ephrem, in meetings to determine how to respond. Rome's ruling had precipitated
a situation which was to affect the congregation significantly for the
next generation and more.

6

A Busy Interim (1945–1946)

The minutes of the provincial council meeting held August 3, 1945, recorded that Frs. Christopher O'Toole and Kerndt Healy as well as Brs. William Mang and Ephrem O'Dwyer were members of the council of Fr. Thomas A. Steiner. This interim group would govern the United States Province of priests and brothers until approval was received from Rome to set up the recently decreed autonomous provinces and until a date could be set to effect the changeover. On September 29 the council approved the designation of Br. Ephrem as provincial steward.[1]

The conclusion of the general chapter of 1945 found Holy Cross religious throughout the congregation in generally good spirits. Though not everyone's expectations had been perfectly fulfilled, the overall outcome of the deliberations of the capitulants was enthusiastically endorsed as a resolution to long-standing problems and as the opening of new horizons for the apostolic mission of the congregation. With autonomy assured for each of the societies, both priests and brothers could move forward with substantive planning and action in establishing themselves and developing in their particular areas of ministerial expertise.

To be sure, many ragged edges remained to be clipped and smoothed out. Despite the excellent preparation by the general council and by special commissions and individuals, the brief time the chapter was in session proved inadequate for legislating and negotiating the finer points governing the monumental alteration of the community. The interim provincial council and the general administration would work closely together in examining questions still requiring resolution.

The *South Bend Tribune* summarized the action of the 1945 chapter: *Autonomous provinces have been set up in each country for the respective and distinct societies of brothers and priests, who, however, follow the same rule and have a common general council in New York City.*

. . . At the general chapter meeting of the delegates of the Congregation of Holy Cross in Washington in July, 1945, it was decided that the two societies of brothers and priests return to

the ideals and plans of the respective founders of the societies, a spokesman for the brothers explained. This early plan required distinct societies with regard to goods, funds and local administration but a union occurred in 1837 when the rapid development of the congregation tended to pool interests and resources in developing various enterprises.

Now that the community has grown large, the brother continued, the chapter of 1945 decreed that each society, priests and brothers, should have the freedom to initiate and carry on its special activities. For this purpose it provided for provincial superiors for both societies retaining, however, the common directive general council as was contemplated at the time the two societies united in 1837.[2]

Br. Ephrem himself in later years recalled the initial intent of the legislation: *A plan for properties, houses, money compensation and all such things was ready for the Chapter. The big point was that the Priests would have NO Brothers; all the Brothers were to be in one Society. The Brothers would pay salary for Chaplains and Priests would pay for Working Brothers.*[3]

Nothing could be initiated, however, until the approval of the Sacred Congregation of Religious was received. Given the nature of the extensive change in focus for the congregation, it was especially important that the Vatican confirm the direction chosen by the congregation and acknowledge the validity of the rationale behind the choice. But no one knew how quickly Rome would move on the matter.

SURPRISES AND REACTIONS

As it turned out, the legislation emerging from the chapter did not wear exactly the same face when approved by Rome on September 29. Between the close of the chapter and the submitting of the documents to the Sacred Congregation, maneuverings had been initiated to alter in a significant fashion the relatively simple solution the chapter had proposed to the problems of union between the societies.

Concerning this, in 1963 Br. Ephrem wrote: *Some Brothers at Notre Dame (Boniface and Seraphim, etc.) heard of this plan* [all brothers in the brothers' province], *and Father Healy and a couple of others encouraged them to send a protest to Rome as soon as the Chapter was over and before the settlement was approved by Rome. Also some Canadian Priests and Brothers protested. Some Brothers wanted to remain with the Priests there.*[4] A decree dated September 29, 1945, from the Sacred Congregation of Religious and signed by the Secretary, Pasetto, announced the approval of the chapter legislation by the Sacred Congregation and authorized Archbishop Amleto Cicognani, Apostolic Delegate to the United States, to issue his executive order for the decree of approval to the Congregation of Holy Cross. Fr. Albert F. Cousineau, superior general, on October 21 wrote Br. Ephrem at the Community House, Notre Dame, where the latter was now a member of the interim provincial council of Fr. Thomas Steiner, saying: *Our big problem is settled and Rome approved the erection of homogeneous provinces in our Congregation. There are changes imposed, but Rome has full authority and we must be pleased to accept the will of God expressed by the Holy See. However, the essential organization of Priests and Brothers provinces with their respective Provincials stands as it was decided by the General Chapter. As the execution of the Decree depends on the Apostolic Delegate in the United States, we have to wait for the last word from His Excellency.*

Couched within the text that eventually became available from the Apostolic Delegate, dated Christmas Eve, 1945, were the alterations "imposed by Rome" which had in fact been requested, or at least acceded to, by Fr. Cousineau as he was submitting the text of the legislation to Rome. Br. Ephrem, in his letter of April 1963 to Br. Maurus O'Malley, said, *Though Father Cousineau agreed in Chapter to the complete plan for only one Society of Brothers, he nevertheless while the decrees were in Rome agreed that the Priests should have Coadjutor Brothers and that other Brothers could stay with the Priests.* Perhaps the change was not entirely Fr. Cousineau's idea. In a letter from Fr. Cousineau to Archbishop Cicognani dated December 8, 1945, the superior general said: *In the several visits Fr. Sauvage and I paid to His Excellency, Msgr. Pasetto* [secretary of the Sacred Congregation of Religious], *His Excellency insisted that the coadjutor brothers must have the right to choose the society to which they wished to belong. This is justice, he told us, because from their entrance into the congregation they have wanted to serve the priests as brothers. His Excellency determined that the two societies would have coadjutors for the same reasons: the two societies, he declared in substance, need these brothers, and both must have the right to receive them and to make use of their services under the control of the general council, which, given its composition of both priests and brothers, is designed to settle all problems concerning the two societies.*[5]

The principal change, then, was that in place of the establishment of two totally distinct homogeneous societies and provinces—priests and brothers—there was authorization for both societies to have coadjutor brothers. Some brothers, those who so chose, would belong to the priests' society and province and would be without active and passive voice—the right to vote and be voted for—in the affairs of the province. Some brothers in the brothers' society would be termed "coadjutors," non-teachers, and they too would be without active and passive voice.

The negative reaction on the part of the brothers was immediate. Fr. Cousineau noted in a letter to Archbishop Cicognani, *On my arrival in New York, I officially communicated the document to my council. I wanted in this way to gain their support. I understood at once that the matter was extremely delicate. Br. Gervais* [Leduc] *declared unequivocally: we the brothers weren't there in Rome, he told me, "to give our point of view."*[6] Br. Ephrem recalled for Br. Maurus, *When Pasetto's action was made known to us, a group of us protested and said that we did not like the plan for Coadjutors in each Society. Heston helped us with the protests at Valatie and we went to see the Delegate in Washington.*[7]

From documentation available it appears that ultimately there was no serious objection among the brothers to the priests' being able to receive newly and specifically recruited candidates for the brotherhood who would be juridically part of the priests' society and province. However, there was very strong reaction against the prospect of having two separate and unequal forms of membership within the brothers' society. Br. Venard Gorman, who had succeeded Br. Ephrem on the general council, was living in Brooklyn, New York, at the primary school conducted by the congregation. He wrote Br. Ephrem: *I can well imagine how you feel about matters and hope that you will "nip it in the bud." One of the reasons why we wanted you there was to break up the gang—you know what I mean. Why wait for the big blowup—why not do it gradually and insist on your place and say. I have longed for the day when all of us could talk things over—if there is anything I dislike it's these secrets which always seem to creep out anyway. Why not broadcast them firsthand? I'm sure if most of us knew what was going on—not everything, but the high spots—there would be a lot more satisfied religious. They would feel that they were part of the organization.*[8] There is no record of Br. Ephrem's reply.

Meanwhile, because the chapter decrees could not be officially promulgated or acted upon in Holy Cross until their official execution by the Apostolic Delegate, those who objected to the substance of the rumors they had heard had no alternative but to await the publication of the legislation. On November 27, Br. Gervais Leduc of the general administration wrote Br. Ephrem: *Father General got off at Staten Island last Thursday the 22nd. . . . We got the dope. I very unfortunately cannot say anything. I never missed you so much . . . I had already a long talk with Brother Venard. . . . Father General wrote you that many changes have been made.* It is clear Br. Gervais had seen the results of the changes, yet through the secrecy he was bound to observe he could not reveal them to Br. Ephrem. Nevertheless, it was his clear objection in council to the changes that made further negotiation possible.

Two weeks later, Fr. Cousineau wrote to Fr. Georges Sauvage, procurator general of the congregation in Rome, *Without fanfare I want to recount what has happened concerning the Decree which I brought from Rome. Upon my arrival after eleven days aboard ship, I very simply and officially revealed to my council the decisions of Rome. Because of the unfavorable reaction of Br. Gervais, I consented to his accompanying me to the Apostolic Delegate. A couple of days after our visit I received a letter from His Excellency in which he asked me to permit my two brother assistants and the two brother provincial councilors each from the United States and from Canada to meet and discuss among themselves the decisions, because, he wrote, "the Society of the Brothers has had no opportunity to make known its viewpoint on the matter." In any case, it seems to me that we faithfully presented the different points of view.*

. . . That is where things are now. You see the danger. Our brothers alone have the right to debate over the decisions of Rome. And what will the priests say when they learn of this, above all if there are important modifications introduced after this intervention? As for me, I have nothing more to say except that I am still superior general and that it seems some doubt has been placed on my activity in Rome. Personally I would not complain, but I have to think of the consequences to the authority of the office of superior general. If authority means anything, the brothers must submit to it just as anyone else must. I believe in my right to defend the decree in whatever way I can, because it is a manifestation of the will of God for us. You see what difficulty we are falling into if

we leave these points unresolved. . . . I hope the response is: What is written is written.[9]

THE VALATIE CONFERENCE

Authorization was given for the two brothers on the general administration—Brothers Venard Gorman and Gervais Leduc—to meet with the two brothers from the United States provincial council and the two from the Canadian council to discuss the implications of the changes supposedly made in the legislation originally sent to Rome. In a letter from Archbishop Cicognani to Fr. Cousineau dated December 4, 1945, the Apostolic Delegate said, *Because of the fear that the sudden and unheralded promulgation of these important changes would give rise to some surprise or disappointment in the minds of several members of the Congregation, I deem it opportune for the minds of the Religious to be properly prepared for the announcement of these documents from Rome. This is particularly important, inasmuch as the Decree from Rome makes mention of the consent of the Religious interested . . . and the Society of the Brothers has had no opportunity to make known its viewpoint on these matters. . . . In any case, the discussion of these points by two Brothers from the United States and two from Canada, in concert with the Brothers of the General Council, would prepare the way for more wholehearted acceptance of the decisions of the Holy See. I dislike greatly to occasion any further delay in the final settlement of a matter on which the entire Community is anxiously awaiting official word, but I feel that the suggested conference with representative Brothers of the Congregation will ultimately contribute in no small degree to the effective application of the will of the Holy See.*[10]

The meeting of the brothers was scheduled to be held at Valatie at the postulate of the brothers, nearly equidistant from Montreal and New York City, a site preferable—from Fr. Cousineau's point of view—to the more visible generalate. The participants were to be, besides Brs. Venard Gorman and Gervais Leduc, Brs. William Mang and Ephrem O'Dwyer from the United States Province, and Brs. Frédéric Dureau and Narcisse Meloche from the Canadian Province.

The meeting was historic and highly significant. The report emerging from it, written by the brothers and delivered by them to the Apostolic Delegate, dated December 9, 1945, appeared as follows.

———

Report to the Apostolic Delegate — Dec. 9, 1945

On December 8, 1945, conformably to the suggestion contained in the letter of His Excellency, the Apostolic Delegate, to the Very Reverend Superior General of the Congregation of Holy Cross on December 4, 1945, Brothers Venard and Gervais, General Councillors, with Brothers William and Ephrem from the United States Province, and Brothers Frédéric and Narcisse from the Province of Canada, met at Saint Joseph of Holy Cross, Valatie, New York, to consider changes in the Constitutions of the Congregation of Holy Cross, as contained in the Decree issued by the Sacred Congregation of Religious relative to the decisions of the General Chapter of 1945. They remained in session until Sunday, December 9th.

The Brothers present at the Conference wish, first of all, to express to His Excellency, the Apostolic Delegate, their sincerest appreciation of his kindly interest in this important matter and to assure him of their gratitude for this opportunity to consider the proposed changes prior to their official execution and promulgation. They feel that their Conference has afforded them an opportunity to express themselves on matters seriously affecting the future of the Congregation, and they deeply appreciate the kindly and helpful interest of the Apostolic Delegate in making this possible.

As the fruit of their discussions the members of the Conference permit themselves to make respectfully the following observations:

I.

The Conference readily recognizes the principle that the Society of Priests shall have the right to accept Coadjutor Brothers. In order to obviate possible confusion, the Brothers of the Conference respectfully suggest that the Brothers to be accepted into the Society of Priests be designated as Coadjutor Brothers of Holy Cross.

With reference to its own Society, the Conference feels that in its constitution up to the present time there have been no Coadjutor Brothers in the strict canonical acceptation of the term. All the members of the Society have always enjoyed the right of suffrage; there has been no postulate prescribed prior to the novitiate of any of the Brothers; there has frequently been an interchange of employment among Brothers engaged in teaching and other occupations.

Because there has never existed a strict line of demarcation between the Brothers engaged in teaching and those devoting themselves to other occupations, the Conference feels that there would be serious difficulty, not to say impossibility, in any attempt to determine definitely who are Coadjutors in the sense of the Decree, and who, consequently, are entitled to the right to choose to which Society they wish to belong. In individual cases insistence on the necessity of choice would give rise to serious difficulty and even personal tragedy.

Hence, the Conference respectfully requests that, while accepting the principle of Coadjutor Brothers in the Society of Priests for the future, all the religious presently belonging to the Society of Brothers be allowed to remain in that Society.

With a view to safeguarding the interests of the Priests, until such time as they will be able to build up their own Coadjutors, the Brother Provincial will continue to provide the Priests [sic; does he omit "with Brothers"?] who have been employed under them in the past, and as agreed by the General Chapter of 1945—that is to say, within the intervention of the General Council in case of negligence or divergence of opinion.

Undoubtedly, certain Brothers who have been engaged in teaching or other employments in conjunction with the Priests will wish to continue in this manner, while still belonging as in the past to the Society of the Brothers. In these cases, the Brother Provincial, in agreement with the Priest Provincial, will endeavor to assign such religious to employments where this desire can be carried out.

In thus urging that the Society of Brothers not oblige its members to make a choice between it and the Society of Priests, the Conference wished to express its earnest desire to further the cause of greater and more harmonious union between the two Societies, while safeguarding its own internal unity, as so strongly reaffirmed by the General Chapter of 1945.

II.

In regard to the right of suffrage, it is the understanding of the Conference that the Coadjutor Brothers who will be recruited by the Society of Priests will not enjoy the right of suffrage in either Society.

As for the Society of the Brothers, the Conference respectfully requests that this Society be allowed, as in the past, to have all its members enjoy the same canonical status and rights, regardless of the type of occupation in which they may be employed. All the Brothers, without distinction of class, would be employed conformably to their individual abilities and inclinations. This principle has been emphasized in the past in all vocational literature, and is the common practice in communities composed exclusively of Brothers—such as the Christian Brothers, the Xaverian Brothers, the Sacred Heart Brothers, the Brothers of Christian Instruction (in whose novitiate the first Brothers of Holy Cross were trained)—as well as in most Congregations of women.

III.

On the question of the ownership and administration of the Sanctuary-Shrine of Saint Joseph in Montreal, the Conference readily accepts the decision of the Chapter, confirmed by Rome, namely, that the Religious administration of the Shrine shall remain entirely in the hands of the Province of Priests. It respectfully makes known its desire, however, that two Brothers be members of the Board of Trustees of the Civil Corporation, and that the co-ownership of the property by Priests and Brothers be made applicable, not only to the present value of the property but also to the future, conformably to the principle voted by the General Chapter.

The Conference presumes to urge these two amendments all the more strongly, inasmuch as the vote of many members of the General Chapter on the acceptance of the principle of autonomy was conditioned by the acceptance of the agreement on the Shrine, as subsequently voted on by the Chapter.[11]

INVOLVEMENT OF ARCHBISHOP CICOGNANI

After the meeting at Valatie, the report was delivered at once by hand to Archbishop Amleto Cicognani, who, on December 17, prepared an accompanying statement to be sent to the Sacred Congregation of Religious in Rome. In it the archbishop acknowledged certain of the points of the letter of approval received from Rome dated September 29. Regarding the decree itself, he wrote in the report: *The Sacred Congregation is petitioned to agree to certain retouchings which, rather than change the Decree in its substance, are rather a brief addition to it, or a benign interpretation of it.* Introducing the brothers' report, he went on to say: *With reference to the Brothers, the Decree, so to speak, appears too radical. And, in consequence, in agreement with the Very Reverend Superior General, it was decided to permit the two Brother members of the General Council, Brother Venard and Brother Gervais, to meet with two Brothers from the United States and two Brothers from Canada, in order to make known their difficulties and their desires, all due care being taken to adhere substantially to the provisions contained in the Decree.*

I must observe here that the above-mentioned Brothers, as spokesmen for their confreres, have given evidence and are presently giving evidence of an excellent spirit and of a lively desire to cooperate with the Fathers in the realization of the high aims of the Congregation of Holy Cross. And it is precisely in view of the realization of this end, whose attainment is so necessary, that we took the above-mentioned liberty of permitting the meeting, which took place on December 8 last.

Archbishop Cicognani then entered into a more detailed description of the requests he was forwarding to Rome, simply stating that the brothers did not desire any distinction of classes among the brothers within the ranks of their own society. He noted eight motives favoring the granting of this request:

(1) This has been the constant practice heretofore, and on this score there are no grounds for complaint;

(2) It was with this understanding that the present members of the Society entered religion and subsequently made their profession, and any other provision would be tantamount to imposing on them an altogether different vocation;

(3) This is the principle enunciated in the vocational literature which is distributed for the recruitment of candidates, and is something generally known by everyone acquainted with the Society;

(4) This same principle of non-distinction is in vogue in other communities of Brothers, such as the Marist Brothers, the Xaverian Brothers, the Sacred Heart Brothers, the Brothers of Christian Instruction, as also in many communities of Sisters;

(5) Not a few of the Brothers pass of their own choice from the employment of teaching to that of manual labor, even to the commonest, according to their capabilities. Sometimes this is done in view of temporary mental rest, or to have a longer period of physical exercise, and then they return to their teaching. This has already become a tradition, and to such an extent that in many cases it would be difficult, if not impossible, to draw a line of demarcation marking out two classes among the Brothers;

(6) The Brothers like this freedom of change of employment and in practice it has been found that it contributes greatly to making them live in genuine and sincere harmony;

(7) In this democratic and American background, especially among the relatives and acquaintances of the religious, it would create a distinctively unfavorable impression were the Holy See to deprive of the right of suffrage those Brothers who render services to their fellow religious, or if it were to be decided that the Brothers engaged in manual labor among their confreres would no longer enjoy a right which was hitherto freely offered them, freely accepted, and freely exercised—and this without any difficulties being thereby engendered;

(Note: The fear which might arise to the effect that the Priests will no longer be able to recruit now or in the future a sufficient number of lay Brothers, or Coadjutors, is groundless, because the General Council will allocate the number of Brothers required for the services of the Priests, as is stipulated in this same No. 1 of the Decree, and has been the practice in the past.)

(8) The fact that the Society of Brothers will provide for the Society of Priests the personnel necessary for its normal services will be a source of union and harmony between the two Societies and will strengthen the common bond of union between the members of the Congregation of Holy Cross. In fact, many of the Brothers wish specifically to be in the service of the Priests and regard this as one of the specific duties of their Society.

The title of Coadjutor Brothers would, in consequence, be reserved for those lay Brothers who will desire to enter as such, for manual labor in the houses of the priests.

Then the archbishop went into a lengthy consideration concerning the Shrine at the Oratory of Saint Joseph in Montreal, noting the need the brothers felt to be included in both the ownership and administration of the shrine. He mentioned having spoken with the superior general and Br. Gervais Leduc, each separately and then together, and of their insistence that for true unity, harmony, and satisfaction in the congregation, the points noted should be conceded.

The archbishop concluded by requesting an answer by telegram so as to speed up the process of facilitating the promulgation of the final form of the legislation from the general chapter.

On December 14, Br. Venard wrote to Br. Ephrem: *Fr. Heston called me tonight to tell me that things looked very bright for us. The Delegate was pleased with the results of our Conference and even suggested himself that we should all stay together for the sake of unity. He is sending a letter at once to Rome for the final approval—if the answer is o.k. they will radiogram back—if not, we'll have to wait for a letter, possibly four or five weeks.*

UNEXPECTED COMPLICATIONS

On January 1, 1946, Br. Venard again contacted Br. Ephrem, this time in a state of unanticipated agitation: *Happy New Year! if such is possible. I am enclosing a copy of the letter which the Delegate had intended sending to Rome until the General stopped it. I thought both you and Br. William would like to see it and possibly make a copy of it. The other is a copy of the paper we submitted to the Delegate. I would like to have both copies back when you are finished with them. Please guard them well. Father Heston was kind enough to send them since the General has never consulted us on them. . . .*

As soon as I hear anything I'll let you know. I wish you could arrange to be here if and when the news breaks.

And then in a poignantly terse postscript, Br. Venard adds: *Do you think Bro. G. [Gervais] and I should resign?* The superior general had changed his mind about supporting the revisions requested by the brothers. He felt his duty was to uphold the decision of the Sacred Congregation of Religious as it had originally come from Rome.[12] In a letter to Fr. Georges Sauvage in Rome, Fr. Cousineau wrote: *I am convinced that it would be better that the decisions of the Sacred Congregation be promulgated as they are: (1) in order to avoid a reaction among the priests which could be productive of disunity when they find out what has happened; (2) in order to establish firmly in heart and spirit . . . that authority, when it speaks—above all from Rome—must by all means be obeyed . . . and (3) in conscience I am convinced that our coadjutors must have the right of choice.*[13]

A few days later, on January 5, Br. Venard wrote again to Br. Ephrem: *I am enclosing a copy of a letter I received from Fr. H. [Fr. Edward Heston, professor of canon law and aide to the Apostolic Delegation in Washington, D.C.] and also one which the Delegate sent to Fr. G. [General], it is marked #2 as I did not wish to put any name on it. . . . Please destroy these or keep them in a very safe place as I wouldn't want to involve H. in any way with any of the stuff I send you. Please show them to Br. William, I'm pretty sure of you being at N.D., hence I send them to you . . . he might be out of town and I wouldn't want them lying around. I'm becoming suspicious in my old age.*

A little more cheerful news came thru last night. . . . Fr. G. answered the Delegate's letter and gave him three choices in which to answer us: (1) To say that he (Gen.) was opposed to the plan; (2) To give no reason at all . . . (3) To send the matter to Rome without his (Gen.) name being mentioned in the proposal.

Fr. H. is going to try and influence the D. to do the last, in any case he will let me know what action is taken. I feel more hopeful about it all but am having a hard time keeping Gervais from swimming to Rome, if necessary, to see the Pope. You can imagine how upset he is, poor fellow.

As soon as the underground speaks, I will let you know. Fr. H. is certainly swell in keeping us informed.

The letter from Father Edward Heston is dated January 1, 1946. It is illustrative of the type of consistent and supportive assistance Fr. Heston was attempting to give the brothers at that time even as he assumed that their request would never reach Rome. Fr. Cousineau considered Fr. Heston's involvement to be ill advised and told him so, but he did not interfere with the priest's determination to assist the brothers, always assuming that only the highest motivation urged Fr. Heston to take the action he did.[14] Fr. Heston wrote:

Happy New Year! I wish that my greetings for this new year could be more hopeful, but I fear that, much against my will, I must strike a pessimistic note. Yesterday Fr. General replied to the Delegate, thanking him for proceeding to the execution of the decree, and asking to be given an appointment to discuss further matters before going ahead with the final steps. The Delegate answered that his work was finished, now that the decree from Rome has been executed and that the General and his Council are empowered to promulgate the decisions of the Chapter in the form approved by the S. Congregation. The Delegate also said that he wished to remain out of the remaining developments, since he had yielded to the insistence of the General that the decree be put into force as prepared in Rome. I am enclosing a copy of the letter. You will see that the whole tenor of the letter aims to impress on the General the fact that he has blocked the way to securing from the Holy See a decision conformable to the desires of the Chapter. The logical consequence is that the entire matter is now his own responsibility. I wrote the letter, it is true, but the Delegate told me beforehand the points which he wished to be stressed. It will be interesting to see what suggestion is made for a reply to the memorandum submitted after the Valatie meeting.

The Delegate's viewpoint on the matter is briefly this: he knew that the General favored the promulgation of the Decree in the form given it in Rome. Still, he thought that the General would cooperate in securing from the S. Congregation an interpretation which would be more in harmony with the wishes of the Chapter— and he really felt that such an interpretation could be obtained without difficulty. Rome is not one to push bullheadedly along a course when the practical difficulties have once been clearly pointed out. When he saw that the General did not wish to give this cooperation, he was very much peeved, and immediately proceeded to throw the whole thing right into his own lap and leave it there.

Personally, I think this was a mistake. Had I been here at the time I would have used every effort to have the memorandum and report sent to Rome notwithstanding the opposition of the General. Then it would have been possible to submit to the decision of the S.C. [Sacred Congregation], whatever it might have been, with the realization that both sides of the question had been adequately represented and weighed in the balance. I was really upset when I found out what had happened in my absence. The only explanation is that the General's letter and stand had so peeved the Delegate that he acted rather impulsively. Right now, I do not suppose there is any hope of getting him to reverse his stand.

And so, as they say in French, we find ourselves face to face with a <u>fait accompli</u>, with all its possible consequences. The Decree from Rome has been executed, and the General and his Council have been authorized to proceed with its promulgation. I fear that the situation has developed much too rapidly for anything to be done to stop it now. The only other alternative is open refusal to accept the decree when promulgated, and that, of course, could not be counselled in any way at all. Anything of that kind would redound to the bad name of the Congregation before Rome, and would foment dissension and bad feeling within the community. I suppose there will be a certain amount of this latter despite all efforts, and it is really disheartening to see the way opened up to such an atmosphere after the golden promises which seemed to shine in our future after the Chapter.

Frankly, I am not too fearful of the consequences in our own province. The two points of the coadjutors having their choice of societies, and of the Brothers having two classes, will be shocks, it is true, but I think that with generous goodwill this shock will *gradually wear off—although with all my heart I wish it would never have to be. The same is true of the admission of coadjutors into the society of the priests. My most serious concern and fear is for the Canadian province and the question of the Oratory. We know the attitude of the Capitulants from the Chapter, and I fear very much that this new provision regarding the ownership and administration of the Oratory is going to strike many so much as a <u>double-cross</u> after the Chapter, that there is liable to be a wide-open split, certainly of spirits and feelings, if of nothing else. I can view the future in our own province with more or less a spirit of equanimity, because I feel that there will be submission and wholehearted efforts to cooperate with the spirit of the Decree. But personal feelings enter much more largely into the Canadian problem than into our own, and that is where the danger lies. So I can only say: Let us wait and pray, and trust to the spirit of obedience to pull us through this tough spot. One of the old priests in France used to say years ago: "You can't kill Holy Cross—no matter how hard its own members try!"*

Because of the very delicate nature of this letter and of the enclosure, I would ask you to destroy both when you have read them. If you wish, you may show them to Brother Gervais, in fact, I would ask you to show them to him. But they should be destroyed immediately after, because my remarks are based on information which neither you nor I are supposed to have, officially.

Let's face the future, not without misgivings, but at the same time without any lack of confidence. We have done everything humanly possible to avert the impending situation, and the realization of duty well done can be a source of gratification and hope. Even tho we have not been responsible for creating the situation, perhaps we can be helpful later on in solving its problems and making even that turn to the benefit of the Congregation.

The letter referred to by Br. Venard as #2 was that of the Apostolic Delegate to Fr. Cousineau, the superior general. Expressing his displeasure with the situation, Archbishop Cicognani said:

I have your letter of Dec. 29, acknowledging receipt of my letter of Dec. 24 and of the Decree authorizing you and your Council to proceed to the promulgation of the decisions of the S. Congregation of Religious regarding the Congregation of Holy Cross. I am happy that these important documents reached you safely notwithstanding the uncertainties of the Christmas mail.

Needless to say, the report of which I sent you a copy will not be forwarded to Rome. From my conversations with you, and after reading the representations prepared by the Brothers in their meeting at Valatie, I had hoped to be of assistance in securing from the S. Congregation an interpretation which would be more conformable to the desires of the General Chapter as manifested last summer. As I stated in my previous letter, I have yielded to your insistence that the Decree be executed in its entirety and as prepared in Rome, and this precludes any further action on my part.

For this same reason, altho I should be happy to receive a visit from you at some later date, I feel that it would be more advisable if you were not to come prior to the promulgation of the Decree. There has already been considerable delay in arriving at the point where this promulgation can be proceeded with, and I should not wish the impression to be given that the Apostolic Delegation is in any way responsible for retarding the announcement which is so eagerly awaited by your Religious. With the execution of the Decree my own part in it is terminated, and I do not feel that I would have any advice or counsel to offer. The decision of Rome is contained in the Decree, and you and your Council can be guided accordingly.

A particular difficulty occurs to me now as I consider your desire that your letter of Dec. 20 be regarded as strictly confidential and personal. This desire, of course, will be respected. But inasmuch as the Brother Councillors and the representatives of the United States and Canada presented to me a Memorandum after their meeting at Valatie, N.Y., I know that they are expecting some kind of a reply from me. It would indeed be a shock to them to receive no word at all from me, and then to learn through your Circular Letter of the promulgation of the Decree as brought from Rome. Out of respect for your wish that your letter be kept confidential, I cannot tell them that I have suspended action because these recommendations could not be sent to Rome with the approval of the Superior General and yet that is the only reason which has motivated my action. I would be grateful if you would suggest to me a mode of action which would enable me to make to the Brothers an appropriate reply in the time intervening before the promulgation of the Decree.

AN EQUALLY UNEXPECTED REVERSAL

The Delegate was placing the burden of initiative on Fr. Cousineau, whose reluctance to allow the brothers' counterproposal to be forwarded to Rome with his approval had angered Archbishop Cicognani. Then, unexpectedly, four days later, on January 9, Br. Venard wrote Br. Ephrem a quick note: *Fr. Heston just called me to say that the document which we drew up at Valatie is going to Rome on Friday just as we wrote it. The General approved it all and said that the whole thing was a misunderstanding. So let's hope and pray that Rome will approve. The Delegate has asked Rome to wire back so as to have the answer by Feb. 2. Fr. H. is delighted with the outcome and feels very hopeful.*

No extant documentation helps to clarify precisely what prompted the superior general's change of mind or how he construed the so-called "misunderstanding." But earlier, in a communique to Archbishop Cicognani dated December 20, Fr. Cousineau said: *If it were not overly bold, I would demand the execution of the Decree exactly as it is. . . . If this decision is no longer possible, I submit myself to your sage discrimination and will rely on obedience to authority as my sole strength.*[15] Then on January 6, 1946, Fr. Cousineau submitted a lengthy document to Msgr. Luca Pasetto, Secretary of the Congregation of Religious in Rome, reviewing the matters at issue and reiterating his sincere belief that for the good of the congregation the decree of the Holy See should be maintained as originally worded.[16] On January 7, 1946, Fr. Cousineau wrote the Apostolic Delegate reiterating that he would prefer the legislative decree from Rome to read as originally worded; *however, I cannot conceive of myself as a barrier to the legitimate desires of my spiritual sons, who always have the right of recourse to the Holy See as they think prudent. Therefore I humbly ask Your Excellency to accede to the wishes of our Brothers and to forward their report to Rome.*[17] The Delegate replied on January 9, expressing his satisfaction over the resolution of the issue. Still, on January 11, Fr. Cousineau sent a letter to Fr. Georges Sauvage, procurator general in Rome, repeating his own preference and clarifying elements of the report from the Delegate, a copy of which Fr. Sauvage had received, and suggesting that Fr. Sauvage might want to stand ready to help the Sacred Congregation judge the question on its own merits should they request his assistance.[18]

On January 19, Br. Gervais Leduc wrote to Br. Ephrem, sending along a copy of Fr. Heston's letter to him dated January 13. Br. Gervais reflected on the assistance that Fr. Heston had given to the brothers in the matter of the request to Rome to overturn certain aspects of the Decree passed by the general chapter. Br. Gervais said: *I think Father Heston is the most wonderful man. No doubt you feel as I do. We were very fortunate to have him occupying the key position he does.* Considering the potentially vulnerable position in which Fr. Heston had placed himself relative to the general administration and his own priest confreres, it was a courageous act on his part, however based on principle, to engage in direct assistance to the brothers in this matter. Br. Gervais went on: *Everybody seems happy and sends you his best regards, including Brother Venard to whom I phoned a few minutes ago.*[19]

Father Heston's January 13 letter to Br. Gervais is worth quoting in its entirety.

Your letter of yesterday made better time than the last special delivery letter you sent me. I found yesterday's letter in my room when I returned just a little while ago from Sunday ministry in St. Martin's parish, and do not wish to lose any time in replying to it at once, in order to answer your questions and put your mind at ease.

I appreciate your kind words regarding anything I may have been able to do for the good cause in the last few weeks. I was convinced that it would turn out this way, although for a while it looked as though the monkey-wrench had really been thrown into the midst of our machinery. But, as I have told you before, I am persuaded that the cause is right and just, and it is sufficient reward to be able to have a part in promoting such a cause.

The documents sent to Rome by the Delegate are as follows: (1) The Italian translation of the Memorandum drawn up at Valatie. In making this translation, I took the liberty of making certain changes, which, however, do not weaken, but rather strengthen the substance of it. I included a little more insistence on the official character of all the Brothers present (General and provincial Councillors from the two Provinces), and stressed a little more the conformity of the petitions of the Memorandum with the decisions of the General Chapter of 1945. For instance, in one part I added: "The Conference permits itself to urge the adoption of the modification regarding the Oratory with all the more insistence, inasmuch as in the minds of many of the Brother Capitulants, their votes in favor of the general principle of autonomy were given after, and on the basis of, the agreement on the Oratory according to the formula drawn up and approved by the General Chapter." Nothing substantial, of course, was changed, but only some minor details which might serve to emphasize certain points in the light of recent discussions and difficulties.

(2) His own report to present the Memorandum for the consideration of the S. Congregation. This text is substantially the same as that of which I sent you the translation some time ago. His Excellency went through the text personally, and deleted from it everything that might give the impression that the General approves of the recommendations therein proposed. He also, in view of the controversy of recent weeks, took out whatever might make it look as though he was asking for the change himself. However, it seems to me that the force of the report did not lose anything by the deletions of his own approval. He left certain other phrases, and introduced certain other expressions which leave no doubt as to his own personal support of the recommendations in question. Anyway, the very fact that he sends a report with the document, instead of just standing on the outside and serving as a clearing-house for the sending of the Memorandum, shows that he favors the requests made in that document.

I think that one new paragraph added to his report is very significant and important: "It is the conviction of the Brothers that, if we wish to safeguard union and harmony, and give general satisfaction to all the members of the Community, the three points above-mentioned are to be conceded as requested. The Very Reverend Superior General would prefer the execution of the Decree as it stands, but the Brothers declare firmly that their position has the support of their confreres and also of the greater number of the priests who took part in the chapter of 1945."

Along with the documents sent to Rome, I despatched a long letter to Father Sauvage—five pages, single space—giving him certain aspects of the question which he would not have gotten from Father General. I did this, as I told him, just in case the S. Congregation should ask his opinion on the matter. Personally, I think Father General plans to wait and do nothing while the document is pending in Rome. At least, that is the impression he has given in his letters to the Delegate in recent days—but, then, you never know! In any case, I don't think there is anything to fear from the influence of Cardinal-Designate McGuigan, or anyone else whose help might be enlisted now. My own impulse would be to let things go for the present, and await the decision of Rome. The Delegate has asked for a prompt reply, and has indicated that it would be desirable to have everything settled so that the first execution date (Feb. 2) of the Decree could be retained. So there will not be much time for negotiating or counter-negotiating, etc. The documents will be in Rome, I think, before Cardinal McGuigan gets there. Bp. O'Hara, I understand, is accompanying Cardinal Spellman, but they will not be in Rome until Feb. 14th or 15th, and by that time, as we hope, everything will already have been decided. So I would think it more advisable not to recruit any supporters right now. I am confident that things will turn out properly, and I feel that this confidence will not be upset.

I most certainly would not even consider the question of asking for the appointment of a Visitor for the Community. That is an extreme step, which becomes known, and which does not do any good for a community, and I would not want to see the entire congregation subjected to the ignominy of an ecclesiastical visitation—which is generally carried out when there is question of general laxness in discipline, etc.

As for my own going to Rome in this connection, I think, in the light of the foregoing, that this will be out of the question. I could not get over there in the immediate future, and by that time everything would be finished.

Most assuredly, Father General cannot proceed to promulgate the decrees before the reply comes from Rome. An appeal, at least in a general sense, has been filed against the contents of the decrees, and that automatically suspends the force of the decree until the appeal is acted upon. When Father said that "la lettre . . . pourrait bien être publiée plus tôt qu'on ne le pense" [the letter . . . could very well be published sooner than one might expect], I think he was referring to the fact that it may be ready for the second of February—which is sooner than anyone thought some time ago. But, again I repeat it, he most certainly cannot lawfully go ahead without some indication of the decisions of the S. Congregation.

I am happy to see the reaction of Br. Ernest, and I think it would be the reaction of 95% of all the religious of the Congregation.

In my letter to Fr. Sauvage, I stressed the fact that, although it would be possible to have recourse to obedience and force submission to the Decree as it stands, such procedure would most certainly not give rise to an atmosphere of cordial and generous cooperation. I told him that if the Decree is published and applied as it stands now, this will mean that autonomy cannot succeed, because it will begin to be applied in a spirit of distrust and discontent born of frustration of legitimate aspirations and aims. I hope that what I said very much at length will help to make him understand that there is at stake in this question much more than mere submission to the decisions of the Holy See.

In the meantime, we must pray and pray much for this big intention. It is in about ten days that the documents should be in Rome, and then we must wheel our armies of prayer into action to get the result we want. You can count on my continued help and prayerful remembrances, as I need not assure you.[20]

The letter from Br. Ernest (in France) to which Fr. Heston referred included this sentiment: *I don't think it fair either, that the Brothers should not be represented in the affairs of the Oratory of St. Joseph. If the Canadian Brothers agree to this, they are surely beneath anything but men of character! I would never accede to such a thing!*

Rome may be Rome, but Holy Cross ought to remain Holy Cross at all cost!!! Please give me your impressions on all these questions! — I'm a fighter, and shall fight to the very last before I would bow to all these new contrivances.[21]

COMPROMISE AND SUCCESS

The subsequent approval of the legislation, as requested by the brothers at their Valatie conference of December 8–9, 1945, and as noted in Fr. Cousineau's Circular Letter No. 21, is adequate documentation of the success of the process initiated through the Apostolic Delegate in early 1946. However, the original target date for promulgation of the legislation, February 2, could not be honored, and it was only on March 21, 1946, that Archbishop Cicognani wrote to Fr. Cousineau advising him of Rome's approval. The superior general's letter to the congregation was dated just four days later, March 25. Thus ended a significant and difficult struggle in the lengthy process of establishing autonomous homogeneous provinces in both Canada and the United States for the religious of Holy Cross. The ramifications and consequences of this whole series of events and arrangements would long be—and still are—felt in the congregation.

Looking back years later, Br. Ephrem wrote: *Through Fr. Heston I sent that particular decision back to Rome and said that the priests could have Coadjutors if they wanted them, but that in the Brothers' Society we wanted no division—that all should have the right to vote and be voted for, to hold any office, none to be called Coadjutors; Rome approved this. Those who were called Coadjutors at the time of the Chapter could decide on staying with the priests or with the Brothers. About 70 decided to stay with the priests. All other so-called Coadjutors decided to stay with the*

Brothers with full voting rights.[22] A document in the Eastern Brothers' Province archives notes that among the non-teaching brothers in the United States 107 men chose to remain with the brothers and 59 went with the priests; and in Canada 57 remained with the brothers and 59 joined the priests' society.[23] Similarly, in his April 1963 letter to Br. Maurus O'Malley, Br. Ephrem wrote: *The only concession we got was that our Brothers' Society would have only one class and since the Priests were having Coadjutors we would have no further obligation of giving them Brothers for their work. Therefore in the spring of 1946 the Decrees came back from Rome giving us the set-up that has since been put into the Constitutions. In many ways it was a blessing, though we thought it bad at the time. It saved us giving workers for the Priests' houses and it let us have only the one Brothers' Society that we had requested.*

Thus the Chapter plans of 1945 were changed by Rome only as regard letting the Priests have Coadjutors and keep those who wanted to stay with them. All else was as in the Chapter approval of the General Council plan. Br. Ephrem here alludes only casually to a major demand of the Valatie Conference, supported by Fr. Heston and Archbishop Cicognani, that was not acceded to by the Sacred Congregation of Religious. The Valatie meeting proposed that, in allowing the priests' society the right to have coadjutor brothers among their members, it would involve only lay religious recruited by the priests *after* the establishment of the separate provinces. All brothers in the congregation prior to the chapter would remain in the brothers' society, whether teachers or not. Rome weighed the possible implications and significantly altered the request, permitting non-teaching brothers already in the congregation to make a selection of the society to which they would belong. To Br. Ephrem, at this time and under the circumstances, it was far more important that the status of all members of the brothers' society be equal than that all non-teaching brothers belong to the brothers' society as such.

FURTHER INVOLVEMENT OF FR. HESTON

Two major documents concerning the Coadjutor Brothers in Holy Cross were written by Rev. Edward Heston, C.S.C., in preparation for the general chapter of 1968. The first document contains ten pages and is entitled "General Chapter 1968, Study on The Coadjutor Brothers." It is divided into six parts: (1) a historical summary of decisions made concerning coadjutor brothers; (2) summary of opinions given by religious during a first consultation; (3) meeting of major superiors in Rome in February 1967; (4) summary of opinions of provincial and vicariate chapters to the second consultation; (5) statistics; and (6) the status of the coadjutor brothers.

The second document is entitled "General Chapter 1968, The History of the Coadjutors in the Congregation of Holy Cross," dated January 15, 1967. It is twenty-nine pages in length and is introduced on the title page by the author: *This work does not pretend to be a scientific historical study. It intends simply to set down the facts (many of which have never been made known) and to cite the documents with the help of the documentation available in the archives of the generalate.* The author goes on to say, *No judgment has been made on the difficult period 1945–1946.* And he adds, *This document is placed in the hands of the major superiors simply in order to furnish them with information.*[24]

Brother Ephrem was intimately involved with events and preparations leading up to the decisions taken in the 1945 general chapter as well as with the subsequent anomaly of a Holy Cross with brothers in both societies of the congregation. Other sources describe his involvement. The value of these 1967 pre-chapter documents is in their historical summary of factual information concerning the establishment of the coadjutors and the exposure of attitudes held on this matter in the congregation following the setting up of the autonomous provinces in 1945.

FR. THOMAS BARROSSE AND THE COADJUTORS

Fr. Thomas Barrosse, superior general of the Congregation of Holy Cross from 1974–1986, wrote "Studies on Union and Collaboration," dated May 1, 1980, as a background document for capitulants to the general chapter of 1980. Under a section entitled "The Coadjutor Brothers in Holy Cross" (pp. 12–18), Fr. Barrosse treated (in points 4 and 5 of eleven points) the role of the general chapter of 1945 and how the chapter's decisions were modified. He wrote:

(4) The general chapter of 1945 restored autonomous government by reorganizing the provinces along societal lines. Provinces were thereafter to be composed exclusively of priests and clerics and exclusively of brothers.

(5) Modification of the chapter's decisions. In approving the chapter's decisions, the Sacred Congregation for Religious introduced an alteration, ordering that there be coadjutor brothers in the juridical sense (conversi, or lay religious without active and

passive voice and engaged in <u>*auxiliary*</u> *services) in both priests' and brothers' provinces; their services were to be used indiscriminately by either society and would be a bond of unity.* The present general administration recently requested the Sacred Congregation for Religious and Secular Institutes to be given the reason for the introduction of this modification into the 1945 chapter's decisions. A subsequent reply from the secretary, Archbishop Meyer, informs us that the archives of the sacred congregation contain no indication whatever of the reason; they contain only the record of the alteration itself. After the 1945 chapter, rumors were rampant, but no documentary evidence exists to justify any explanation.

The brothers immediately appealed for abolition of all class distinction in their society, and this was granted by the sacred congregation. This left coadjutor brothers in the priests' provinces only. Brothers engaged in activities other than teaching would have to choose whether to remain in a brothers' province or to transfer to a priests' province. The superior general appealed that, in this case, brothers transferring to priests' provinces would not lose their right to vote or to be voted for, rights they had always enjoyed. The sacred congregation then ruled that they would not lose their active and passive voice, but that these rights would be exercised in the provinces of the brothers. The confusion generated by this ruling was finally dissipated by yet another Roman decision: brothers engaged in manual labor choosing to transfer to a priests' province would thereby lose active and passive voice. It was understood, of course, that those who joined priests' provinces as coadjutor brothers in the future (after 1945) would not have active or passive voice.

THE EVENTUAL OUTCOME

The confusion and dissatisfaction engendered by this set of circumstances and decisions led to continued controversy over the nature, role, and rights of the coadjutor brothers. As he assumed office as the first brother provincial, Br. Ephrem wrote in his Circular Letter No. 1 to the province: *You are all aware of the great organizational changes that have occurred in our Congregation during the past year. The General Chapter of 1945 decreed the establishment of homogeneous Provinces, that is, autonomous Provinces of Priests and Brothers, each Society having its Provincial Administration and administering a specified portion of the Community's assets and activities. This modification in government has in no way changed the ideals and mission of the Congregation. Indeed it rather takes us back to the founding concept of Holy Cross— two Societies distinct but not separate. The distinction has been emphasized, and the unity has been protected by our following the same Rule, having a common General Council and Superior General, and a General Chapter composed of priests and Brothers, as has been the case all through our history. In the past year we have had Local Superiors in each Society, and now separate Provincials have been added.*

The General Chapter's plan for homogeneous Provinces was modified by the Holy See, which permitted Brothers engaged in manual labor to transfer to the Priests' Society if they so wished. A number of Brothers exercised this right, and as a consequence some situations arose for which the Chapter had not legislated. These are being taken care of by the Administrations of the co-Provinces, cooperating with the Superior General and his Council. Some of the agreements thus reached will no doubt be matter for review at the next General Chapter.[25]

Subsequent general chapters did indeed deal with the issue, never, however, fully resolving the continuing uneasiness generated by the existence of brothers in both societies. In 1976 Br. Renatus Foldenauer, provincial of the Eastern Province of Brothers, asked for advice from Br. Ephrem regarding the ongoing pursuit of a lasting resolution to the question of the coadjutor brothers. Br. Ephrem, at that time eighty-eight and in the infirmary at Notre Dame, responded that, if the matter were still an issue in the congregation, then he would suggest that the priests have *no* brothers and that the brothers furnish whatever assistance was needed by the priests on a contractual basis as was done regularly by the brothers' society in securing chaplains from among the priests. Br. Ephrem allowed that, if some of the present brothers wanted to remain with the priests, they could do so, but the priests ought not to take in any more brothers through their own recruiting, but should rely on the brothers' society to recruit and supply those men required by the priests.[26] Finally in 1986, with the substantive revision of the constitutions of the congregation, the status of coadjutor was definitively terminated through a return to the denomination of all lay religious as members of the brothers' society, whatever their province affiliation, and the renewed structural possibility of *mixed* provinces, that is, provinces comprised of both lay and clerical religious, all enjoying equal juridical status and rights.

OTHER ELEMENTS OF TRANSITION

Apart from the issue of the coadjutors, a multitude of technical details demanded consideration during the interim year. While theoretically it had been relatively easy to decree the separation of the brothers and priests into autonomous provinces, legally and practically many complexities arose, among them the determination of corporate identity. A document dated May 24, 1943, outlined how the corporation known as "Brothers of St. Joseph" had functioned from its establishment in 1844 for nearly a hundred years, and suggested that, were its existence to cause problems in the determination of an equitable division of properties, it could be dissolved after deeding all property under its name to the University of Notre Dame.[27] Because of the often unclear distinction between property and other assets owned by the congregation and those owned by the university, the niceties of determining formal proprietorship had sometimes been obfuscated. Practically, there had been no need for clarity; if brothers, priests, and the university were essentially one unit, there was no concern over precisely in which branch of this triumvirate lay the legal corporate ownership of the shared property or assets. The Holy Cross legal entity capable in Indiana law of owning property had been from 1844, the year the University of Notre Dame was formally incorporated (January 15), "The Brothers of St. Joseph." The Congregation of Holy Cross, at that time thirteen years away from official approval by Rome, did not yet have official recognition in France or in the Church, and Fr. Sorin and the brothers at Notre Dame were pressed to denote some form of corporate identity by which they could legally own and develop properties in the United States. Apparently no move was subsequently made until the provinces separated to render themselves legally independent of one another by individual incorporation under more up-to-date identities.

Nevertheless, it is interesting to note that in 1943, two years in advance of actual separation, a serious look was being taken at potential complications requiring resolution in the event of separation into autonomous groups.

MIXED EMOTIONS OVER AUTONOMY'S IMPLICATIONS

Though in a position of having to prepare for the governing of a newly structured province comprised wholly of brothers for the first time in the congregation's history, Br. Ephrem continued to serve on the interim provincial council of the single province of priests and brothers. All about him at Notre Dame were the conversations which revealed formally or informally, placidly or heatedly, the reactions of the membership of the congregation to the general chapter decrees and the subsequent modification of them by Rome at the request of some concerned or dissatisfied religious. There was tension in the air, particularly in a local community such as the Community House, home to both priests and brothers and surely to be seriously disrupted by the pending changes. Within houses of brothers, there were conversations, even arguments, regarding brothers engaged in manual labor. A choice was being given to each of them to become a member of the priests' society or to remain with the brothers, and many questions arose. What would it now mean for a brother to be governed by a priest provincial? Indeed, what would it mean for brothers heretofore governed only by priests to be ruled by one of their own? What were the implications of giving up one's active and passive voice? What value was there in retaining these prerogatives? Would it make any difference now or in the future in the context of daily life?

Works which up till then had been undertaken by both brothers and priests were overnight to become apostolates juridically governed by one group or the other, even if collaborative involvement of manpower were retained. The changes implied in such moves were considerable.

Yet until the official date for the formal establishment of the two autonomous provinces arrived, the congregation moved forward as the traditional single province. Finally, on June 29, 1946, the minutes of the provincial council meeting tersely noted: *The Provincial Council will cease to function as of July 1, 1946.*[28] On that day the new governmental structures were to begin to function, an extremely significant moment in the evolving history of Holy Cross.

III

Provincial:
A Man of Character
and Talent

7

A Man for His Time (1946–1956)

EXCITEMENT AND OPTIMISM

On July 1, 1946, the official transition was made from a single United States Province to autonomous, homogeneous provinces of brothers and priests, each with its own provincial superior and administration. That day found Br. Ephrem hard at work finalizing preparations for the first all-brothers' provincial chapter, set to begin on July 7, 1946: *The brothers will hold their first provincial chapter meeting since the administrative change beginning at 8 a.m. today in Dujarie Hall at Notre Dame. Thirty-eight delegates will attend to consider all business, religious, and educational matters of the society.*[1]

The excitement surrounding the opening of the chapter arose out of two sources. The first was without doubt the optimistic spirit with which the membership of the new province approached the future. For the first time in the history of the congregation's one hundred and eleven years the brothers were to be fully responsible for their own destiny in pursuing life and ministry in Holy Cross. Still bound by the same rules and constitutions as the priests, still participating in the overall government of the congregation on the general level, still open to collaborative ventures with the priests, the brothers nevertheless through the separation of the societies into provinces had been accorded by the chapter the liberty to explore heretofore circumscribed areas of mission and to assume direct and full responsibility for their own growth and development in any works they chose to undertake. Indeed, the excitement was not unilateral; the priests were equally enthusiastic about their own freedom to move forward in those ministerial areas more proper to their clerical state, not constrained by the basically scholastic parameters influencing the brothers' interests, but by the same token not ruled out of such endeavors.

The second source of excitement for the brothers was that at the helm of leadership in the new province stood the one man acknowledged by everyone as the most logical and capable choice to hold the office of provincial, Br. Ephrem O'Dwyer. For the first time the brothers had over them a major superior from among their own

131

number. The implications of this new application of canonical authority were to call the congregation to a formal restatement of its rules and constitutions in the 1950 general chapter. In the meantime, however, there was complete confidence among the brothers in the ability of this man to motivate them toward the firm establishment of educational apostolates throughout the country, to encourage them in their religious profession, and to supervise the formation of the large number of young men joining their ranks at the close of the Second World War. These activities stood out as priorities for the incipient province, and no one was better qualified by age, experience, wisdom, and forceful diplomacy to coordinate the efforts of the 338 brothers in perpetual vows, the 81 men in temporary vows, and the 26 novices who at the outset made up the membership of the province.

After the general chapter of 1945, the process set up by the delegates for the selection of the first brother provincials in Canada and the United States was completed, and the general council appointed Brs. Narcisse Meloche in Canada and Ephrem O'Dwyer in the United States. Br. Ephrem was not the only person considered for the American position. Br. Venard Gorman, a member of the general administration after the 1945 chapter, was another popular candidate. The choice of Br. Ephrem was providential in some respects, because the congregation unexpectedly lost the considerable administrative capabilities of Br. Venard with his death three years later at the age of fifty-four.

AN IMPOSING MAN OF EXPERIENCE

Br. Ephrem was widely known among province members. His experience as a teacher, founder, and administrator in several schools; his years on the provincial council of Fr. James Burns; his university exposure as treasurer, teacher, and secretary to the board of lay trustees; his term on the general council; his membership on the interim provincial council of Fr. Thomas Steiner; and his widespread visibility and many friendships in the priests' society were qualifications not to be underestimated or dismissed. His personality, demanding of himself as much as of others, his intellectual capacity, his wit, straightforwardness, tireless perseverance in the pursuit of his goals, and quiet and gentle compassion were characteristics contributing to the brothers' confidence in Br. Ephrem.

To be sure, the man had his less attractive side. As well as anyone, he was aware of his quick temper. When convinced of the correctness of his directions, he could be stubborn, manipulative and demanding, sometimes giving others the impression that he counted their viewpoint worthless and had little time or patience for them. He has been called obstreperous. He respected strong personalities, his being such itself, and enjoyed witty repartee and challenging conversation. According to those who knew him well, there were some men with whom he regularly had difficulty getting along, but others whose friendship he cultivated and cherished. Still, some say he had no intimate friends among community members. His independent nature, which often proved itself capable of resolving thorny issues completely and satisfactorily, did not seem to want or need close companions or advisers. The invisible but nearly tangible barrier he maintained between his deepest self and others was, perhaps, as much a result of a strict adherence to the rule against particular friendships between religious as it was anything inherent in his personality. Though no taller than five feet seven inches, with a full head of hair changing over the years from auburn to grey to white, his bearing was formal, almost imperious. His voice was somewhat high-pitched and his language clipped and tinged with the Irish brogue which never disappeared even after long years in the United States; his rapid speech pattern occasionally made it difficult for some to understand him. The penetrating gaze of his steely blue-grey eyes and the firm set of his jaw were imposing, sometimes intimidating. Whatever the cause, surely not wholly physical, Br. Ephrem was a man who valued his independence and utilized it to forge ahead with little thought given to human respect, within or outside of Holy Cross. He was a man in charge, and he exerted no effort to dispel that impression.

THE TASK AT HAND

The task that faced Br. Ephrem as he brought down the opening gavel on July 7 at the chapter of the brothers' province appeared monumental. He knew well enough what confronted him and the entire membership. Having been an integral part of the lengthy process leading up to the declaration of autonomous provinces, he was acutely aware of the difficulties which lay ahead. The settlement resulting from the chapter decree on the division of assets between the priests and the brothers turned out, as already noted, somewhat short of his expectations, certainly significantly short of those of many province members. Yet pragmatically he had not demanded anything for the brothers beyond the fair share of assets that would enable them to strike out on their own and give them reasonable hope of success in the wake of the enthusiastic effort and determination their development would require. Several recall that as he stood before the delegates to the chapter he exuded an aura of confidence and assurance. Beholden to no one, capable of whatever they wished to accomplish, the brothers were embarking on a journey into the future whose horizons, always focused within the constitutional imperatives of the mission of the Congregation of Holy Cross, were unlimited. Men left the chapter enthusiastic about the leadership and about the future. As Br. Elmo Bransby wrote of Br. Ephrem, *It is evident that from this strong central leadership came a unity of purpose. There was no searching for a new asceticism so much as following an asceticism of forbearance and acceptance of conditions together with a willingness to deal with and to solve the issues at hand. These efforts became socially rewarding and engendered a vibrant sharing. There was a pulling together, and a walking hand in hand, motivated no doubt by the newness of the venture that came with the new autonomy.*[2]

From developments, and from his own correspondence, it is not inaccurate to say that Br. Ephrem began his term as provincial of the brothers' province with three major goals in mind, none of which took priority over the others, each forming an essential element in the development of the province as envisaged by the new provincial.

First, the brothers needed at once to establish secondary schools owned and operated by the province. Many of the teachers were already engaged in several diocesan secondary schools, and, as Br. Ephrem would point out, there was no money to be made in diocesan schools. Each brother committed to a diocesan (salary) school meant that a layman had to be hired for a position in a community-owned (property) school. He was not denigrating the teaching of laymen or the ministry performed by brothers in diocesan schools. He simply recognized that the funds required for the ongoing growth of the brothers' apostolates would never come from the diocesan schools because Holy Cross did not own them or determine the use of funds accruing from them.

Next, Br. Ephrem realized that whatever they undertook, the brothers had to prove their capacity to function independently of the priests as successful owners and operators of institutional ministries. As alluded to by Fr. James Burns several years earlier, the brothers at this stage required total autonomy and full freedom to pursue their own future. Br. Ephrem was determined that nothing would prevent the brothers from achieving success. He saw from a practical and realistic perspective the money and manpower required to accomplish the goal, and both were now available and at the disposal of the province. With the advent of autonomy came the opportunity to recruit and form young men for the specific ministries of the brothers, and with the postwar influx of vocations, especially men who had completed high school and had served in the armed forces, there was almost no limit to what might be achieved.

And thirdly, Br. Ephrem envisaged an imminent division of the single U.S. brothers' province into three separate provinces or vice provinces, though prior to the chapter he had other things on his mind than this possibility: *Bonny* [Br. Bonaventure Foley] *wrote me about some ideas he had on three or four Brother Provinces in U.S. I would prefer to let that rest to see if the Brothers need any such plan after the Chapter is over. I see no rush on that idea; one big problem is enough for this year.*[3] Nevertheless, in the planning for the division of properties prior to the 1945 chapter, the brothers involved were sensitive to the geographical location of the properties, schools, formation houses, and other institutions they might be assigned. Already, the grouping of ministries in the eastern, midwestern, and the southern and western areas of the U.S. was foreseen. Though it was assumed that those clustered in the South and West would need to be administered as a single unit for a time, even in these years thought was given to their subdividing into a southern province and a western province as soon as feasible. An alternative geographical division of the single U.S. Brothers' Province was also considered. Under this proposal California was to be a unit unto itself, an *Indiana* province was to incorporate Texas and Louisiana, and an eastern division was to have Michigan and Ohio as part of it.[4] Br. Ephrem hoped to be able to effect some form of subdivision before the convoking of the general chapter of 1950, but the time proved too short. To prepare a firm enough foundation for each geographical area to be assured of adequate property, income, leadership and institutional ministry to function independently, and to do so within the five years available, was clearly out of the question. Instead, the goal was pushed forward to 1956, with emphasis placed on cementing the establishment of new apostolic works in those areas needing them. As will be seen, the expectation was fulfilled, perhaps even more expeditiously than anticipated simply because circumstances conspired to demand such a division.

As tools by which he could help craft a firm future for the brothers, Br. Ephrem had the money, properties, and other assets assigned to the brothers in the settlement decreed by the general chapter of 1945. He could rely as well on a trend toward growth in the membership of the province. Vocation recruiting was highly successful at this period immediately following the war, and young men were coming not only directly out of high school but also fresh out of the service. As schools opened, new sources of ready vocations were effectively tapped. A major challenge to the young province was the staffing and supporting of its houses of formation—its postulates, novitiate, and scholasticates. Br. Ephrem, perhaps as a result of his own work on vocation promotion in the thirties and certainly because he was an astute and practical businessman, realized the importance of a constant stream of new recruits for the province in the perpetuation of its mission and in the plan to increase its ministries throughout the United States and to develop sufficient stability and strength for subdividing into provinces or vice provinces. Thus, the availability of adequate if not abundant resources challenged the initiative and ingenuity of the fledgling province but gave it at the same time some assurance of success.

To assist him on the administrative level in carrying forward his plans and those of the first provincial chapter for the development of the province, Br. Ephrem needed men qualified by both training and experience. He chose as his first assistant Br. William Mang, an eminent and respected educator whose earlier participation in both provincial council work and the commission for the division of assets familiarized him with province government and the practicalities implied. As secretary Br. Ephrem engaged Br. Columba Curran, a highly capable young academic whose special field at the University of Notre Dame was chemistry. The treasurer was Br. Chrysostom Schaefer, a financial specialist who had also been a member of the commission to determine the division of assets before the general chapter of 1945. Rounding off the first council was Br. Nilus Grix, an astute and experienced farmer recognized by his peers throughout the region. Br. Nilus, along with Br. Chrysostom, represented the brothers engaged in ministries other than teaching. These four men helped Br. Ephrem guide the province from its establishment until 1950. From then until the end of his term in 1956, Br. Ephrem was assisted by Br. John Baptist Titzer as first assistant and Br. Bonaventure Foley as secretary, both experienced educational administrators, and Brs. Chrysostom Schaefer and Columba Curran, who remained on the council, the former continuing as treasurer.

It is curious to find that the majority of religious who were contemporaries of Br. Ephrem remained for the most part unaware of the serious health problems that plagued him during the years of his administration and that occasionally drew him into a mild depression and at one point a desire to resign his office. The asthma from which he suffered periodically affected not only his breathing but his heart, which in turn rendered him on those occasions physically less capable of responding to the demands of his office. He was hospitalized several times for various types of treatment. He was sometimes prevented from attending meetings or making provincial visits and was unable to preside at the 1952 provincial chapter. His most serious bouts of illness were in 1951–1952, but once he recuperated in late summer of the latter year, he seemed to be in relatively good condition, having accepted the fact—as his doctors predicted—that he would continue throughout his life to experience health problems.

ADMINISTRATIVE METHODOLOGY

Subsequent chapters will focus on various aspects of Br. Ephrem's personality and capabilities through the use of anecdotal information culled from Br. Ephrem's own correspondence or from that of others about him. Reference will be made as well in special appendixes to data on Br. Ephrem gathered in interviews, on tapes or in writing from religious who were contemporaries of the first provincial. First, however, it is helpful to have something of an overview of Br. Ephrem's administrative methodology to serve as a backdrop against which a more specific depiction of his characteristics can be projected.

Setting up and organizing an entirely new provincial administration could not have been simple or easy. Br. Ephrem had been part of other congregational administrations, all of which had been in existence before his arrival on the scene. Even the new school offices he moved into as principal demanded routines and methods relatively determined by traditional academic practices and procedures. In every situation he fitted into an already established office structure. With the advent of autonomy, however, came the need for him to plan and execute the setting up of a completely new administrative unit. Starting from his own pragmatic bent, he had as examples to follow only those administrations on which he had served.

From the outset and throughout his term of office he never utilized the services of a personal secretary. For the most part, he wrote all his own letters, typing them rapidly with a skill acquired over years of practice, in length virtually always no more than a single page. He spent hours each working day at his typewriter and sometimes humorously complained the machine was heating up from overwork. Infrequently Br. Ephrem would commission a letter to be written in his name by the council secretary; this delegation was somewhat more common after Br. Bonaventure assumed that office in 1950. Sometimes the provincial requested his assistant to pen a letter for him. No matter whose signature appeared, the responsibility for the decision expressed in the content rested with Br. Ephrem, as both author and provincial made patently clear.

Though it seems he normally made and filed carbon copies of letters he wrote, Br. Ephrem calculated at one point that he did not make carbons of up to fifty percent of his correspondence. The process of researching Br. Ephrem's files supports the suspicion that some carbons were either never made or were subsequently extirpated for one reason or another. No doubt he replied to some urgent letters by telephone or, if the source were local, in person, and he made no record of these communications.

Br. Ephrem's economical use of language in his letters was further supported by his overall method of replying to inquiries. He tended to respond in proportion to the depth and detail of the questions or problems posed. He offered as a rule neither more nor less than required from his perspective and his level of authority to address the matters at hand. Never at a loss for words, it seems likely this somewhat terse method was pursued in deference to the confidence he had in his appointed superiors and administrators to resolve issues locally, something of a hint that, with some thought and a bit of common sense, they themselves could as easily find a solution for the problems.

Though he was capable of foresight and planning, Br. Ephrem was more comfortable in the role of doer than in that of sedentary thinker. His talent was in making things happen. A train ticket in one hand and a set of blueprints in the other would depict him accurately. Though there was never a question as to who was the chief administrative and executive officer in the province, Br. Ephrem delegated first to Br. William Mang, and then in the second ad-ministration to Brs. John Baptist Titzer and Bonaventure Foley, a great deal of authority in the ordinary areas of province life and development, and spent time himself involved in institutional planning and in traveling to sites of new construction. And these men were eminently qualified. There were times when Br. John Baptist signed his name to correspondence as "Assistant Provincial" and on occa-sion as "Acting Provincial," the latter generally being during periods when Br. Ephrem was away or incapacitated by illness. Br. Ephrem affirmed Br. John Baptist's role when writing to him during his travels. And no one in the province questioned Br. John Baptist's authority, delegated though it was. When Br. Ephrem doubted his own capacity to continue as provincial during a difficult bout of illness in 1951, he wrote to Fr. Christopher J. O'Toole, superior general, that he had complete confidence in Br. John Baptist's ability to assume the office of provincial if necessary.

The constitutions required that the provincial or his delegate make an official visit to each house of the province once a year. A record of provincial visitations during the years of Br. Ephrem's term of office indicates that the majority of such visits were delegated by him to others, usually Brs. William, John Baptist, and Bonaventure, and he considered any visit made by the superior general to substitute for the one normally done by the provincial. Nevertheless, Br. Ephrem maintained an active and involved interest in the entire membership of the province and its institutions, and he had a prodigious knowledge and understanding of his men and ministries.

He scheduled regular provincial council meetings, ordinarily once or twice a month on Sunday mornings. When he presided, the agenda was specific, the discussion relatively brief, and the decisions definitive. There is little doubt that the provincial steered these meetings with a strong hand on the tiller. If he had to be on the road because of contract negotiations or the investigation of properties, or perhaps because of some personnel issue, or if he were ill, he felt that the council meetings could and should still be held in his absence to settle ordinary matters, and many such meetings in fact took place. He freely delegated his authority to his assistant to conduct meetings, and he upheld the decisions taken by the council, even if reluctantly now and then.

RELIGIOUS LIFE

In administering the province, whatever its structural needs and complexities at the beginning, Br. Ephrem had to bear in mind that he was governing a province of dedicated vowed religious, not merely a federation of independent business associates. His role as provincial obliged him to supervise, lead, and give example in the living of the religious life. Br. Ephrem interpreted strictly the rules and constitutions of the congregation, and considered it incumbent upon himself as provincial to see to the exact carrying out of the prescriptions of the rule in every house. Some thought him too demanding in this, but he sincerely believed, and often said, that only by adherence to the rule would God's blessing come to Holy Cross, and in particular to the brothers' province. Beyond the financial exigencies requiring extreme care in monitoring expenses in the early years of the province, the demands of the evangelical counsels called each religious to abstemious living, and Br. Ephrem not only preached but practiced the requirements of the rule as he scrupulously interpreted it. Nevertheless, when an individual's special needs called for pastoral concern in the application of the rule, he was compassionate and generous and counselled superiors to be likewise.

During his term of office it was customary at the beginning of the academic year for the daily schedule of the local religious houses of the province to be submitted by the superior to the provincial for approval. Often Br. Ephrem would make some notations on the schedule, and occasionally he would write a full-length letter back to the local superior with directives for changes to be made. There were principles to be observed: meditation was to be made half an hour following rising; recreation in the evening was not normally to be extended beyond the prescribed half hour even if visitors were present in the house; the use of radio and television was strictly limited so that the time, occasion, and atmosphere for fraternal conversation could be preserved; evening socials, or *soirées*, were to be held only occasionally, and beer was not to be served more than once a week; spiritual exercises in chapel were not to be *telescoped* together without absolute necessity and then never regularly; and night prayer was normally to be held at 7:30 seven nights a week. Br. Ephrem was convinced that religious discipline in the common life was the spiritual underpinning of the apostolic outreach of the community, and he demanded fidelity to the rigors of the schedule as an essential spiritual component of the apostolic religious life.[5]

When called upon by local superiors for advice or rulings on the practices of the common life, Br. Ephrem was quite strict on the requirements of regular discipline in the province and on interpretations of the communal practice of the vow of poverty. Several times, especially in circular letters, he alluded to the necessity for regular observance if the province expected to benefit from God's blessings.

During the years Br. Ephrem held the office of provincial, there were not many occasions for him to collaborate with the administrators of other men's communities in assemblies, meetings, or discussions on the nature of the religious life. Pope John XXIII and Vatican II with its call for adaptation and renewal in the religious life had not yet entered upon the scene, but the roots of change were already grasping a firm hold in the soil of an enormously altered postwar world. Br. Ephrem did become involved with such national religious life leadership as there was. In an undated newspaper clipping from the archives, probably from 1952 or 1953, a short article, *"Male*

Religious Form Association in U.S," states: *Ninety-five superiors of religious societies in the U.S. formed an "Association of Religious Superiors" at a meeting here* [Washington, D.C.]. *Objectives are the promotion of the spiritual welfare of the religious and an increase in the efficacy of their apostolate. Officers are . . . and Br. Ephrem O'Dwyer, C.S.C., on the board.* This is the only mention in available resource material of any official involvement on the part of Br. Ephrem in any religious life organizations in the United States. Such organizations were in their infancy at the time and developed substantially and effectively only after Vatican II.

PERSONNEL ADMINISTRATION

Perhaps the greatest and most continuously challenging task facing the new provincial was the effective administration of the province personnel. Determining the needs of the institutions and locating and assigning to them appropriately prepared and fit religious was never a simple matter. The complications involved in this never-ending task were in themselves enough to create physical and mental stress, as changes were necessitated in one location or another throughout the year for any of several reasons, usually having to do with the health, death or departure—unexpected or otherwise—of key religious.

It seems certain that few, if any, anticipated the heavy influx of vocations to the community in the late forties and early fifties. Br. Ephrem remarked about his being pleasantly surprised by the numbers presenting themselves at Sacred Heart Juniorate at Watertown, Wisconsin, and subsequently going on to the novitiate at Rolling Prairie, Indiana. Yet these men, especially the veterans, brought with them wide varieties of experience and background, and did not fit easily into any preconceived mold out of which acceptably prepared teachers could be made immediately available. Regardless of the numbers of men joining the province, there were members on whom no firm reliance could be placed, and the apparently rapid growth was seriously offset by deaths or departures.

The period of strongest institutional development in the province was accompanied and made possible by the many vocations to Holy Cross following the Second World War. Theoretically, Br. Ephrem ought to have been able to keep pace with the personnel required to staff the various schools, old and new alike. Several factors, however, must be kept in mind: (1) the new religious, some of whom were veterans and therefore older than the usual high school graduate candidates, still needed several years of preparation before being fully ready for assignment; (2) not only the recently acquired schools, but the older ones which were expanding their programs, needed additional staff; (3) though new men were coming into Holy Cross, a significant number of their predecessors, both in temporary and perpetual vows, did not persevere, thus somewhat offsetting the numbers entering (an average loss of just over seventeen men per year through death and departure was documented over a nine-year period in a statistical survey prepared for the provincial chapter of 1955); (4) not all the new men were capable of or interested in teaching, and experience proved this by the many transfers necessitated at assignment time; (5) changes of obedience had to be geared to skills and subject area capabilities as well as personality, compatibility, experience, and the like. According to the mode of the time, few individuals—if any—were directly consulted as to their next obedience, yet Br. Ephrem and his council spent months each year working on assignments. They wrote or talked with the superiors and principals of individuals involved and utilized unsolicited suggestions from some brothers, as well as information gathered during the provincial visits. A significant number of religious in the province at this time were frankly untested by reason of youth and inexperience. Thus what appeared to be an unimpeded opportunity for expansion and entrenchment was continuously and severely tempered by the realities of the multitudinous personnel issues. Br. Ephrem, frustrated that he could not ever expect to exert total control over the situation, was nevertheless philosophical, and in his always practical and energetic way he dealt with it courageously in a spirit of faith and trust in God's providence for Holy Cross.

Br. Ephrem interested himself directly in the concerns of veterans joining the province. He specified resolutions to particular problems they raised concerning benefits, the rights of individuals to dispose of their property and money, and many other confusing canonical issues resulting from the intricacies of the veterans' educational benefits under the GI Bill.

It is clear from the minutes of provincial council meetings in the late forties and early to mid-fifties that a surprising percentage of those entering Holy Cross during those years subsequently asked for dispensations from their temporary or perpetual vows, and some who had been members for many years also requested dispensations. Curiously, four or five who asked for dispensations from perpetual vows and whose requests were approved and forwarded to the superior general remained indefinitely in Holy Cross.

Once a man had left Holy Cross, it appears that, with few exceptions, Br. Ephrem's policy was that the individual, should he change his mind, not be considered for readmission. This pertained whether the man had been simply a novice or a religious in temporary or perpetual vows. It is not clear from available documentation what criteria were used in judging applications for returning to the congregation. Yet it is likely that experience had shown the provincial that almost invariably these cases did not work out in the long run. He knew his men generally and had the capability of judging character and potential even in men with whom he was not well acquainted personally. There were, however, a few atypical cases in which petitioners were readmitted to the congregation.

During Br. Ephrem's term as provincial, the appointment of superiors and principals (the same individual held both positions simultaneously) was made by the provincial with the consent of his council, ordinarily without the consultative involvement of the individual concerned. Experience showed who could manage the responsibilities, and often the same persons, when their terms expired, were simply moved from one institution to another to continue in a similar role. Not infrequently, however, a religious found himself unequal to the administrative task for any of several reasons and requested that he be allowed to resign. Br. Ephrem was understanding, and it appears he never exerted undue pressure on his men to continue in such situations. Naturally, finding replacements, sometimes at short notice, was not easy; yet wise choices were almost invariably made, and made quickly. Br. Ephrem was a realist: he asked great things from his men, especially sacrifice, but was not overly disappointed when one or the other of them in the end did not respond positively and effectively.

Once a superior was appointed, Br. Ephrem's policy was never to burden him with an undesirable, counterproductive or ineffective religious in his house or on his faculty longer than the superior felt he could tolerate or work with such a person. And Br. Ephrem always proposed a concrete alternative solution as part of his reply to any letter regarding serious personnel problems.

OVERALL IMPACT

The impact made by Br. Ephrem as he assumed office in 1946 and then led the brothers through the next ten significant and momentous years is summarized well in a reflection on the provincial written a year before Br. Ephrem's death by Br. Columba Curran, one of the two men who remained as provincial councilors during the entire ten-year period 1946–1956.

To appreciate the impact of Brother Ephrem in the development of the Brothers of Holy Cross in the United States, one must look at the situation just prior to 1946, the year the Brothers' Province was formed. After a hundred years in the U.S. we had only one school of our own, in New Orleans, where the Brothers taught and lived in dilapidated buildings. In the diocesan high schools which we staffed we were at the mercy of priest diocesan superintendents of schools, some of whom had no experience in school administration and who interfered in many ways with the operation of the schools. For over thirty years we taught at Central Catholic High School in Fort Wayne under very primitive conditions. A new high school was constructed in the late 30's and designated as coeducational—forcing us out, as at that time we were not permitted to teach girls below the college level. There were rumors that we would lose at least one additional school for the same reason. We staffed the new Monsignor Coyle High School in Taunton, Mass., in 1933 and in 1940 (or '39) the provincial administration at Notre Dame acceded to the demands of the Bishop of Fall River to have a diocesan priest as principal. In all schools our salaries were inadequate for us to be self sufficient. Needless to say, our overall morale was low.

When Brother Ephrem took office as the first Brother Provincial in 1946 he lost no time in making many changes. He wrote to the Bishops or pastors in the dioceses in which we had schools, respectfully and discreetly, but very firmly (I saw the letters), demanding higher salaries if we were to continue teaching. And the Bishop of Fall River was informed that our continued presence in Taunton was contingent on a Brother principal at Coyle. His diplomacy is evidenced by the fact that we did not lose a single school.

Those who were present at our first provincial chapter in 1946 experienced a tremendous uplift. We were on our own; our destiny was in our own hands; and we had a leader in whom we had the utmost confidence. In the succeeding years the Brothers of Holy Cross experienced a second spring. In ten years our numbers doubled and we had eleven schools of our own (including one in Brazil), with more on the drawing board. Holy Cross School in New Orleans had new buildings, and Saint Edward's University was making splendid progress. Our Gilmour Academy brought us in contact with Bishop Edward Hoban, the best friend in all our history. He and Brother Ephrem had a great respect for, and trust in, one another—each recognizing the other's greatness. Bishop

Hoban gave us far more financial support and independence than we had received elsewhere, and Brother Ephrem was to carry with him the Bishop Hoban plan for financing new schools when he went East as Provincial in 1956.

And what about the man himself during those years? He was all Holy Cross. His guides in developing our spirituality were Father Moreau and the Constitutions. He displayed a wisdom and a vision and a vigor that were remarkable, and for which we should be forever grateful. He was very astute in financial matters and was a keen judge of character and potentialities. More than any other man I have known, he had courage. When he was convinced of the validity of a certain principle, a certain cause, a certain procedure, he never hesitated. The word compromise was not in his vocabulary. He met every challenge head-on, never sidestepping an issue.

Brother Ephrem had a great heart. In little things he could be over-strict and disconcerting. But when a Brother was in real trouble he would rush to his defense. I often thought that if ever I had a serious problem, he would be the first I would go to for help. He had a keen sense of humor that helped to relieve the strain of the many problems he faced in the province. He had a great faith, and a great trust in the God Whom he served so faithfully. He had a great esteem for the apostolate of teaching in Catholic schools. For him this is where we were needed, and I am sure that many thousands of persons who benefited by our teaching and counseling agree with him and are grateful for his efforts.[6]

And *The Brothers of Holy Cross*, a periodic four-page news publication aimed at province members, associates in prayer, parents, prospective candidates, and others, and put out by the province during Br. Ephrem's term of office, wrote of him in 1950: *Characteristically, when discussing the progress of the work of the Brothers of Holy Cross, Brother Ephrem calls attention to a provident God, to his very able council, and to the many loyal religious as being responsible for whatever success there may be. It is certain, however, that history will attest the vision and quick-wittedness of this selfless man.*[7]

Br. Ephrem did in fact often defer credit for any success he apparently had achieved to God's grace, to his associates, and to the hard work and loyalty of the province membership. Yet no one who recalls the first provincial and the progress made by the brothers during their first ten years as an autonomous province denies the integral and essential role played by the man himself as a leader who inspired and led others, motivating them by his own apparently indefatigable energy and enthusiasm, his sense of mission, his vision, his determination to make of the brothers significant contributors to the apostolic work of Catholic education for the Church in the United States.

Having seen in general who this man was as he assumed office on July 1, 1946, and what qualities he brought to his position and relied upon throughout his term as provincial, it will be useful to examine more closely some of his fundamental characteristics. The following several chapters will provide, as evidenced in his personal correspondence and sometimes through the eyes of others, a few anecdotes illustrating Br. Ephrem's administrative astuteness, his involvement in the educational administration of the province's institutions, his dealings with his religious personnel, his efforts to enhance the image and identity of the brothers, his fundamental spirituality, his humanity, and a bit of the wit and humor for which he was noted.

8

An Astute Administrator

A REPUTATION TO UPHOLD

Whatever differences of opinion Holy Cross men may have concerning Br. Ephrem, none will deny that he was an exceptionally shrewd and capable administrator. He had proved himself long before being chosen as the first brother provincial, and he did nothing during his ten years in office to contradict his reputation. His accomplishments were numerous, significant, and honestly directed especially toward the welfare of the Brothers of Holy Cross, but also toward the benefit of the entire congregation and the mission of the Church in education. He established new apostolic works and houses at the rate of one and a half per year.

From the correspondence files of Br. Ephrem, letters written to and by him during his years as provincial, especially during the early years of the founding of the province, attest to his capabilities as an administrator. This chapter will relate several incidents illustrating his astuteness.

ADMINISTRATIVE POLICY

In his correspondence with bishops, superintendents of schools, principals, community authorities, and others Br. Ephrem showed the practical wisdom which sprang from his experience as a school administrator years earlier. No doubt some of this acumen resulted from his sound upbringing and early life, influenced as it was by the folk wisdom common to so many, even among the less educated.

New beginnings call for solid, confident leadership. Br. Ephrem believed in the capacity of the province to develop almost without limit but always according to a carefully conceived and well-executed plan. He had clearly in mind the goals toward which he felt the brothers could and should move. He realized that the young administrators of the province with whom he was to work as founders of new educational institutions had practically no experience and that he himself would have to exemplify the qualities all of them needed, not the least of which was a certain bold assurance. Policy was not an established

tradition in the province at this point; it had to be formulated, sometimes on the spot, but always according to the goals envisioned and
the overall plan conceived to bring about those ends. Br. Ephrem
was an expert at policy formulation. He had operated within policy constraints established by others—governmental, congregational,
and educational authorities alike—and knew the importance of clear
guidelines by which team effort could move large organizations toward
desired goals. When he became provincial, he was primed to exercise
the leadership qualities which illustrated his capacity to forge policy
and to assure its implementation.

Br. Ephrem's financial background enabled him to project achievable aims realistically. It is said that his overall fiscal plan for building
up the school system of the province, a plan for which he owed
some credit to Archbishop Edward F. Hoban of Cleveland, was so
unconventional that most people had trouble grasping its intricacies.
On one occasion, it is told, the provincial was discussing his plan for
financing a new school with a representative of a banking firm in
the East. After some time the man confessed Br. Ephrem had lost
him somewhere in the process and called in the senior partner to
continue the discussion. The newcomer to the conversation found
himself intrigued that someone outside the banking profession could
have conceived such an ingeniously audacious yet quite workable
financial scheme. Members of the province became familiar enough
with it in time. Fundamentally, it relied on an initial investment of
available capital for the first institution, and then the subsequent mort-
gaging of that and each succeeding structure, in some cases twice,
to begin further building projects. An illustration of this is found in
Br. Ephrem's own words in a letter to Br. William Mang in February
of 1952: *A note from Br. Chrysostom says the Archbishop has
cashed our final check for Lakewood. Now the problem is to get
some money for Bayside. I am afraid title to Lakewood will not
come fast enough to let us borrow there.*[1] And in October of the
same year: *Among ourselves, we would borrow on Lakewood to
pay for Akron; then later borrow on Akron if we get the Bayside
project.*[2] His fiscal vision focused on the whole, not on any of the
parts, and the administrators of individual institutions, whatever their
needs during the early years, had to be willing to sacrifice for the
benefit of the many until such a time as the basic province expansion plan had been achieved. The plan was provincially owned and
operated, so to speak, with Br. Ephrem as the chief proprietor and
executor. Confident and optimistic himself, he did not expect to be
challenged in his methodology and demanded complete cooperation

from the brother-administrators and other religious he appointed to the new schools. And because of their implicit trust in his abilities, they collaborated, though occasionally not too wholeheartedly, and inspired the cooperation of their entire faculty and staff.

———

In early 1947 Fr. Louis Kelley, assistant general, wrote from the generalate to Fr. Albert Cousineau, superior general, who was traveling: *Br. Ephrem is here after an operation on his legs. . . . From his sickbed he carried on a battle with the Bishop of Fall River about the school in Taunton. The Bishop tried to get our Cardinal and the Bishop of Brooklyn in on it. It looks as though Brother has won.*[3] A few days later Fr. Kelley wrote, this time to Fr. Georges Sauvage, Procurator General in Rome: *The Bishop merely accepted Brother's two demands. A Bishop has no chance in a fight with Brother Ephrem. Of course Brother was right in this case and Bishop Connolly knew it. The whole difficulty was to get the old Bishop to observe the contract that he had made. The Cardinal's appeal through Bishop O'Hara did not help any. Bishop Connolly said to Brother, "I believe you do not like to be pushed around."*[4]

———

Later that same year, Br. Ephrem was distressed by a seeming lack of sensitivity to the financial realities constraining the young province. He wrote to Br. William Mang, *Expensive ideas here and there are getting me. . . . So many houses have no idea of economy or good business.*[5]

———

Br. Alcuin Nuss, business manager of the Ave Maria Press at Notre Dame, which in 1950 employed approximately twenty brothers, had written to Br. Ephrem concerning a labor organization established on the premises, to which some of the brothers wished to belong. Br. Ephrem responded: *If it does not require a person to take sides or issue between employers and employees there shouldn't be any harm in being a member.*

As far as attending a banquet or social affair now and then, there should be no problem there if the participation has some direct or indirect benefit for the <u>Ave Maria</u>.

Of course our members <u>may not hold any office</u> either in an Employers' or in a Workers' Association, and must remain free of responsibility for determining policies for or against labor. It *is certainly in order to keep in touch with what is going on, but it is not wise to be on committees or to hold any office beyond honorary or actual membership.*[6]

Br. Sabinus Herbert submitted an article to Br. Ephrem for approval to have it printed in a Catholic magazine. In his reply, the provincial expressed his philosophy of involvement in writing for the Catholic press: *In principle I have no objection to their [the brothers] writing articles on vocations in general if the theology, discipline and traditions of the Church have the approval of a competent censor. Where there is question of history, government or purpose of our Society, or the personal experiences of our members, I believe it my duty to be particular about what should appear in print. For this reason, we have been most critical as to the type and need of vocation articles required for our Province; and in order to maintain this position it has been a tradition to ask certain Brothers to write the type of articles desired.*

After reading this particular article, and having it read by the council, Br. Ephrem would not permit its publication, citing its content as a "griping" article. Even Br. Sabinus's subsequent revision work did not qualify for Br. Ephrem's approval, and the suggestion was made that Br. Sabinus might well concentrate on writing books for youth through the Dujarie Press, for which avocation he seemed well qualified. Br. Ephrem mollified his criticism by saying: *All of us agree that your recent book for that press was well done.*[7]

In 1951, five years after becoming provincial, Br. Ephrem still had not had the opportunity to travel to Bengal to visit the brothers there. In writing to Br. Jude Costello, religious superior of the brothers in that mission, Br. Ephrem said: *For years I have thought of visiting Bengal, and it is not a dislike to do so that keeps me back. It is just time. I hope I can manage that soon, when things here in the administration get built up to a point when three or four will be on hand to do the work of the administration and all have an equal knowledge of the many problems.* This is a key expression of Br. Ephrem's administrative policy. His always-present health consideration aside, he felt he personally must be present and on top of issues of importance in any area of province administration, especially expansion, and his hope was to train his assistants through experience to cope with matters should the provincial himself be absent or incapacitated. The trust and authority he placed on Brothers John Baptist Titzer, his assistant, and Bonaventure Foley, the council secretary, are illustrative of the effectiveness of Br. Ephrem's approach. In the meantime, however, the missions in Asia lacked the benefit of even the brief presence of the dynamic and inspirational provincial.[8]

Br. Ephrem was meticulous in observing ethical standards in dealing with the financial matters relating to diocesan institutions. He wanted the Brothers of Holy Cross to benefit, of course, but never unduly, from their presence at a given school or boys' home. In writing to Br. Lawrence Miller, director of St. Charles Boys' Home, Milwaukee, about services performed by brothers resident at St. Charles but doing full-time studies elsewhere, Br. Ephrem directed: *Our only interest is in the consideration that we take no advantage of what we may morally owe the institution. We are presuming that your viewpoint is that the services of the student Brothers are of some value to the institution.*[9]

The Notre Dame post office was, from the outset, staffed by brothers, including—after Fr. Sorin—the position of postmaster. The provincial thus became responsible for finding brothers to fill the needed positions for a government agency. Br. Ephrem was well aware of the proper authority of the brother postmaster in his own right, yet in areas of religious discipline and harmony the provincial had to intervene when necessary, and this created a climate of thorny sensitivity at times. On one such occasion, when complaints were emanating from the post office about preferential treatment accorded some customers, Br. Ephrem wrote to the brother-postmaster: *It does seem to me that the positive policies of the Post Office Department should be strictly followed and then there would be no complaints among the Brothers, since all customers would be treated alike. The Brothers at the Post Office don't owe any favors to students or to professors or even to Community members. The Post Office is an independent organization, and customers should realize that it has the same rules as South Bend or other places.*[10]

In the 1950s it was not the policy of the province to have student brothers do part-time outside apostolic ministry. Fr. Charles Delaney,

C.S.C., pastor of Dolores Church in Austin, Texas, wrote Br. Ephrem asking whether some brothers from Vincent Hall might assist him apostolically in some minor capacities, and Br. Ephrem wrote back: *It is our policy that Scholastics remain strictly in scholastic status and confine their activities to their house or campus.* He went on to explain his decision: *I know you realize that it will be all too soon that our young Brothers must take up their regular teaching and regular school activities, and even in such school activities we prefer that the older Brothers handle them. I know that there is a tendency among the young to want to get out and "do something worthwhile," little realizing that the strict formation is the thing most worthwhile for them now and most worthwhile for the Community.*[11]

In 1947 Br. Eymard Salzman, director of vocations for the province, wrote Br. Ephrem asking whether it would be advisable and permissible to admit a candidate from the Philippines. Br. Ephrem, interpreting province policy on vocation recruitment, replied: *If he has all the qualifications I see nothing against accepting him. Take the matter slowly, however. . . . The time is not far away when it will be necessary, I believe, to make no distinction in color or nationality. And a time may come when a house in the Philippines would be desirable.*[12] Following World War II, the winds of social change were beginning to blow noticeably and Br. Ephrem was sensitive to the stirrings within Holy Cross.

On one occasion Br. Ephrem took exception to the vocation director's philosophy concerning personal contact with potential candidates and his visitation of schools and institutions from which those candidates might come. Br. Ephrem wrote him, calling into question the need for a particular journey and reminding the vocation director that it was especially important that the superiors and local communities of brothers in the schools and institutions become directly and chiefly responsible for promoting vocations and maintaining contact with the young men. This principle, Br. Ephrem felt, could well be compromised by frequent visits from the vocation director. Knowing that there was a distinct difference of opinion on this point, Br. Ephrem did not want to discourage the vocation director and in fact hastened to congratulate him on his energy and enthusiasm. He felt it wise, however, to transfer responsibility for planning vocation trips to the local superior of the Watertown, Wisconsin, house in which the vocation director lived, reserving for himself as provincial only those decisions pertaining directly to novitiate admission, which by rule he had to deal with in any case.[13]

Even in the latter years of Br. Ephrem's term as provincial of the U.S. Brothers' Province, missionaries from East Pakistan [Bangladesh] returned home only every five to seven years. When they did, they spent an entire year in the States before returning to Asia. There had been no specific program established to occupy the vacationers' time, and several signified that they expected to be kept profitably occupied once their three-month stay at home with relatives was completed. On an *ad hoc* basis some brothers were asked to work at the Bengalese, the central mission office of Holy Cross in Washington, D.C. As his term was drawing to an end, Br. Ephrem felt it useful to lay down some principles for stabilizing the situation for returning brother missionaries. He wrote Fr. Thomas Fitzpatrick, superior of the Foreign Mission Seminary in Washington, where the Bengalese offices were located, saying he thought it best if vacationing missionaries from among the brothers were to teach one semester in the schools of the province. He considered that this would be more of a vacation than traveling about the country soliciting funds for the missions. He concluded logically: *In view of the future returnees teaching a semester in the States, I think it would be best that their whole period in the States be under the direction of the Brother Provincial rather than under the Bengalese as is substantially the custom now.*[14]

Br. Ephrem kept in touch with his assistant, Br. John Baptist Titzer, while the latter was in California visiting the province institutions. Apparently Br. John had stopped at one of the boys' homes just prior to leaving for California and had written a memo to Br. Ephrem about his brief visit. Always the practical administrator, Br. Ephrem responded sardonically to one point: [The director] *believes that only men with at least one year's experience can handle the delinquent boy. This reminds me of the fellow who had trouble putting on a new pair of shoes: "I can never get these on till I have worn them a while...." I am particularly interested to know WHO should get a year's experience and WHERE. If Brother answers that question, a solution may be found. If we cannot adjust our men to the institution, the institution should be adjusted to our men.*[15]

———————

At times requests came from family members of religious concerning special permissions they sought to have granted. One such request came from the mother of two young sibling religious about their spending their vacations at home together rather than following the strict regimen of vacation schedules set by the provincial chapter that, in this case, prevented their being at home at the same time. Br. Ephrem, in trying to find a reasonable solution without violating his principle of rigid adherence to the legislation of the provincial chapters, wrote back: *As you can imagine, we must treat all Brothers the same. . . .* Nevertheless he found a way for one of the brothers to be at home during at least part of the time the other was to be there and remarked: *I hope all this will be satisfactory with you. It is the most I can do under the ruling of the Provincial Chapter about vacations, for I may not go beyond the ruling of the Chapters.*[16]

———————

Some administrative methods were no doubt forged only after years of Br. Ephrem's experience as provincial. However, certain decisions were required of him very early in his career. For example, on July 15, 1946, only two weeks after the province was officially established, a group of local superiors met in the Law Building at the University of Notre Dame to discuss issues affecting common observance in their houses and to make a report of their informal findings to the provincial, Br. Ephrem, who had assumed office only days earlier. The first brothers' provincial chapter had just been held on the campus of Notre Dame as well, and the meeting of superiors immediately followed the chapter.

Br. Ephrem received the brief resume of topics discussed and consensus reached among the men, and from it he constructed a list of directives for use in local houses. He said in his introduction: *The aim is not so much to restrict as to bring under proper control certain privileges and customs. Even in the case of rights there is often need for uniformity and regulation. If our houses can be operated along well established lines we shall grow in helpful traditions. . . . Time will naturally bring modifications in customs, but even then the modifications should have rather general Community sanction and be supported by official approval. We all have a tendency to interpret life as we locally find it. If the house in which we live is on an up or a down grade we take it for granted that the Community as a whole is on a corresponding up or down grade. Our ideas and interests are in danger of becoming localized. The remedy is to keep the whole Community in view and to be interested in all its major problems.* He then listed eleven directives corresponding to the eleven topics brought up by the local superiors. They had to do with smoking, frequency of soirées [socials], recreation schedules, pocket money, visiting homes, radios, brothers as athletic coaches, etc.[17] Even this early, especially at the outset of the new province's autonomy, Br. Ephrem recognized the importance of strict uniformity in disciplinary traditions among the brothers, practices that of necessity and out of prudence could and would change in later years, but that at the moment contributed to a sense of pioneering sacrifice, camaraderie, and unity among the brothers.

On this same matter some seven years later, following a meeting of the superiors of formation houses on August 13 and 14, 1953, Brother Ephrem issued a list of "Regulations for Houses of Formation" based on suggestions submitted by the superiors. It is worth noting here the entire list, as the directives—outmoded though the years may have rendered some of them—illustrate not only issues which perhaps had become problems in various houses, but also the concern of the superiors, including Br. Ephrem, over forging a unified approach toward enforcing the essentials of regular discipline among the young religious being formed in their houses.

01. Only those pages of the daily secular newspapers dealing exclusively with sports should be made available regularly to the aspirants and scholastics. Other selected clippings from newspapers having educational values may be given them from time to time.

02. Secular news magazines such as U.S. World News and Newsweek may be made available to aspirants and scholastics after any objectionable features have been removed. Scholastics may be given permission to read <u>non-picture</u> literary magazines such as Harpers and Atlantic Monthly at the University Library. Recreational reading of a type that is intellectually stimulating should be encouraged.

03. Musical records should be carefully selected. Classical music and the best in popular music should be made available.

04. Campus movies attended should be restricted to those of high caliber irrespective of the intervals between them.

05. Visits of relatives should not normally exceed one or two days' duration.

06. The taking of photographs is to be limited and should not become an expensive hobby.

07. Gift watches may be accepted from relatives, but repairs to them should be limited in the interests of economy. An inexpensive watch may be supplied a scholastic who has incurred excessive expenses in watch repairs or if a contemplated repair is too costly.

08. The interests of parents as well as the training of those in formation should be considered in formulating rules for correspondence. Permission to write letters should not be withdrawn from aspirants and scholastics during Lent and Advent. Christmas, Easter and Mother's Day cards may be sent by all those in formation. When necessary, novices may write home at any time of the year. Incoming mail to novices should be opened immediately and urgent messages should be transmitted to them without undue delay.

09. To relieve himself of routine work a Superior may pass on limited authority to an aspirant, novice or scholastic.

10. Limited pipe smoking is permitted to scholastics. Only on rare occasions may cigars or cigarettes be passed around (not more than about ten times a year).

11. Definite rules should be drawn up by the Superiors of scholasticates for camp life during the summer holidays. These should provide against any danger of a let-down.

These directives were approved by Br. Ephrem. Despite the seeming severity of some of the regulations, common religious discipline in Holy Cross was in the postwar years much less demanding than in most other communities of brothers. Stress was placed on common life and uniformity of practice.[18]

ADMINISTRATIVE COUNSELS

When asked for counsel on various administrative matters, Br. Ephrem was never reluctant to give advice, at times more as terse directives than as suggestions. There were, however, areas in which he did not wish or need to become involved, either because policy already existed on the issue or because he wanted the administrator on location to use his own initiative, for it was on his shoulders the burden of responsiblity would fall. Several incidents help to illustrate how Br. Ephrem sometimes offered counsel in place of formulating strict policy.

In 1949 there seems to have been a disagreement between Br. Ernest Ryan, author and director of Dujarie Press, which was preparing and publishing manuscripts on lives of the saints for younger readers, and Br. Alcuin Nuss, business manager of the Ave Maria Press, which did the printing and binding. Br. Ernest had written to Br. Ephrem, who responded:

In any matters of business controversy I like to get the variant views in writing.

As Business Manager of the Ave Maria it is apparent that Brother Alcuin has reserved to himself confirmation of all estimates and contracts, and his letter of May 24 is based on that procedure.

I have at no time questioned Ave Maria charges for work done for the Provincial Office, and I do not feel I should question the charges for any other job work in the Province. After a conversation with Brother Alcuin I asked him to be good enough to give a written comment to the statements I had asked you to put in writing. This he has courteously done. I therefore consider all past agreements closed in conformity with his bills.

In future transactions I recommend that you get (1) flat contract price from Brother Alcuin, or (2) cost-plus as may seem best to you. All agreements should be in writing in presentation and acceptance.[19]

Br. Sabinus Herbert was dedicated to enhancing the popularity of Br. Columba O'Neill, the community cobbler who, living and working at the Community House, had become widely known for his intense devotion to the Sacred Heart. Both before and after Br. Columba's death on November 20, 1923, favors, even cures, were attributed to the Sacred Heart through the humble brother's intercession. On April 19, 1955, Br. Sabinus wrote Br. Ephrem asking permission to establish a public shrine to the Sacred Heart in one of the rooms of Columba Hall, formerly known as the Community House, and to set up in the shrine mementos of Br. Columba, such as the statue of the Sacred Heart he kept in his shoe repair shop and tools he used in his trade.

Br. Ephrem, sensitive to the implications of such a move, wrote back on April 23 saying: *Your communication . . . relative to having Room 109 in Columba Hall turned into a Sacred Heart Shrine as a memorial to Br. Columba was discussed in the Provincial Council today.*

All angles to the proposal were considered, with the result that neither the Provincial nor any member of the Council favors such a move. For the present it is considered sufficient that the Community House has been re-named Columba Hall.

Father General will be here within a few weeks and it is probable that I shall ask his views on the matter, as in any case nothing could be done without his permission.[20] Br. Ephrem recognized the seriousness of establishing an ambience in which encouragement of a cult could thrive prior to official Church recognition of the individuals and circumstances involved.

Advising Br. Theophane Schmitt, headmaster at Gilmour Academy in 1950, on issues which arose surrounding the role of the Director of Studies at the academy, Br. Ephrem expanded a bit on the relative power of superiors and councils: *About Committees in general, I believe they are useful for discussion, but I do not think that when anyone has charge of something he should be ruled by a Committee vote. Since a Superior cannot be ruled by his Council, it somewhat follows that a Head of something should have similar recognition, else he would be but a mere agent of a Committee.*

While I am on Councils I should add that no vote of the Local Council can force the Superior to act on anything he doesn't want to act on. For example, if all his Council voted for a new auto, he doesn't have to get one. But if he wants a new auto he must have the consent of the Council. And in Council no one may bring up something for discussion without the permission of the superior.[21]

Though contrary to his usual philosophy and practice, when he was asked to do so, Br. Ephrem took decisions for administrators who specifically sought his guidance. What is more, he expected that in such cases these decisions of the provincial and his council would govern the subsequent actions of those who had asked for assistance, even if such decisions turned out not to be those the administrators had anticipated. He wrote to one such administrator: *We prefer cooperation without pressure. Good judgment would be indicated by your Council members to readily agree to decisions from this office as being economical for your house. We eased Gilmour's burdens by giving extra help, and by not billing for summer services as we do at Lawton. We must soon advance money to finish the gym too.*[22]

Br. Jude Costello cabled from Bengal asking that five thousand dollars be sent to the mission at once; a letter would follow with explanations. Br. Ephrem was away when the wire was received, but its apparent urgency prompted the provincial councilors to send the money immediately. When Br. Ephrem returned he was advised of the request and subsequent action. Displeased, he wrote to Br. Jude: *First of all, no individual on our Council, nor the whole Council put together, had any constitutional right to send you the amount your requested. ALL MONEY GOING TO THE DIOCESE GOES THROUGH THE BENGALESE AND IS HANDLED BY THE BISHOP. Why a request from your Council to our Council should come is beyond me, and what it has to do with C.S.C. I can't guess. I should think that the whole matter, whatever it was, was one for the Bishop and the Bengalese and not a matter for our Brothers in Pakistan or here.* He went on to clarify his interpretation of the nature of the transaction *ex post facto* not as a gift from the province but as a loan which must be repaid, and he had clear suggestions as to just how the repayment might be handled. He also alluded to Br. Jude's consideration of building a provincial house in Bengal and said that *our Council favors nothing until we see what is going to happen in the General Chapter. Why should we have a Provincial House till we first have and own schools and other property?*[23]

Br. Jude replied immediately upon receiving Br. Ephrem's letter: *Our request to you was for the Brothers, not for the diocese. We consider it as a loan and will repay you. We did not know that we were asking for something unconstitutional. . . . We should have been more explicit, I know, and we are sorry that we gave the impression that we were in danger here in Dacca. My letter must have allayed that feeling.*[24]

In discussing a possible purchase of some property in Dhaka, Br. Jude had written Br. Ephrem suggesting that though property might be expensive in Bangladesh, it was a very small investment when compared to similar property investments in the United States.

Br. Ephrem, practical as always in matters of money and not happy being tutored in his field of expertise, wrote back: *You make reference to the fact that the outlay needed in Pakistan would not buy so much property in the States. Quite true, but here is the difference. In the U.S. the outlay would produce a real good income, but in Pakistan it is not probable that you could ever earn back the capital you would invest. You may not even be able to support the teachers. So comparisons are not just.*[25]

Details surrounding the establishment and running of a major property school such as St. Edward High School, Lakewood, Ohio, consumed a great deal of attention both for the provincial administration and the faculty at Lakewood. Many questions needed clarification throughout the process, as well as a keen sensitivity to levels of responsibility. In reply to one letter from Br. John William Donoghue, principal, Br. Ephrem showed a bit of pique: *You may not know, but I am very particular about little points I mention in my letters. It would be well to read them carefully.* He then plunged into several items which apparently were either misinterpreted or not alluded to at all by the school administrator. Later in the letter, however, not wanting the principal to be discouraged, Br. Ephrem tempered the message with a supportive postscript, *Needless to say we were all delighted with what we saw at Lakewood on our recent visit. We pray God to continue to bless your prudent efforts.* The visit referred to had coincided with the official dedication of the new school by Archbishop Edward Hoban of Cleveland.[26]

Br. Ephrem wrote again to Br. John William Donoghue at St. Edward High School regarding proper procedures to be followed in filling in forms for consideration by the provincial council as they addressed requests and permissions at their usual Sunday morning meetings. Br. Ephrem said: *This is but one of the letters I have to write to property schools to get them into the swing of the required procedures.* Though the letter was written in 1952, six years into Br. Ephrem's term as provincial, it was still early in the period of development during which schools wholly owned and operated by the brothers were being established, and many details that did not apply in diocesan (salary) schools were arising and had to be thought out, explained, and implemented. Even as provincial, Br. Ephrem remained something of a teacher among his own membership.[27]

AUTONOMY AND COLLABORATION

The conclusion of the 1945 chapter may have ushered in a new era in the history of the congregation by the creation of autonomous provinces, but even the detailed legislation which emerged could in no way address the multitude of complexities which would have to be resolved over time by the newly established provinces through dialogue and collaboration with one another. Because of his reputation and his experience and knowledge of the workings of the entire congregation, Br. Ephrem was well suited to supervise the cooperative efforts of the priests and the brothers in implementing the intent of the chapter delegates. Several houses and works remained part of the apostolic life of both societies, especially the Ave Maria Press, the Foreign Mission Seminary, and for a brief time the novitiate. Sensitive questions or problems regarding administrative responsibility naturally arose with the implementation of the new structures, and occasionally Br. Ephrem had to deal with the consequent complications.

Within six weeks of becoming provincial of the newly established Brothers' Province, Br. Ephrem was faced with some decisions regarding the Ave Maria Press, an apostolate served by both brothers and priests. Brothers Alcuin Nuss, business manager of the Ave Maria, and Jacob Eppley, superior of the Community House, where brothers working at the Ave Maria lived, had written Br. Ephrem asking about the proper division of and accounting for expenses incurred by the brothers. Br. Ephrem responded:

June 30, 1946, I submitted proposals to Father Steiner [the priests' provincial], *among them being the following;*

(1) AVE MARIA. Seems best for the Community House to pay all expenses—board, room, laundry, travel, clothes, medical care, perquisites, and charge the AVE MARIA a flat rate of $650 a year. This simplifies the work and puts the AVE MARIA on a business basis. Profits after this to be shared as provided for by the General Chapter. [And to Alcuin and Jacob he adds:] *(Clothes and travel-vacation for the summer of 1946 are an expense of the year 1945–46.)*

(2) CANVASSERS. Expenses are irregular. AVE MARIA directly stands all expenses, and pays the Community House $60 a month for summer board, room, laundry, etc. [And to Alcuin and Jacob he adds:] *(Vacation and clothes during the summer of 1946 belong to the 1945–46 account.)*

I have no written confirmation of this proposal from Father Steiner, but I presume he has found it the best and most satisfactory way to handle the problem.

Brother Jacob, therefore, would take care of all the needs in #1. Brother Jacob would delegate Brother Alcuin to provide for the Canvassers as in #2.

I know you have much trouble and confusion already in not knowing how to proceed, but this is the best solution I can offer to simplify accounting. If I get a different proposal I shall reply without delay.[28]

On June 13, 1953, in a letter to Fr. Theodore Mehling, then provincial of the Priests' Province, Br. Ephrem passed along a letter written by Br. Kenneth Hopkinson, leading canvasser for the *Ave Maria* magazine. The letter is not extant, nor the focus of its contents, but Br. Ephrem wrote in an accompanying note: *I know that by the ruling of the General Chapter the AVE MARIA plant is owned by the Priests' Society; that profits are to be divided 50-50; that capital expenditures are to be made from the profits received by the Priests' Society; that reasonable depreciation on equipment is to be charged to operational expenses.*

This depreciation clause really means that over a period of time the Brothers' Society pays for 50% of the capital expenditures. Therefore, as regards profits, losses, capital expenditures, the Brothers' Society is affected to the extent of 50% in loss or gain returns. And from this it follows that every major decision taken by the AVE MARIA Editor means either loss or gain for the Brothers' Province.

I know that the aim of the Editor is to do the best thing for both Provinces and that he has your prudent approval in all things. But since we are to some extent concerned in AVE MARIA policies it might help things if we were aware of policies which are being initiated.[29] Though not directly responsible for the press, Br. Ephrem wanted to be included in all decisions which affected the brothers, whose stake in the press was significant.

On January 19, 1952, Br. Ephrem, in reply to some queries made about authority and responsibility, wrote to Br. Alcuin Nuss, business manager of the Ave Maria Press, explaining some details of the relationship between the priests and brothers in the operation of the press. He said:

By the set-up of the autonomous Provinces the Priests' Society (represented by Father Mehling and his Council) is the sole and exclusive owner of the AVE MARIA and the Notre Dame Farm.

Our interest in both of these places, guaranteed by the Chapter Agreement approved by Rome, is to share 50-50 in profits before capital expenditures of whatever nature are made. All increase in property belongs to the Priests' Society since that Society pays for such increases out of its share of profits.

The 50% comes to us under two considerations: (1) The rights of the Brothers as part owners before the agreement was made. (2) Services to be performed by the Brothers equivalent to what the Brothers were performing at the time of the set-up of Provinces.

I might note here that in the setting up of the Provinces it was not thought desirable by either Society to give the Brothers a cash settlement on the property and then agree on a considerable salary for the Brothers employed. Chapter records and the notes of the two Societies prior to the Chapter bring out this point.

The two points concerning us are the right of the Brothers to work at the AVE and the right to 50% of the profits.

I do not think that the AVE MARIA policies that do not affect either of these points need be any concern of the Brothers' Province. Important new ventures that might diminish profits would be considered a matter for discussion between the two Provincial Councils.[30]

It seems that the letter of January 19 did not satisfy Br. Alcuin. Br. Ephrem wrote to Fr. Mehling, the priests' provincial, on April 17 of the same year, noting at the top of a copy of the letter to Br. Alcuin these words: *Because of problems at the AVE MARIA I sent the following letter to Brother Alcuin on the date given. He did not gratefully accept what I believe to be the intent of the Provinces' Agreement. He wants a change. We should give it. We have been discussing some possible new men.*[31]

Br. Ephrem was at times placed in delicate situations by the precipitant or unilateral actions of others, yet he had the knack of diplomatically and effectively extricating both himself and the others concerned. One time while Br. Ephrem was away on a journey, some of his provincial council members, acting on a provincial chapter decision, made a request of Fr. Felix Duffey, editor of the *Ave Maria* magazine, that the annual stipend given to the brothers working for the *Ave* to cover board and room at the Community House be increased by ten percent. Br. Ephrem returned to find that the request had been made without going through what he knew to be proper channels. He wrote Fr. Duffey: *In an agreement made October 29, 1946, with Father Steiner, the living allowance for Brothers at the* <u>AVE MARIA</u> *was fixed at $650 a year for a minimum period of two years. That is the allowance that has been operating since.*

In the Brothers' Chapter last summer, it was decided to increase the allowance to the Community House Superior for board, etc., of all members living in the house.

That regulation, as I see it, was simply between the Brothers' Province and the Superior of the Community House. In my absence, some of the Council members here asked Brother Manuel or you for a 10% increase in allowance. I regret that the matter was so handled without going through the procedures agreed to in the Agreement of October 1946.

He seized on the situation, though, to confirm the request, inadequate as he felt it would be, saying: *Since Br. Chrysostom* [Provincial Treasurer] *has already mentioned a 10% increase over the $650 I cannot very well suggest more, though it is probable that living expenses are up 15 to 20% since 1946.*

As Father Mehling [Provincial of the Priests' Province] *will be consulting you on the increase we are requesting, I shall be very grateful if you will favor this increase of at least 10%.*[32]

With the separation of the priests and brothers into homogeneous provinces in 1946, there were many issues concerning the division of property and the relationship of authority structures in the congregation, not the least of which was evident in areas where priests and brothers lived and worked closely together, such as Bengal. Apparently the mission had been placed juridically under the title of "vice province," and Br. Jude Costello was named first religious superior and vice provincial of the brothers, a position which, though Bengal remained dependent for money and manpower on the Bengalese and on the province, effectively made him a major superior, in many ways equivalent in authority to Br. Ephrem.

A year following the establishment of this structure, Br. Jude wrote Br. Ephrem asking for some response on questions submitted in several letters prior to that. Br. Ephrem wrote back: *You mention that I have not been answering letters. You say I must be busy. That is true, but frankly it is not the chief reason for my delay in answering letters. The primary reason is that I don't know how to answer the type of letters I have been getting.* He went on to detail the questions posed in the letters referred to, and to elaborate on why he could not respond. The relationship between the missions and the general administration, and the structuring of the area into vice provinces rendered the direct responsibility of the provincial in the United States much weaker than it had been before 1946, and Br. Ephrem complained that he was now expected by Br. Jude to be concerned with matters which legally were no longer strictly within his jurisdiction. Still, he attempted to point out how he had cooperated with the continuing growth of brother personnel in Bengal. This letter is one of the lengthier ones Br. Ephrem wrote, and toward its conclusion he said with a tinge of sarcasm: *I hope that the Brothers in India can see that we have problems too—and that unless we get a chance to solve them there will be neither men or money for India in the future. God expects us to be practical—to plan ways and means of financing and training teachers. Our Brothers here have piety and zeal too, and they are all overworked trying to run schools with too few teachers. Sure, we can close a school and ease up on our teachers and have a couple of men for India! Yes, and if we close a school, lessening our income, we can cut down on the number of students at Watertown and Dujarie!* [houses of formation]. *That would be wisdom indeed for our Province and for India!*

Definitely all the men in India will have our help and cooperation, but in return we expect that they be a bit considerate and try to see the total Community problem.[33]

Sometimes the epitome of administrative astuteness and sensitivity was called for by seemingly minor questions of peculiar detail and delicacy. On one occasion Br. Ephrem received a letter from the novice master relating an incident during which the superior of the novitiate community complained that a novice had come late for supper by reason of being detained by a priest hearing his confession after the supper bell had rung. The superior felt that at the sound of the bell the confessor ought to have released the novice so as not to prevent his being on time for a regular exercise. Br. Nicholas, the novice master, referred the matter to Br. Ephrem for comment.

Br. Ephrem replied delicately and at length: *Neither priests nor penitents in the confessional when the supper bell rings should be bound by the bell. It is for the confessor to decide when the penitent should leave the confessional, irrespective of whether or not both confessor and penitent are late for supper. There is no breach of proper discipline here and no remarks should be made.*

If confessions are to be resumed after supper, then it seems proper that those not already in the confessional should go to supper and go to confession after.

If confessions are not to be resumed after supper, then one of two things should be done: (1) delay supper till all have confessed, (2) let those who come late for supper be excused without comment.

A third solution might be: (3) Allow a longer period for confessions before supper even if some other religious exercise or work has to be dispensed with.

The third solution, a compromise suggested by Br. Ephrem, is typical of his sincere concern in responding to the needs of those he placed in roles of authority in the province and in assuring a peaceful environment in which collaboration between the societies could flourish.[34]

———

In the late forties there were adjustments to be made because of the relatively new situation of the brothers themselves operating a novitiate, which up to October 1946 had been done always in concert with the priests. During the process of evolving principles by which the brothers' society would conduct a suitable novitiate program, Br. Ephrem wrote philosophically to Br. Dominic Elder, superior of the novitiate community, and Br. Nicholas Ochs, novice master: *As I said above, our autonomous position is new; we have little or no tradition to guide us, and consequently our aim should be to create traditions. Tradition in the sense of custom, however, is always subject to modifications made imperative or desirable by the times in which we live.*[35]

———

Following the general chapter of 1945 and its decisions regarding the establishment of autonomous provinces for the two societies, there was need for a period during which the decrees of the chapter and their implications could be tested and refined. Br. Ephrem was in touch with Fr. John J. Cavanaugh, president of the University of

Notre Dame, concerning the precise interpretation of the financial settlement regarding tuition for the brothers, and in the course of his reply Fr. Cavanaugh said: *My own desire and that of all of us here is, of course, to be faithful to the arrangements officially determined. I have always been edified by your sense of fairness and I certainly hope that you will never have reason to find anything but a similar disposition in us.*[36]

During the period of transition between the one province of priests and brothers to that of two separate provinces, questions arose over propriety in handling situations about which there had previously been no difficulties. One such case was the canonical classification of brother postulants not destined for teaching, the coadjutor brothers. Br. Ephrem wrote to Br. Bonaventure Foley, superior of Sacred Heart Juniorate, Watertown, on June 5, 1946: *As you know, there are some new problems as to admission of coadjutors to the Novitiate. According to all the remarks of the Holy See only those devoted to manual labor are coadjutors. These must be at the Postulate six months. It appears that others, office men and others who may help in schools, such as priests do at Notre Dame, may be considered as teachers, and may help out in classes commensurate with their ability or education, if requested to do so.*[37] Coadjutor novices were expected to have undergone a six-month postulancy; teaching brother novices did not fall under that requirement. It was a matter of determining precisely which brothers not strictly destined for teaching fell officially under which category so that the province could deal uniformly with requests for admission to the congregation.

At the time of the separation into provinces but before the decrees had been approved by Rome, Fr. Albert F. Cousineau, superior general, replied on June 7, 1946, to Br. Ephrem regarding a potentially sensitive situation about which the new provincial of the brothers had written him. The superior general said: *I would appreciate it very much if you can meet with Father Steiner [provincial of the priests' society] and take at least a temporary decision about priests and coadjutors in the Community House. We have not indeed to sacrifice any principle but we have to keep peace and a friendly union between the two Societies. How to proceed in the case of the Community House? It is your duty and Father Steiner's to find out a means to assure our Religious a way of living. It was not very easy, without betraying the secret of the decisions of the General Chapter, to provide an abode for the priests and the coadjutors of the Community House. This is an excuse for Father Steiner's delay. In any case it would spoil our whole plan if we do not solve our unavoidable practical problems with the proper consideration. I know you will do your best in this matter and I thank you for your cooperation.*[38] Both Br. Ephrem and the superior general were well aware that the manner in which the local housing situations were resolved would set a tone for the future of close collaboration between the societies, and they were sensitive to the needs of each group, particularly the newly established coadjutor brothers.

It is not clear whether a letter from Br. Ephrem to Fr. Cousineau dated the same day, June 7, 1946, preceded or followed reception of Fr. Cousineau's communication. A letter similar to Br. Ephrem's from Fr. Cousineau but addressed to Fr. Thomas Steiner and dated the same day urged the priests' provincial to come to some agreement, even a temporary one, with Br. Ephrem on the matter of the Community House.[39] There is no record of any reply from Fr. Steiner to this letter. From the papers of Fr. Christopher J. O'Toole, assistant provincial at that time, a letter to him from Fr. Cousineau, also dated June 7, is found asking Fr. O'Toole to use his good offices to bring Fr. Steiner and Br. Ephrem together to discuss the situation and take the necessary decisions. *I heard that Father Steiner and Brother Ephrem did not agree at their first meeting and that they did not meet since. I do not see how the problem could be settled if both of them remain apart. I ask you to be the mediator and to try by all means to have those two provincials sit together, consider the situation seriously and religiously and decide a way of living for priests and coadjutors of the Community House.*[40] Br. Ephrem's June 7 letter expressed these problems quite clearly. It is useful to quote this significant document almost in its entirety:

A month ago I wrote Father Steiner about accommodation in the Community House, offering him the Annex, where for the past few years five priests and eight Brothers have been living. He did not answer my offer. At the same time I said it was my desire, according to the specifications of Rome, that only the members of the Brothers' Society live under the Brother Superior in the Community House proper. Any other arrangement would deprive us of the right given by the decree from Rome that the Community House is for the Brothers. I thought I was being very considerate in offering the Annex.

With regard to the Novitiate, I was not consulted by Father Steiner. I believe that any concession from Constitution V, page 43 Circular Letter, should be voluntary on my part and not forced upon me. If asked about a joint Novitiate for a short time I would have agreed (using the term of the Constitution) to a priest as Novice Master and a Brother Superior. The Novitiate is a Brothers' House, and I cannot see otherwise than that they should have a Brother Superior. Actually the Master of Novices is not supposed to be a Superior. We would board the seminarians there at a reasonable cost.

Frankly I am disappointed in Father Steiner's having gone to the General Administration to put pressure on me. He should first have written me and asked for the cooperation he wanted. I am also disappointed in the second paragraph, page 2, of the letter from you I found this morning, as it is in the nature of a directive without the trial of agreement provided for in the Constitution. I owe you respect always and obedience according to the Constitution, and that I would give to the very letter and even more; but it seems to me that things are being forced upon me and that my position as Provincial is considered secondary to that of Father Steiner's.

I wrote Father Steiner two letters manifesting a spirit of cooperation, and he did not have the courtesy to acknowledge them, nor to write me about what he wanted. I naturally protest this procedure.

I accepted this job because the Brothers wanted me to take it and because the General Council elected me, and I accepted it with the absolute intention of full cooperation with the administration officers of the Priests' Province, and I am still in that spirit.

But I do not see how I can keep this job and be faithful to my trust if I am denied the right to make the agreements provided for in the Constitution and Decrees mentioned in your Circular Letter. . . .

We have suffered in many ways by the change of coadjutor Brothers, and the question of adjustment must undoubtedly come up later. With a burden like that, and no consideration of my analysis of the situation at the Community House, and the problem of trying to lay a financial basis for the future security of the Brothers' Province—I find the whole pressure a bit too much. If I hold on it will be because most of the Brothers believe I am competent to see them through these first critical years. . . .

I regret having to write a letter like this, but it is the only thing I can do. I have tried to base my public acts, at least, on principle. I have tried to be open and honest always, and this is the only road that satisfies my conscience.

You have my honest assurance of cooperation, but I feel a moral obligation to the full rights of my office as long as I hold it.[41] Clearly and insistently Br. Ephrem intended to utilize to the fullest extent the canonical authority of the office of provincial as he understood it and as he was expected to fulfill it by those who placed him in the position and those who relied on his prudent and perceptive manner of exercising it. He wanted to establish at once that there was no question in his mind as to the equality between societies and their administrations.

On June 11, Fr. Cousineau wrote Br. Ephrem exclaiming, *I knew there was misinterpretation of my letter of June 7. Be assured that as long as I am Superior General—for the next four years—I will consider and treat our Provincials, Fathers or Brothers, from the constitutional viewpoint, on equal terms. It is prudence, it is also justice. And for you, you have been too much close to me and too much a cooperator in my work to follow another way of proceeding.*

As Brother Venard explained to you through the phone, nobody has gone to the General Administration to put pressure on you. But in an informal talk with my Council I considered the different points of the actual situation in this Province and I wrote you to present suggestions only in order to execute the plan of autonomous Provinces. I pointed out that you and Father Steiner have to meet and assured you that any cooperative suggestion from you will be welcome.[42] On the same day, June 11, Fr. O'Toole wrote Fr. Cousineau saying, *You can count on me to do everything that I can to smooth the way for the official beginning of the homogeneous Provinces on July 1. This afternoon Brothers Ephrem and William, Father Provincial [Steiner] and myself are going to meet to lay plans for the housing of the coadjutor Brothers and to decide upon the changes of both priests and brothers.*

. . . It is true that when Brother met Father Provincial there was some table thumping, but the Council has met since that time very amicably. Some of the difficulty has arisen not so much on important issues as through lack of diplomacy and tact.[43]

In any event, there appears to have been no settlement made for some time regarding a formal lease for the Community House.

Three months later, on September 13, 1946, Fr. Steiner wrote to Fr. Cousineau, *I had hoped before this time to sit down with Brother Ephrem to settle many details that must be settled soon. There are such things as working up a lease for the Community House. . . .*[44] A formal ninety-nine-year lease was in fact not executed until late 1948.

———

Always conscious of financial implications and still smarting to some extent over the post-chapter maneuverings which resulted in a significant alteration of the general chapter legislation, Br. Ephrem wrote Fr. Albert Cousineau, superior general, in April 1947 regarding the allotment the Brothers' Province was expected to submit for the maintenance of the general administration: *Because of transfer of "coadjutors" to Priests' Province (not contemplated by General Chapter) we suffer at least $10,000 a year loss. Considering that we have less than one-fifth of the U.S. Community assets, I would be interested in knowing what fraction of the $20,000 allotment to the Gen. Admin. would be expected of us. If a settlement is under discussion I respectfully suggest that until next General Chapter we stand the coadjutor loss and the Priests' Province take care of the total Gen. Admin. budget.*[45] Br. Ephrem continuously alluded to the justice of an appropriate settlement in the division of assets, and in his mind this particular facet precisely fit that category.

———

Whatever the difficulties in the early months of organizing into two autonomous homogeneous provinces, Br. Ephrem appreciated the assistance the general administration gave in their resolution: *At this time I wish to express my sincere thanks for all the help and consideration given us during this first year of organization— thanks to you personally and to all the members of your Council.*[46]

———

On June 6, 1946, Br. Venard Gorman, general councilor, wrote Br. Ephrem about the two principal points of ongoing contention with Father Steiner, provincial of the priests' province—the novitiate and the Community House. Br. Venard asked several questions, and Br. Ephrem responded, quoting the Constitution: *The Provincial Superiors of co-Provinces . . . are free to agree among themselves as to the use of a common novitiate. In this case the Master of Novices will always be a priest.*

This is a Constitution, and no Council can step over it. Father Steiner has not approached me about the Novitiate, and no one can do anything till he does, and he can do nothing unless he does. It is up to him to make the first move if he wants something. When he does, my Council will consider his request. If he tries to go to the General Council without going to our Council (or to me as Provincial) as the Constitution says, I shall constitutionally refuse action by the General Council and appeal to Rome for the observance of the Constitution. He must first find out whether or not we want to agree, and on what terms, before he can approach the General Council. You might suggest to Father General that Father Steiner proceed according to the Constitution. . . .

With regard to the Annex [of the Community House], *he did not answer my offer, so I don't know what he intends to do. I intend to cooperate, but not be forced. Five priests and eight Brothers have lived in the Annex since September. . . . If the Annex was good enough for two years it should still be good enough. The Brothers have an exclusive right to the Community House. Here again I shall stand for cooperation but not force. We need all but the Annex.*

If Father Steiner does not approach me about the Novitiate, I shall send not only the name for a Brother Superior but the name of a Brother Novice Master to the General Council, according to the Constitution. I have full confidence in Father General, but if Father Steiner is trying to side-step me and get something over my head, I would not be worthy to be Brother Provincial if I stood for it.[47] Here is found the usual adamant determination in Br. Ephrem's interpretation of his role as provincial.

In negotiating with bishops for new schools Br. Ephrem sometimes ran into erroneous assumptions on the part of the hierarchy about the status of the brothers. In 1954 he wrote Fr. Christopher J. O'Toole, superior general: *Some of the Bishops think that in the setting up of Provinces for the Brothers enough money to build institutions without borrowing was provided by the Congregation. How such reports got out I don't know, but even Bishop Cassidy was among the first to ask me this direct question: What are you going to do with all the money you received from the Priests?*[48] Apparently in the minds of some of the hierarchy, association with the University of Notre Dame was tantamount to association with wealth, and it was with difficulty that Br. Ephrem convinced those prelates with whom he dealt that the brothers were acting entirely on their own with no assistance whatever from either the priests or the university apart from the relatively meager initial settlement.

PROPOSAL FOR A PROVINCE JUNIOR COLLEGE

A direct consequence of the split into autonomous provinces was the settling onto the brothers of full responsibility for the education of their own men. Policies had to be established governing the training of young religious in the various fields of educational expertise needed in the schools. Some determination also had to be made as to how much education beyond the bachelors degree would be needed and by whom. Br. Ephrem set as a priority the swift, economical, and adequate academic formation of teachers, which meant that postgraduate study was perceived, in the early stages of province development, as more a luxury than a necessity.

It seemed logical to Br. Ephrem to take even greater control not only of the religious formation of his brothers but of their academic education as well. Given the growing number of scholastic brothers in the early fifties, he dreamed of establishing a program of studies for them that would assure province responsibility for the entire first two years of university training for the brothers. A preliminary plan was to set up a junior college at Sacred Heart Juniorate at Watertown, where classes would be taught entirely by brothers from the province. After some consideration of this plan, suggestions were subsequently accepted for establishing the program instead at Dujarie Hall, Notre Dame, and a serious dialogue with university officials was initiated toward this end. The difficulties encountered, however, prompted the provincial council eventually to discontinue the plan for the time being. Br. Ephrem wrote to Father Christopher J. O'Toole, superior general, on April 14, 1952: *In conjunction with the members of the Provincial Council I wish to thank you sincerely for your interest and efforts to bring about some plan at Dujarie whereby our Brothers could teach the first and second years in Arts and Letters courses to our scholastics.*

. . . The Council voted to drop all consideration of the project for the present. We cannot say that Father Beichner's [in charge of Academic Affairs] *conditions are unjust, but they definitely are restrictive and stringent.*

To accede to all his conditions would cost us more than the project would be worth. Then Br. Ephrem went on to explain his decision: Fr. Beichner felt the brothers teaching in the junior college program would have to shift to a "college-minded" attitude from one more characteristically "high school-minded," would have to become part of a "community of scholars" as opposed to "teachers of a class." Secondly, regardless of the experiential capability of brothers with bachelors' degrees to teach a given area, the university required a masters in the subject to be taught. Thirdly, further specialization within areas such as English was required beyond that possessed by the proposed teachers among the brothers. And finally, the province calculated it would have to withdraw as many as thirteen *specialists* at one time from teaching in various other institutions to work at Dujarie, an unacceptable initial sacrifice.

Br. Ephrem concluded his letter: *It is plain that we had to let the matter drop for the present. We are under pressure to meet the spread out requirements for high school and we cannot go into the perpendicular for college.* It was not until 1966 with the opening of Holy Cross Junior College at the Holy Cross Brothers Center, Notre Dame, by Br. Donatus Schmitz, provincial, that the junior college concept at last became a reality in the province.[49]

MANY REQUESTS, FEW ACCEPTANCES

One objective of autonomy was to allow both priests and brothers to develop apostolically to the extent they wished and were capable. Numerous opportunities were offered even before the separation of the provinces, and Br. Ephrem had begun planning how he might respond to such requests when he assumed office in July of 1946. Little would be left to chance. His desire to subdivide the province into at least three units had motivated him and his associates to envision the nature of institutional presence toward which the province should develop, as well as its geographical situation, so that when the time came for permitting units to function independently, formation houses, provincial offices, and adequately productive apostolates would be in place and either operative or ready to begin, and directions would already be set for future growth in each area.

Unsolicited sources for possible expansion continued to pour into his office. Throughout the war years (1941–1945) and beyond, right up through the separation into homogeneous provinces and during the full ten years of Br. Ephrem's administration, numerous requests from bishops, pastors, superintendents of schools, and concerned laity to undertake the staffing of schools and institutions came from all sides. The Midwest Archives files indicate that requests reached

Br. Ephrem from every corner of the United States plus Jamaica, Brazil, Colombia, Japan, Kenya, the Philippines, both English and French Canada, and Australia. These were invitations for brothers to come and assist in existing or planned educational or social welfare apostolates. While many offers were quite enticing during these years of growth, it is clear that Br. Ephrem and his council had a long-range plan for the expansion of the province, eventually expecting to divide it into three separate provinces, and unless a particular request fit specifically into the plan, they felt they could not consider it. In 1942 serious thought was being given by the congregation to some form of presence in Panama. In a letter to Br. William Mang, Br. Ephrem referred to this possibility and gave his opinion of what ought to be done. *Frankly I am not hot about Panama or any such place until we have positive strength in U.S.A. You know the climate is malarial. We shall be filled with all kinds of offers from those Central American countries, such as the San Domingo or Haiti offer, and whoever would go to such places would have to be vocationally very strong, and you know we need even home strength there. Other communities have more men and are better prepared, and we shall need good men for India when the war is over, for many will be sick by that time.*[50]

Br. Ephrem was gracious but direct in his refusals. In writing to one pastor he said: *We are not able to meet ten percent of the requests.* To another he wrote: *Almost every day we have to refuse requests for Brothers.* And to a Kentucky pastor who wanted the brothers to assist in a salary school, he replied: *We are only open to proposals for property schools.* To Msgr. Bernard Dolan of Long Beach, California—where the brothers were already established—Br. Ephrem wrote when turning down a newly offered section of property in Anaheim: *Every school is growing so rapidly that it is a problem to keep them staffed, for though we have a reasonable supply of vocations we never have enough. And any financial profits we make have to be plowed into the houses of formation as our best hope for the future.*

While requests streamed in, the long-range plan suggested that Br. Ephrem himself take initiative and cast a few inquiries into various sectors to see if the local ordinaries might be interested in having brothers in the diocese. He wrote to San Diego, Galveston, and Chicago in the U.S. and to Manila in the Philippines, the latter at the suggestion of the superior general, though in this case Br. Ephrem made it quite clear to the apostolic delegate there that no commitment was being made through the inquiry, and that much would depend on whether certain factors pertained in the diocese. Br. Ephrem saw the Philippines as a possible stepping-stone into other areas of the Orient such as China and Japan, as he noted to Fr. O'Toole in a letter written December 7, 1953.[51] Of these investigations it appears only the Chicago inquiry evolved into something concrete with the eventual administration and staffing of Holy Cross High School in River Grove. The San Diego and Galveston dioceses were being looked into in the light of an eventual province in the South and West.[52]

Excited though he and his council had to have been over the potential for expanding the presence of the brothers into nearly every corner of the globe, Br. Ephrem remained realist enough to recognize that he could so severely fragment the apostolic outreach of the province as to render it relatively impotent and perhaps even to endanger the wider plan of subdividing into vice provinces. He trusted his own intuitive caution and determined to place emphasis in predetermined areas and according to principles which would safeguard the financial capability of the province to manage regular but appropriate growth.

INCIDENTAL DECISIONS

Less momentous but intriguing administrative decisions had to be taken by the provincial during his term, decisions which had lasting effects.

In mid-1954, at the request of Br. Gerard Fitz, local superior of the Community House at Notre Dame, and Br. Sabinus Herbert, responsible for the Br. Columba O'Neill Apostolate of the Sacred Heart, Br. Ephrem—with the consent of his council—wrote to Rev. Christopher J. O'Toole, superior general, to ask that the name of the Community House officially be changed to Columba Hall in honor of the brother whose devotion to the Sacred Heart was well known and was believed to be the source of possible cures and favors received. Fr. O'Toole, responding to the appeal of Br. Ephrem in a letter written August 25,[53] acceded to the request on September 2, 1954, and from that date the Community House was known as Columba Hall.[54]

Earlier, Br. Barry Lambour, superior of the scholasticate at St. Edward's University, Austin, wrote Br. Ephrem in 1952 shortly after assuming his position, asking whether it might be possible for the

sake of clarity and propriety to name the scholasticate Aidan Hall
after Br. Aidan O'Reilly, a prominent and gifted teaching brother who
had died in 1948. Br. Ephrem wrote back after he had discussed the
matter with the council: *I have talked with some members of the
Council . . . and we are all of the opinion that VINCENT HALL
would be a possible name for your scholasticate. Not St. Vincent,
but VINCENT HALL. It will not confuse or conflict with any other
building. Brother Vincent was the first teaching Brother in U.S.A.
in our Society. He was also the first Novice Master and was even
a while in Texas.* Br. Barry replied that the suggestion was a fine one
and would be accepted.[55] The scholasticate was consequently named
Vincent Hall.

The problems which plagued Br. Ephrem and his administration extended far beyond personnel and other community issues.
Plans were being laid during the administration of President Dwight
D. Eisenhower to structure an intricate system of interstate super-
highways throughout the country. A section of one major 300-foot-
wide artery (Interstate 80–90) was originally planned to cut diagonally
through the heart of the property of St. Joseph Farm, Granger, Indiana, a few miles east of Notre Dame. Br. Ephrem mustered enough
local Holy Cross and political pressure to alter the plan. He wrote to
Father Christopher J. O'Toole, superior general, on September 23,
1953: *At first the 300 foot wide highway was to run diagonally
through the whole St. Joseph Farm, but with the help of Brother
Nilus* [Br. Nilus Grix, farmer, county leader and former provincial
councilor] *and Judge Farabaugh the Baltimore Office has agreed
to cut only a small portion of the farm off. We hope things will
stay thus.*[56]

Before negotiations were entered into for the building of either
a Notre Dame Preparatory High School (boarding) or a diocesan
Catholic high school on the brothers' property in South Bend north of
Angela Boulevard along U.S. 31, the provincial council had received
requests for permission to purchase or lease a portion of the property.
One such request was from a dentist who wished to build a small
office on the corner of the property and deed the structure over to
the province after eight years. Also, a fruit vendor wished to set up a
fruit stand on the corner. Both requests were turned down. However,
when in June 1952 the Roseland Police Department planned to stage

a five-day carnival and requested the use of a portion of the property just south of Dorr Road for the purpose, permission was granted. Nor was there a problem for Br. Ephrem and his council to agree to the proposed construction of a Howard Johnson restaurant on the southwest corner of Michigan and Angela directly across from what would eventually become St. Joseph High School. Though having no legal claim on this parcel of land, they felt that such an establishment would assure a relatively secure gentility to the neighborhood. For some reason the restaurant was never built at that location.

EXTERNAL AFFIRMATION

Br. Ephrem was recognized as an astute administrator not only by Holy Cross but by outside professionals as well. In May 1955, after an informal tour of province institutions in Ohio, Mr. James E. Armstrong, Alumni Secretary for the University of Notre Dame and long-time friend of Br. Ephrem from Brother's days as treasurer and teacher at the university, wrote: *Mainly, I am writing to you as a cherished friend, because everywhere I go, among lay people who are informed, and—perhaps even more significantly—among the Religious I meet, they attribute this wonderful picture of progress to your leadership. I know what your modesty is shaping in rebuttal. But if you will file this letter under* encouragement, *it need not violate your humility, and it reflects not only my appreciation but my hope for many more years of progress and happiness.*[57]

Another description of Br. Ephrem's administrative capabilities had come many years earlier from Msgr. George Finnigan, C.S.C., former provincial and then bishop of Helena, Montana, when he wrote Br. Ephrem after learning he had been made superior of Holy Cross College in New Orleans: *Be to your subjects as you have always been. I remember the fine house you had in Indianapolis. You were kind and democratic, but you were always right from the shoulder when you needed to be. Be that way always.*[58] He was.

9

Educational Supervision

Perhaps the greatest practical contribution made by Br. Ephrem O'Dwyer to the development of the Brothers of Holy Cross was in the field of education. Three factors influenced his capacity in this regard. The first was his broad experience both in teaching and administration in several of the congregation's institutions. Secondly, he was involved in both provincial and general government in Holy Cross, which exposed him to the broader planning, operation, and evaluation of the community's institutions. And thirdly, he harbored an enthusiastic vision of what the brothers could become through the proliferation of their educational institutions at a time Catholic secondary education was being given such high priority in every diocese in the United States.

Having been principal in three Holy Cross schools—Evansville, Indianapolis, and New Orleans—Br. Ephrem understood the issues underlying the operation of a well-run secondary school. As he began his term as provincial, he was filled with an exuberant but tempered excitement. The possibilities were nearly unlimited. Offers were arriving from bishops everywhere begging the brothers to establish secondary schools to accommodate the fast-growing surburban population that had no ready access to Catholic education beyond the parochial level, if that.

If the brothers' province were to expand and eventually subdivide, it needed a well-planned blueprint for development. Such a plan Br. Ephrem envisioned even before assuming office. Each geographical area later to become a vice province, then a province, would have two or more large secondary schools owned and operated by the brothers. Out of these would come not only the revenue to assure continued expansion, but the young men who would enter the congregation as brothers and contribute to the ongoing mission of Holy Cross.

Besides these property schools there would be the occasional diocesan, or salary, high school such as those in which the brothers already taught and administered. The brothers would remain in them, but, by the very nature of the institution, would never fully determine their policy or exercise ownership of them. From these

179

diocesan schools came only a small salary covering local expenses and a meager contribution to the formation of scholastic brothers, and such institutions were not relied on to contribute substantially to the growth of the province. However, they responded to a real need in the Church, and Br. Ephrem was sensitive to the urgent pleas of bishops to assist them in their role as educators in the faith.

He also felt that homes for boys—delinquent, orphaned, disadvantaged—were a valid and much-needed apostolate for the brothers. Their experience in Gibault Home for Boys in Terre Haute, Indiana, and St. Charles Boys Home in Milwaukee showed both the value of this work for the brothers and their capacity to perform it with remarkable success.

At least one boarding school would also be welcome in each geographical area. A well-run preparatory boarding school could not only offer quality alternative education, but also furnish substantial income for the province.

And finally there was hope that each geographical area would eventually have an institution of higher learning both as a source of education for young religious and as a scholastic outreach beyond the secondary level. With the division of assets came the ownership and operation by the brothers of St. Edward's University in Austin, and plans were laid immediately for the province's own program of at least the first two years of university education for student brothers in the midwestern area of the country, either at Sacred Heart College in Wisconsin, or in conjunction with the University of Notre Dame. Some encouragement toward this end had come from Fr. Christopher J. O'Toole, superior general. On November 20, 1951, Br. William Mang wrote to Br. Ephrem regarding the superior general's suggestion to the provincial that he might initiate a junior college program at Watertown, Wisconsin. Fr. O'Toole thought three brothers would be adequate for teaching there in that aspect of the program and that it would be a way of avoiding tuition costs for the freshman year at Notre Dame.[1] A search also began early in Br. Ephrem's term to locate a possible higher education site in the East. In April of 1951 Br. Ephrem wrote to Br. William, *Since sooner or later we must develop an Eastern Province, a college of some kind in the East would be the ideal thing to take care of Eastern scholastics. This would enable us to keep the minimum number at Notre Dame, allow St. Ed's to use its space for paying students, and give us almost free tuition for Eastern scholastics in the East. Moreover, with scholastics distributed for their education we could more easily meet area state requirements.*[2]

Each of these branches of the educational apostolate—property schools, salary schools, boys' homes, boarding schools, and higher education—was considered essential to all three geographical areas of the country before the subdivision into vice provinces was feasible, and Br. Ephrem set about creating an overall plan of development geared toward this goal. In the process he kept in mind that, even if at first the southern and western portions of the country were to be united as a single vice province, it was expected that eventually they would subdivide into separate governmental units.

Br. Ephrem understood that in order to embody his vision, he needed the collaboration of qualified and energetic administrators throughout the province. The selection of such men was of prime importance, as well as the maintaining of a constant, close, and cordial relationship with them. The provincial's acumen in this area proved itself in nearly every appointment of a principal and local superior throughout his term. He chose and encouraged each administrator and kept a close eye on local developments, especially where construction was involved, sometimes finding it useful or necessary to make suggestions or to reprimand when there was an overstepping of the limits of the authority held by the appointee. In the early days some technicalities either were not spelled out clearly or were not easily interpreted, and it had to be the firm hand of the provincial—whose perspective was founded on his vast and productive experience—which guided and assured the successful accomplishment of each apostolic initiative.

To understand the man and his contribution to Holy Cross in education, one must examine his approach as well as his accomplishments. From correspondence available, especially between the provincial and bishops, superintendents of schools and principals, the spark of administrative vision, tenacity and shrewdness in education which marked Br. Ephrem's term can be clearly seen.

CONTRACTS

In the course of planning the construction of schools, through his dealings with various authorities Br. Ephrem had naturally to work with the multitude of details involved in contracts. As an astute businessman, he was anxious to have everything spelled out and understood by all parties. If he himself could not oversee each step of the planning and implementation of new institutional presence for the brothers, he delegated one of his councilors to do so, without at any point relinquishing responsibility for the overall supervision of the process. Underlying his natural inclination to become involved in a practical way was his ardent determination to expand the independent presence of the brothers throughout the United States. Any impatience shown relative to shortcomings exhibited by congregational or diocesan parties in contractual dealings was fueled more by this determination than by the personal inadequacies or ineptitude of others.

Delegated authority was one of Br. Ephrem's strong points in administration. Regarding the negotiations for staffing a proposed boys' home [eventually Boysville] in Michigan, Br. William Mang, assistant provincial and supervisor of studies for the province till 1950, was put in charge of dealing with Detroit archdiocesan authorities, particularly Msgr. Carroll Deady, Superintendent of Schools. But Br. Ephrem kept his finger on the pulse of developments and when the appropriate time came, inserted himself into the process, recognizing that as provincial he not only bore the responsibility for decisions taken, but that negotiators wanted to deal in the final stages of canonical and business arrangements directly with the person highest in authority.

So on March 22, 1948, Br. Ephrem wrote Msgr. Deady: *Now that I have a couple of weeks at home I have an opportunity to thank you and all concerned for the invitation to Holy Cross Brothers to conduct the institution. On behalf of the Provincial Council I heartily accept the appreciated invitation, while awaiting discussion of details and contract for which it will be necessary for us to obtain formal approval of our Provincial and General Councils.*

He went on to discuss policy items and remuneration for the brothers and added that, if a choice were possible, he would prefer to have a Holy Cross priest as chaplain. He nevertheless acknowledged the diocesan role in the chaplaincy question and was aware that *we would both have to consult Father Steiner, Provincial of our priests.* He confirmed Br. William's proposal of four brothers the first year, with two additional men being assigned over each following year.[3]

Subsequent to Br. Ephrem's first letter to Msgr. Deady, he wrote rather regularly during the fast-moving process of finalizing contractual agreements for the brothers' taking on the directorship and running of Boysville of Michigan. With an early fall opening date anticipated, Br. Ephrem contacted the monsignor in late August reminding him that the contract had not yet been finalized and that even when it was received from the archdiocese, it still had to be studied and approved by both provincial and general councils. On September 7, Br. Ephrem was able to thank the monsignor for the contract. He announced provincial council approval of it and predicted approval by the general council. He went into some detail concerning the community's view of the role and authority of the director he had appointed, Br. Patrick Cain.

On December 9, well after the school had opened, Br. Ephrem had reason to write Msgr. Deady again on the basis of a letter from Br. Patrick notifying the provincial of several serious predicaments which had arisen. Br. Ephrem wrote: *The Brothers are finding the situation difficult and inconvenient. Brother Patrick mentions that neither he nor Brother Carlos has a room; that there is no hot water; that classes are conducted in the end of the dining room, etc. He further mentions that there are no facilities for indoor recreation during the winter months.*

He says that even under these conditions boys are still being sent to the institution, even though there are no proper facilities for sleeping and for wardrobe.

. . . All of us here realize that this institution is still being founded and that there will be certain inconveniences for a time, but we would appreciate whatever amelioration you can provide at this time so that the morale of our Brothers, at least, may not become such as to give the institution a bad start.

We are interested in doing a first-class job at Boysville, but we feel that excellent morale among both Brothers and boys the first year is a definite requisite for this purpose.

Msgr. Deady replied on December 13 that concrete action was being taken to look into and address the issues raised by Br. Patrick. The monsignor alluded to apparently conflicting reports he had received on the progress and condition of facilities at the school and announced his determination to go to Boysville personally within the week to assess the situation. Br. Ephrem appreciated the monsignor's efforts and wrote to him: *I am sincerely grateful to you for your letter of December 13. . . .*

I really regret having written you, as I am convinced from your letter that I should not have taken the Director's letter too seriously. He probably was feeling a bit down the day he wrote, his mind being in the past rather than in the present.

Be assured that our sole aim is to cooperate with you in doing everything we can for the success of Boysville, for we definitely appreciate the opportunity of being in Boysville.[4]

Br. Ephrem remained in close contact with Msgr. Deady, especially during the period following the conclusion of the first year of the school's operation, at which time the Board of Trustees of Boysville suggested that the director be replaced. Br. Patrick by that time had for his own reasons already submitted his resignation to Br. Ephrem, and eventually during the summer the situation was resolved by the reassignment of Br. Patrick elsewhere and the appointment of Br. Hilarion Brezik as the new director.[5]

The superior of another institution informed a local architect that he would assuredly be engaged for the planning of a new building and conveyed this expectation to Br. Ephrem. He suspected as he did so that he might possibly have acted a bit precipitantly and overstepped his bounds in presuming permission from the provincial. Br. Ephrem quickly replied: *We do not wish any contract signed till full approval is given here for architect's ideas. In most cases architects draw competitive sketches and give cost estimates. Cost is the important thing, not the architect.*[6] The provincial reserved the right of final approval not only of plans, but also of architects and contractors. It was the province, not the local institution, which bore ultimate responsibility.

Following a visit to Catholic Central High School, a salary institution in Monroe, Michigan, Br. Ephrem wrote to the diocesan superintendent, whom the provincial had met during his official visit to the brothers. In the letter he reflected on the conversation the superintendent and he had held and on points arising from the visit. Showing concern for the situation of the brothers in their living accommodations, Br. Ephrem wrote: *I mentioned that the house needed three or four additional rooms now, and that if 100 additional students were to be enrolled the faculty would need still another three or four rooms for additional members. I referred to the present fact that contrary to our discipline each Brother did not have an individual room now. When I mentioned that furthermore a Brother had to give up his room to me and sleep on a parlor couch, you simply said something to this effect: "What of it if a Brother has to sleep on a couch in the parlor?" I did not expect that lack of appreciation or interest.*

Correctly interpreting the provincial's expectations, within a month's time the superintendent began investigating the possibility of expanding the residence by six rooms or more, at least one of which was to be available for the second semester.[7]

Br. Ephrem experienced a degree of exasperation in dealing with a certain bishop over the potential opening of a new school, and, in the course of writing to the first assistant superior general, he referred to prior problems encountered with the same bishop and included correspondence to that effect. He wrote: *I shall be grateful if you will kindly return the enclosed letters. I simply submit them to show that I am not "holding back" if a man has played fair and has evident good qualities. I feel you believe this already, but it is only fair that the General Council should have written evidence. I am, and I intend to be, tough where I think I should be.*[8]

Br. Ephrem also encountered difficulties negotiating with Bishop Molloy of Brooklyn concerning the establishment of a secondary school in Bayside, Long Island (the Flushing school). It was a case of Br. Ephrem's proposal for financing running counter to the specific interests of the bishop involved. The provincial wrote to the superior general, Fr. Albert Cousineau: *As you saw, the last letter from Bishop Molloy was not so satisfactory as I would wish it. So I have thought it better to let things simmer for a while, at least till he gets back from his vacation. I have a notion he is just as anxious as we are for the high school, and a little lack of enthusiasm on our part now may make him more anxious. I know he wants Holy Cross Brothers and thinks them the best, but I don't blame him in going slow in making a total loan—as I requested. If he made a total loan he would appreciate a large bulk payment within a few years. We could not promise that. All we could promise would be about a 25 year distribution in repayment, as from now on we must depend on annual earnings, since all our capital is being put to work in various schools.*[9]

Contractual negotiations constituted sensitive areas of business, not only between Br. Ephrem and the bishop, but for the local superior/principal as well. Early in 1951 Br. John William Donoghue, principal of St. Edward High School in Lakewood, Ohio, reported to Br. Ephrem on the progress of the new school. Some questions about responsibility for financial and contractual matters arose, and Br. Ephrem wrote back: *In all that is being done now, you are simply the agent of the Bishop—who is incurring the obligations. All property and equipment remains his and in his name till our 25 years are up. And we should not let our contract information get outside yourself. The faculty and public should not know unless the Bishop wants to tell them. My letters on these matters are also private.*[10]

Always concerned about the rights of the brothers in conducting their own property schools, even beyond fiscal and proprietary issues, Br. Ephrem wrote to Br. John William: *In our property schools we must hold on to all privileges we have according to canon law and not give diocesan authorities jurisdiction that does not belong to them. Superintendents and others often want to cut in and make us fill out more forms than we have to. Keep us posted if any pressure is put on you.*[11]

Shortly after Br. John William's appointment as principal of the still temporarily quartered St. Edward, Br. Ephrem offered some practical guidance for the new principal: *Since till we enter the new school the Bishop will get all the return from clubs and the like it would be well for us not to make these contributions too high. After the $400 deal* [which the brothers received net per man, all else going to the diocese] *passes out and we have to live on our own when we enter the new school, such funds and contributions will come to us to augment our tuition receipts. We wouldn't want it to appear that we were getting much in receipts from clubs and activities, as the Bishop may (because of any big receipts now) want us to cut out some money-raising doings. After we were in the new place and going our own way he would have no idea of our returns, since he would have no right to see our books. He would simply get his $25 annually for each student. Our contract leaves us the specials* <u>after</u> *we enter the new school. NO MORE SPACE. YOU GET THE POINT.* The point with Br. Ephrem was always a candidly practical one aimed at the interests of the brothers.[12]

In the early phases of development in some of the province-owned schools, requests were made to Br. Ephrem by local superiors to allow brothers who had building skills to assist in minor school or house construction projects to keep costs down. Though keenly aware of the need for frugality, Br. Ephrem was even more conscious of legal liability under contract, and wrote to Br. John William Donoghue at St. Edward after one such request: *In my letters of May 14 and 19 I was rather expressive in having all the work done under proper direction or contract. We do not want to get into trouble with Lakewood Education Board or with Engineers. I think it was somewhat of a risk to remove the dirt with assurance of engineers there foundations would not be hurt.*

I don't want the Brothers to do any physical work on what can be let out on contract under the direction of Mr. Stock. The Brothers are not to lay any cement or build any wall that has to do with the floor or the foundations. The problems of partitions later is not of so much consequence, as these do not affect the structure. And I think our Brothers will have plenty of work in their ordinary summer assignments. Money saving is not the problem— what we want is guaranteed satisfaction in construction according to a plan to be made out by proper architects or engineers and approved by the Provincial Council. *Kindly do not make any bargains or contracts until you have approval of details from here.*

As I mentioned in previous letters, I want to know about windows, ventilation, built-up foundations, etc. No Brothers *are to do work on floors, walls, ventilation, etc. They may be able to do cinder block partitions later on.*[13]

Br. Ephrem was adept at dealing out of strength with other parties in contractual negotiations. Early in 1956, noting the prognosis regarding the ever-increasing cost of operating St. Edward High School, he wrote to Most Rev. Edward F. Hoban, Archbishop of Cleveland, citing the following factors: *According to the contract agreement the tuition rate for the year is $115 a student. Though this rate is low compared with that of the local Catholic boys' high schools, it is entirely sufficient, on the basis of a complete staff of Brothers, to give the Provincial Administration the usual tax of $450 per Brother, to cover operating expenses, to meet interest and amortization, and to allow for some capital improvements each year.*

However, the picture changes somewhat when a number of lay teachers have to be employed. As we shall endeavor to show here, the present tuition income per student would not pay lay teachers. It would be to our financial advantage to limit enrollment to about 1200 students and then employ only such lay teachers *as help with coaching. If this should not meet with your approval, we then respectfully ask that the tuition be raised from $115 to a minimum of $120.*

Br. Ephrem knew that given the great need for Catholic high schools in the diocese, the archbishop was not likely to agree to a decrease in enrollment from 1400 to 1200. And he was right. Three days later the archbishop wrote the provincial: *Recognizing the need of operating on a sound financial basis, and our obligation of providing a Catholic education to the greatest possible number of boys, it is not advisable to reduce the enrollment from the present 1400 to 1200. Accordingly, acting upon the alternative solution which you propose, I hereby authorize you to increase the tuition rate from the present $115.00 to $120.00 per student.*[14]

Although Central Catholic High School in South Bend, Indiana, had been in existence some fourteen years on the upper floor of St. Matthew's Grade School, the brothers continued to encounter administrative and financial difficulties. Br. Ephrem, in writing to Fr. Albert Cousineau, superior general, on April 5, 1948, complained: *The South Bend school has been a load for years. . . . This school has been made "our baby" for some years. Neither Bishop nor parishes help. I was down to see Monsignor Sabo, the District Dean, lately and I told him we did not own "the baby" but that we would continue as nurses if we got the same consideration as in other high schools. As Brothers we owe South Bend nothing. . . . So for business and morale we want some sort of agreement. Originally the Bishop subsidized the school, but he soon left us holding the bag. We desire a contract that will be independent of any interests of the University or of C.S.C. parishes.* Br. Ephrem's dream of establishing a boarding preparatory school owned and operated by the brothers adjacent to Notre Dame shortly after the 1945 separation of provinces had never materialized, partly because of the bishop's desire to build his own new boys' Catholic high school which he wanted staffed by the brothers. But neither had this plan yet come to fruition. Meanwhile, circumstances remained both primitive and largely unacceptable in the temporary quarters occupied by the high school.[15]

DEALINGS WITH PRINCIPALS

Br. Ephrem may have been the prime mover behind the expansion of the brothers' apostolates in the late forties and early fifties, in various ways cementing his authority as chief negotiator and architect of policy. Yet it was the men in the field, primarily the principals and directors of boys' homes, who took responsibility for setting the plans into motion in the daily arena of school office, classroom, and dormitory. They were the men who, along with those assisting them, truly represented what Holy Cross meant to the parents and young men to whom they were ministering. Br. Ephrem recognized the crucial role played by these brothers, most of them in their thirties and forties, and was in close touch with them regularly during the early years of each new institution.

On March 2, 1948, Br. Ephrem wrote to Br. Reginald Justak, principal of Holy Trinity High School, Chicago, regarding staffing questions for the upcoming academic year. He announced there would be no additional brothers available for Holy Trinity because of the low remuneration received from the parish. He explained: *We shall cooperate as much as possible, but our future value to any day school depends on the growth and development of our Society. Those who want our services in their schools should cooperate with us in providing and educating teachers in our Society. You have men on your faculty who have devoted 20–30–40 years to the interests of Holy Trinity. It takes men and money to replace these when they retire. We are on our own and do not share in the splendid returns from the parish to Fr. Steiner* [provincial of the Indiana Province, which staffed the parish]. *There is no longer a "common treasury" in Holy Cross. We must approximate $400 a man in order to keep our formation houses going and take care of our infirm and sick.*[16]

Illustrative of the practical administrative detail the provincial not only was expected to command, but of the expert knowledge and experience which in fact Br. Ephrem did possess, is a paragraph from a letter he wrote Br. Reginald on March 24, 1948, after hearing from the principal about the academic program in place in the Chicago school.
About your typing. I gather that you have only two sections a day in typing. This means that each machine earns only $20 a year, and that if a machine costs $120 it would take 6 years to pay for the machine, not counting underline{interest on the $120 invested or the cost of upkeep, repairs, ribbons, etc.} So you can see that we lose on typing unless you can keep the machine going all day. Talk

this over with your Council and plan for next year. Each machine should bring a gross income of $50 a year.[17]

———————

Br. Ephrem laid out clearly defined parameters of authority for his provincial administration and presumed that institutional heads would abide by established regulations. On one occasion the headmaster of Gilmour Academy, elated that funds were apparently about to become available for a long-awaited outdoor swimming pool, without referring the matter to Br. Ephrem approved the announcement in the school paper that the pool would soon be built. The provincial learned of the announcement and contacted the headmaster at once: *As you know, there has not yet been any approval for this by the Provincial Council or the General Council. It was consequently rather out of order to announce that a swimming pool was to be built. Announcements of that nature should not be made until all the necessary approval is obtained.*[18]

In reply to this letter, the headmaster wrote: *I am sorry that the article in The Tower gave the idea we were going ahead. Its purpose was to inform the public that we are interested in getting a pool. We felt we might get some donations. Its purpose was to let the public know we were trying to get money for a pool, not that we had one already. I must assume responsibility for the article since it cleared my office.*[19]

And Br. Ephrem responded: *I note what you say about the Tower article. You say: Its purpose was to inform the public that you were interested in a pool so that you might get some donations. I believe the article went much farther and said a pool was planned and would be built by summer. If it is not built by summer you will be somewhat on the spot. It would have been much better to say it was decided—for this latter requires the action of the Provincial and General Councils.* He then softened his tone a bit to say that in fact that very day the provincial council had approved the construction of the pool, and that he was sending the request on to the general council.[20]

———————

A parent of one student requested not to return to St. Edward High School for the 1954–55 academic year wrote to Br. Ephrem asking him to intervene. Br. Ephrem wrote back: *The Principal of each of our schools has a Local Council for making decisions in all school problems, and it has not been our custom, nor do we think it wise, to interfere in the local operations of our schools.* However, Br. Ephrem said he would forward the letter to the principal for appropriate action.[21]

———————

Concerning minor points of discipline to be observed by the brother faculty members, Br. Ephrem offered this advice to a principal in 1954: *I am very anxious that the Brothers do not smoke or chew gum in school. The boys must get good example in this respect. It does not look good to see cigarettes hanging from the lips of Brothers or to see the clip-clap of their jaws on gum-chewing.*[22]

———————

In reply to a principal's request for guidance in disciplinary procedure, Br. Ephrem wrote back giving a detailed explanation of some basic tenets he thought ought to be observed. The first among them focused on justice: *A higher Superior cannot support a lower Superior against a subject if in his judgment the subject is in the right. On the same principle of justice a local Superior cannot support a subject against a student if in his judgment the student is in the right.* On a separate sheet Br. Ephrem added: *Positively no teacher must be a law unto himself even if it means he has to be taken out of teaching. . . . Our moral obligation to students is the same as to our own members. There is no distinction in justice. Parents trust us and pay for the education of their children. We have a serious obligation and God will not bless our schools if we are not just. As far as possible the teacher must be supported if he has any reasonable complaint against a boy.*[23]

———————

As a result of the provincial visit to the religious house and the school at Akron, Ohio, by Br. Bonaventure Foley, provincial secretary, some sensitive interpersonal items came to Br. Ephrem's attention and he wrote to Br. Noel Romanek, local superior and principal: *You no doubt realize that the strength of any house is the full cooperation of the faculty and giving them part in the administration as being all Holy Cross men having the Community at heart. And of course our men are to be considered ahead of any hired person and are to be respected as such.*

Then, sympathetically, Br. Ephrem went on, *When you get time, I would like to have your comment on things in general . . . , also plans for enrollment and teacher needs for next year. I can feel for*

you in the load you are carrying, but as you know I have also the
job of helping keep the men satisfied and keeping places in close
touch with the Provincial Administration. From here we can plan
to improve a faculty, but we must depend on local men for the
impression made on the public and for the future of the school.[24]

In corresponding with the director of Boysville of Michigan as the
school entered its second year of existence, Br. Ephrem expressed
his own philosophy about intake policies and wrote supportively to
Br. Hilarion Brezik, newly appointed director, concerning the type of
boy the archdiocese desired the school to accept: *I think it would*
be just and wise for us to take the kind of boy the admission
boards favor, making it plain that the unmanageable ones should
not be retained in case any such should be sent to the institution.
The greater good of the greater number is a good philosophical
and Catholic principle, and it holds good for all organized groups,
even for religious communities. It has all the more application to
custodial care institutions.[25]

During the academic year 1948–49 a brother in one of the
schools wrote to Br. Ephrem complaining about an edict from his
principal stating that no more than 10 percent of a class could be
given failing marks by an individual teacher without permission from
the principal. The brother's immediate response was one of defiance,
considering the classroom his own castle and himself the best judge of
who should or should not be failed. He wrote to Br. Ephrem about the
matter. Br. Ephrem replied in his diplomatic yet direct way, clarifying
one or two points misinterpreted by the brother and offering an
opportunity for personal discussion should the brother wish to pursue
the matter. Though not at first intending to elaborate on reasons why
the principal had in fact the right to issue such an edict, Br. Ephrem
supplied a whole page of principles of school administration covering
the point at issue. Having been principal himself in three schools, the
administrator in him surfaced when occasion demanded.[26]

The principal of a diocesan school where the brothers administered and taught informed Br. Ephrem that the priest superintendent, a man new to the role, expected to have control over any
dismissals the brothers wished to make. Br. Ephrem wrote directly

to the superintendent and asked him for a clarification of his understanding of the relationship supposed to exist between the brothers
and that office. Receiving no answer from the superintendent, Br.
Ephrem wrote to the principal: *We want to hold strictly to our
authority in the contract, the right of our Principal to suspend
and dismiss without permission or veto from anyone. We shall
not give in on this point no matter what row it may raise.*

*. . . We do not accept the principle that the superintendent
delegates the principal to dismiss a boy. That is a right of our
principal by his office. It's the contract, not the superintendent,
that gives our teachers their authority.*

*. . . While we must respect the superintendent appointed by
the Bishop, it is not to be expected that we give up our customs and
principles to satisfy his concepts of how a school should be run.*[27]

Further difficulties with the newly appointed superintendent of
schools for the diocese were reported by the principal to Br. Ephrem,
despite the principal's insistence on the substance of things as outlined in Br. Ephrem's letter of October 24. The provincial wrote:
*As I mentioned in a previous letter we wish all relations to be
polite and amicable, but we have no inclination to weaken our
traditional control and administration. . . . Should a real problem
arise you may write me or tell Father . . . to write me. Contracts
are bilateral, not unilateral.*[28]

Eventually the superintendent wrote Br. Ephrem, asking for the
change of both the principal and another brother whom he accused
of undermining his authority. Br. Ephrem replied, requesting *detailed reasons for your recommending that [they] be changed. I
am particularly anxious to know if either member has failed in
the performance of his duties as outlined in our contract to teach
at . . . that school.* The superintendent responded at length, and Br.
Ephrem wrote back that as a result of the provincial visit done by
one of the assistants, the teacher was in fact going to be changed;
however, the principal would remain officially, though serious but
unrelated health reasons would necessitate the interim appointment of
an acting superior/principal. Br. Ephrem advised the superintendent:
*It is my feeling that the problem . . . is not so much with the men
we send . . . as with the <u>modus operandi</u> of the school. Since it was
my privilege to open the . . . school 34 years ago, and even be the
first principal, . . . there has been no administrative conflict until
the school year that has just ended. It was recognized that our
Principals were such in fact as well as in title. We naturally expect
them to acknowledge and respect the Superintendent both in his*

office and as the representative of the Ordinary of the Diocese in matters determined by canon law or by mutual contract. At the same time they are bound by their vow of obedience to follow the advice and directives of their Provincial and his Council in adhering to the policies and principles which govern our Society and its activities.

It is my sincere hope that during the coming year a plan of operations can be worked out in which the specific duties of the Superintendent and the Principal will be more clearly understood and executed without conflict in personalities or policies. Thus in his usual diplomatic manner Br. Ephrem was able in part to placate the superintendent, who apparently had at least some grounds for his requests, while simultaneously upholding the rights of the provincial and the principal and clarifying their stance in the matter.[29]

When asked for an interpretation concerning cooperation with a diocesan school office that had asked for the submission of certain information on property schools, Br. Ephrem wrote: *I shall answer . . . some of the matters referred to in your recent letter relative to jurisdiction of the Office of Superintendent of Schools.*

In one of my talks with Father General in New York he advised me that our schools must be operated according to our Constitutional rights, which in fact means that we operate them independently of Diocesan authorities except where canon law gives jurisdiction. In brief we are accountable for proper moral and religious instruction of the young people entrusted to us.

. . . Of course it is our wish to extend all courtesies to the Diocesan School Board and to cooperate in all things that do not take away from the authority we have to operate our own schools according to our Constitutions. We at least want the goodwill of those in whose diocese we labor and where we can concede a point we shall do so.[30]

Br. Laurian LaForest, headmaster at Gilmour, wrote Br. Ephrem in the early fall of 1954 about a request made by the diocesan Superintendent of Schools for certain background information on teachers. Br. Ephrem's reply was made not only to Br. Laurian, but to Brothers John William Donoghue, principal of St. Edward High School in Lakewood, and Br. Noel Romanek, principal of Archbishop Hoban High School in Akron, both of which schools were also in the diocese.

Br. Ephrem wrote: *We do not wish any form or reports sent in for our Brothers, since our schools are private and do not in the usual way come under the Superintendent of Schools.*

Though we hold that Sister Patricia [diocesan superintendent] *has no right to visit our schools, we think it better at this time not to put any obstacles in her way in case she comes of her own accord to visit our schools. If she comes she should be accorded normal courtesy if she visits classes. She is not, however, to get any information about the qualifications of our brothers. When the school is properly underway such information is listed with the State Board or with the North Central, as the case may be.*

Any problems arising should be referred to the Provincial Office.[31]

A principal was experiencing difficulties relating administratively with the superintendent of the salary school in which the brothers were teaching and wrote Br. Ephrem for advice. The provincial replied: *At this point I do not wish to have* [the superintendent] *know I am writing this letter. Make your own judgments along any hints I have mentioned. Then if there is a clash I won't be committed ahead of time. I may have reason before the year is over to see the Archbishop about some of these things, for I am sure he does not understand the weaknesses in the methods used by the Superintendent. I do not wish at all sacrifices of prestige to have the Principal and Brothers be mere teachers under a Superintendent. For this reason I wish you to keep an exact record of things happening that indicate that so that I shall have talking points if necessary.*[32]

At the beginning of the academic year in 1953, the principal of a diocesan school informed Br. Ephrem that the superintendent and coaches, who were non-C.S.C. men, expected to be present at faculty meetings. Br. Ephrem replied, explaining that *when we speak of faculty meetings once a month, we really have in mind only the Brothers and not the coaches and superintendent. Faculty meetings are to build up the inside Community morale and settle problems and policies among ourselves.* He went on to say that the other men might be invited to participate once in a while, but if so, the brothers ought to have met prior to that time among themselves, and at the combined meeting only the principal ought to speak out and the other brothers should remain relatively silent, particularly concerning strictly community matters. Br. Ephrem continued: *My own wish would be that the Superintendent have nothing to do with the members or be present to hear them talk. . . . The Superintendent should talk only with the principal. . . . If you get into a hole at the meetings, say you must refer the policy to the Provincial. This will save an argument. My chief interest is to preserve the position of the principal.* Considering the era, and acknowledging circumstances that directed focus toward the firm establishment of the presence of the brothers and on their authority and impact in educational institutions, this approach to very limited lay faculty involvement in meetings was not wholly inappropriate, however puzzling or ill-advised it might seem in more recent times.[33]

Early in his term as provincial of the Brothers' Province, Br. Ephrem approved the establishment of Gilmour Academy, a day/residential preparatory school for boys east of Cleveland in Gates Mills, Ohio. The first superior and headmaster, Br. Theophane Schmitt, was given significant leeway in making arrangements for the adaptation of the buildings of the old Drury Estate to scholastic and boarding purposes, but apparently Br. Ephrem felt the headmaster had at one point overstepped his bounds and wrote: *I allowed for plenty of initiative in the organizing of Gilmour Academy, and I am satisfied that most things have been done well.*

However, since I am responsible for all houses and their development and welfare, it is essential that my directions be carried out. Contrary to my wishes a stairway was cut in the inside of the gymnasium and a different lower-floor plan was made. I let these things go. According to our Rule all plans and serious changes have to be approved by the Provincial or his Council.

The more serious matter is that of detrimental advertising. I objected once to mention of MILLION DOLLAR UNIVERSE, with its reference to MILLION dollar this and that and even to possibly spoiled boys. It is an article of bad taste and bad advertising. The harm cannot be undone now, but since my first hint was not taken, I must now forbid all such articles and any other type of printed literature unless I have first approved it. I am very much upset about the Universe [the *Universe Bulletin*, the Catholic diocesan newspaper] *article. I must insist that whoever is Superior at Gilmour will follow my instructions.*

I appreciate all the good things you have done, but I cannot overlook the type of advertising that hurts us.[34]

A day later Br. Ephrem learned that Br. Theophane was planning dedication services and other celebrations before school opened. He wrote at once: *I don't recall having given any permission for these things, and unless I give permission they are not to be held. There are expenses and other things involved that should not be undertaken without the consent of the Provincial. It is better to realize at the beginning that Directors or Local Superiors are not to presume that they have authority for certain things without the consent of the Provincial.*[35]

To Br. Theophane's credit, and illustrative of the type of man he was, he replied to Br. Ephrem's letters this way: *Your letters of July 31 and August 1 have been received and appreciated. We have in Holy Cross been hungry for years for some semblance of authority, but it has been hard to find. We have suffered much for lack of it. I am happy that you are taking a firm stand and enforcing some program of administration and fulfillment of Rule and Constitutions. I shall appreciate corrections and suggestions. I am not deceived in my abilities and in all probability I shall make many blunders that will worry and irritate higher superiors but you know these are not intended. I am not assured of success at Gilmour but I pray for it daily, not as much for my own sake as for what it may mean for Holy Cross.* But he concluded candidly: *I must confess I have felt the burden, the blunt burden of starting this institution without the interest or single visit of the Provinicial whom I had to rely on for permissions but from whom hardly any were received. That is history and forgotten [except] only in so far as it has enriched our experience.*

Then he explained he had known nothing about the *Universe Bulletin* article and was unhappy about it. Nor was he aware of any plans for the dedication of the school and wondered where the brother who passed the information on to Br. Ephrem got the story.[36]

It was not yet the end of the affair concerning adverse advertising. Another article appeared in a newspaper, about which Br. Ephrem wrote: *Darn that Akron paper that mentioned the <u>million dollars</u> again. That's what makes communists and keeps people from giving to communities. Catholics are hurting themselves and religion by advertising the "million dollar estates" they grab. No wonder tax payers get mad. Why can't nice things be said about the place without referring to the gold this, the bronze that, etc. No wonder the Cleveland priest said we should take in some poor boys to* *show the others what they look like. Otherwise that Akron page was splendid and fine advertising.*[37]

———————

Another case arose which aroused the ire of Br. Ephrem. Replacing Br. Nicholas Ochs, whose age and health required him to distance himself from active teaching, Br. Theophane Schmitt, headmaster of Gilmour Academy, hired a lay teacher without requesting permission to do so from Br. Ephrem. The provincial wrote on November 22, 1950: *I still find it impossible to believe that you hired a teacher without referring the matter here or without asking me if we could send one if a replacement were needed for Br. Nicholas.*

It is really the business of the provincial to provide teachers for our schools and to notify the Superior to hire a man if the provincial cannot supply a Brother. It is not for the Local Superior or his Council to make such a decision.

In addition to being contrary to policy, I think an unauthorized expenditure has been incurred. . . .[38]

Br. Theophane once more acknowledged that he perhaps acted out of line, but defended himself: *Your letter of November 22 at first reading was quite a surprise to me but after reading it several times and thinking it over objectively from angles other than our own I understand its contents. I realize now for the first time in this hiring affair that we were out of step. I should have written for permission to hire a man but I must say I thought it was implied from your letter of October 30 and my remarks and "complaints" from last Jan. to June.*

He went on to elaborate on the conditions at Gilmour which caused overburdening the brothers with classroom, extracurricular and prefecting duties, but closes: *All this and more does not excuse us from following a policy that is community custom. Let me assure you that it was not my intention or that of the Council to go over anyone's head or to incur an unauthorized expenditure. Probably our own desperation and the remark of your letter of October 30 caused us to meet the situation without using the ordinary procedure.*[39]

———————

Another headmaster of Gilmour Academy, Br. Laurian LaForest, asked Br. Ephrem whether the academy might replace a female receptionist/secretary who was leaving the school. Br. Ephrem wrote back on August 22, 1953: *I shall be grateful if at present you will*

*not hire any lady to replace Miss Day as "receptionist-secretary."
I think that title is far too high-sounding anyway. Your place
is not like a downtown doctor's office, or similar places, where
trained help is needed.*[40] The brothers' talents should be considered
adequate for the clerical staffing of their own institutions.

While attempting in his first years as provincial to afford brothers
with continuing education opportunities to upgrade their certification,
Br. Ephrem ran into the practical difficulties attendant on such a
surge of educational activity. He wrote to the principal of Cathedral
High School in Indianapolis on April 30, 1949: *As you saw by our
schedule, every Brother is busy this summer and there are still a
couple of tight spots. A Circular Letter from Father General soon
to appear has much to say on poverty and will furnish matter for
the Chapter. There are other reasons why we have to cut annual
and summer expenses too. And too much "education" may be
a luxury.* Br. Ephrem suspected that a corporate tendency could
develop toward the accumulation of degrees beyond the needs of the
secondary schools that were at that time the principal focus of the
province's educational apostolate, and he was determined to limit the
higher educational opportunities of his membership to those strictly
required and within the capabilities of a quite limited budget.[41]

In the first days of St. Edward High School, Lakewood, Ohio,
Br. John William Donoghue, principal, wrote Br. Ephrem, giving
a report on conditions in the temporary quarters for both faculty
residence and school. Br. Ephrem replied two weeks later upon returning from a trip East: *I shall have particular interest in plans and
projects for the new school and will want to see and check all plans
for school and house. Since we are directly and indirectly to pay
for all <u>by cash and low tuition</u> the utility of the future school and
house will be our concern. In any conversations with Monsignor
Whitehead [superintendent of schools], kindly inform him that the
Provincial Council is to be kept up to time. I am not concerned
much about what you do at the old school and how you change
and fix things. All those expenses belong to Monsignor Whitehead.
With regard to the <u>new school, kindly approve nothing</u>, but refer
all to the Provincial Council. This will save you trouble later on,
as our Council is very definite as regards what is wanted. This is
our position in all our property schools.*[42]

For some time the brothers did not accept administrative or teaching roles in coeducational institutions. They did, however, serve in co-institutional settings where the girls' department was basically separate and relatively autonomous, and only such common facilities as a gym, cafeteria, or library were shared. In Evansville some discussion arose as to the better administration of activities within the co-institutional school, and the principal of the boys' department wrote Br. Ephrem with some suggestions approved by his local council. The provincial replied, reiterating the policy of the administration: *All right to cooperate with Sisters, but the less we have to do with Girls' Department the better even in joint programs. Positively no Brother should direct an all-girls chorus or any other all-girls activity. Neither should any Brother direct even in practice girl groups as such. If combinations are necessary we should only reluctantly tolerate the system.*[43]

While the first faculty at St. Edward High School was still in the temporary buildings in Lakewood and establishing itself and its philosophy of operation, Br. John William Donoghue, principal and superior, wrote to Br. Ephrem asking whether two of his brother faculty members might be allowed to use the house car to travel to Notre Dame to attend a football game in the fall of 1949. Br. Ephrem replied: *While we are anxious to be reasonable about our Brothers seeing a football game here, I think Cleveland is a bit out of our area. Nor do I wish to see the car start in on a "faculty entertainment basis." It is essential that we limit the use of that car very much—almost strictly to business.* But the provincial tempered his refusal: *In place of coming to Notre Dame for the game I suggest that Brothers Paul and Regius go to Gilmour or some other place and take advantage of television, etc. Both are fine workers and I appreciate their contribution to Holy Cross. But a new school must be more particular than other schools in many things. "At home and on the job" should be our slogan.*[44]

In March 1953 Br. Ephrem wrote to Br. John William Donoghue about the likelihood there would be insufficient brothers available the following school year to accommodate all of the Lakewood school's staffing needs. He said: *You know we shall be scarce in teachers for many years to come, and you may have a lower quota of C.S.C. men next year with Akron opening (I fear). I hope you don't overcrowd your school beyond its real facilities. There is no profit if we have to hire teachers. It takes 35 boys to pay for a teacher (hired), or near that number. So crowding is no profit. Hiring should be because of shortage of Brothers, not for school expansion. When I see you, you can let me know how many you can comfortably take care of. More schools, not bigger schools, should be our policy.*[45]

In the spring of 1954, Br. John William Donoghue contacted Br. Ephrem saying that the local council agreed it would be good to do something concerning tenure for lay teachers at the school. Br. John William, affirming his strong belief that lay teachers were going to be around for a long time in province institutions, realized that the formulation of a policy on tenure was the responsibility of the provincial council. Br. Ephrem wrote back asking for information on what was being done in other schools, public and private alike. Br. John supplied some information. Br. Ephrem asked for a list of the present teachers and coaches at St. Edward and their contract terms, including increments earned and foreseen. He added: *I am interested in what the private high schools pay and what kind of contracts they make. We do not intend to do as the public schools do unless the other private high schools are doing the same as the public high schools.* Br. Ephrem recognized the validity of Br. John's request, but understood its implications as well and felt the province needed not only to be well educated on policies already in place in the Cleveland area educational field, but be self-determining and firm in setting up a tenure policy for the province.[46]

In 1956, realizing that his term as provincial was coming to an end and desiring to complete certain institutional negotiations prior to having to alter the nature of the Board of Trustees of the Brothers of Holy Cross, Br. Ephrem wrote to Archbishop Edward F. Hoban of Cleveland regarding the new school at Akron: *My term of office as Provincial will end this summer, and I am most anxious to complete all official business before June. . . . Since the Akron Agreement has my signature in the name of the present Trustees of the Brothers of Holy Cross, it would simplify matters if title could be transferred and payment made under our present Administration, preferably by Easter.*[47]

LAY TEACHERS AND COACHES

Br. Ephrem recognized the difficulty of retaining qualified and effective teachers/coaches on the salaries Holy Cross schools were capable of paying in the early days of the province. He had a theory on that subject: *No matter what you pay you won't be able to hold men very long. They will go to public schools after they have experience with you, and we never can, on your tuition, compete with public schools, and we shouldn't try to. I think you will find St. Joseph's* [on Cleveland's east side] *and the other schools, who have even higher tuition, paying less for teachers.*[48]

Apparently the provincial council was receiving data of varying natures from the property school administrators concerning the salary scale for lay teachers and coaches. The council met, made decisions, and the results were forwarded by Br. Ephrem to the superiors of the property schools.

Br. Ephrem's basic philosophy was that no more lay teachers and coaches be hired than absolutely necessary to fill out a faculty made up primarily of brothers. Because most teachers, coaches especially, would ordinarily seek higher paying employment in the public system after a few years' experience with Holy Cross, the salary ought to be kept as low as possible. Certainly Br. Ephrem was not fundamentally prejudiced against lay teachers and coaches as such; he knew they had to pursue their own interests. Instead, the rationale was to keep the brother ratio high and tuition costs down for the young men attending the schools and to make the Holy Cross institutions more than competitive with their Catholic counterparts.

Br. Ephrem wrote: *There should be no intention of trying to keep up with the public school salaries and the increases planned for each year of service. In almost every instance coaches and teachers will try to get into the public schools anyway after a few years' experience with us. And coaches are especially known for going after larger salaries.* He added sardonically: *In practice, contracts are only unilateral, as the teacher or coach is always considered free to leave when he wishes—if he is offered a better job.*[49]

In 1960 Br. Ephrem visited the little church in Hollyford, Ireland, where he was baptized seventy-two years earlier.

Br. Ephrem, on the left, with Br. Anthony Von Bersum, two of the brothers drafted into the army in 1918.

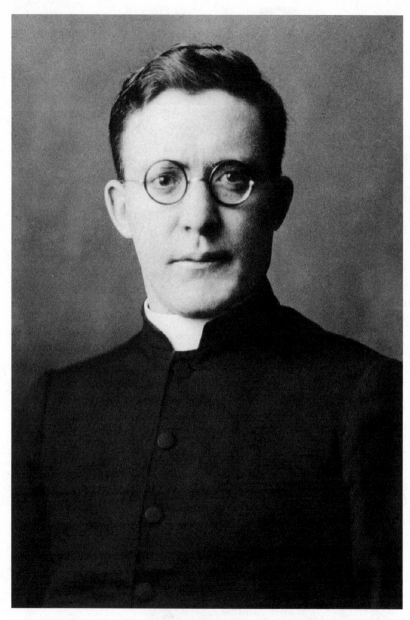

A portrait of Br. Ephrem taken probably when he was in his late twenties.

Br. Ephrem in the
1930s.

On a hike with Fr.
Cornelius Hagerty
in the 1940s. Fr.
Hagerty, a long-
time chaplain to
the brothers at
their house of
studies, was an
avid outdoors-
man. The STOP
sign is an ironic
and inappropriate
symbol of Br.
Ephrem's nor-
mally aggressive
nature.

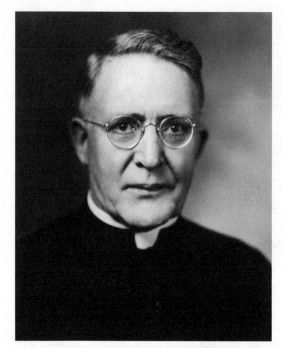

An often used photo-
graph of Br. Ephrem as
provincial in 1950.

Outside of Columba Hall at Notre Dame in the early 1950s, Br. Ephrem
with the visiting Cardinal Tien, S.V.D., of China.

In Rome at the 1956 general chapter, the three provincials of the brothers' newly established provinces: Br. John Baptist Titzer, South-West; Br. Donatus Schmitz, Midwest; and Br. Ephrem, East.

Br. Ephrem takes a turn on a bicycle in New Orleans in January 1957.

Br. Ephrem addressing the assembly on the occasion of his fiftieth anniversary of religious profession, July 5, 1959.

Aboard ship heading for Europe in March 1960 are Br. Ephrem and Br. Bertram Madden.

Br. Ephrem is shown in an informal pose chatting with Br. Albert Rimlinger and Br. John Tryon in 1976 at Le Mans Academy, Rolling Prairie, Indiana, formerly the brothers' novitiate.

Br. Ephrem's last formal portrait, taken in the early 1970s.

Br. Ephrem's philosophy about coaches in schools conducted by Holy Cross men was illustrated in another case. One such individual, a fine Catholic gentleman, serious, honest, but having evidenced little talent for coaching, was resigning at the end of the year, and the principal was happy because he felt he could not afford to keep such a man. Br. Ephrem wrote: *Never need to worry about coaches. They are easy to get. All our schools pay too much for their services.*[50]

In replying to a request from Br. Laurian LaForest, headmaster at Gilmour Academy, to approve the hiring of lay coaches and teachers, Br. Ephrem wrote: *Coaches should teach a regular schedule and give full time to athletics, not having any job or activity that would impair their efficiency. This, as you suggest, should be in the contract. Also the question of good moral conduct. If the question of outside activities is not in the contract, the new coach or teacher should be told verbally.* Clearly Br. Ephrem was concerned over the image of lay involvement in the brothers' schools, and he set out principles to which any employee was expected to adhere.[51]

THE POSSIBILITY OF SISTER COLLABORATORS

Early in his term as provincial of the brothers' province, Br. Ephrem was interested in obtaining sisters to supervise and per- form domestic work in the boarding institutions at which the brothers taught. He was firmly opposed to the establishment of a coadjutor class of brothers, even *de facto*, in the province and, apart from necessary exceptions, purposefully refused to assign brothers to tasks ordinarily associated with such a status in the community. Fr. Edward Heston, procurator general in Rome, the Holy Cross priest who had been so helpful to Br. Ephrem and the brothers in general when the question of the coadjutors surfaced immediately after the 1945 chapter, was asked to check into possibilities of recruiting domestics among Italian sisters, and in August of 1947 he wrote Br. Ephrem concerning a group of possibly interested sisters. Br. Ephrem wrote back: *I presume your cablegram was in response to a letter from Brother Alfonso* [Br. Alfonso Comeau, at Gilmour Academy], *who asked me if he could write you. I had been talking to him how much we needed Sisters, and he said you could do anything. I am sorry I did not write you myself, but it did not dawn on me that Rome was a good place to make contacts.*

Now that you feel you have some prospect of getting some Sisters, you can rely on our gratitude and our full cooperation in the whole matter. Nationality does not make any difference, but if all could be of the same Community it would make it easier to change around and make life more pleasant for all of them.[52]

On an accompanying sheet, Br. Ephrem estimated for Fr. Heston the province's need for sisters. Acknowledging that the permission of the local ordinaries would have to be asked before sisters could be assigned to institutions, Br. Ephrem listed the immediate requirements: New Orleans, Austin, Gates Mills, and Watertown, a total of some fifteen sisters, all young enough to perform useful household service. He said these religious could be received *without delay* so they could become somewhat Americanized by learning English before being placed. Ten more sisters the following summer would be welcome. The financial offer Fr. Heston was authorized to tender was a dollar a day plus board and room.[53]

After formalities had been undertaken to secure the necessary permissions and documentation for the sisters, an unexpected barrier was met at Immigration. The sisters, who Fr. Heston thought were not subject to the usual U.S. quota of immigrants, were in fact declared to come under that quota. As such, it might be years before their turn came to emigrate to the United States, even for purely religious purposes. Fr. Heston said: *I am sorry that your hopes, and mine, have been so unceremoniously dashed to the ground.* He promised to keep his attention focused on possible alternatives, which, in the development of events, never materialized despite a further promising possibility in early 1953 of some sisters from a diocesan community. Arrangements were foiled when that community's bishop refused permission for the sisters to leave Italy, much to the disappointment of the Mother General.[54]

ACADEMIC POLICIES FOR COMMUNITY MEMBERS

In a letter to Br. Elmo Bransby, superior of Dujarie Hall, written August 17, 1947, Brother Ephrem revealed his attitude concerning the education of the brothers at the scholasticate. Two brothers were following a special program leading apparently to an A.B. degree in religion. Brother Ephrem said, *It may be too late to change their program now, but it is not my wish that any Brother specialize in religion until he has obtained A.B. or B.S. in regular secular studies first.*

Brother Ephrem continued in another vein: *I believe that by watching every <u>required</u> credit hour we can get our Brothers faster through Dujarie than in the past. "Luxuries and hobbies" can come after graduation.*

Not that he denigrated the study of religion. Rather, he went on to say: *It may be that our Brothers need more academic religious training than required for graduation, and that, credit or no credit, we should offer a more extensive program in religion at Dujarie.*[55]

On a three-by-five memo slip filed between two documents from an August 2, 1954, meeting of a province Committee on Studies, Br. Ephrem had typed in some questions he apparently wanted addressed by this gathering. From their practicality, it is obvious that some immediate manpower issues were at the forefront; but a few also address more general or future needs. The hastily formulated questions were:

Latin or Modern Language Community needs for Texas Scholasticate?
Are religion courses satisfactory?
In what fields do we need more A.B. men? Commerce?
In what fields do we need more M.A. men?
Any more needed for M.A. in social work?
The future of shop work in our property schools?
The future of art work in our property schools?
More band directors needed?
It appears that we have men advanced enough in science for Texas. What is our next most urgent need for some men with Ph.D.?
How to emphasize Latin in our high schools?[56]

From these notes it is possible to see the educational issues which occupied Br. Ephrem's mind. They had primarily to do with the preparation of religious to fill the surprisingly large number of special needs in the schools. They are the remarks and questions of a school administrator, one who knew the problems from experience, who had the prudence and vision to foresee solutions over time and to engage selected religious in the process.

Determining the optimal involvement of over four hundred men in the multitude of tasks inherent in the institutional apostolates of the congregation was not an easy task. The relatively numerous applicants wishing to join the brothers' province made planning easier for providing teachers and administrators for both existing and new schools but simultaneously produced complications in the staffing and operation of the postulates, novitiate, and scholasticates. Significant growth had its blessings, true, but afforded its complexities as well. Nevertheless, Br. Ephrem looked upon such problems as signs of God's beneficence to the brothers as they struck out for the first time wholly in reliance on their own resources. That he was able to accomplish within a ten-year period all that he had envisioned and to have done so on such a meager material foundation suggests that he was governed and motivated not only by his confident awareness of his own personal capabilities and convictions, but by the providence of God, in which he, like the founder before him, was such a firm believer.

10

Personnel Issues

A MAJOR OCCUPATION

Br. Ephrem began his term of office in an era when the practice if not the essence of the vow of obedience was given a far different interpretation from that of the post-Vatican II period. It was in his time customary for provincials to determine assignments—or "obediences" —for their subjects and simply to notify an individual of his occupation and residence for the coming year, usually by the posting of an obedience roster in each house. Seldom was there consultation before the formal announcements were made. The provincial and his council knew their men, were aware of their experience and areas of competence, and usually understood their personal circumstances wherever they were. The individual was not customarily brought into the dialogue on assignments. The needs of the province and the presumed availability of each of its members for appointment to any aspect of its mission were taken for granted, and it was the role of the provincial council to determine who could best help in the carrying out of the province apostolates. In a pioneering era the provincial administration had to enjoy nearly total freedom in arranging the optimal placement of its personnel.

It should not be assumed, however, that no consideration was ever given to personal preference or to academic capacity or skill. On the contrary, it fell to the provincial and his council to know their men well enough to be able to incorporate these considerations—normally determined during provincial visits or other consultations—in any discussion concerning placement of personnel. When Br. John Baptist Titzer replaced Br. William Mang as assistant provincial, Br. Ephrem requested Br. John to make all the provincial visits for the 1950–51 academic year so that he might get to know the membership of the province better.[1] The drawing up of lists of obediences was never a wholly mechanical process; yet literally hundreds of influential factors entered into the procedure three times a year—prior to each semester and shortly before summertime. And between times individual changes had to be made, as occasion frequently enough dictated.

Since some activity calendars differed from others, the requirements of each apostolate had to be taken into account and numerous other aspects as well, such as the cost of travel between assignments, the fitting of individual vacations into schedules, and, most importantly, the capability of the individual to handle the position assigned. Surely thought was given to the compatibility of individuals in certain community living situations, but this was not a priority unless a person were known to constitute a potential source of difficulty. All in all, the engineering of a suitable and effective roster of assignments was a major task, one which regularly occupied vast amounts of time and challenged the ingenuity of the whole provincial council.

Br. Ephrem was certainly capable of mastering the technical side of personnel management. To him it was probably something akin to working a large jigsaw puzzle, the multiple pieces of which had to fit properly together in order to effect the desired result. It was a chore; it took time; but eventually, sometimes after much reshuffling, each element fell into place and the whole assumed coherence and life. As the number of religious increased, Br. Ephrem wrote to Br. William in 1954, *We are trying to look into the future. One big problem is that the province is too big for efficiency, and for all the contacts with houses necessary.*[2]

However unwieldy the size of the province, for Br. Ephrem there was always more than the mere filling of positions. Underlying each move rested an awareness of the overall mission of the Brothers of Holy Cross. What configuration of assignments would best assure the effectiveness of that mission? The *who* and the *where* were essential components in the decision-making process. Some men were leaders and known to be so, others followers, most of them entirely loyal and quite capable, but there were also a few whose personal agendas might not always have been in perfect synchronization with the provincial's perspective of province ministry.

Br. Ephrem registered more sensitivity to the individual than might have appeared on the surface. Many incidents and the recollection of several religious clearly show his very human side and his sympathetic response to the needs of his men. What stands out in most people's memories, however, are the relatively impersonal, curt, and autocratic methods he employed in resolving personnel issues. This mix of characteristics may be judged incompatible, but in Br. Ephrem they were never so. A bit of the martinet had to be evidenced in anyone who undertook to lead over four hundred men of varying ages, backgrounds, interests, and talents into an entirely unknown arena of independent growth and development toward goals whose attainability had never before been tested experientially. Someone had to exert the right to speak and act unambiguously, forcefully, effectively, and that right had been granted to Br. Ephrem through his election as the first brother provincial and by his virtually universal acceptance among the members of the brothers' society. There was a willingness among them to be led, because he who led was recognized as having those traits essential to a master of diplomatic but effective personnel management.

Thus Br. Ephrem assumed control of the lives of several hundred religious knowing that he would encounter complexities of enormous proportions. Yet he entertained hopeful and optimistic enthusiasm regarding the capacity of his men to continue their former responsibilities and to begin and bring to a high level of achievement the new apostolic endeavors that were part and parcel of his plan for the brothers' society.

He knew there were, and would always be, innumerable human issues to be dealt with among his religious. He was a man who assumed the existence of a definite policy in any given area of responsibility. He adopted successful policies and created new ones governing personnel placement. The key question facing him always was how to fit the reality of the province manpower with all its limitations into the vision of ministerial expansion he intended. Whatever number of religious joined the ranks of the professed members each year, there were never enough fully qualified men to satisfy the needs of the schools and institutions. Yet ironically there could be no continuing potential for vocations to the province unless there were more and more institutions to serve young people and to acquaint them directly with the brothers, their life, and their work. Numbers relied on exposure, and exposure depended on numbers.

Br. Ephrem, always an astute judge of human nature, probably had as thorough a knowledge of his men as any leader of a similarly sized group. His peers he naturally knew relatively well, though he had not developed any remarkably close friendships among them. He did his best to become acquainted with the younger men, especially those pointed out to him as having notable academic or leadership potential. He let others, usually the province director of studies, determine their course of studies according to needs in major fields of academic expertise, but he familiarized himself with these particulars for each individual as successive rounds of assignment considerations began.

Several anecdotes illustrate Br. Ephrem's methodology of personnel management as provincial.

DETERMINING ASSIGNMENTS

When the superior and principal of an institution which offered multiple programs during the summer wrote to Br. Ephrem asking whether locally he had the freedom to assign brothers on the summer roster to more than one program, Br. Ephrem wrote back: *You have but <u>one</u> faculty for the summer, and all those in your house are under your direction in the distribution of work regardless of overlapping between one department and another. Everything is under your direction to plan as you see fit to move Brothers part-time or full-time from one department to another as you see the need. The programs, length of day and all other things are to be approved by you. There is no independent unit or activity at your school.*[3]

On one occasion a young brother wrote to Br. Ephrem that his spiritual director had suggested he request a change of obedience to an outdoor activity, as the present obedience *is a detriment to my living the religious life as I should.*

Recognizing the sensitive role of a spiritual director, but also aware of potential self-interest on the part of the brother in question, Br. Ephrem replied: *April 22 you wrote me* [and here he quotes the request made by the brother]. *You may show this letter to your spiritual director and ask him to be good enough to write me a note stating that a change is necessary.*

Of course you are free at any time to call at my office and discuss the question of change insofar as it may be discussed outside the field of conscience.[4]

In correspondence with Br. Lawrence Miller, director of St. Charles Boys Home in Milwaukee, Br. Ephrem revealed an interesting fact about his method of conducting the official visit and revealed a memory sometimes burdened with too many details: *I usually destroy the individual notes I make at the time of the visit and keep only a general write-up of the house. I find nothing in my summary notes about a summer assignment for Brother* [name]. *I shall be grateful if you will remind me of anything you mentioned to me in this regard or of anything Brother himself may have told me. Did I promise a new assignment for the summer or a new permanent assignment? When I hear from you on these points I shall know what to do with the summer schedule.*[5]

In sharing with the same director the problems connected with formulating summer placements for brothers, including the boys' homes, and elaborating several examples of the difficulties encountered, Br. Ephrem philosophically noted: *This summer blocking is a trial. One obstacle here, another there. So all we can do is trust the good Lord and make the best selections we can.*[6]

Upon hearing from Br. Cyprian Milke, principal of the diocesan-owned Monroe Catholic Central High School, that both the principal and another brother intended to remain in Monroe during the summer and assist the janitor by cutting grass and doing other odd jobs, Br. Ephrem wrote back: *You mention that Father Shaw objects to such work for you. He is right, and had we known your intent we would not give permission for any janitorial work. I am surprised that you got such an idea.* He went on to say that no brother would remain at Monroe during the summer for any reason at all unless Fr. Shaw was willing to allow two men to stay on salary there.[7]

Br. John Baptist Titzer, assistant provincial, was in the process of making the official annual visit to the religious at St. Edward's University, Austin, and wrote to Br. Ephrem about the results of a conversation he had had with a religious who apparently had pleaded for an additional man for the faculty. Br. John took the liberty as visitor of promising him one. Br. Ephrem, slightly piqued, wrote: *I doubt if this can be done even if I were inclined to make such an assignment. . . . But all matters can wait for discussion when you return, but I feel I must reserve the right of obediences.*[8]

In a further letter, Br. Ephrem alluded once more to this situation: *As I said before, the Rule says that the Visitor shall draw up regulations for the house and give what advice to each member he thinks necessary. The question of any changes in obediences will be discussed when you return.*[9]

In writing the earlier letter to Br. John Baptist in Texas, Br. Ephrem alluded with a sense of realism and subdued humor to remarks made by Br. John in his report on the visit to the university and the high school in Austin: *About houses: Superiors always want changes and best men, but they must understand that every house must take some of the "lesser best."*[10]

In 1956 Br. Ephrem contacted Mr. James O. Cherry, board president of the Bedford, Texas, Variety Club Boys' Ranch, regarding manpower problems, particularly in the staffing of boys' homes. He acknowledged, *Our greatest hindrance in doing more of this work is our shortage in man-power, as each time we take over the operation of such an institution, we have to withdraw teachers from our high schools and replace them by secular teachers. We have about 750 members and all but six, whom ill-health has retired, are fully busy in matters directly or indirectly concerned with Christian education.*[11]

THE ACADEMIC SIDE

In a letter of January 14, 1951, to Br. Hilarion Brezik, director of Boysville, Br. Ephrem remarked about difficulties affecting the province, particularly in the light of the Korean War and a sensitive financial climate. He said: *And this summer our hands will be full with many projects tending to save money in times that are already pressing us. We hope to have some high school summer schools going to help feed our men for the summer. You can guess that Texas [St. Edward's University] will be knocked out by September if the army takes all possible students. We may have to depend on the high school there.*[12]

––––––––

In 1954 Br. Ephrem was approached by a brother who wished to take time off to study for a doctorate in an academic area that the provincial council decided was not a priority for the province. In conveying this decision to the brother, the provincial thought it would be prudent to give a somewhat thorough explanation of the rationale behind the fairly terse decision as worded in the minutes of the council meeting. In the course of his explanation, Br. Ephrem alluded to the policy of his administration: *Because our resources in men and money are limited, not all our teaching Brothers have received A.B. degrees, but most men being brought back to study are finishing in summer school. As many as possible are being given a summer opportunity to work for an M.A. According to the needs in Texas, a few are working for the Ph.D.*

It is only because so many Brothers are earning in summer by working in the camps and in teaching summer high school, that we are able to keep others on working for an M.A. Our net returns from any day high school are so small that it would not take care of summer work for an M.A. A Brother taking time out for study is a double loss: (a) we have to hire a man in his place, for day schools will not hire men; (b) we not only lose his earnings while studying but it also costs money to keep a man studying.

In view of all these things it is a wonder that we can get money enough to keep formation houses going and still provide the advanced education that we have absolute need of. Were it not for the St. Joseph Farm, the Ave Maria and the Post Office, not many of our Brothers could get as far as the M.A.

I believe you can readily see why we must limit graduate study whether during the year or in summer school to what is necessary and desirable for the Province.[13]

When a young religious in his first year teaching wrote Br. Ephrem that he would rather do manual work during the coming summer than return to Notre Dame to begin graduate studies, Br. Ephrem replied: *I simply want to assure you now that if a summer out of "education" will help, I shall be happy to grant it.*

Often when our young Brothers finish at Dujarie they have ideals that the "mission work" jolts and may need some readjustment. Our whole philosophy is to serve and forget self. This is the foundation of religious happiness. I need not say more about this.

Don't let the graduate work worry you now. Life is long enough for that, and a summer or two in other fields may be a great advantage to you.[14]

Concluding a letter in which he had taken a young religious rather severely to task for changing the major focus of his doctoral studies on his own authority without specific permission to do so, Br. Ephrem said: *Finally I wish to assure you that I shall be fair in every respect and that the same letter would be written to anyone else under the same circumstances.*[15]

Br. Ephrem was himself sometimes in direct contact with prospective candidates for the congregation, particularly if there were some issue at stake referred to the provincial by Br. Eymard Salzman, the vocation director. One such case was that of a young veteran who had already obtained an M.S. in botany and wished after joining Holy Cross to pursue a Ph.D. in the same subject and teach botany in one of the community's universities. In writing, Br. Ephrem was careful to send along vocation literature which stressed the principles of the religious life: *We are naturally pleased with your interest in the Congregation of Holy Cross, and we believe that your desires as to vocation and avocation can be satisfied in our Congregation.*

After reading the booklet you will readily see that the religious vocation is the primary thing in a Community, and that studies and occupations, though of great importance, are considered secondary. We have room for teachers of botany, as we have for other sciences, but a vocation might be doubtful if the major aim was to be professor of a certain field or subject.

The whole aim of the religious life is to make it easier for men to save their souls. With this thought in mind, a very definite effort is made to have each member labor in an avocation for which nature, grace or study has prepared him. We wish each to use his talents for God in the furtherance of our general work in education.[16]

From the time the brothers' province became autonomous in 1946, Br. Ephrem sought to collaborate with Br. Narcisse Meloche, his counterpart in the brothers' province headquartered in Montreal, Quebec. Br. Meloche inquired into having some brothers from Canada study English during the summers in the U.S., and about the feasibility of having two of his men do their undergraduate work at the University of Notre Dame. Br. Ephrem wrote in March of 1949 to Br. Meloche, himself proposing two young American brothers to study for a masters in French at the University of Montreal during four successive summer sessions on condition that they live with the brothers at Collège Notre-Dame or some similar community house. Br. Meloche replied in the affirmative at once, offering lodging gratis to the U.S. brothers. The two brothers subsequently began studies at the university as planned, and reported very favorably to Br. Ephrem upon returning from their first summer. Contrary to arrangements, a statement was sent for the brothers' board and room. Br. Ephrem paid it without question. Br. Meloche learned of this and quickly cancelled the charges. Returning the check, he reaffirmed his invitation and his offer of free board and room for any subsequent summers. At the foot of the letter from Br. Meloche Br. Ephrem appended a note relevant to his subsequent reply: *Check was for $161. I said that since our Brothers would be in Canada for four summers we wish to make some compensation in the future. Invited his Brothers here.*

The following spring, in order to forestall further awkwardness in this matter Br. Ephrem wrote to Br. Meloche requesting the same accommodations for the two brothers during a second summer of studies, remarking that unless the Canadian brothers had men to send in exchange for studies, the U.S. Province would feel obligated to offer some financial compensation. Br. Meloche replied at once, welcoming the two brothers and announcing that two of his men would indeed be ready to study English in the U.S. Br. Ephrem subsequently received another bill for the board and room of the two U.S. brothers. He sent a check covering the amount, and shortly after that Br. Sylvester Crête, superior of the house at Collège Notre-Dame, wrote back saying that his intention had always been to receive the two brothers in the same manner the U.S. had always received young Canadians studying in the U.S. He added that he did not understand why the steward in Montreal persisted, despite instructions to the contrary, in billing Br. Ephrem. He concluded: *I beg you, therefore, once again to excuse his zeal or his absentmindedness.* Br. Ephrem insisted, though, that unless there was an equitable exchange of men, he wished to contribute on a business basis to the cost of the upkeep of the two American brothers. He wrote Br. Crête: *I know you will be good enough not to interpret this "business" proposal as in any way operative in the case of Brothers from either Province enjoying the hospitality of the other Province according to the traditions of the Holy Cross spirit.*

One of the two American brothers completed the full four summers of study, the other completed three.[17]

PROFESSIONAL QUESTIONS

A local superior had written Br. Ephrem about a brother in his house who desired general permission to attend the monthly meetings of a particular organization to which he wanted to belong. The superior had reservations about giving the permission, principally because the religious was not consistent in rising and arriving on time for morning prayer with the local community. The superior wrote to Br. Ephrem, in effect asking the provincial to make the decision for him. Br. Ephrem replied: *You mention you would prefer not to give . . . permission to go to . . . unless he gets up on time every day. I suggest you tell him that, and make it clear that you have approbation to do so from the Provincial Office. I would say that it is generally good policy to let your men know exactly where they stand, rather than to keep them guessing.*[18]

One brother attached to the Notre Dame Post Office asked Br. Ephrem whether he might be allowed to join a postal organization for supervisors. Br. Ephrem, conscious of the delicate distinction between membership in a religious community and a profession in a secular governmental agency, but equally intent on clarity for the individual making the request, wrote back this advice: *I see no objection to your becoming a member of the National Association of Postal Supervisors.*

However, because of your position as a religious it would not be compatible or prudent to accept any office or membership on any committee, to attend any convention or meeting, such as the secular members may be expected to do. As you are aware, your identity as a religious is unknown to the Association.

You are free to pay the dues of membership and if necessary add your name to any resolutions that would not jeopardize your standing as a member of the Congregation or your position in the post office. Membership therefore indicates only your moral support of efforts to better the members of the Association.[19]

The director of vocations, Br. Eymard Salzman, gave a talk at a vocation convention during the summer of 1953. From some of his listeners he received encouragement to publish the text. He sent a copy to Br. Ephrem asking whether in the provincial's judgment the talk should be published, and if so, what suggestions would he have for emendation? Br. Ephrem, his usual diplomatic but straightforward self, wrote back: *While I think the address was a very good one to deliver at a vocations institute, I do not think it is the kind we should publish. What is said at a convention is one thing; what goes out in print is another.*

My whole philosophy about vocations to the Brotherhood leans to the positive rather than to the negative. I believe in praising Sisters, Pastors and Bishops for what they have done and are doing for the Brotherhoods. Praise will make them do more. I would thank them for the fine intellectual vocations they are sending, showing that they realize that talent and apostolic spirit are necessary for religious teachers who are to form others to virtue and scholarship and to exemplify ideals that will lead others to the religious life and the priesthood. They will say, "Why, if so many are boosting the Brothers, we should do so too."

Your papers would offend pastors for not knowing their theology; sisters for wanting to suggest only rubbish vocations for us. The paper has a rather complaining and defensive attitude. . . .

You have matter enough for a shorter and more positive paper. You might think it over.[20] There is no record of any revision or its publication.

COLLABORATIVE COOPERATION

On April 4, 1952, Br. John Baptist Titzer, assistant provincial, wrote in Br. Ephrem's name to Fr. Theodore Mehling, provincial of the Priests' Province: *Brother Alcuin has requested a change from his position as Business Manager of the AVE MARIA, and, under the present organizational circumstances, Brother Ephrem believes that a change is necessary.*

To fill this position, we will probably have to depend upon Brother Manuel, whose head position at the BENGALESE could be taken care of by Brother Casimir. Of course, we shall see that the BENGALESE staff will be kept at the usual quota.

This incident illustrates both the type of personnel tensions arising in the administration of a single apostolate by two provinces and the thorough but economic manner in which Br. Ephrem approached the concrete settlement of such personnel issues.[21]

Br. Ephrem was well aware of the tremendous toll that canvassing for subscriptions to the *Ave Maria* magazine was taking on brothers assigned to that exhausting work. Reviewing the personnel situation in a letter to Fr. John Reedy, editor of the *Ave Maria*, on February 22, 1956, Br. Ephrem said: *Each year it becomes more difficult to keep up the quota of canvassers. Scarcely anyone desires the job, and a couple who might are not the type for it. . . .*

Then he went into some detail about individuals presently canvassing, their strengths and weaknesses, and the reason why he could not assign to canvassing one or two proven men who were needed elsewhere for various reasons. He concluded: *This is the position of the present group as I see it. . . . The picture is not very encouraging, and I fear that in the future it will be worse. Separation from the Community and other problems are too trying. There are no new prospects for the work; and it appears to me that it is an occupation that a Brother should not be pressed into. It requires a special vocation—if such a vocation does exist.*

I mention these things now in the hope that you may see some alternative plan that would limit the canvassing problem. It appears to me that the day of the Brother canvasser is about over. I am far from wishing this, but the conclusion is forced upon me from what I know of the men who have tried or are trying to live the religious life as canvassers for the AVE MARIA.

On February 28, Fr. Reedy responded, thanking Br. Ephrem for his comprehensive report. He pointed out that though he realized no Catholic magazine *must* have canvassers to solicit subscriptions, the manner in which the *Ave Maria* was financially structured relied on such a practice, and it would properly be the business of the two provincial councils—priests and brothers—to discuss the implications of the phasing out of brother canvassers.[22]

Needs in the expanding institutional system being developed in the early years of Br. Ephrem's administration of the province prompted him to remark to Rev. Vincent J. McCauley, superior of the collaborative Holy Cross Foreign Mission Seminary in Washington, D.C.: *This year hits us very hard in men. We must send out 31, and we have but 10 finishing college. We are sorry to have to dip down among the student Brothers. Every school is expanding.* Br. Ephrem had earlier in the letter notified Fr. McCauley of the names of the three men being assigned to Bengal in the fall.[23]

RELIGIOUS DISCIPLINE

In explaining details of administration to Br. Sigismund Danielski, who had been named summer superior of Holy Trinity High School, Chicago—the residence of many brothers taking summer courses in various institutions in the city—Br. Ephrem dealt with the matter of clothing for the men studying at VanderCook College of Music: *Our regular community garb is to be worn under the same circumstances as during the school year. But during the hours for those taking band lessons, not during other hours, the members may wear collar and tie if this is considered necessary or has been the custom in the past. Such attire may be necessary for drill, etc. Except on a picnic or trip outing, black clothes are to be worn by our religious. If permission is given for a show or a concert, the full religious garb is to be worn—we are always Brothers.*[24]

The local superior of an institution mentioned to Br. Ephrem that one of the brothers who was assigned to do development work for the institution was, on the average, spending three weeks out of a month on the road and wondered whether, from the perspective of regular discipline, that might be too much. Br. Ephrem agreed. He wrote directly to the brother in question saying, *I would like to see a plan worked out whereby you would be two weeks with the community and two weeks on the road. As you know, community life is always first as a moral obligation.*[25]

A brother who had been assigned to work at the Community Infirmary at Notre Dame wanted in 1949 to return to his former work in Texas among the African Americans there. His request was, unfortunately for him, couched more as a demand, and Br. Ephrem straightaway informed him that for two reasons he could not grant the permission: there would be no community life, and a brother does not choose his own obedience. The brother responded that, one way or another, he was going to return to Texas to that particular apostolate—either by obedience or on his own after dispensation from vows. Br. Ephrem advised the brother that it would not be under obedience, and, as provincial, he had no power or authority to grant a dispensation but would refer the matter to the superior general if the brother so wished. He meanwhile reminded the brother that if indeed he felt a change of obedience necessary, he should say so and leave the details to the provincial.

The brother continued to insist on Texas or else. Br. Ephrem asked the superior of the Infirmary to talk with the brother, and he did so, reporting that the religious was *not so certain as the first time. We will have to wait and see.* Four months later Br. Ephrem received another letter from the brother renewing his request to go to Texas or, if this were not granted, to apply for a dispensation. Br. Ephrem replied at once that he would refer the matter to the superior general, which he did, and within three weeks he had an answer to pass along to the brother. *No one may select his formal obedience in the religious life or say that he wants a certain obedience and no other.* And the superior general said that even if Br. Ephrem were to grant the brother a change of obedience it should not be to Texas, *for that would be going contrary to the meaning of the vow of obedience in acceding to the specific "demand" you made.* And he reminded the brother that the priest in Texas with whom he had worked and thought he could work again would not be permitted to hire him if the brother left and became a layman again. Br. Ephrem reminded the brother of his long and admirable record in Holy Cross and said he would be making a "regrettable mistake" in continuing to insist on Texas or a dispensation. However, if the brother stood firm, Br. Ephrem and the superior general would consider the request for a dispensation. He concluded: *I hope you will not unwisely insist on such a choice which would be so much to your detriment from every angle.* There is no further documentation on this matter, but in the end the brother did not leave Holy Cross and several years later died a member of the congregation.[26]

In January 1950 Br. Regis Regensberger, principal and superior of Cathedral High School, Indianapolis, wrote to Br. Ephrem requesting permission for twelve of the brothers on the faculty to accompany the school basketball team to Evansville, Indiana, for their game against Reitz Memorial High School, another of the brothers' schools. The brothers, the superior noted, would be accommodated overnight in the faculty residence. Br. Ephrem wrote back to Br. Regis for further details because of the unusual nature of the request, warning that even with clarification, the request was still likely to be refused. He concluded: *The proposal is indeed extraordinary. And it should not be part of our philosophy of the religious life that such group trips are necessary for morale. Our morale must be built on a higher plane—frankly the plane of sacrifice, if we are to merit respect and vocations. I wonder how the idea of 12 for the trip originated.*[27]

As was to be expected, from time to time Br. Ephrem received from administrators various complaints about men assigned to their institutions. The provincial's customary manner of responding was to trust fully the report of the administrator but also to write personally and frankly to the individual in question to allow him to present his side of the affair. Having received a report from a principal/superior about an incident which illustrated a certain brother's unacceptable behavior and seeming disrespect for authority, Br. Ephrem wrote directly to the alleged offender: *I need not tell you that I am much surprised at this turn in events, as I had every reason to believe you were an exemplary Brother of Holy Cross, and feel sure that with your cooperation I can permanently retain this belief. I have experience enough to make allowances for some things done under excitement which would not be done in normal circumstances.*[28]

Another such letter from Br. Ephrem contained the following: *Brother* [name of the superior] *has written to me informing me that you manifest an attitude of disrespect towards him, and that along such lines your conduct is far from exemplary. He suggests that I remove you from* [the institution].

Before taking any steps in the matter I would like to hear your comment on this. I intend to support Brother [name]'s *authority without question as local superior, and unless you manifest a willingness to cooperate fully with him I may find it necessary to assign you to some other type of work than that in the Homes or Schools. Especially where there are boys it is imperative that every faculty member shows proper respect for the person and orders of his Superior.*

I do not wish to take any step until I hear from you. I even suggest that you see Brother [name] *and talk the matter over with him. There is no objection to your showing him this letter. I would prefer a local solution to the problem.*

This example may be taken as the general policy, and is illustrative of the pastoral but firm method followed by Br. Ephrem in dealing with such matters. In principle Br. Ephrem supported the superiors he appointed; in justice he wanted all the facts before taking action.[29]

One brother wrote Br. Ephrem from Sacred Heart Juniorate in Watertown to ask about proceeding with structural improvements which he could arrange to be made through donations to that house and to the novitiate at Rolling Prairie, Indiana, by reason of influential contacts he had cultivated. Br. Ephrem, never reluctant to accept generosity but aware of potentially undesirable perceptions, wrote back: *Another angle on our formation houses is that they are better equipped and have more luxuries than have the houses in which our school faculties live, and that is bad for morale. After our members go on the missions they are asked to do with fewer conveniences than they have in their years of training.*[30]

In 1948, shortly after receiving a report from the superior general, Fr. Albert Cousineau, on the recently completed general visit to the brothers' province, Br. Ephrem wrote to the province membership, commenting on the praise given by Fr. Cousineau for the spirit of loyalty and cooperation of both subjects and superiors locally as well as generally throughout the province. Br. Ephrem wrote: *The numerous little problems that come to the attention of the Provincial tend to make him more conscious of your small weaknesses rather than of your major accomplishments in spiritual and intellectual growth. Open compliments may not be so numerous as they should be, but this should lead no one to feel that the manifest good he is doing is not appreciated. Though all of us are usually benefited by encouragement, our merit would be very much diminished should we seek glory from men. There is meritorious consolation in remembering that God rewards more abundantly the unnoticed and the unmentioned good if we have made that our objective.*[31]

A similar note was appended to a circular letter sent to the province membership in August of 1954: *There is very little to complain of regarding the administration and spirit of our houses. There is much to praise: a spirit of devotion, economy, loyalty, a willingness on the part of the members to do extra work for the intellectual advancement of the faculty and for the material upkeep of the house. Most Superiors are making an effort to aid beginning teachers as part of their responsibility, and this is most important because of our heavy quota of young members. If a young member has weaknesses or defects, often due to lack of adjustment, it is the office of the Local Superior to take up these matters in the monthly interviews. Local Councillors have the duty of calling the Superior's attention to any neglect in holding Council meetings and the faculty meetings and when the neglect is grave informing the Provincial.*[32]

In a brief introduction to one of his annual visit reports sent to the superior general, Rev. Albert Cousineau, Br. Ephrem tersely remarked: *We have about half a dozen "odd" members. All others are apparently cooperative. There is an excellent spirit of work and zeal.*[33]

In a bulletin to the membership dated August 22, 1954, Br. Ephrem emphasized among other things some points on regular discipline which apparently were drawing attention as the new academic year got underway. Concerning late evening work, he wrote: *The school or business offices are not places for work after supper or after night prayers. The evening work should be confined to the house, except when conditions make it necessary to direct plays, basketball games, etc. Grand Silence requires that members are not to be annoyed or disturbed in the evenings. You already have rules governing the use of radios, typewriters, etc. Besides, all are to retire at a reasonable hour, allowing at least seven hours of sleep. It is unreasonable to sleep part of the afternoon and then stay up late at night to pound a typewriter or create other disturbances.*[34]

VACATION REGULATIONS

Br. Ephrem laid down fairly stringent policies regarding the taking of vacations and personally monitored this facet of province life. The permitted length of a vacation was two weeks plus travel time to and from the vacation site. Apart from adherence to religious simplicity, the young province needed every religious in place and every cent for development and could not afford lenient and overly generous vacation expectations, either within the province or with family. When Br. Donatus Schmitz, superior at Sacred Heart Juniorate, Watertown, wrote concerning vacations for the brothers on his staff, Br. Ephrem replied with some specifics: *I wish to mention three points first: (1) Brothers who have not been a full year on the mission do not get a vacation at full Community expense. (2) Except where there is long-distance travel the Community stands the expense of an annual vacation. (3) Those who are to be at Notre Dame for the summer may see me there unless they wish to make expense arrangements with you now.* Funds were already stretched to the limit by expansion of both personnel and institutions, and Br. Ephrem felt it an obligation to be extremely strict on vacation expenses. It was a time of sacrifice for the whole province, and its leader was not afraid to ask for it from the membership, recognizing at the same time the human factor and the requirements of necessary relaxation for all, regardless of occupation. He did not want loose interpretations and practices gradually taking hold to the eventual detriment of discipline in the matter of vacation control.[35]

On June 1, 1948, Br. Ephrem issued a further specification of policy concerning vacations for men in the Notre Dame area: *(1) All who have had a regular assignment during the year and are not going home this summer may have up to $25 for a vacation. The vacation may include trip to Chicago (or other city), all or part-time at Bankson Lake or at any other house in the Province within* *the travel range of the allowance. Local Superior to approve time and place. Cash at Treasurer's office. (2) All whose vacation will cost more than $25 will get voucher from the Provincial for cash at Treasurer's Office. The normal allowance is $15 plus travel expenses. Time for vacation is to be approved by the Local Superior or his delegate. (3) Any surplus in travel or vacation allowance should be returned to Treasurer. Retention as pocket-money would be contrary to poverty.*[36]

In May, 1947, Br. Ephrem wrote to Br. Octavius Franke, superior of Notre Dame High School, Biloxi, concerning several points, principally vacations. He closed his letter: *Your year has been heavy and tough, and all men should get a couple of weeks rest someplace, but with times as they are we must save every possible dollar.* Concern for the religious was necessarily tempered by the fiscal realities of province expansion.[37]

By 1951 the situation had become even more serious. Writing to Br. Maurus O'Malley, superior of one of the primary schools in New York, Br. Ephrem reiterated some of the standing policies and noted a personal interpretation or two of new conditions levied on vacations. Br. Maurus had asked about vacation policy for those in temporary vows. *Under new planning, Brothers who have not put down the same time as the Brothers in Dujarie before getting vacations are not entitled to vacations home. You have two in this position. . . . However, if those wish a vacation this summer, they may have it at their own expense.*

At Dujarie the Brothers go home at their own expense at the end of their freshman year and also at their own expense the year they get their degree.

Even the Brothers who have been doing manual work here at the Community House, living in the Annex for a full year, go home this summer at their own expense.

Applying the same principle, the Brothers who are in their first year of teaching without a degree take their first mission vacation at their own expense. They even get a better break here than the Brothers who spend a year working after leaving the Novitiate.

You might inform the two Brothers concerned, for the same rule is being applied to other houses. It follows the idea that members under temporary vows are still in formation no matter what house they are in.[38]

On May 21, 1951, Br. Ephrem wrote Br. Rex Hennel, superior of Notre Dame High School, Biloxi: *In the discussion of trying to keep up annual vacations home for most Brothers it appeared financially possible if travel expenses were held to a minimum. This means that pullman and meals on train should practically be eliminated.*

In the directions this year there is no allowance for pullman except for the second night if one has to spend two nights on a train. If one wants to take pullman for only one night on a train he will have to economize on the $15 allowance or on something else.[39]

And in a letter to Br. Christian Stinnet at Vincentian Institute, Albany, Br. Ephrem wrote similarly: *We are making an effort to cut out all pullman travel when there is only one night on a train, and particularly where the ride is not more than 16 hours. Even all mid-year transfers to Texas were without pullman. Expenses are such that every dollar must be saved.*[40]

A day later, Br. Ephrem wrote Br. Ellis Greene, superior of Mt. Carmel School in the Bronx: *According to our present policy, Brothers who have not degrees do not get a vacation at community expense during or at the end of their first year of teaching. They are really on Dujarie status. However, if the Brother is free and can conveniently take vacation at his own expense he will get permission to do so.*[41]

Some brothers stationed a great distance from their homes who were due vacations inquired about taking vacation in their local California communities. Br. Ephrem saw no problem with this and wrote back to Br. Francis Assisi Davis, superior at Long Beach, California: *For those who hang around Long Beach or Sherman Oaks for the summer some little trips or little spending should be arranged not to average more than $25 per man. This does not mean that each man gets $25 to spend as he wishes. The group or individual spending is under the direction of the Superior. For one who does not want to join in trips or common recreations, I think summer cash of $10 is enough for personal spending. That will leave more for the group activities of others, if the Superior wants to plan things that way.*[42]

———————

Writing to Br. Theophane Schmitt, superior of Gilmour Academy, Gates Mills, Ohio, on May 23, 1951, Br. Ephrem said: *About over-night travel, or travel under 20 hours, there is very little need for our young Brothers to take pullman. I am asking this bit of economy and religious poverty in all places possible this year unless men are old, nervous, etc. Unless men have business the next morning one night in a coach does not knock young men out. Use your judgment in special cases. Some allowance for meals too, but even here a [brown bag] lunch or two can cut down part of the travel bill.*[43]

———————

And in 1953 Br. Ephrem wrote Br. Alfonso Comeau, headmaster of Gilmour Academy, saying, *I need the help of every local Superior to discourage all unnecessary travel, not only for economy but for many other reasons. I have tried to be very fair and liberal in the questions of regular vacations, moreso than finances would warrant, but there are always some who want more and more.*[44]

SENSITIVE RESPONSES

At times the resolution of specific personnel cases or of matters pertaining to certain individuals called for extreme sensitivity on the part of Br. Ephrem. A case arose in which the local superior felt that a brother needed to be changed immediately to another location and occupation. After assessing the situation through a personal representative and additional correspondence, Br. Ephrem wrote: *Brother [name] is to come to Notre Dame, the sooner the better. Have Brother [the representative] decide with you when Brother . . . can leave. He should bring trunk and all. If there is any trouble, phone me. I am enclosing a note for him. He is to get no permission home. If that is necessary, it will be taken care of here.*

To the brother in question, Br. Ephrem wrote: *When [your replacement] arrives, or when Brother . . . or [the local superior] shall decide, after perhaps a couple of days, you will come to Notre Dame and bring personal belongings. Here we can talk things over and provide for some rest.*[45]

———————

In reply to a local superior/principal who was worried about the effect in the neighborhood of the lingering presence of a brother who had been granted a dispensation, Br. Ephrem wrote: *As regards [name], there is no way of controlling where he will live or what occupation he will follow. You will suffer nothing from his absence from Holy Cross or his presence in [the city]. There need be no hiding from the boys that he is no longer with us. To any inquiry: "He asked for a dispensation and got it." Actually your other members gain in the esteem of the public. In no town has the presence of an "ex" hurt us. Even among the clergy there are such.*[46]

Br. Gerontius McCarthy, novice master, wrote Br. Ephrem in 1956 about a novice who had recently left, apparently filling in some details in the letter. Br. Ephrem responded typically: *We should thank God he is gone; but the wonder is why he ever came in or how he got in. Never worry about those who should go. The dear Lord will always send enough and good ones.*[47]

Br. Ephrem, though sometimes brusque and terse in his communications and in his official relationships with members of the province, appreciated the efforts of his men and used opportunities that arose to convey this appreciation to them. One such instance was a letter to Br. Eymard Salzman, vocation promoter, with questions and suggestions about four candidates for the novitiate. Br. Ephrem began the letter by saying: *For something you have done so exceptionally well I owe you a line of appreciation, not only from myself but from all the Brothers in the Province: your most efficient work as a Recruiter. God has certainly blessed your zeal and sincerity, and I can say your personal sacrifices also. The large groups you have for the Novitiate each half year are a blessed surprise. May God continue to bless your labors for Holy Cross.*[48]

In the spring of 1947 Br. Ephrem wrote to Fr. Albert Cousineau, superior general, at his office in New York, saying that he would like to visit the generalate in connection with a difficult personnel situation in one of the New York houses. Br. Ephrem wrote: *At Albany there seems to be much vocational trouble. One temporary professed will leave August 16. One professed wants to enter a seminary, another is anxious for ordinary dispensation, and the Superior himself wants to resign his job—and may even want a dispensation. There are no moral problems, and probably no general house problems—but there are unstable vocations. I want to see the situation, general and individual, and then presume the privilege of being able to see you in New York before you go to Canada.*[49]

Br. Ephrem, as conscious as he was by training, experience, and necessity of fiscal responsibility and frugality, still regarded the individual as more important than rigidly unbending principles. He wrote in a circular to the membership in 1952: *The pressure of work in all our houses is intense and the strain on some members may be provoking too much. More members would remedy the situation, but until this is in sight all legitimate means possible for saving time and energy should be used, and material expense should not be spared in this regard. Young teachers especially need help and encouragement and they should be assigned a veteran faculty member with whom they can discuss their problems. The excellent spirit of work reported from every house is a blessing for which we should all be grateful. Let us continue private prayers and novenas for the additional members we need to carry on our apostolate and promote the Kingdom of Christ.*[50]

In Br. John Baptist Titzer's first few months as assistant provincial, he was sent out on a series of visits to the province to familiarize himself better with the membership. He sent copies of his reports back to Br. Ephrem, wondering whether they were properly and clearly rendered. Br. Ephrem wrote back: *No, your reports are not too long. I like the way you do them. They are complete, to the point and comprehensive. Your comment on each man is fairly well in line with what I know. I think you got the weak and good spots rather rapidly. There is, however, a background to many of the characters and to the things reported to you that I can supplement here in conversations when you return. It will explain some things that you mentioned and some things that were said to you.*[51]

Br. Ephrem appreciated the dedication of his religious to their calling to the vowed life. A little more than a year after becoming provincial he decided to act formally on a suggestion he was hearing repeatedly about initiating some type of celebration of the 25th anniversary of profession. On November 1, 1947, he wrote to the superiors of the houses: *Many Brothers have recommended that the Silver Jubilee of First Profession be given a primary place of importance in our Community celebrations. In Canon Law, seniority and eligibility to hold office date from First Vows. Final Profession is but a confirmation of the vows taken at the end of the novitiate period. A member is truly a Religious from the date of his First Vows.*

By having the Silver Jubilee celebration based on the year of First Vows, each novitiate group will have the same Year of Jubilee, and will, so to say, constitute a Twenty-fifth Anniversary Class.

In agreement, therefore, with the members of the Provincial Council, I ask that Jubilee recognition be given to the following Brothers during the year 1948 [here are listed twenty-seven brothers whose twenty-fifth anniversaries were being celebrated in 1948].

There can be a common celebration at the Community House for those who will be at Notre Dame in July 1948. In addition, each house away from Notre Dame in which jubilarians of the year reside should have its own recognition program some time before school closes in June.

Each year following 1948 there will consequently be but a single Jubilee Class, based on the twenty-fifth year of vows, the occasion to be celebrated in the house of assignment, and, when possible, a common celebration at Notre Dame that summer.[52]

A similar message was written to the membership in a bulletin dated May 13, 1948. Br. Ephrem concluded: *The summer activities of our Brothers have become so extensive that only a limited number can be spared to attend summer school at Notre Dame. These I hope to meet on a couple of evenings for an exchange of ideas. I wish I had more time to keep the problems and work of the Provincial Administration before those who will not be at Notre Dame this summer. I hope these few lines will be accepted as a manifestation of our intention to make our problems the problems of our whole Society, and to enlist the aid of each one in furthering our apostolate as Brothers.*[53]

HEALTH ISSUES

A brother experiencing some anxiety wrote to Br. Ephrem requesting a change at the end of the semester from the school where he was teaching. Br. Ephrem wrote: *I am sorry to hear that your health is not good and the classroom is a worry for you. The news is somewhat of a surprise, as when I last saw you you were apparently in fine shape and very happy with* [the school] *and your work. You remember that we had a long talk this summer.*

Then practicality surfaced. . . . *We certainly wish and hope you will be able to carry on at least till the end of January.* . . . [The request was made in November.]

Be assured that if your health requires a change it will be provided.

. . . *We have time enough to think of a place where you could fit in for a year or half-year, and something will be worked out by the end of the semester. Meanwhile, take the problem philosophically.*

Subsequently Br. Ephrem received a letter from the brother's doctor certifying that a change would be beneficial by reason of colitis due to nervous tension. Br. Ephrem wrote the doctor assuring him that a change could be conveniently made at the end of the semester and thanking him for his interest.[54]

Br. Ephrem, under his apparently imperious exterior, could exhibit kindness and gentleness, as many attest. On one occasion a brother was having psychological difficulties and requested a change from his assignment. When the crisis passed, however, he decided to remain where he was. Br. Ephrem wrote to him, having been kept informed by the local superior.

I am writing this note to assure you that I shall do all I can to help you out of your present state. I have been very pleased with your work and your dispositions . . . and I want to let you know that your services are appreciated.

You are free to visit me any time you wish. As I told [the local superior], *you may give up your work . . . and come to Notre Dame, but if at all possible I would prefer that you finish the year. I think you should get a rest or a trip this summer, and I would like to have your suggestions about this and about next year. We are making out some summer assignments now but you need not be governed by them. I want to do whatever is best for your state of mind, and if we both work together on this the result will be better. Expense will not be a question in restoring you to better health. Don't be concerned about any listing you may get for the summer; it will be changed if not for your benefit.*

. . . *Let me again assure you of my interest and desire to help you all I can.*[55]

Br. Ephrem was always solicitous for the health and welfare of the members of the province. Br. George Biadaszkiewicz, seriously ill in Chicago, was being cared for by his sister during the nights at the hospital. Br. Ephrem wrote Br. Reginald Justak, superior of the brothers at Holy Trinity High School, saying that he felt that Br. George's condition and the less adequate facilities available at the Community Infirmary at Notre Dame warranted his remaining in Chicago, but that the province was in no way disclaiming its responsibility toward his care. In fact, a brother had been sent from Notre Dame to help care for Br. George, and Br. Ephrem was trying to locate someone more or less full time to do that service. Br. Reginald was instructed to find a nurse to assist, but in the meantime a brother would be provided. He concluded: *With regard to Brother George's sister, she certainly is doing us a big favor, even if Brother George is her brother. Let me know how she is fixed financially. If we had to pay for what she is doing it would cost us something. We would be readily disposed to make her a present of a check from this office. Let me know exactly what services she has been performing and how long.*

Be assured for the sake of your faculty and for Brother George we shall do everything we can.[56]

One brother who was a patient in the Community Infirmary wrote Br. Ephrem in November 1950 that, though he was diagnosed as a diabetic and also had angina, he was fit enough in the doctor's opinion to travel if he wished. The brother had a free railway pass to New Orleans and was asking Br. Ephrem if he could take the second week of his vacation by going to New Orleans. Br. Ephrem replied that patients in the Infirmary did not take vacations, and that *since your health is good, it is evident that you should be living at the Community House.* Only after such a move could the subject of a vacation be further discussed.[57]

In the early 1950s several Holy Cross Brothers were afflicted to a greater or lesser degree with tuberculosis or other lung ailments. Br. Ephrem, after seeing to the proper care of one such brother suspected of having the disease, and clearly concerned about the anxiety of the brother's relatives, wrote to the parents, who lived at a distance from the Notre Dame area where treatment was to be administered. He said: *Healthwin is a very fine place. It is the regular place where we send such patients. Dr. Carter is a Catholic, and the Hospital has a private chapel. Brother will be well taken care of. So kindly do not feel worried about him.*[58]

When one brother wrote to Br. Ephrem requesting for reasons of economy and health that he be permitted to spend full time in the printing shop of the school to which he was assigned, Br. Ephrem wrote back to the principal/superior, expressing something of a personnel policy: *At the present time I cannot see the problem that way, and I am writing you rather than [the brother involved], as all ideas on school policies should come through you. First of all we don't desire a* <u>one-man job</u> *in any of our schools. We want only* <u>jobs and classes</u> *for which we can provide successors and retain the freedom to make all necessary changes in obediences.*[59]

Br. Ephrem showed a deep concern for the health and overall welfare of those administering the brothers' institutions. After listing a number of impending changes to be made for a variety of reasons at St. Charles Boys' Home, Milwaukee, Br. Ephrem encouraged the director, Br. Lawrence Miller, by asking: *Any possibility of your taking a few days off during the Christmas holidays if you get some assistance from Chicago?*[60]

In 1948 the director of Gibault Home for Boys in Terre Haute, Indiana, felt that for reasons of health he ought to resign before the completion of his three-year term, and had the support of a doctor in the matter. He wrote to Br. Ephrem conveying this message but allowing that there might be a possibility he could stay on for another year. Br. Ephrem had to have certainty on the issue and wrote back: *Our Council has been pleased and has appreciated your work as Local Superior during the past two years, and if you are at all able to stay on the job the Council would be pleased to have you finish your three year term.*

If, however, for health reasons now, or to safeguard your health during the coming year and later, you and the doctor think you should be relieved of the responsibility of the Superiorship, the Provincial will agree, though regretfully, to present your resignation which, should you feel compelled to take it, should be formal, to the Superior General.

If for health reasons, inability to continue your work as Superior, you feel you must resign, write a formal note to the Provincial asking him to present your request to the Superior General. Put nothing else in that note.[61]

THE INTERIOR LIFE

On one occasion a religious wrote Br. Ephrem claiming that though he was happy in his work at a particular institution, it was at the same time, he felt, injurious to his spiritual growth. He asked for a change if possible but invited the provincial to decide. Br. Ephrem wrote back: *Always feel free to write your mind. Your opinion will be given all possible consideration.* The rest of the letter reflected a sincere concern for the welfare of the brother in question.[62]

One brother was seriously contemplating leaving the community and had spoken with his retreat director about it. He wrote to Br. Ephrem about his situation and felt that he might want to try the Trappists as an alternative. Br. Ephrem wrote back: *You should not come to any decision immediately, as you are now much under the influence of the retreat and you must think out your problems coldly. Abbot Fox and some others usually think that the Trappists are the only solution to "conversions." But there are some others who are as much convinced that living one's Rules and Constitutions is in many cases a better solution. However after your visit now for a couple of days we can talk things over after you come back or during the summer.*

You are aware that for some years you were in the proper swing in Holy Cross, and, though I may be mistaken, I believe that it was too much interest in athletics that caused the let-down. You came to C.S.C. with the needed great ideals, but time wore you down somewhat and you probably did not put all you should into prayer and daily life. The means were there all the time.

An effort was being made by Br. Ephrem to offer gentle guidance and enlightenment to the individual without being judgmental and overly directive.[63]

Br. Ephrem was approached several times by members who requested either to leave the religious life entirely or to transfer to the Trappists. In writing to the superior general, Fr. Albert Cousineau, in

1948, Br. Ephrem remarked: *We have two extremes: Trappists calling some and the "world" calling others. We are trying for regular
Community discipline, and I can see why both extremes. Trappists
do God's work; and we shouldn't regret losing the "worldly" if they
can't accept the ideal of Holy Cross. If we have a worthy goal, God
will send replacements, and He is.*[64]

At the same time, several requests were made in the early 1950s
by religious of other institutes to be incorporated into Holy Cross.
Br. Ephrem, in a letter posted from the generalate in New York, wrote
Br. John Baptist, assistant provincial, with some advice: *On principle
we should not encourage Brothers from other Communities to
come to us while they are still bound elsewhere.* He had no problem
considering men who had been in other congregations, had allowed
their temporary vows to expire, and then applied to Holy Cross free
and clear of other obligations.[65]

Br. Ephrem showed sensitivity to the feelings of his religious,
regardless of the brusque exterior he sometimes manifested and the
terseness he employed in communicating with them. Notifying a
young brother his petition for renewal of temporary vows had been
denied, Br. Ephrem wrote him personally: *I regret to inform you
that the Provincial Council and the General Council did not favor renewal of vows for you on February 2. You should not feel
disappointed about this, as I think you realize that the religious
life has been very difficult for you and no doubt you yourself have
had serious doubts about your vocation.*

*This decision regarding vows carries with it only the conviction
that you have not a vocation to the Brothers of Holy Cross. It in
no way reflects on your character or other qualifications.*

*I assure you of our good will and prayers and of any recom-
mendations you may need or desire, but I do think it would be
best for you to believe that God wants you to be a good Catholic
layman rather than a religious.*[66]

Often Br. Ephrem was approached by superiors of scholasticates
about personal problems affecting the lives of individual religious.
Br. Ephrem had dealt with such questions before, and had established
a relatively firm policy: *It is a policy for everybody's good that*

scholastics under stress or strain or in doubt about their vocations go to the missions [an assignment in any one of the institutions] *without delay. After all, a teacher's vocation is not given a fair chance until he has spent some time in the classroom.*[67]

Br. Elmo Bransby, superior of the scholasticate in Austin, wrote Br. Ephrem on one occasion about the apparently singular behavior and attitudes of a young brother and suggested that perhaps a change to active teaching life might be beneficial to the individual. Br. Ephrem wrote back: *Offhand I would say you shouldn't get too serious about his "ideas on the interior life." Young people are inclined to get their own notions about things, but unless things go too far we can expect that time will solve the problems, and there are a number of moves that can be made to bring people down to the actualities of life.* Then Br. Ephrem went on to say that he would assign the religious to some mission at the semester, as *we must do what we can for every vocation.*[68]

A scholastic brother in Texas informed Br. Ephrem in January 1951 that he did not intend to renew his temporary vows when his profession expired a month later. The brother was scheduled to receive his degree in June of that year. Br. Ephrem thoughtfully stated in his reply that he would in no way place a barrier in the brother's way to leaving at the appropriate time, but that if the brother felt he could live another year under vows, it would be to his advantage later on to have completed his degree. Br. Ephrem suggested he might wish to renew his vows, complete his degree, then remain in Holy Cross for the rest of the term of the vows. No dispensation would be given in the meantime. *After you got your degree in June you would complete the vow-year in one of our schools or other institutions. You would make a definite decision in January 1952.* This incident is illustrative of the unusual perspective of personal interest Br. Ephrem brought to personnel matters.[69]

It goes without saying that the vocation of many young religious was often severely tried by suggestions or even stronger forms of communication from relatives attempting to influence a brother to discontinue the formation program in favor of personal or family considerations. One young brother wrote of his parents' interference to Br. Ephrem, who replied with his usual wisdom and kindness, expressing in the process something of a policy statement regarding the issue: *It is really unfortunate that your parents, especially your mother, take the viewpoint they do. I must agree with you that they are making a mistake in trying to influence you in the manner in which you believe you ought to live your religious vocation. History is full of situations like yours: Saint Thomas Aquinas, Saint Stanislaus, and others.*

However, take your trial as patiently as you possibly can. Things will work out in time, and your parents will see that it is the vocation and not the occupation that counts. Give them credit for meaning well even though they be mistaken in their judgment. Morally they should not interfere with your vocation—and this is the teaching of the Church; but you can assume that they do not feel the responsibility of their attitude. Pray confidently for a change of view on their part. You have a right to remain fixed in your intention, but at the same time you will show them all the respect and devotion due them. In future letters or contacts, do not argue the problem; rather treat it lightly and cheerfully, informing them that they should be glad you are happy and endeavoring to save your soul according to your conscience.[70]

These illustrations offer a fairly typical image of Br. Ephrem in his dealings with his men. The perspective he enjoyed as provincial, as chief architect of the province's future, afforded him the bigger picture whose details had to be addressed even when others could not appreciate them by reason of a certain tunnel vision caused by focusing on local issues alone. He respected his religious, acknowledged the sacrifice they had made in joining Holy Cross, supported each person's search for God in the religious life, and encouraged them repeatedly. But he demanded of everyone total dedication to the commitment made, part of which was unflinching loyalty to being an integral part of the institutional presence of the brothers in a specific apostolate. He asked no more of others than he did of himself.

11

Societal Image and Identity

For the one hundred and nine years between 1837, when the Brothers of St. Joseph became part of the Association of Holy Cross in Le Mans, France, and 1946, when the newly autonomous United States Province of Brothers was legislated into legal existence, the brothers' society of the congregation had never functioned separately from that of the priests. It had not determined its own apostolic goals, independently governed its own institutions, or made its own decisions as to the education and development of its members.

As evidenced in the usually minor but persistent difficulties between societies, more serious examples of which came to a head in the United States during the general chapters of 1906 and 1932 and which led to the momentous decisions of the 1945 general chapter, there were potential causes of tension in the very nature of the congregation and in the manner in which it evolved in North America. The priests were concerned during one era that a preponderance of members in the lay society could threaten to interfere with, envelop, even denigrate the clerics; and the brothers were anxious in another period that a numerically weighted clerical status could cause the priests to dominate and obfuscate the vocational identity of the brothers. The latter concern was perhaps the more common down through the years. At the time of the separation into autonomous provinces, neither cause predominated but both were operative enough in the minds of the religious in Canada and the United States to suggest that it was indeed time for a creative resolution to be implemented.

So when, on July 1, 1946, Br. Ephrem O'Dwyer became the first provincial of the newly established homogeneous brothers' province in the United States, he faced an entirely novel situation regarding the brothers. For the first time in their history as part of Holy Cross they were fully responsible for their own future, reliant only on the supervisory role of the general administration to assure their remaining within the constitutional parameters of the congregation's overall mission to the world.

Br. Ephrem was no stranger to issues concerning the brothers' image and identity in the congregation. Chapter 3 has dealt with the matter of his letter to Fr. John F. O'Hara and the atmosphere at the University of Notre Dame at the time that ignited his determination to lodge a formal protest against the treatment he perceived the brothers were receiving on the campus. In chapter 4 two significant letters of Br. Ephrem were quoted nearly in full, one to Br. Justin Dwyer and the other to Fr. Thomas A. Steiner, in which he expressed his concern over the image of the brothers and his rationale for writing the history of the brothers in the United States. Chapters 5 and 6 outlined his formal involvement in the preparation of the general chapter of 1945 with its agenda of autonomy and in the resolution of the coadjutor brother issue which arose consequent to the chapter.

He knew that there had been plenty of rough pavement on the road leading to autonomy, and the apparently smooth surface which now lay stretched out toward the horizon could conceal potentially disastrous cracks and crevices. The concept of autonomy was new; living its principles harmoniously and effectively would take time, experience, and patient compromise on the part of both societies. It was the task of Br. Ephrem as the brothers' first provincial to lead them toward the achievement of two specific goals, each of which was difficult but nevertheless essential if autonomy were to succeed.

The first goal focused on the apostolic mission of the congregation as specified in the brothers' ministries, especially in education and youth care. Br. Ephrem intended to lead the brothers toward the independent ownership and administration of its institutions to the extent that these ventures would support other apostolic works in diocesesan institutions, would provide the housing, staffing, and forming of new young religious, and would assure the financing of ongoing education among the province members. The settlement that came to the brothers in the division of assets at the 1945 chapter was basically adequate, as it involved most of the saleable properties of the priests and brothers. However, Br. Ephrem did not see such assets as tangible sources of income except through their development and use for mission. Thus he enjoyed only the bare necessities from which to launch his ambitious program of development. But they were enough.

The second goal was not nearly so openly expressed or embraced by Br. Ephrem, but it was fixed in his mind and heart and had been for years. Throughout their existence the brothers almost naturally had been identified exclusively in relation to the priests. The brothers assisted the priests in their ministries. The brothers held auxiliary roles in the institutions operated by the congregation, especially the University of Notre Dame. However influential its presence was in any situation, the brothers' society was recognized both within and outside Holy Cross fundamentally as an adjunct to the priests' society. Despite significant exceptions to the contrary, the attitude most often expressed among the priests was that of the superiority of status accorded by the hierarchical structure of the institutional Church to the vocational role of the priest. The brothers could not exert total authority in the operation of even those schools which nominally were theirs. Often priest superiors presided in the community houses and brother administrators were *advised* by diocesan superintendents of schools from among the local clergy. The brothers taught in and operated schools for others; the fruits of their labors could never benefit them directly, certainly never toward independent expansion. Autonomy changed all that. Now the potential of the future was limited only by the creative imagination of Br. Ephrem, his chosen advisers, and the potential of the province membership, and by external fiscal and social realities over which they had little or no control.

Thus, in the process of achieving apostolic prominence and effectiveness, a major goal was also to enhance the image of the brothers' vocation and to clarify the identity of the brother in the apostolic mission of the congregation and the Church.

Though it is relatively easy to document Br. Ephrem's intent to create a powerful apostolic dynamic in the province and to cite his fairly consistent exhortation toward that end, it is not so simple to find written examples of the provincial's determination to raise the image of the brother in the minds and hearts of everyone in any way connected with the works of the brothers' society. Yet that determination was there. It had been clearly defined in earlier years and nothing had changed in Br. Ephrem's vision of the lay religious life and its mission in the Church. To be sure, he operated out of the context of the times in which he lived, and was influenced by the ecclesiological and theological perspectives of the day as well as by the spirituality of brotherhood which was current at that time. But to him the brother was a valid, essential, and effective minister in the Church, particularly in the education of young people, and, while he might not be a cleric and enjoy the image generally conceded by the faithful to that status, he could be not only equally effective but perhaps even more so by reason of his capacity to focus his energies exclusively and collectively on his religious life and apostolic work. Brothers might be fewer in number, might have responded to a calling less known and appreciated in the Church, might function in the shadow of the clerical image, but they had an identity of their own which commanded respect and the acknowledgement of their contribution to the welfare of a whole segment of the People of God.

This they deserved from the clergy and bishops who conscientiously aspired to respond to the needs of their flock and the parents who sought a formative Christian experience for their youngsters in Catholic schools governed by men and women who had dedicated their lives to the service of God through the Church. The brotherhood was to Br. Ephrem a dignified, respected calling in the Church, and he intended to promote that image through the apostolic outreach of the Brothers of Holy Cross.

It should not be thought that Br. Ephrem or any of the brothers came by their determination to enhance the image of the male lay religious because of any serious rupture in their relationship with the priests of the congregation. Surely there were more or less sensitive incidents from time to time, based usually on personality or on conflict of community or apostolic interest rather than on strictly interpretive or ideological differences over the basic nature of the congregation; but these were to be expected in the normal course of events as the single province of brothers and clerics grew and developed.

Br. Ephrem's own relationship with the members of the priests' society was virtually always cordial, even friendly. His letter to Father O'Hara was clearly indicative of a delicate sensitivity to the distinction between an individual and the position he occupied. Br. Ephrem recognized and respected commitment, intelligence, common sense, cleverness and wit, whoever might possess these qualities. He was himself a match for anyone in conversation and never allowed himself to be awed into a sense of inadequacy by the color or cut of a clerical cassock. He tolerated as exceptions—not always graciously, however—the errant reasoning or attitudes he sometimes experienced among both Holy Cross brothers and priests and did not censure the whole because of the ineptitude of the few. Respecting religious, especially priests, and their rank in ecclesial circles, he simply assumed his own place in the ranks of Church personnel and considered himself one of them; and rightly so. In turn he was accepted and admired by priests throughout the congregation, especially those who had come to know him by association either at work or in community. Br. Ephrem appreciated the intuition of Fr. Basil Moreau in founding Holy Cross and worked throughout his life to preserve and protect the fundamental nature of the congregation. The awarding of an honorary doctorate to Br. Ephrem in 1976 by the University of Notre Dame was a belated but nevertheless sincere acknowledgement of his considerable place in the history of the institution and in that of Holy Cross.

EXAMPLES OF HIS CONVICTION

In December 1933 while a member of the provincial council, Br. Ephrem wrote a memo to Fr. James Burns, provincial, making a suggestion which he felt would respond to some uneasiness which apparently existed in the formal governing of the University of Notre Dame through its Board of Trustees. The "trend of recent discussions" and "the recent history of the Community" perhaps refer to the serious consideration given at the general chapter of 1932 to legislating some type of separation between the priests and brothers in Holy Cross; or these phrases may allude to more recent efforts to effect the chapter's decisions regarding the relationship between the two societies, or to the possible followup given to Br. Ephrem's recent letter to Fr. John F. O'Hara about the brothers and the university. Precisely to what the "St. Joseph Properties" refers is unclear, but it should be borne in mind that for decades after the founding of the university, at least some of the property was owned by the priests and brothers in common under the legal corporate identity of "The Brothers of St. Joseph."

Dear Father Provincial,

I had intended to defer the request I am now making until the "Province of Indiana" was incorporated. The trend of recent discussions, however, prompts me to place the matter before you at this time.

Considering the recent history of the Community and the desire all of us now have to give greater permanency in fact and in principle to the future well-being of the community, I am respectfully requesting official consideration, at the proper time, of vacancies on the Board of Trustees of the University of Notre Dame. It is probably not necessary for me to give in detail my reasons for this request. In brief, I have in mind constitutional, moral, legal, and diplomatic necessities or values.

At the time of the transfer of the "St. Joseph Properties" from the Brothers, I would suggest that there be Three Brothers (3) on the Board of University Trustees and Four Priests (4).

At the present time there are but four (4) active priests on the Board, and in view of the work ahead the present is a most opportune time to make the adjustments.[1] The *Bulletin* of the university for the years 1934–1938 shows no evidence that any action was taken on this request.

On July 10, 1937, Br. Ephrem wrote again to Fr. Burns, this time concerning the issue of brothers transferring to the society of priests. In a congregation composed of both clerics and lay religious, each society receiving candidates called to that specific way of life, it had been considered prudent from the outset for Holy Cross officially to recognize the distinction in the nature of each vocation. Br. Ephrem, referring to a letter he had received from the director of one of the postulates, probably Valatie, said: *In a note from Br. Jude he says: "Stafford withdrew with the intention of entering the seminary at North Easton."*

I do not know whether Br. Jude states this as news or as a matter which I should mention to you. There are numerous old decrees and comments touching such transfer, but all I find in the Rule is: "A candidate who has entered the Novitiate as a Brother cannot become a priest in the Congregation." This taken literally would leave the transfer clear.

However, such a transfer has not been a policy in the past, and I believe there is a general opinion that it is not expected to occur.

There is some support of this opinion in the question asked in the questionnaire filled by each Brother-postulant: "Do you understand that you are entering the Congregation to become a Brother, not a priest?"

Should there be such changes contemplated I desire to be in the position of saying that I respectfully stated the case to the Provincial and gave my personal opinion.

Only one such case came up within the last six years; but I do not think there was any transfer. Such cases are rare, but they may become more numerous (and cause some serious discussion) should the spiritual director in a Juniorate feel free to encourage such transfers. Naturally he has the right to judge a vocation to the priesthood and to so advise, but the only point here is: "Is he or the candidate free to consider the priesthood in Holy Cross?"

Even in the Decree of the Propaganda [Fide] of 1856, there is a strong implication against encouraging Holy Cross Brothers to become priests even outside the Congregation: "Let it not be easy for the Brothers of St. Joseph to enter the priesthood."

I do not think I have sufficient grounds for a formal protest, but I do believe that there are some good reasons why it would be better not to make such transfers.[2]

Nearly twenty years later in a letter to Rev. Richard H. Sullivan, C.S.C., of Stonehill College, Br. Ephrem wrote on March 14, 1956, concerning the request of a brother of the priests' society (forwarded in Fr. Sullivan's letter of March 10 to Br. Ephrem) to transfer to the society of brothers so that he might teach.

Brother Ephrem noted, *Article 132 of the Constitutions, as well as certain directives from Rome, do not permit transfers from the Brothers' Society to the Society of Priests. I do not find any mention anywhere about transfers in the other direction. Probably the only consideration here would be a matter of prudent policy.*

In general we would not favor transfers from the Brothers in the Society of Priests, but if the Provincial of the Priests' Society and the Very Reverend Superior General favor such a move in individual cases which may deserve special consideration because of any unusual circumstances, I am sure our Council would have no objection to transfer.

Brother Ephrem then referred to the one such case of transfer which took place in the ten years 1946–1956, simply pointing out that in that circumstance a new novitiate was not required and that the annual vows made in the priests' society were continued until the time of perpetual profession.[3]

An interesting letter from Br. Ephrem to Fr. Albert F. Cousineau, superior general, written on April 21, 1941, from the generalate while Fr. Cousineau was making a visit at Notre Dame, is indicative of some of the tensions building up which eventually encouraged the separation of priests and brothers into autonomous provinces in 1945.

Remarking about an influential brother whose patience was wearing thin and who had made some statements about the treatment the brothers habitually received at the hands of the priests, Br. Ephrem said: *I might add that many other Brothers are discontentedly bearing with the same problem. First of all they believe that there is lack of common Christian charity and justice on the part of those who are above all people expected to manifest and practice these virtues. After a few years the Brothers lose their ideals; some lose their vocations and several who are persevering are doing so under the most trying conditions, but without much joy or contentment in life. . . .*

As regards this Province, it would take several letters to even mention the problems—many of which are never mentioned

outside groups, for several members have accepted the philosophy: What's the Use? I don't know if there is a remedy. Talent,
as Father Burns said in one of the General Chapters, is not a
prerogative of the priesthood; the Brothers may also have talents.
But it is presumed, and the presumption is not confined to our
Community, that they are not supposed to have either talents
or feelings. There is supposed to be an ideal in the religious life
even for Brothers; most of our Brothers don't know what this
ideal is. The goal of course is salvation; but what about the means
one expects the Community to furnish? Apart from special graces
there is the routine of daily devotions. But what one might call
the atmosphere appears to be lacking. It is reasonable to expect
union and community spirit, recognition of the natural gifts that
God has bestowed and a proper outlet provided for the exercise
of these gifts.

In many things outside the sacerdotal field the Rules and
Constitutions have provided for this recognition; but that appears
to be the end—a theory rather than a practice. It seems to me that
when the Church approves a theory it presumes that the practice
will follow. I have heard many Brothers ask the question: What
is the Brother's vocation anyway? Do the priests believe there is
such a vocation? In any case the ideal disappears and then an
effort is made to seek natural comforts or to settle down to some
indifferent type of life and let the others do the worrying about
Community problems. . . .

It would not be honest if I did not say all these things have
not bothered me. Very much so.

These matters and the routine of life at the generalate were
weighing on Br. Ephrem. For a man to whom action was a way of life,
the more sedentary if essential preoccupations of the general council
were a real challenge, and, though Fr. Cousineau's plan for separating
into autonomous provinces was in the process of formulation, it had
not yet taken enough shape to offer a real sense of hope for the
immediate future of the brothers.

Perhaps at the present time I am taking too blue an outlook on
things; and I fear I am getting more that way from day to day. My
inclination is more to action than to contemplation, or perhaps
to a balance of both. Right now three more years—or rather three
years just beginning—looks like an eternity to me in the stiff and
artificial life of this house. Honestly I don't know how long I
can hold up under such a life of stagnation and inactivity. The
whole day—even so-called recreation—is a monotonous strain,

and sometimes I get so nervous I can't think straight. I am living in a mechanized and formalized atmosphere. My time seems to be wasted without benefit to myself or anyone else.[4]

But the separation did eventually occur, and 1946 was a year of transition following upon the 1945 general chapter decision to establish autonomous homogeneous provinces of brothers and priests. Up to late October 1946 the single novitiate at Rolling Prairie continued to function for both societies while another location was being sought by the priests. Problems or questions naturally continued to arise, particularly concerning authority in the administration of the novitiate, and Br. Ephrem had occasion to write Fr. Felix Duffey, Novice Master, on October 14, 1946: *In this transition period it is natural that some unforeseen problems should arise, but I think we are still enough the single Congregation of Holy Cross to be able to settle them in an amicable way.*[5]

In the first years of the autonomous provinces, there were questions about continuing practices which had heretofore affected both societies of the congregation equally. One such custom had to do with the free use of facilities and attendance at events on the campus of the University of Notre Dame. Father John J. Cavanaugh, president, conferred with Br. Ephrem on the matter, and Br. Ephrem wrote the superior general, Fr. Albert Cousineau, afterward: *Father Cavanaugh cordially came over to my office last Saturday and we had a friendly discussion about some of the matters you mentioned to him and some that we mentioned ourselves. I am agreeing with his point of view that one Province or a house in one Province should deal with the other Province in a business way. Any comments by the members of the Brothers Province (and some members of the Priests' Provinces made comments in our favor) had to do with "methods of business" rather than with "business" as such. I believe the question of the Golf Course, Athletic Contests and the like, can be worked out without having the Brothers feel they belong to a different Community. Strictly speaking the Brothers have no claim to University concessions, but it will take a little while to accustom them to procedures that will remove the "charity" angle and put "privileges" on a business basis which will eventually strengthen morale and create a spirit of self-reliance and friendly business cooperation. Any other procedure would* make "concessions" dependent on the personal notions of the University officials. I want to assure you that Father Cavanaugh is very reasonable in his "business proposals."[6]

During the early years of autonomy, the members of the brothers' society, so long reliant on the priests and now responsible for their own apostolic development, were in need of occasional reminders to that effect. In a circular letter to the membership written May 13, 1948, Br. Ephrem wrote: *Our stability must be founded on the conviction that we have a God-given mission, that our labors of every sort infallibly lead to our own salvation and to that of those whom, directly or indirectly, we train in the Catholic ideals of our establishments, or whom our daily lives edify.*[7]

The clear distinction demanded in 1946 by Br. Ephrem and others that in the brothers' society there were to be no differences in status between teaching and non-teaching brothers was not fully understood or appreciated by some, even three years later. In responding to questions from a brother superior about a request from one of the local men to recite the *Paters* [seven Our Fathers prayed by non-teaching brothers] in place of the Little Office of the Blessed Virgin [recited by the teaching brothers], Br. Ephrem wrote: *Encourage all about the Little Office they get in the Novitiate, but, if the case requires it for workers (who haven't convenience or time to read) you may give the permission for the Paters while you are Superior. We can't change our old Brothers, but we must try to impress on the young that there is but one kind of Brother in our Society.*[8]

In 1949, while lines of authority and responsibility were still being clarified between the two societies in Holy Cross, Br. Ephrem had occasion to write to Br. Jude Costello, vice provincial of the brothers in Bengal, India, concerning the presumption of Bishop Lawrence Graner, C.S.C., of Dhaka, that he could exert some degree of control over the appointment of brothers teaching in the diocesan school, St. Gregory's. Br. Ephrem wrote: *I see no reason why in India, as here, we should not have contracts to staff or man such or such an activity by a mutual contract, <u>not an obedience from the Bishop</u>.* He elaborated further. *In 1912 Rome advised that the Brothers* *be given their own schools. The recent Autonomy made this a condition of our set-up, with properties owned by the Brothers. We are separate Societies with respective properties. I can see no canonical or Autonomy grounds for making it imperative that we teach in a diocesan college, or jointly in a Community College, unless we so elect. We cannot demand priests to teach in our high schools or in our College in Texas, nor can the priests demand that we teach at Notre Dame or in a high school that the priests may elect to conduct. There would be no Autonomy for either party in that. Obviously we don't want to run a college in India, and if we are to run (in our own right) a couple of high schools it will take all the men that can be spared for that purpose.*[9]

In 1953 some issues arose relative to the Ave Maria Press, one of the apostolates which continued to operate under both societies even though it legally belonged to the priests. Br. Ephrem, in a letter to Fr. Theodore Mehling, provincial of the Priests' Province, wrote: *You will recall the agreements relative to the AVE MARIA made at the General Chapter of 1945. It was presumed at that time that the operation of the plant would continue as in former years, that there would be a Brother Business Manager and a Brother Superintendent.*

It could be recognized that the Editor should have an important say in all business matters, but it was never contemplated that the Editor would take over the management of the office or of the shops; still less was it assumed that a layman would be given jurisdictional authority over the Brother heads of departments.

Br. Ephrem went on to relate how it had been necessary for him to remove the Business Manager as a result of a conflict with the Editor, and how the replacement did not work out well because the brother seemed "little more than a figurehead." Br. Ephrem explained how he had hoped to "keep out of AVE MARIA problems," but a note received from one of the brothers working there alerted him to new difficulties. Br. Ephrem related the discontent among many of the brothers over the past year. *They complain that Father Duffey is running everything and makes himself head of every department and that Brothers no longer have their historical position at the AVE MARIA.*

In seeking a solution together with Fr. Mehling, Br. Ephrem expected the brothers to be treated as equals, not only because of the agreements of 1945, but because the brothers had functioned impressively in these important positions for years. *I passed over their comments lightly, as I had hoped Brother Sabinus would be able to bridge the troubles. Things are now coming to a head, and I think that our mutual interests in the AVE MARIA call for a solution that will be practical and in harmony with the business and social status of the Brothers as exemplified through the years.*[10]

In 1953 a principal complained that at a public religious function when salutations were being extended by the bishop, mention of the brothers, as seemed all too usual, was omitted and only clergy and sisters were recognized. The principal wondered whether some reaction on his part ought to be forthcoming and asked Br. Ephrem for his advice. The provincial surely had strong feelings on this matter, but recognized that diplomacy might achieve the best results. He wrote back: *Sorry to hear about the omission of reference to the Brothers at . . . the celebration. I wish you would send me a list of times and places during the past couple of years (ask the other Brothers) when His Excellency made the same omissions.*

I believe the omissions are unintentional and entirely due to thoughtlessness, but I can realize they still hurt. Better make no comments about the matter locally. The problem is a bit delicate, and I may have an opportunity to get the matter across without offending him.[11]

Br. Lambert Barbier, who, with the priests, previously had been an extremely effective missionary among minority groups in Texas, in the early 1950s was, behind the scenes, a notable if somewhat eccentric fund raiser and public relations voice for the brothers' province. On one occasion he wrote Br. Ephrem, apparently about a potential donor whose understanding was that the brothers were still intimately tied into the ownership and operation of the University of Notre Dame. Br. Ephrem wrote back: *You know he is mostly a Notre Dame booster, and we find that problem everywhere. Wherever we have schools or institutions, the Big Men think of the University first, and in doing so some of them think we are being favored at the same time, not knowing we have a separate treasury to maintain.*[12]

Br. Ephrem was sensitive to the rather universal lack of understanding of the brother's vocation, and when this was exhibited in various ways by those expected to know better, he seized the opportunity to say something about it. Fr. John Reedy, editor of the *Ave Maria*, had a regular column, "The Editor's Desk," which appeared weekly in the magazine and served as a literary pulpit through which the editor could express himself on some aspect of Catholic life. One such column caused a brother-reader concern, and he placed a copy of the *Ave* under Br. Ephrem's door. After reading the column, Br. Ephrem wrote to Fr. Reedy: *He* [the brother] *had marked the second last paragraph of* The Editor's Desk *dealing with retreatants who were recently at Notre Dame, underlining your words:* From their families come nuns and priests and Bishops.

Br. Ephrem went on to say: *Logically he and most people, including myself, expected Brothers to be included among those who come from such families.*

At various times Catholic periodicals have been guilty of this sin of omission, but it is certainly a regretful surprise to see such an omission made by the Editor of the AVE MARIA whose daily life and duties must make him conscious of the existence of Brothers.

Why such omissions occur it would be uncharitable for me to guess. I am nearing fifty years as a Brother, and I have no reason to believe that Brothers are spiritually, intellectually or socially inferior to nuns or priests or that they do not come from the same families that you credit with giving nuns and priests to the Church.

We have at least three sons of Notre Dame professors among the Brothers of Holy Cross; we have Brothers who have priests of their families in Holy Cross; we have Brothers who are the sons of Notre Dame retreatants. And we have a few Brothers who have the trying task of selling the very AVE MARIA that does not recognize the vocation of a Brother.

I hope that in some way The Editor's Desk *will find means of recognizing the Brother's vocation for what it is worth in the eyes of the Church and of the public.*

That admonition was written September 3, 1955. On the 6th of that month, Fr. Reedy wrote back to Br. Ephrem apologizing *to you and to all the Brothers,* acknowledging it as simply an oversight, one he ought to have caught before it went to press. Fr. Reedy then went on to express his recognition of the brothers' vocation and their essential role at the Ave Maria Press. He concluded: *Having received an official reprimand from the Provincial's Office, I assure you I'll be more careful in the future.*

In fact, on September 19 Fr. Reedy wrote Br. Ephrem enclosing an article from the diocesan newspaper of Newark and Paterson, New Jersey, which highlighted the canvassing work of the brothers for the *Ave Maria*. He wrote: *I might add that I was working on this* [convincing the author of the article to write it] *several weeks before I committed the faux pas in my column.*

And in the December 10, 1955, issue of the *Ave Maria*, Fr. Reedy devoted his entire column to the brothers working at the press, concluding: *Each week, when you receive your copy of the magazine, you are receiving the benefits of the work, the sacrifice, and the zeal of this hidden vocation.*[13]

These examples are characteristic of the habitual attitude expressed over the years, sometimes forcefully, by Br. Ephrem when the image or identity of the brothers' vocation—in Holy Cross or outside it—was clearly misunderstood or demeaned, even unintentionally. His vision of the brothers was that of a growing band of men whose influence in Catholic education and child care would be increasingly effective, proliferating throughout the United States and into the overseas mission areas undertaken by the province. Nothing less than full recognition of their capabilities and qualifications would do. Where there was ignorance of the brothers' vocation, Br. Ephrem, like St. Francis before him, wanted to sow truth and knowledge. But he was always concerned that this be done more by deed than by word and that patient diplomacy rule the brothers' own direct efforts to make themselves known and accepted as equal partners in the mission of the Church.

That such an approach was successful is evident in the continuing appreciation and respect the brothers have enjoyed in every area of their presence in ministry, particularly those localities in which they have been functioning for decades. From the outset this was the intent of the brothers' provincial, and nothing less than full cooperation from the province members themselves through their efforts locally would be tolerated. But it was easy for them, because they had as an example the man who himself, in a multitude of ways, had proved over many, many years his convictions and his determination to enhance the image and identity of the lay religious life and its unique contribution to the mission of the Church.

12

The Spiritual Underpinning

AN UNDERSTATED ASSUMPTION

Whatever is said about Br. Ephrem and his leadership of the brothers' society in the United States, surprisingly little is either documented or recalled of his deeply motivating spirituality, a trait not worn on his sleeve but nevertheless animating his entire life.

Springing from the solid folk spirituality of the Irish countryside and from the close ties to Catholicism in school and parish there, young Dennis O'Dwyer benefitted from the example of his relatives, friends and elders and carried this sound foundation in religiosity with him when he emigrated to the United States to join Holy Cross.

Never afraid to assert the source of the motivation compelling him into action, he seldom did so unless the occasion demanded it of him. Spirituality was such an integral part of his life that in no way did he consider it simply an adjunct to the intellectual and physical characteristics necessary for living the religious life. If one was a religious, it was presumed he was aware of God's call and its implications and exigencies in every circumstance throughout his life, whatever his role. One assumed spiritual motivation rather than talked about it.

Br. Ephrem was perhaps not pictured by his religious as a man of prayer in the sense that he spent long periods in the chapel or referred habitually in conversation to the presence of God in his life and work and in the unfolding of province development. Yet his letters, his conversations with individuals, his speeches all give clear though sporadic notice that he was constantly aware of the providential God who supported and encouraged him throughout his life. At times he stated this belief unambiguously; usually he did not. He was not a sentimental man, though he was fully capable of the sentiment which contributed to the pastoral compassion he regularly showed in dealing with his men. His spirituality was not primarily devotional, yet a more devoted religious could not have been found who would dedicate himself so thoroughly and perseveringly to the momentous challenges he and the congregation faced throughout most of his active life.

The spirituality of the religious life current in Br. Ephrem's time proclaimed that "if you keep the rule, the rule will keep you." Perfect

251

fidelity in obedience to one's assignment and way of life assured sanctity. There was no need for the extraordinary proliferation of prayers, devotions, time in chapel. If a religious, any religious, faithfully followed the approved schedule of events in his daily life, including those elements which governed his prayer life, he could be assured he was fulfilling God's will and could not fail to achieve his salvation if he persevered accordingly.

There is no question Br. Ephrem was faithful to the requirements of his religious life. Far from their being routine practices he was obligated to fulfill in order to assure ongoing association with Holy Cross and God's friendship, he saw them as substantive to the entire unfolding of one's apostolic endeavor. Prayer underlay action. Action for its own sake, even work aimed at benefitting others, was for a religious empty of meaning. One could not give what he did not have. If God was not part and parcel of one's daily existence, God could not be the product of one's ministry, whatever the intent or the name given to it. Br. Ephrem participated regularly and faithfully in the spiritual exercises of whatever house he was living in or visiting. He insisted repeatedly and vehemently that every house of the province must have a regular life of prayer or its apostolic outreach would be fruitless, appearances to the contrary notwithstanding. Each individual must cultivate a strong and abiding relationship with God in order to be able to enter into the mission of the congregation and the Church.

There were occasions on which Br. Ephrem did write about such matters, and this chapter will gather several instances as illustrative of his attitudes and activity in this area. Sections of this book focused on other characteristics of Br. Ephrem also provide glimpses here and there of his substantial spiritual underpinning.

A BASIC SPIRITUALITY

In his first circular letter to the province membership following the establishment of the United States Brothers' Province and the first provincial chapter, Br. Ephrem wrote: *Such, my dear Brothers in Christ, are the Decrees and Recommendations of our first Provincial Chapter. I have no doubt of their cordial acceptance by all of us, for there is among our members an excellent spirit of obedience, admirable Community morale, and a keen appreciation of the new destiny that is ours. There is evidence everywhere of sincere loyalty and a hearty willingness to cooperate for the common good and the greater glory of God. All this is a source of joy for me, and I thank God for this great blessing and take* comfort in the task of organizing the Provincial Administration. The problems confronting our new organization are many, but God has blessed our Society with the means necessary for this purpose. We have reasonable material resources, we have well trained members, we have an approved mission in the Church, and we have the benediction of the Holy Father in our new evolution.

. . . More subjects is our chief need at the present time. Without an increase in membership we cannot make much material progress, and above all we cannot do the things for God that it is the desire of our Society to do. There is probably no community in the Church that has such a wide range of apostolates as the Congregation of Holy Cross. The active congregations are founded to preach the word of God, to conduct schools, hospitals and the like. Communities, as such, are not founded to operate farms or printing plants, but these and kindred activities may well be part of the program destined to achieve the objective approved by the Church. The first aim of every religious is personal sanctification, and the second aim is to promote directly or indirectly the composite aim of his Society. In Holy Cross we have many auxiliary activities, all leading to the same general goal—the glory of God. We need more religious for all our undertakings. There is not and there cannot be a standard for measuring any member's worth to the Congregation. The sick and the incapacitated may be the ones who are doing most to enable the Community to reach its goal.

Those who love their community never fail to express their appreciation by praying for more subjects. They want others to share the happiness and blessings they enjoy; they want God's work to go on. Christ gave the injunction to pray for vocations, and they are heeding it.

. . . My dear Brothers, there is no reason for me to write more. We are all of one mind in our vocation, in our hopes, our problems and our projects. We must all use the same means—prayer and sacrifice. We are not many. But if we are united for God our works will be great.[1]

In a bulletin to the membership written May 13, 1948, Br. Ephrem concluded: Our stability must be founded on the conviction that we have a God-given mission, that our labors of every sort infallibly lead to our own salvation and to that of those whom, directly or indirectly, we train in the Catholic ideals of our establishments, or whom our daily lives edify.[2]

———

A few days later, in a bulletin to the membership Br. Ephrem appealed to those who could do so to help with financial contributions from friends or from their personal accounts to defray the cost of printing booklets written by Br. Ernest Ryan about Br. Aidan O'Reilly and Br. Columba O'Neill. Concluding, Br. Ephrem wrote: *Keep the development of our Community and its apostolic mission constantly in your prayers. Only through Jesus, Mary and Joseph can any of our undertakings have real success. Some of us may have no money and but few friends to further our works, but all of us can contribute the heavenly coin of prayers and good works. In this, at least, we can be generous.*[3]

———

The provincial chapter of 1949 was held from July 1 to 10 at Notre Dame in the Community House. As soon as the documentation was approved by the general council, Br. Ephrem wrote the province on August 15 promulgating the legislation. In that letter he indicated that he wanted to speak at greater length about the situation of the province, but he did not wish to delay the promulgation. In fact, on November 1 he did write a full circular letter to the province which focused significantly on the spiritual and material welfare of the province, highlighting regular discipline, the spiritual life, poverty, and the apostolates.

———

Fr. Thomas A. Steiner, provincial of the priests' province, wrote Br. Ephrem on April 29, 1949, about the availability of copies of an English translation of Fr. Hervé Morin's French version of the *Commentary on the Rules.* Fr. Steiner wanted to know how many copies the brothers would be interested in having, suggesting that perhaps not everyone would need to possess a personal copy. The same day Br. Ephrem responded, and in the course of his letter he said: *Frankly I had looked forward to a Commentary that would give a real understanding of the Rules. For some months I have had the French copy. I had the pages trimmed at the Ave Maria and I read all about the book, but I cannot say with pleasure, interest or benefit. I do not think I gained anything by reading it, at least nothing new. I had hoped for an* <u>actual commentary</u> *on our Rules, an interpretation such as a novice master would give or should give, even if some points were backed up by the writings of*

Fr. Moreau or some other superior generals.[4] Clearly Br. Ephrem had expected something of substantive value in the interpretation of the rules governing the congregation's way of life, including resource material which could serve as exhortative encouragement in the training of young religious.

In a letter sent to his new assistant, Br. John Baptist Titzer, who at that time was in Texas making the official visit to province institutions, Br. Ephrem reflected on reports Br. John had sent concerning houses he had already visited in California and elsewhere. He wrote: *THERE IS SO MUCH GROUND WE HAVE TO COVER YET IN STRENGTHENING THE PROVINCE. But if we can get the religious life going first, the other things—finances, educational standards, etc., can be attained more easily, as the religious life will establish the moral obligation in these matters.*[5]

Responding to the suggestion of Fr. Christopher J. O'Toole, superior general, regarding enhanced spiritual growth opportunities for brothers, Br. Ephrem wrote the general: *As you mention, something should be done to renew the religious life and ideals of the Brothers. We already have sheets of matter from Brothers for conferences, but as yet no one has found time to coordinate it. Furthermore I think we should work for something like 30 days "seclusion" for several members each year in a house where there would be no other activity. Something like a retreat. Maybe more can be done. The trouble now is man-power pressure—and too much of this can become expensive as to ideals and contemplation. Brothers Dominic, Lawrence, Hilarion, Gerontius, etc., got much spiritual pep and ideals from their work at Dominican Institute; but what we need is something that can be developed internally under the direction of a priest and some Brothers. It will come.*[6] This proposal was realized half a dozen years later in the establishment of the *second novitiate*, begun during the summer of 1961 at Archbishop Hoban High School, Akron. The program served its purpose over several summers. In the 1970s a house of prayer was organized at Le Mans Academy, Rolling Prairie, for one or two summers. Opportunities for ongoing renewal remained available subsequently, primarily through programs offered and staffed by other congregations.

PERSONNEL CONCERNS

Br. Ephrem's fundamental belief was that in committing himself to Holy Cross each religious bound himself to the full development and use of his gifts and talents for the benefit of others in and through the congregation. In a letter written in 1942 to Br. William Mang, Br. Ephrem stated: *Your remark about the man whose talents "the Community had used" amuses me. What do men come to the Community for but to offer their talents? Where is the merit if one wants his talents for himself? Are we in the Community for self-development? It's a sad ideal for any man to have. And if the Community were to offer exceptional opportunities to such a one he would hold to the theory that it was done for self-development. Some encouragement may be necessary for weaker souls, but I hope we can develop a higher type of men. And about higher studies, no doubt many could be found who would want to take such studies for the intellectual pleasure or to become great teachers. But it's a great Community we must keep in mind, and no man can be great unless he puts the Community before himself. Common needs and common good must come first. Personal glory in getting out a year book, managing a team, running a school, etc., won't end well for the individual.*[7]

From time to time in contacting individual religious regarding obediences, Br. Ephrem would allude to the spiritual motivation or communal benefits underlying personal sacrifice and effort in the apostolate. In notifying Brothers Hobart Pieper, Martinian Wilson, Fulgence Dougherty, and Ivan Dolan that they had been selected to go as missionaries to Bengal in 1947, Br. Ephrem wrote: *Were I to express my appreciation of our foreign mission work, the part it plays in the individual salvation of the missionary, its promotion of the kingdom of Christ, its blessings for our Society and our Congregation, this would indeed be a long letter. But even if I were not pressed for time there would still be no need to make this letter long.*[8]

A brother assigned to work at the Foreign Mission Seminary in Washington, D.C., wrote Br. Ephrem after only a short time on the job complaining about the monotonous nature of his work. Br. Ephrem, noting that this particular brother had expressed dissatisfaction in several prior positions in the community, replied: *As you know, our merit is in not working for ourselves but for something bigger than ourselves. What we do may not appear to be much, but it is doing it for God that counts. Should we care to do only what pleases us personally, it is doubtful if we could have any reward. I could give you case after case of Brothers who found happiness and sanctity in doing the things that were not at first to their taste.*

I would like to believe that you value your vocation more than all else and that your spirit in Holy Cross is to work for God alone. . . .[9]

In 1949 through some omission no vocation advertisement was inserted by the province in the *Signpost*, a publication that highlighted for young people the characteristics of religious communities in the United States. Br. Ephrem, upon learning of this, wrote Br. Donatus Schmitz, superior of Sacred Heart Juniorate, Watertown, where the vocations office was located and directed by Br. Eymard Salzman. *We are much pleased with all things at Watertown and with Brother Eymard's vocations work. He is worried about omission in Signpost. No form or request was sent to us to fill in. We knew nothing about the book till it came out. Sorry we did not get word to put in a page. Will inquire if there is a reprint. Anyway no need to worry: THE MORE MEN NEGLECT US, THE MORE GOD HELPS US. This is being proved. Vocations come from prayers, not from signposts. . . . Let us not worry too much about the natural.*[10]

One brother wrote Br. Ephrem in December of 1950 asking for permission to spend some time in a Trappist monastery during the Christmas holidays because he yearned for a "week of complete shut-off from the world." Br. Ephrem replied at once denying permission, but he indicated that when there was sufficient reason the provincial could grant permission to spend some time in another house of the community. He suggested the brother take a week in the rural setting of the novitiate at Rolling Prairie. Later, if the brother so wished, he might do his annual retreat with the Trappists. Then Br. Ephrem wrote: *I am naturally anxious to aid you achieve the perfection we all are expected to achieve, but I cannot help remarking that the daily effort to meet our daily problems is in itself very much achieving perfection. As the Imitation says, wherever we go we carry ourselves with ourselves; and that very much means we should make a fight where we are. If we win that fight we may with reason think of other victories.*

If you haven't done so already, it might be well to get in close touch with a spiritual director and expose your worries and thoughts. We are poor doctors for ourselves.[11]

In reply to the lament of a boys' home director that he had unexpectedly been burdened with responsibility for supervising a construction project on the campus, Br. Ephrem wrote: *Try not to take all the work, building programs, etc., too seriously. You can't afford to get worried or get headaches. The good Lord takes care of all our unintentional mistakes and our natural inability to do the work of several men.*[12]

A religious asked for permission to visit whenever he wished his long time spiritual director, who had moved several hundred miles away to another house of his own community. Br. Ephrem had to refuse him even though the religious had a railway pass permitting free travel. Br. Ephrem wrote: *Your request about visiting . . . for spiritual direction from Father . . . is most unusual. The fact that you have a railroad pass cannot be given much weight in considering your request.* He then went on to explain that canon law provided freedom for an individual to correspond by mail with his director if the distance was too great, and that the best arrangement was to have a locally available director. Tempering his refusal, Br. Ephrem allowed the religious one visit to the distant location and ordered that subsequent trips be requested individually if the religious felt he must continue seeing the same director. The principle appealed to by Br. Ephrem was that correspondence was permitted by canon law and that the area in which the religious was stationed had adequate religious and diocesan priests from whom to choose another director.[13]

SPIRITUALITY BUILT ON DISCIPLINE

Though solicitous for the spiritual welfare of the membership, Br. Ephrem never lost sight of the essential role played by regular discipline—living strictly in accord with the rules of community and apostolic life in the congregation. To live the rule was to live one's vocation.

In 1948 the superior general, Rev. Albert Cousineau, made a general visit to the membership of the province, and on August 2 submitted a report to Br. Ephrem. The provincial, utilizing the content of that report, wrote a circular letter to the province on August 15. Concerning Fr. Cousineau's remarks on the spiritual life Br. Ephrem said: *Personal sanctification is made doubly imperative by our vows. It is the primary work of all of us, and everything must be subordinated to it. All our activities must be but means to this end. Being too busy can never be a valid excuse for consistently missing spiritual exercises. Anyone who claims that he has so much work that he has no time to say the Little Office, for example, should present his case to the Provincial. Superiors have the duty of seeing that members say the Little Office or the Paters (if approved by the Provincial), of making the weekly hour of adoration, etc. Our spiritual exercises are determined by our Rule. Their aim is to keep alive and strengthen our supernatural life. The religious vocation is something supernatural, and it cannot be sustained by mere natural activities. All we do should have a supernatural motive, and when we have such a motive our ordinary work becomes a prayer also. The first duty of Superiors is to do everything possible for the personal sanctification of their members, not hesitating to give conferences and exhortations on the means and obligation of reaching sanctity.*

In viewing the means of reaching sanctity I fear that many of us do not attach sufficient importance to the vow of poverty, and particularly to the virtue of poverty. Abuses are creeping in in obtaining, carrying and using pocket money. Surplus travel money, for example, is not intended to be pocket money. It should be turned over to the local treasurer. The use of personal gifts, whether in goods or money, must definitely have the permission of the Superior. No matter by whom paid for, we have the use rather than the ownership of books, radios, etc. Our Rule is plain on who owns gifts. And personal accounts carry no rights or privileges beyond that of mere ownership. The right to spend or dispose of comes from the Superior acting in harmony with the Rule. Negligence in poverty leads to many abuses, and no doubt to loss of vocation in more instances than we suspect. The Superior should be informed of a presumed permission with respect to poverty, else the subject might develop a habit of presuming, and thus offend against poverty.[14]

―――――――

Noting some scheduling problems regarding religious exercises in the house at St. Edward High School, Lakewood, Br. Ephrem wrote the superior, Br. John William Donoghue: *The zeal of your members is wonderful and you should be happy about it, as you say you are; but keep the brakes on so that work and occupations do not cut in on religious exercises and community silence. The Brother who misses Office because of some job or hobby (even for the C.S.C.) is getting no blessing on himself or on C.S.C. even though the world may praise him. Natural efficiency of itself will get us no place.*[15]

―――――――

For some years the provincial administration was housed in the Community House (later Columba Hall) at Notre Dame. Thus the provincial and his council participated in many facets of the life of the local community, at times giving rise to situations in which the authority of the provincial crossed lines normally reserved to the local superior. From his office Br. Ephrem wrote a note to Br. Gerard Fitz, the superior, on October 8, 1952: *Being in the Community House I cannot very well escape noticing deviations from Constitutions and customs. There is one innovation that I wish to call attention to now lest some other houses start the same thing. It refers to the type of reading in the refectory, particularly at breakfast. Today, for example, the subject was* <u>The Democratic Convention in Chicago</u>.

Article 373 of the Constitutions covers the nature of the reading in the refectory. The first few lines read as follows: "During meals the life of Our Lord Jesus Christ, or the lives of the saints, shall be read, and may be followed by some <u>instructive and edifying</u> *book."*

The same day Br. Gerard thanked Br. Ephrem for calling his attention to this deviation from the Constitutions and assured him that appropriate material would henceforth be provided for public reading. He in fact named a particular spiritual book chosen for the purpose.[16]

―――――――

On one occasion Br. Ephrem found that the superior of the Community House had changed the chaplain's room into a storehouse for Dujarie Press, which was housed in that building. Br. Ephrem wrote to him ordering the room to be restored to its use for the chaplain, as all arrangements in all houses regarding chaplains were determined by the provincial; it was through the provincial that the "agreements for chaplains" were arranged with the provincial of the priests' province. Furthermore, Br. Ephrem had already designated a special room in the Annex for Dujarie Press. And he reminded the superior that Dujarie Press was subject to the provincial, not the local superior, even though it was housed in the local residence. In the same letter Br. Ephrem called attention to abuses in the schedule of the house regarding recreation periods, citing specific examples and calling for a return to the observance of the approved house schedule.[17]

Br. Ephrem's permission was requested by a local superior to purchase a relatively large and powerful car at a reduced price available to the brothers through business connections enjoyed by a brother from another school in the area. The provincial wrote back: *Getting a high-priced, high-powered car at a reduced price may in itself be a financial bargain, but there are certain other angles to be considered, and I think some of these are so vital that our houses should not take a fancy car as a gift.*

. . . Communities are expected to be poor and humble, and the Brothers of Holy Cross cannot afford being considered rich . . . enough to have a high bracket car.

Your parents' club has been wonderful; they will continue to help you if they see you are trying to live humbly and economically, proving to them that you need for necessities every dollar they contribute.[18]

In reply to a request from the novice master to append to the schedule an additional hour of adoration per week and other extra devotions, Br. Ephrem reminded the novice master that it was the provincial and his council, with the consent of the superior general, who approved the program of the novitiate: *It is my opinion that the Novitiate should have no extra devotions* [other] *than those specifically requested by the Superior General. I am not in favor of adding to the devotions in our Directory or in adding to what is required by the Constitutions.*[19]

In an era absorbed with the legalities and precision of private and common prayer, occasionally Br. Ephrem was requested to interpret the appropriateness of the structure of spiritual exercises for particular local communities. One such request came from Boysville's director, Br. Hilarion Brezik, in March 1955. The house members wished to hold a common hour of adoration each week and the question dealt with how this holy hour might dovetail with already prescribed daily religious exercises. Br. Ephrem replied: *With regard to Holy Hour, there is freedom for each individual to select his own hour, and that stipulation should remain and the superior has a right to see that the Hour is made. For all those that are willing (indicates selection) there is nothing wrong in having a common hour whether before the Tabernacle or before the Blessed Sacrament exposed, and each member attending can consider this his Holy Hour. Of course it is understood that such an hour would not be pushing out a regular Community exercise of some length, say 10 or 15 minutes. Essentially the Holy Hour is* extra, *though there may be a little leeway.*

Prayers during a common Holy Hour may be individual, but whether the Blessed Sacrament is exposed or not the Superior or any other delegated member may read some prayers aloud or all may join in common prayer at different times during the Hour. I am also of the opinion that common rosary during such Hour would count for the daily rosary. There would still be a substantial hour of adoration. Similarly it is true, but better not done, that a person could say Office for about 10 minutes during his Holy Hours if no common exercises are being pushed out by the Hour. Of course it is always better not to telescope exercises.[20]

In the late 1950s, Br. Ephrem was provincial of the Eastern Province. The day he celebrated his golden jubilee of religious profession Br. Ephrem gave a short talk to the novices and postulants. He said metaphorically: *You came to Holy Cross to give and not to get. Give all you have. Never think you are giving something to Holy Cross. Holy Cross is giving something to you. This is your ticket to heaven. You have the ticket when you have your vocation. Don't get off the train unless you are told you are on the wrong train. Then change trains.*[21]

A few months earlier he had spoken to the novices at Valatie on the occasion of the feast day of Br. Maurus O'Malley, novice master. *This particular life in Holy Cross is a very happy one. If you are always ready to turn on the tears you do not belong in*

*Holy Cross. We need tough men in Holy Cross! If you are entirely
sentimental, it just will not work. You have to be able to stand on
your own two feet—I don't think you'll ever have anyone else's
feet to stand on.*[22]

A SPIRITUAL LEGACY

Though documentable evidence is scarce, even these few examples show fairly forcefully the spiritual underpinning integral to Br.
Ephrem's whole personality. He was a man for whom the providence
of God was tangible, compensating for the inadequacies of each
religious, including the provincial. The mission of Holy Cross was
God-given and bound to succeed, though it could be disrupted or
rendered less effective by individual or corporate infidelity. The faithful
execution of one's duties through obedience and living a simple life-
style in the spirit of poverty would bring God's blessings upon the
province and assure the necessary augmentation of membership. Br.
Ephrem asserted that work could become prayer when undertaken
and carried out with the proper intentions. Above all, he believed
that *the religious life is something supernatural, and it cannot be
sustained by mere natural activity.*

This principle governed his own life and contributed to his habitual
expectation that it must govern the lives of others as well. Whether
tangibly projected or not, whether perceptible or hidden in his day-to-
day dealings with his religious and with others, the rich spirituality of
Br. Ephrem sustained him personally and apostolically throughout his
life. On the occasion of his leaving office as provincial of the Eastern
Province of Brothers in 1962, he remarked, *My uppermost thought
is one of sincere gratitude to God for granting me the necessary
health to carry out the obedience given me. . . .*

*Though material progress is necessary it is but a means to
an end—the salvation of our members and the spread of Christ's
kingdom by our apostolate of education. The material things are
but of time; their proper use is to purchase eternal values.*[23]

Thoughts such as these were characteristic of a man for whom
God's presence was real, constant, and supportive. His legacy to his
religious was both the conviction and the proof that this was so.

13

A Man Like Us

SPIRIT RAISED, FEET FIRMLY PLANTED

Observers of highly competent and efficient men and women in history are inclined to emphasize the attractive, largely positive traits of the individuals concerned. Less engaging attributes, even clearly negative ones, tend to be relegated to the background, if acknowledged at all.

With Br. Ephrem this temptation toward deifying the subject exists simply because absolutely no one denies the enormous contribution made by the man to the growth and development of the Brothers of Holy Cross, to the ongoing stability of the Holy Cross congregation as a whole, and to Catholic education and child care in the United States. Nevertheless, Br. Ephrem was an eminently human individual who never pretended to be anything else. He acknowledged his faults, among which was his temper—allegedly a shortcoming that at the age of fifteen earned his dismissal as a postulant from the Irish Christian Brothers—and his overall lack of patience with those less gifted with common sense or slow to grasp what he considered the obvious. He knew his bent toward imperiousness irritated others, and he tried to soften it by a more conscious pastoral compassion and interest in others. In short, the man was human. He was not a saint by any ordinary stretch of either imagination or popular definition, and given the swift affirmation of that fact from those who knew him well, it is not likely he will anytime soon become a subject of consideration by the Congregation for the Causes of the Saints.

But sanctity is not the point. Though the man had his undeniable virtues he was primarily a pragmatic leader, an administrator, a motivator of men toward realistic and achievable concrete goals in the religious life and in education. His eyes were firmly fixed on earth and its accoutrements even as his mind and soul were raised in humble acknowledgement of the presence and providence of a loving God. As noted in the chapter on the spirituality which contributed to the unflagging determination of Br. Ephrem to pursue and achieve one goal after another, he was suffused with the awareness of God in his life, and his personal motivation functioned exclusively on this assumption. He admitted to the influence of sinful human nature upon

him even as he strove through ascetical self-discipline to rise above
its deleterious effects toward the achievement of the ideals he kept
always in his heart.

The chief constraint affecting Br. Ephrem's career in province
administration was his health. Though apparently sound, he suffered
from asthma, at some times more seriously than others, and the physical afflictions springing from this condition contributed to and perhaps
were the major sources of the mental and emotional reverberations
which occasionally plunged him into near clinical depression, a fact
not widely known by the province membership. His image was that of
a man always in total control. A man of iron will and determination,
from time to time he experienced—unwillingly but admittedly and
concretely—the limitations of the human condition. When he had
to bow to inadequate strength and restricted capacity at any point,
he considered it something of a personal defeat that he only grudg-
ingly accepted as inevitable. As provincial, his health at one point
led Br. Ephrem to suggest that his resignation would be beneficial
to the congregation, and he submitted a letter to this effect to the
superior general. That Br. Ephrem served the congregation in roles
of authority for over forty years—until he was in his mid-seventies—
and then led a relatively active retirement until he was ninety, albeit
with the aid of a pacemaker in his final few years, suggests that he
had long since learned to live with, indeed to dominate, the influence
of any health problems he experienced.

As would be expected, Br. Ephrem was an intense worker. He
functioned, as noted earlier, as his own secretary except for the
occasional use of the assistant provincial or the provincial secretary
to help with correspondence. When in his office, he devoted much of
each day to work at his desk. He traveled extensively to provide the
personal expertise and contact only he could bring to his religious and
to on-site planning of expansion projects and the supervision required
as a followup.

Nevertheless, occasions served over the years to illustrate his
fundamental humanness, and it is to several such examples recorded
in his correspondence that attention will now be turned.

AN INDEFATIGABLE WORKER

Br. Ephrem's correspondence was voluminous. A pecunious administrator in days when each penny counted toward the formation of
young brothers and the development of the apostolic presence of the
province, he seldom used or encouraged others to use long distance

telephone calls for business, but rather relied on the mail. The postal system was such that next day delivery was the rule rather than an expensive exception. He was an administrator of the old school. From his office he initiated action or dealt with requests received, on which he made decisions unilaterally or with advice from one or more of his councilors. He usually made carbon copies of his correspondence but admitted to neglecting this practice with some frequency.

In 1942 Br. Ephrem concluded a letter to Br. William Mang saying, *This is enough for today, and besides I am always inclined to write too much, but, dogonnit, my heart is in the Community and its problems.*[1]

An optimist despite many reasons to be otherwise, Br. Ephrem sometimes buoyed up the spirits of others by terse endings to his letters, such as one to Br. William in 1943: *Enjoy the sunny South and don't take problems too hard. They always existed and always will.*[2]

On January 28, 1948, Br. Ephrem wrote Fr. Louis Kelley, C.S.C., vice superior general: *I hope I am not missing any replies to your very cordial and professionally helpful letters. I have filled two cabinets of carbon copies (only for half the letters I write) since I got the job as provincial. Two inches thick for Texas alone. California worse; and as a Cleveland sample I had to read and file a nine page finely written contract to get city water for the place.*[3]

Br. Ephrem had many questions, problems, or requests to submit to the general administration. On one occasion he wrote: *This is the fourth and last letter of mine that will bother you today. But I know you will try to spare the time, and I feel it a policy, a duty, and a comfort to keep in touch with the Generalate in all things concerning the Brothers' Province.*[4]

Fr. Frank Gartland, C.S.C., editor in 1949 of *The Catholic Boy* magazine, when sending along a copy invited Br. Ephrem to come visit his offices in South Bend sometime soon. Br. Ephrem thanked

Fr. Gartland for his thoughtfulness and concluded: *But to get back to your cordial invitation to visit your editorial office at the Novitiate. I shall phone you when a nice day comes. . . . The pressure of time and work almost makes me a hermit when home and a train jumper when on the road.*[5]

In preparation for staff scheduling during Boysville of Michigan's first summer, Br. Ephrem wrote to Br. Patrick Cain, director, on April 30, 1949: *If the balancing* [of faculty vacations, retreats, presence at Boysville] *is not correct, you can let me know. It is quite a job to lay out summer assignments, vacations, etc. But I guess I can't escape it—part of a tough job.*[6]

In September 1950 Br. Lawrence Miller, director of St. Charles Boys Home in Milwaukee, wrote to the provincial office about some problems he was experiencing. Br. Ephrem was at the time away in the East, and the letter was answered by one of the councilors, presumably Br. John Baptist Titzer, assistant provincial. In concluding, the writer said: *I have been here since the first of September and Br. Ephrem has done his best to inform me of community matters as quickly as possible. His problems, too, have been multitudinous and overwhelming, and I marvel at his capacity to solve them.*[7]

Fr. Vincent J. McCauley, C.S.C., superior of the Holy Cross Foreign Mission Seminary, wrote to Br. Ephrem: *You certainly are a fast man with the typewriter. I wish I could emulate you, but before you bother to answer my last one—which must have passed yours at Pittsburgh—let me thank you for the very welcome letter that arrived today.*[8]

Brother Ephrem spent long hours at his typewriter in communication with community members and others. At one point in December 1950 when Br. Charles Andersen was in the process of preparing Notre Dame Camp at Bankson Lake, Lawton, Michigan, for the upcoming summer boys' camping program, Br. Ephrem responded to a letter by saying: *Would write you more but must let the pleasures pass and get on to business. I wear out a typewriter ribbon each week.*[9]

In 1951 Br. Ephrem wrote to Br. John William Donoghue, principal of St. Edward High School in Cleveland, at a time he was extremely busy with province affairs. He confided: *I almost live at the typewriter.*

And in a letter five days later, he said: *This typewriter is used so much it is getting jittery.*[10]

In 1954 Br. Ephrem noted to Br. William Mang, *We have many irons in the fire and we hope to hammer some of them at least.*[11] His typical dedication to duty shows through this folksy description of the situation.

Br. Ephrem remarked to Fr. Thomas Fitzpatrick, director of the Foreign Mission Seminary in Washington, D.C., in February of 1956: *We are busy with all kinds of jobs—never so rushed. This is a clean-up year for our Provincial Administration.*[12]

HEALTH AND RELATED CONCERNS

During the time of preparation for the general chapter of 1945 and the imminent decision to split the one U.S. Province into two autonomous provinces, Br. Ephrem, a general councilor but spending a good bit of time teaching at the postulate in Valatie, was in contact with many brothers by letter. Several communications came from Br. William Mang. In reply to one on February 9, 1945, Br. Ephrem admitted near the end: *Having no official vacation last summer I may take some time off this spring before much typing begins. It will depend on when the next Circular has to be translated. If I get off, I may pass in your direction for a couple of hours. I shall be on full schedule here—three English classes, two Latin classes, one typing class—until February 22. My day is over at 3:15. But the work is not too heavy.*

I'm weary of the typewriter just now; so I shall quit it. Write when you can. Your letters are always welcome. My greatest interest is in seeing a future for our young Brothers. If all is settled this summer, I shall welcome the rest of old age. The years have been tough but worthwhile. It seems Br. Ephrem, then in his late fifties, entertained hopes of being relieved of the responsibility of authority for a while if not permanently.[13]

In a letter from Fr. Felix Duffey, novice master, dated October 11, 1946, the priest referred to the state of Br. Ephrem's health, which had been alluded to in a prior letter from Br. Ephrem to Fr. Duffey. Fr. Duffey said that he hoped Br. Ephrem had completely recovered from his "recent illness." There is no indication as to what the illness was or whether it was considered more than just passing.[14]

Br. Ephrem suffered a serious circulation problem in one leg in late 1946. On September 19 a letter from Br. William Mang referred to Br. Ephrem's getting out of the hospital and going to the generalate in New York for recuperation. While the malady was not specifically identified, it is probable that it involved the leg, because in January of 1947 he went to the French Hospital at 24 W. 30th St. in New York to have a vein removed from hip to ankle. He wrote on February 9, 1947, that he was taped and bandaged and was on crutches. He had instructed Br. William earlier, on January 29, not to mention this leg problem to the membership.[15]

Later in 1947 Br. Ephrem wrote Br. William from New Orleans. *Weather has been pretty hot, and the gas pressure makes the old heart jump a few times at night, but all in all I'm feeling pretty well.*[16]

A significant revelation was made by Br. Ephrem to Br. William in an undated letter probably written sometime in 1948 or 1949, but marked only "Thursday evening." He said, *I just got back from the Mayo Clinic after waiting three hours to see some docs. The upshot appears to be that I have not much organically wrong. Slight asthmatic condition. Spastic condition of diaphragm is rather intense— called a "sleep spasm." Must be stopped by some "dope" I am to get or rendered inoperative by drink or some other form of "stupor." Some nervous basis. The diaphragm violence knocked the air out of lungs and caused choking sensation.* This situation was exacerbated in 1951. The reference to the form of medication prescribed to alleviate the choking sensation might serve to explain in part the origin of Br. Ephrem's sometimes liberal use of alcoholic beverages in later years.[17]

In writing to his friend Fr. Edward Heston, C.S.C., procurator general in Rome, in August 1947, Br. Ephrem admitted: *Personally I am rather tired, as I have more things to attend to than I can conveniently handle. Buildings, corporations, everything all in one year constitute a load. One great consolation is that Father General and his Council have been most helpful and cooperative, and Father Steiner has been all that could be expected too. There is much I have to thank God for and much for which I should be grateful to the Community. Not only I but our whole Society.*[18]

Br. Ephrem was in the East in February 1951, visiting the elementary schools and taking some rest to alleviate his asthmatic condition. He was about to leave for West Haven in Connecticut. He wrote Br. John Baptist Titzer, assistant provincial, who was doing most of the major visits in the province: *Sometime after the 19th I shall go on to West Haven. Then I shall stop in Brooklyn for a day or two on the way back. I am planning on staying away during February. Still a bit slow on some things, but I feel mentally eased up.* Br. Ephrem was not averse to considering his own health needs but felt it an inappropriate use of rest and relaxation if they were not taken within a context of province business, such as visits to brothers in the houses and institutions.[19]

In mid-1951 Br. Ephrem was in touch with Br. Dominique Leclerc, provincial of the brothers' province in Canada, concerning his possibly being a traveling companion to Bangladesh, a trip Br. Ephrem was not looking forward to although he was being pressured to make it. Asking for a complete rundown of Br. Dominique's plans, Br. Ephrem wrote: *It is probable that if I make the trip I would stop off in Ireland to see the folks, etc. In that case I would plan on meeting you in Rome or someplace when you would be starting for India. I would not be interested in any stay for me in France or Rome.* This trip was eventually postponed for nearly eighteen months by reason of the provincial's health.[20]

Br. Ephrem was on a western trip in September 1951 to alleviate asthmatic complications which had begun to show themselves at Notre Dame. He was staying at St. Anthony's High School in Long Beach, California, and wrote Br. John Baptist, assistant provincial, about his health situation, which was unexpectedly on the verge of becoming quite critical. *Don't wait on me in deciding business or other problems. My plans and time of return are indefinite.*

I had two good days after arriving at Sherman Oaks and then the trouble set in worse than ever—lungs feeling closed and as if paralyzed with much coughing trying to open them. Dr. McDermott gave me some capsules but after the first day they did no good.

Then I came down to try Long Beach, but the very day I arrived I choked up again and went to St. Mary's Hospital for full checkup. X-Ray heart and lungs, etc. Only apparent trouble is thickening of bronchial tubes causing wheezing and hardness of breathing— asthmatic condition. Got all kinds of pills and injections every day. Condition relieved now, but doctor says condition will probably continue depending on climate, etc. I can continue the pills, but injections could only come from a doctor.

. . . At present I am feeling rather well but that is due no doubt to the three daily injections of 10 cc of some dope.

Doctor says that dampness and the ocean fogs each morning here do not help. He thinks that dryness will help. So I may as well experiment. You can send me news if you wish, but yourself and Council can decide all business matters and assignments, etc. I have no worries about yourself and Council.[21]

Two days later he wrote Br. John Baptist: *I am feeling rotten today. Seems if I don't get shots regularly I shall not get much relief. I go to Sherman Oaks tomorrow. Will leave Sunday for Texas, arriving Tuesday. . . .*

I am sorry about the delays in answering your letters, as they get forwarded down here from Sherman Oaks [he was at Long Beach]. *I am perfectly satisfied that you take care of everything and make what decisions you wish. I cannot tell you how useless I feel when I get choked up. The nights and early mornings are hopeless, and I have no pep. I hope I pick up in Texas, but I doubt it. So save time by handling all you can. I would not stay around California, but since I'm here I want to make the Visit.*[22]

Eventually Br. Ephrem's asthmatic condition forced him to seek a more thorough examination and treatment at the Mayo Clinic in Rochester, Minnesota. The day after Br. Ephrem had left with

Br. John Baptist for Mayo's Br. Bonaventure contacted Fr. Christopher J. O'Toole, superior general, about Br. Ephrem. He wrote:

Dear Father General:

Your letter of September 23rd to Brother Ephrem was passed on to me by Brother John Baptist for attention. I hope the findings and the statistics contain the information you wish to furnish Canon Catta for his epilogue to the second volume of the life of Father Moreau.

Brother Ephrem and Brother John Baptist left yesterday noon for the Mayo Clinic at Rochester, Minn.

I do not know if you have been informed about Brother Ephrem's health and I do not know if I am in order to pass on this information but I am going to act boldly and give you a summary as I know it.

During the early part of August, Brother Ephrem was stricken with what seemed to be an asthmatic condition. He attended the Reception on August 15th at St. Joseph's Novitiate and during the meal he was seized with a very bad attack. When I returned from my vacation on the evening of August 16th, he was in a miserable condition and was having great difficulty getting his breath. He sought some relief from the atomizer. On Thursday he left for New York thinking that it was the climate here in Northern Indiana that was causing his trouble. He found very little relief in New York and returned to Notre Dame the following Thursday morning. Brother John Baptist, seeing that Brother was getting worse to what he was the week before, insisted that Brother go to Calif. The Provincial finally agreed and said if he would go then he would stay and make the Visits while out there. He left that same afternoon for the West and arrived there Saturday morning. While in the west he spent 5 days at the hospital in Long Beach. He made the Visits and left the West on Sunday the 16th. When he arrived in Austin he was feeling very bad and was taken at once to the hospital for a shot of something and then went out to the College to wait for the regular doctor to come and see him. When the doctor came to the college he ordered Brother to go to the hospital at once and he stayed there till he returned to Notre Dame last Friday evening.

In a phone call from Brother Edmund and a letter from Brother Stephen we learned that Brother Ephrem was in a very bad condition. For four days they fed him intravenous[ly] and [he] was in an oxygen tent. Last Thursday the Doctor told him they could do nothing for him and that he should take a train and a traveling companion and go back North. He recommended that he go to

Mayos for a check-up. Brother would not listen to a traveling companion and said he would go by plane, which would make the flight to Chicago in 4 and one half hours. Since he insisted on doing that the doctor pumped him full of dope and when he arrived in Chicago he was feeling rather well. Brothers John Baptist and Eymard met him with the car at the airport. Brother John wanted him to go right on from there to Mayos but Brother insisted that he wanted to return to Notre Dame and said he would wait for ten days before he would do anything. Saturday morning he ate breakfast in his room and came to my room about 10:00 saying he was feeling fine but he sure looked drawn and white. He went to the refectory for dinner and at 11:00 seemed to be in good spirits. But in the afternoon the dope began to leave him and as the afternoon went on he began to feel bad. At 5:30 Brother John Baptist drove him over to the Community Infirmary to see Brother Michael and get another shot which gave him some relief.

Saturday evening Brother John Baptist mentioned Mayos again and Brother said he would wait for 3 days. Saturday night was terrible for him. He couldn't sleep. Sunday morning he went to the early Mass. After breakfast Brother John went to him again and insisted that he go to Mayos and told him that he would go along with him. By that time Brother Ephrem was ready to listen and agreed to do whatever Brother John suggested. Brother John then called Sister William at St. Mary's Hospital and told her they would be in that evening on the plane and Sister said they would be ready for them. Thus Brother Eymard drove them to Chicago. Before they left they had to go to the Infirmary and get another shot for Brother.

When talking to me Sunday morning he said: "I don't think this can be due to pollen. It must be something else." He was exhausted, in great distress. It was pitiful to see him sit there in such a condition. He said: "I have no pain but a very distressing feeling."

I am sure when Brother Ephrem left us yesterday he realized very well that his condition was serious. He said that when he was in the hospital in Texas was the first time he didn't care if he lived or died.

In expressing these facts about Brother Ephrem's condition, I don't think I have over stated the seriousness of his physical condition; and if you have not heard about it, I am sure you should know.

Sincerely yours in Christ,
/s/ Brother Bonaventure Foley, C.S.C.[23]

On October 4, Fr. O'Toole replied: *Personally, I think Br. Ephrem is exhausted, both physically and nervously. He needs a thorough rest, but, as you know, it is very difficult for a man of Br. Ephrem's activity to take a rest. He always carries the business of the Province about with him, even on vacation, and that is no way at all to get the relaxation he needs. Possibly, these attacks will convince him that he must take things a little bit easier. It may be, too, that the doctors at Mayo's will be able to give him a regime which will prevent any further distressing occurrences. Of course, we have him in our prayers each day and I have celebrated Mass for his speedy recovery.*[24]

After Br. John Baptist had returned to Notre Dame, Br. Ephrem kept him and the other councilors apprised of his condition by regular but very brief notes.[25]

So far little change in myself—one test after another. Shots every 4 hours night and day. Oxygen every night. Time is tough. Tonight I think I am to have the "drip" bottle again which you saw. Don't know yet results of X-Rays and other tests. Seems not common asthma. [October 3, 1951]

Sorry I can't report much change. I get adrenal every hour and half. Last night at 10 got Intravenous bottle of glucose with amophyllin. At 12 took oxygen, also at 3. Had adrenal shots all night. Lungs just seem to be closed and chest will not expand. Wednesday was down at Clinic for skin allergy tests. I believe the 30 different scratches showed no reaction to pollen. Dr. Peters says I may have dust allergy. [October 5, 1951]

I think "cycle" has been broken. Had special nurse Friday and Saturday nights. Figure I won't need her tonight. . . . Still slow problem, but lungs are not so raw. [October 7, 1951]

I don't know how long more, but I feel there is a change for the better. . . . I have spent the $100 Brother John gave me. Costs run about $20 a day, and I owe a nurse for two nights. [October 8, 1951]

Slow business. Much same since Eymard was here. [Br. Eymard Salzman apparently had driven up from Watertown, where he was director of vocations.] *Nerves probably worse than asthma. Today or tomorrow a special Doc will try to find out why I am so nervous. I know no reason.* [October 9, 1951]

Don't expect any positive news or reports for some time. Things change much from day to day—up and down. Was feeling fine at 6 a.m. today. As usual, went to bathroom to wash before Holy Communion at 6:45. As soon as I started to damp a towel at 6:10 I saw the bathroom turn dark. Perhaps 5 minutes later I came to on the floor gasping for air. Crawled back towards bed to pull cord for nurse. Immediate oxygen, etc. By 7 I quit perspiring and could breathe pretty well. The staff has been around since— Morlock, Peters, etc. There seems to be a change in blood pressure when I lie down and when I stand. Even low in both cases. So a bed correction is necessary. I am feeling pretty good at the moment. [October 11, 1951]

The night was good. Today I feel pretty solid. [October 12, 1951]

I believe tests and medicines are about over, and I shall probably get thrown out some time this week. Asthma is under control but is going to be a permanent thing according to Doctor. Relief is to come from adjustments in life, occupation, etc. All this later. I simply want to mention now that there is no use calling here. When I learn the leaving day from the Doctors I shall let you know and plan to get to Chicago by plane. [October 14, 1951]

Will be in Chicago, please God, at 2:44 Sunday as mentioned. . . . Am taking physical therapy (breathing exercises) this week. Pulse still jumps between 78 and 130. Temperature stays fixed. [October 18, 1951]

Br. Ephrem suffered this especially difficult period in 1951 when he was hospitalized in Long Beach, Austin, and finally the Mayo Clinic in Rochester. While treatment was beneficial, Br. John Baptist Titzer, assistant provincial, nevertheless sent out a bulletin to the province membership on October 17, 1951, announcing Br. Ephrem's release from Mayo's: *The asthma is under control, but the doctors have indicated that he will be bothered with it more or less permanently.*[26]

On October 22, 1951, Br. Ephrem, influenced by his serious bout of asthma and discouraged by its implications, wrote a significant and disconcerting letter to Fr. Christopher J. O'Toole, superior general, concerning his health and his future. It deserves to be quoted in its entirety.

I am very grateful for your kind letter of October 5 addressed to me at the Mayo Clinic. I got back to Notre Dame last evening. This is my first letter, and I owe a large number of little notes.

The asthma trouble is under control, thank God, but according to the doctors the asthmatic condition will remain. No particular allergy found, so I come under the "dust" classification. My chest has no contraction to get the air out of the lungs, so I have been given some diaphragmatic breathing lessons which I must keep up till the action becomes automatic.

When I started running a fast pulse I don't know, but it's usually close to 100 and sometimes up to 120 or 130. Doctor says situation could be due to nerves, thyroid, or even to the strong medicines given me at the clinic. May have to take a metabolism test in So. Bend at a later date. Dr. Egan is to get report.

As you said in your letter many others also advise rest, but I am convinced a more radical remedy is needed. More and more each year I have been developing a dislike for the position I hold. Though individual and group cooperation have been wonderful, I positively fear and dislike the work. I had hoped not to bring this matter up for your official consideration till next June, but I now feel that such a delay would be a detriment all around as well as to myself personally.

Since August 17 Brother John Baptist has been virtually Acting Provincial, and he does a good job. When I got back yesterday I asked him to continue to handle all business with the Council. I do not wish to start in again except by way of cooperation and for taking care of unfinished business. I should be pleased if you would now name Brother John Acting Provincial, releasing me now or by January 1. If you see your way clear to make a permanent appointment before January 1, all the better as far as I am concerned.

If I can get the health situation sufficiently under control I should be most happy to do some teaching in one of the schools in the semester beginning February 1. I wish to be as far as possible from Councils, Chapters and Administrative work.

I shall deeply appreciate your paternal consideration of the request I am respectfully making.[27]

A few days later, on October 25, Fr. O'Toole, sensitive to the provincial's health situation but most reluctant for several reasons to accede to his request, replied: *The main thing right now, Brother, is for you to follow the doctor's instructions and gain back your health just as perfectly as you can. That is the immediate problem. I understand perfectly your reaction to the strains of the Provincialship, but I really feel, Brother, that we cannot act on your suggestion of a resignation hurriedly. We should give this a lot of serious thought for several reasons. First of all, you know how much the General Administration counts on your devotedness and your good judgment and, for that reason, particularly since the Brothers' province, as such, in the United States is comparatively young, we would like to see you at the helm as long as possible. Secondly, I do not think that the present moment is exactly the best one for coming immediately to the decision that you have indicated. After all, you are just out of the hospital, after having gone through a difficult siege of sickness. You should give yourself a little more time before you begin to think about whether or not you should continue as Provincial. Then, as I have already indicated, you can understand how here at the General Administration we would have to consider such a step very carefully and prudently.*

At the same time, we are not forgetting the question of your own personal welfare. In any case, I feel, Brother, that if you let Brother John and the Council carry along as they have been when you were at the hospital, you will be able to get the rest that you need and so give yourself more leisure and more time for prayerful reflection before this question is decided upon definitively. From the supernatural point of view, your spirit is wonderful, and that is a great grace of God. At the same time, let us not hurry into this thing with too much urgency.[28] Apparently there was never any official follow-up from either party regarding this situation.

The province membership was aware of Br. Ephrem's spell of illness, and Br. Hilarion Brezik, director of Boysville, wrote him: *Our Community here has been remembering you in our prayers, for without any obsequiousness, we think the Community in general has been missing your steadying and vigorous guidance.*[29]

Br. Ephrem returned to Notre Dame on October 21, 1951, and his general health seemed to improve gradually throughout the fall. Still, given his active nature, it was difficult for him to take the rest prescribed. On November 2, Br. William Mang, former assistant provincial under Br. Ephrem and currently assistant general, wrote from New York to Br. Bonaventure Foley, provincial secretary: *It's good news that Brother Ephrem seems to be on the mend and I hope the colder weather will be a help to him, but I know he won't find it _easy_ to take it easy. He's just not constituted that way. I hope he'll gradually get back into the swing of things.*[30]

———————

In writing on November 9, 1951, to Br. Jude Costello, religious superior of the brothers in Bangladesh, Br. Ephrem referred to the recent bout of illness which had forced him to seek treatment. He said: *For a couple of weeks after getting back from the Mayo Clinic I felt a bit knocked out, but thank God I am in mighty fine condition again. Of course there remains some asthma trouble, as that usually hangs on in more or less intensity.*

Sorry I cannot travel this year for any length of time, as the doctor says I must observe some conditions regarding the rooms I inhabit—air, etc.[31]

———————

Brother Léopold Taillon of Canada wrote Br. Ephrem in December of 1951 with best wishes for good health. The provincial responded: *As to myself, my health has come on fine, thank God. At the present time I am about back to where I was a year ago. But in the late summer and fall I had quite a knockout and tried three hospitals for relief from some unusual form of asthma and the attendant nervous choking. The Mayo Clinic produced good results. I guess old age and too much work have something to do with health conditions. Administratively our Province has men qualified for all necessary positions; so there is no reason for me to think I am necessary or that I should conserve my health.*[32] Thoughts of possible resignation from his office had not wholly disappeared, and Br. Ephrem's accurate assessment of the administrative capabilities of others in the province, if it were necessary to replace him, encouraged his natural inclination toward total absorption in his work with only minimum concern for his own overall welfare.

———————

At Notre Dame the following spring Br. Ephrem experienced another serious health condition, forcing him to miss the triennial provincial chapter in July. Earlier, on June 10, 1952, Br. Bonaventure Foley, provincial secretary, wrote Br. William Mang, assistant general, about Br. Ephrem's health: *Brother Ephrem is still at the hospital. Yesterday he insisted that he did not need the private nurses any longer so they didn't report today. But today at 9:30 the Sister called and said that someone should be with him all the time. They just found him out of his room and he seemed to be somewhat confused. Brother John Baptist is going down now to see what he can do about the situation. You know as well as we do that when he makes up his mind on something it is very hard to do anything with him. I was in hopes that Father General would lay down the law to him but he sort of pushed it off on to Brother John. I feel certain that he would make much better progress if he had private nurses taking care of him than if a Community person was in the room with him. For, whenever one of us go down to see him he will talk the whole time about Community affairs and it is such talk as that (I think) which makes him tense. But when he has a lay person in the room, he has to get his mind off of Community affairs.* Clearly the old tension had returned and was affecting Br. Ephrem's asthmatic condition once more.[33]

In Rome during the winter of 1952, finally on his way to East Pakistan (later Bangladesh), Br. Ephrem wrote to Br. William, *Two idle weeks here will kill me. Don't want to walk, don't know the buses, and the station wagon has not come yet. And, as I said, the weather is cold.*[34]

Br. Ephrem made his visit to East Pakistan only when he had been provincial for seven years, a trip two years earlier having been postponed by his serious asthma attacks. While he was in Asia, Br. John Baptist Titzer and Br. Bonaventure Foley kept him abreast of developments in the province, particularly regarding the expansion of the educational institutions. Closing one letter to Br. John Baptist, Br. Ephrem wrote back: *I was much pleased with my visit. . . . I shall visit Chittagong with Br. Jude (courtesy visit). By plane or train—both bad. Eleven hours in train by night (all coach) and plane three times a week. Narcisse and Dominic visited here, and I can't avoid this trip very well. Of course Br. Jude wants me to visit all around, but I don't think I should. Travel is not easy. My mind is to leave not later than the end of January. Health fine, thank God, just a little asthma trouble when I awake in the morning.*[35]

Br. Ephrem was never a great long-distance traveler, and it took willpower for him to make the required visitations of houses overseas. When writing Fr. Christopher J. O'Toole, superior general, who had just returned from visiting East Pakistan, he remarked: *I am certainly happy to hear that your health is good and that you are back from that long and busy Pakistan trip. As for myself, I am glad I went and glad I am back.*[36]

When Br. Kieran Ryan was experiencing medical problems and was hospitalized in Austin in August of 1954, Br. Ephrem wrote replying sympathetically to a status report Br. Kieran sent in which he mentioned a reaction to some drugs he was being given: *I am familiar with drugs and their reactions. I nearly got drugged to death a couple of years ago, and I have a mean reaction towards drugs from cortizone down. And some of them knock you out and make you cry in bed.*[37]

The asthma was never far from Br. Ephrem's experience. *Under some pressure I feel some asthma pop up, but the coming trip to the South will ease that up.*[38]

An undocumented assertion voiced about Br. Ephrem is that sometimes he actually feared to open his mail in the morning. The closest direct reference from the man himself to any truth in the matter is a very short, undated, handwritten note, apparently sent by Br. Ephrem to Br. John Baptist, his assistant, sometime in 1954. Br. Ephrem tersely noted: *Take care of every letter you can without waiting for me. Letters to answer always make me on edge, after I am absent.*[39] The provincial who seemed always so much in control suffered from apprehension at times and, to some degree, anxiety. The question may be posed as to whether it was the asthma which contributed to these symptoms or vice-versa. In any case, admirable fidelity to a sense of duty kept Br. Ephrem at his post throughout the mandate of his terms of office, whatever the condition of his overall health.

In early 1955 Br. Ephrem wrote Br. William Mang about his difficulties in dealing with personnel issues. He remarked, *So far I can't complain of health, thank God, but the load till summer will be heavy. Many expiring superiorships will be hard to fill.*[40]

OTHER ILLUSTRATIONS

Other examples of the more human side of Br. Ephrem which are not easily categorized under work habits or health-related issues are also available from his correspondence.

Though a constant proponent of fraternal relationships between the priests and brothers, Br. Ephrem was enough of a realist to recognize that occasionally circumstances arose which ruffled the smoothness of the desired mutual compatibility. Brother Aidan O'Reilly, a friend of Br. Ephrem and a notable figure among the brothers as a teacher of English at the University of Notre Dame, wrote Br. Ephrem in January 1943 concerning a recent history of the university authored by one of the priests, Fr. Arthur J. Hope, C.S.C.: *We're reading at breakfast the Hope book. It's easy reading, too. He might have mentioned in his ample bibliography your two books. After reading it, I recalled what you wisely said last fall: "We shall have to write our own history. . . ." Few pages are devoted to our Brothers whose work largely made ND possible. That was to be expected. We shall survive it as we survived the Zahm regime. I could supply him with some choice Zahmiana.*[41]

Br. Ephrem had no doubt shared with others his belief that there were several brothers in the congregation who could handle the responsibility of guiding their province into the future, allowing him to return to teaching and other less taxing ministries. As noted in an earlier chapter, Br. William Mang, in a letter to Br. Ephrem on February 28, 1945, had written about Br. Ephrem's allusion to possible retirement from congregational administration at the age of fifty-seven following the general chapter. Br. William suggested that Holy Cross needed the strong leadership of men in their sixties, which was the experience of several other congregations of brothers in the U.S. at that time. He hinted that perhaps in another ten years both Br. Ephrem and he could think of retiring to some less demanding apostolate.[42]

Following the division into homogeneous provinces it was necessary for the priests and brothers to continue for a short time to share the same novitiate program at Rolling Prairie. Fr. Albert Cousineau, superior general, wrote on June 7, 1946, to Fr. Thomas A. Steiner, the priests' provincial, concerning the need to negotiate with Br. Ephrem on collaboration in the program until the priests could organize their own novitiate. Fr. Steiner had apparently alluded to some reservations he had in dealing with Br. Ephrem on this matter. Among other details covered in the letter (treated in an earlier chapter), Fr. Cousineau revealed an interesting insight into Br. Ephrem's temperament. *And so, as you say it is impossible to find a place for the Seminarian novices that will be given the habit on August 15th, you have to meet Brother Ephrem and come to an understanding with him. I feel he wants to cooperate and you know as well as I do that sometimes, because of his character, he will say and do things he does not mean so much. For the sake of peace do not pay too much attention if he breaks out and slow him down by your patience.* It would seem the so-called "ungovernable temper" which allegedly caused Br. Ephrem's dismissal from the Irish Christian Brothers' postulate had, at least at that time, never been wholly mastered.[43]

———

On December 10, 1946, Brother Dominic Elder, superior of Dujarie Hall, wrote to Brother Ephrem on some matters of business. In a postscript, he added: *Brother, I wonder if it would be possible to get a picture of yourself? We would like to remove Father Steiner's picture from our house as he is no longer our Provincial. I know that you personally do not care about your picture being taken, but I think the office almost places this unpleasant task upon you. It seems that in the past all of our houses had the picture of the Provincial along with that of the General. I think this would be a nice Christmas present for us.*[44] Br. Ephrem's tolerance for portrait sitting was only slightly greater than the proverbial reluctance of the congregation's founder, Fr. Basil Moreau.

———

On June 21, 1947, Br. Ephrem wrote Fr. Albert Cousineau, superior general, about decisions taken by the provincial council regarding a request received from Br. Nicholas Ochs, novice master. Among other things the council determined: *that "unity between the two Societies" be never a public intention (bad psychology).*[45] A strong proponent of unity between priests and brothers, Br. Ephrem felt it would be a mistake to call attention to its incidental absence or deficiency by assigning it as a special intention for public prayer among the membership.

———

On occasion when he thought proper procedures or responsibility were not being exercised on the local level, Br. Ephrem could be somewhat caustic: *How much local superiors put the Provincial on the spot in trying to make or get decisions for them!* He was referring to some questions asked by a local superior and his council. Apparently there had not been sufficient data provided the provincial from which he and his council could determine solutions at that level, and Br. Ephrem continued: *Don't blame the Council, don't blame me.* But then in his typical fashion, after having vented his frustration, he did in fact address the issues presented and finished by giving the advice the local superior sought.[46]

Brother John Baptist Titzer, assistant provincial, responding to a letter from the scholasticate superior in Texas, explained that Br. Ephrem had left for the East after seeing off the young scholastics who were heading by train for St. Edward's University in Austin. After treating the business at hand, Br. John Baptist said: *Brother Ephrem gave all the men going to Texas a fine talk which should carry them through for a while. Something must be done to have him speak oftener to the Scholastics and Novices—even if I have to drive him out to the novitiate myself. All of us need a lift occasionally—and the higher the authority that gives it, the better it works.*[47] Many of these young men were leaving their home areas for the first time and needed the inspired encouragement only a figure such as Br. Ephrem could give them.

Br. Ephrem was generally considered an entertaining speaker at functions of various types but felt more comfortable on informal occasions. He was invited in 1951 by Br. Donatus Schmitz, principal of Notre Dame High School, West Haven, Connecticut, to give the commencement address. About this, Br. Ephrem wrote to Br. John Baptist, assistant provincial: *I doubt if I should try it. I don't write or memorize speeches, even though I can talk about many things for any length of time whether I say anything or not. I shall try to hold him off till you come back.*[48] Br. Ephrem had some sense of his own capabilities—and limitations—as a speaker, recognizing that some appreciated his efforts more than others.

In corresponding with Fr. Christopher J. O'Toole, superior general, about plans for the Bayside [Flushing] high school, negotiations for which were being carried forward, the subject of a name for the school came up. It had been decided at some point that it would be called "Notre Dame High School." Br. Ephrem wrote: *The "Notre*

Dame" name got into the Bayside project before Sherman Oaks or West Haven got that name. I have been in favor of a different name for both Bayside and Akron, and the Council members are thinking that way too. Unless some local name is picked up, we favor "Holy Cross." In fact, I would have favored that for Rome, if it were not for Father Heston. I still would favor that name for Rome. Recalling some of the difficult times at the university, he continued: While we might like Notre Dame as "Our Lady" we have little reason to like Notre Dame University as such.[49] The Flushing school was eventually named Holy Cross High School.

Br. Ephrem understood the problems inherent in being local superior and principal of a major high school. Relative to a personnel issue in one institution, Br. Ephrem counseled the principal: Your six years at Lakewood are giving you much experience with men and with business and with many other things. There are many who never guess that responsibility has all these burdens. I can believe that it is one of the trials that helps towards salvation; at least, in my own case, I hope so.[50] He certainly had the experience on which to base his remarks.

A substantial supplementary collection of anecdotal information on Br. Ephrem will be found in the appendixes to this book among the reminiscences furnished by numerous Holy Cross brothers who knew him personally and perhaps a bit more intimately than others. What stands out always is the reality of his humanness, in terms of strengths and weaknesses, whatever skills he might have possessed which thrust him to the forefront of congregational leadership. An inherent, deep-seated humility prevented his arrogating to himself exclusive credit for his many accomplishments. He acknowledged his gifts, was grateful to God for them, knew he must use them for the glory of his creator and the good of the congregation, and did so with confidence and in full anticipation of success. His consciousness of his limitations prevented an unbalanced view of himself from forming in his mind and assured all those with and for whom he worked of being the beneficiaries of his talents through his determined and skillful fulfillment of the duties entrusted to him through the years.

14

The Lighter Side

SHORT IN STATURE, TALL IN WIT

Being Irish, short, and from a large family, Br. Ephrem could hardly have escaped needing a keen wit and a sense of humor, if for no other reason than self-defense. There are few who dispute his ability to hold his own in any conversation, formal or otherwise. He enjoyed laughter and its causes. His wit, sharpened by years of verbal repartee in family, school, and community, was the perfect foil for the depth of native common sense and wisdom he both possessed and developed. In an argument one did not expect to get the better of Br. Ephrem, and if pure logic or craftiness were wanting in the Irishman's effort to win a point, they were more than compensated for by his bold aggressiveness. Many are the religious who went before their provincial literally trembling in anticipation of the worst—however the worst might be imagined. No one assumed he would emerge having carried the day.

Yet Br. Ephrem, as seen earlier, could be both an entertaining conversationalist and a compassionate and sympathetic listener and adviser. The same sharp intellect and insight into human nature which enabled him to meet both friend and potential adversary on equal terms made it possible for him to be almost literally all things to all people. He enjoyed recreation periods among his confreres. Though he was never on particularly intimate terms with any of his religious, he did have favorite companions for pleasant games of bridge or canasta, for short drives in the countryside, for the infrequent walks he took as relaxation, and for travel. While some might suggest that Br. Ephrem seldom if ever forged a relationship without calculating in advance the benefits and the costs, one must suppose that he truly and honestly enjoyed the fraternal exchanges which were an inherent part of community life.

If few abide fools gladly, Br. Ephrem did so with even less tolerance than most. He might have admitted the reality of human nature and accepted the fact that not every bishop or priest with whom he had to deal was a pure image of the Redeemer and that not every religious admitted to profession in Holy Cross was a paradigm of perfection, but he found it difficult indeed to understand, much less

285

to work with, a lack of common sense, sincerity, basic intelligence, determination, and loyalty. All these characteristics he possessed in abundance, and he could not understand how any one of them, let alone several, could be missing from the repertory of essential elements proper to any Holy Cross religious. Whether he understood or not, he acknowledged the reality and learned not only to allow for weakness, stubbornness, selfishness, short-sightedness, and lack of tact and prudence, but fully to accept his confreres and to do his best to compensate along with them for what both of them might lack.

A sense of humor was an essential component in the portfolio of gifts Br. Ephrem brought to religious life in Holy Cross, both as an equal in community and as a leader over the years. His smile was broad and contagious, his laughter unrestrained and sincere. He enjoyed jokes and humorous stories and retained a loosely organized file of several which he used, some repeatedly, when he spoke to various audiences. Today few of these dated anecdotes would evoke laughter of themselves, and perhaps even in his day they were not nearly so humorous as he made them sound by the very manner of his telling them; but he relished speaking before groups and being the center of attention through the various contrivances he used to hold their attention.

In theory he was able to laugh at himself, and though he expected much of others, he demanded even more of himself. His own weaknesses were less tolerable to him than those of others. It took his profound spirituality to provide an acceptable sense of balance for him among the conflicting exigencies of his life.

His conviviality was legendary. He loved entertaining and being entertained. He enjoyed a drink or two on occasion and was usually among the last to bring a party to a close. There are those who recall his needing from time to time later on in his life a bit of assistance in returning to his room. This fact never seemed to influence the agenda of the following day or his perspicacious intensity in addressing it.

A FEW EXAMPLES

Br. Ephrem's characteristic wit and humor can be seen, at least to some degree, from his correspondence. His normal posture in writing was serious and businesslike, so examples do not abound, and little remains of his personal correspondence, if indeed he wrote much of it at all, which could exhibit these qualities more openly. In his less formal moments he displays a wittiness and irony which are engaging.

As principal, Br. Ephrem wrote from Cathedral High School, Indianapolis, in April of 1927 asking Fr. Finnigan, then the provincial, to be the speaker at commencement a couple of months later, or if he could not be present himself, to send an appropriate substitute. In his letter Br. Ephrem said: *Thirty minutes is our normal. You know the line—wonderful bishop—wonderful pastors—wonderful building—wonderful school—wonderful parents—wonderful boys —WONDERFUL faculty, and the people will go home and say you are a WONDERFUL speaker!*

Fr. Finnigan replied, regretting his inability to accept. He himself repeated the overuse of the word *wonderful* throughout the first paragraph of his letter.[1]

Responding to Br. Reginald Justak's informative letter about the impending construction of a new faculty house for Holy Trinity High School in Chicago and about the role the brothers ought to have in helping the parish (operated by Holy Cross priests) determine the incidental details about the house, Br. Ephrem, recalling some earlier misunderstandings with various pastors, wrote back with a tongue-in-cheek cautionary piece of advice: *Be sure you count each brick that goes into the new house.*[2]

One brother on the staff of the postulate in Wisconsin wrote Br. Ephrem suggesting that it would be a good idea to have a capable cook come to work there so that while doing his own work he could at the same time teach the trade to some of the aspirants and in the process supply the province with much-needed cooks for its houses. Br. Ephrem wrote back: *We would like to have a capable Brother in Watertown to train cooks, but we haven't got even enough of incapable cooks to go around.*[3]

The question of food service in community houses was traditionally resolved by the appointment of brother cooks wherever possible. In 1948, however, it was becoming evident that the number of houses being opened was outstripping the availability of brothers to cook, no matter how optimistic the vocation picture appeared at that time. Br. Reginald Justak, principal of Holy Trinity High School, Chicago, had written Br. Ephrem on April 6 asking whether as an alternative the provincial thought there was any possibility of securing some nuns to do the cooking for the brother faculty at Trinity. The reply came: *I see no hope for you to get Sisters for the house. We can't even get them for houses where we have accommodations for them. Cooks' wages are high everywhere, and we must stand it. It is one of our reasons for "living salaries." The Brothers should be patient with the cook in her job. It is probably harder to get a cook than a Brother. Talk to your faculty on being considerate to her unless they want to take turns cooking.* A dose of realism would not hurt the brothers, some of whom were accustomed to having their food prepared for them regularly, sometimes unmindful of the demanding task food preparation entails.[4]

Br. Ephrem began a letter to Fr. Louis Kelley, assistant superior general, with the following: *Your telegram spread it on thick for my feastday, but even if the water does run off the duck's back, the duck likes it! Anyway, I am grateful for all the good wishes from yourself and the members at the Generalate. I shall try to repay with a little prayer.*

Funny, isn't it? — compliments on Province success from the Generalate, and compliments in a brief letter today from Father General, and all the time it's one problem after another. But maybe that's one of the ways the Lord wants me to earn salvation. If I'm short on prayers I must make it up some other way.[5]

Br. Nicholas Ochs, novice master, wrote Br. Ephrem asking about adding books to the library of the novitiate in 1949 to accommodate the needs of a burgeoning population. Br. Ephrem replied that he had not seen the list drawn up by Br. William Mang of possible books that Br. Dominic Elder (on the staff of the novitiate) was to discuss with Br. Nicholas. But he went on to say that he relied wholly on Br. Nicholas's judgment to provide suitable reading material. Apparently one specific book was referred to by Br. Nicholas, and Br. Ephrem stated: *I have never read Makers of the Modern Mind (I think my own modern enough).*[6]

More than one novice approached Br. Nicholas about leaving Holy Cross to join a more demanding form of religious life with the Trappists. The novice master referred to this phenomenon in a letter to Br. Ephrem, who replied: *Reformers are seldom good Holy Cross material. . . . Two temporarily professed have Trappist notions now. I said to one, "You are a cigarette fiend. Quit smoking for the next six months and then come and see me." Looks like some people either want to be Trappists or get married (maybe several times). Pray that I keep faith in humankind.* He well knew that these men were not guaranteed a resolution to their restlessness in either way of life, both of which were a distinct change from Holy Cross where, if they remained faithful, they would, he believed, fulfill themselves and unerringly do God's will.[7]

In response to another letter from Br. Nicholas regarding health-related issues, Br. Ephrem, aware of his possibly deceiving himself, drolly declared: *Nothing the matter with me (in my own eyes) but too much work.*[8]

Responding to information from Br. John Baptist Titzer, assistant provincial, who was on visitation to St. Edward's University, Austin, and who had reported a donation given by a prominent person known to Br. Ephrem, the provincial wrote back: *Dr. [name] promised, when I saw him over a year ago, $1000 for the gym. I am glad he went to $1500. He is a Protestant Irishman. He would do more if the wife were not so watchful.*[9]

Br. Ephrem knew of people's tendency to let difficulties overcome their normally optimistic outlook. After hearing from a local superior and principal about several problems he was dealing with, the provincial responded to each point, concluding light-heartedly: *All good wishes, and don't look at any blue clouds.* Blue clouds were distinctly different from blue skies for Br. Ephrem.[10]

A principal wrote Br. Ephrem asking advice on how to find the money to buy new laundry equipment and an addressograph machine. The provincial replied with barely concealed sarcasm: *Your latest letter mentions the need of larger laundry equipment and a better addressograph, and that you may have to pick these up when you find a bargain.*

You ask—what to do? Well, Constitutions neglected to provide for bargains, but they did contemplate a budget for the year. The normal thing to do, therefore, is to list on the regular requisition forms the things you need and give the top amount you would like to pay. . . .

Then, as he often did after venting his irritation, he grew serious and sympathetic. *For the things you really need—laundry equipment, addressograph, and other practical bargain items wherever found—you may take advantage of the opportunities even if the approval from here cannot be secured in time.*[11]

———

Brother Ambrose Nowak had been a faculty member at Gilmour Academy but had recently been transferred to Reitz Memorial High School in Evansville, Indiana. Apparently Br. Ambrose had been in touch with Br. Ephrem at some point and had mentioned being short of alarm clocks for the brothers' house in Evansville, whereas they must have abounded at Gilmour. Br. Ephrem wrote to Br. Laurian LaForest, headmaster of Gilmour, and said: *Br. Ambrose says he is short some alarm clocks, and in case you have a surplus he may be asking a favor of you.* He added humorously, *I know you would like the Evansville faculty to be in time for meditation.*[12]

———

In reply to the principal of Reitz Memorial High School's grievance about dealings with the sister who was principal of the girls' department, Br. Ephrem replied: *If the Sisters complain too much, I think the best thing to do would be to let* [the Superintendent] *know their complaints. After all, he can be a useful buffer in keeping you out of conflicts with Sister. One never wins with a woman. So pass the burdens on to someone else.* Apart from periodic contacts with his relatives in the U.S. and abroad, there are few if any extant examples in his correspondence of Br. Ephrem's formal dealings with women, religious or lay, if in fact he ever had occasion to engage in any. One suspects a bit of unjustifiably flippant and chauvinistic prejudice in his reply here.[13]

———

The father of a student at Reitz Memorial High School in Evansville was a dealer in a particular brand of soft drink. He suggested to Br. Ephrem, at that time principal of the school, that because his boy was at Memorial it would be fitting if the Brothers switched from

Coca-Cola to his brand. Years later, reflecting on this incident in a letter to the current principal, the provincial said: *I refused. He said he was keeping his son in school keeping us in bread and butter. I told him if he felt that way he could take the boy out and we would have bread and jam. He walked away with his tail between his legs. The boy finished at Memorial and finished in Commerce at Notre Dame.*[14]

As a rule Br. Ephrem did not attempt to be humorous in his correspondence. He was generally all business. However, from time to time his wit would show through. On one occasion he was writing to a local superior who had informed him that a brother with psychological problems was before long probably going to cause the local superior himself to need psychiatric treatment. Br. Ephrem wrote back: *You mention that the Superior might soon want a straightjacket because of the worry of the problem, and I am beginning to wonder if with this and similar problems I shall not need about six straightjackets. It might be easier to have several wear one than have one wear six.*[15] For Br. Ephrem it was a matter of "divide and survive." He did suffer from the problems which beset his men, sometimes taking them too much upon himself, but attempting nevertheless to put on a good face as seen here and to make light of a serious situation.

Br. Alfonso Comeau, headmaster of Gilmour Academy in 1956, was consulting Br. Ephrem about the new gymnasium recently constructed and what name might be given to it at the time of its dedication in June of that year. The suggestion Br. Alfonso passed along was "Lancer Gym." Br. Ephrem wrote back, and it is clear that at this stage of his administration, as he was wrapping up ten years as provincial, such a relatively insignificant issue was not high on his list of priorities for excitement: *About a name for your Gym. It is just a gym, so why should it have any other name? But least of all why should it have a name like Lancer? I believe the Lancers is a name like Knights, Tigers, Rams, etc. You wouldn't like a name like Tiger Gymnasium or Ram Gymnasium. Buildings are usually named after individuals or after something local that is not abstract. Theophane would be appropriate as the founder of the school, but the name may be a bit long. He started plans for a fieldhouse. You say you want a name "consistent with its use," so why not Brawn or Muscle or Dribble?*[16]

Whether through clever witticism, irony, or good-natured sarcasm, Br. Ephrem could and did show on occasion the lighter side of his personality even as the more serious elements of life in a growing province of brothers were consistently challenged by the need for more men, more money, more capability in order to respond to the call of bishops and pastors everywhere to establish schools and boys' homes and overseas missions. Responsibility for increasing numbers of men and vastly augmented properties and investments required and even imposed a solemn seriousness—which Br. Ephrem was not only able to exemplify but which depicted his characteristic mode of operation; yet at the same time balanced health of both mind and body called for a capacity to put matters in perspective, to see everything as relative to the larger picture which governed far more than the administration of a province, even one as large and flourishing as the brothers in the United States. Beyond that view lay the role all of this played in the plan of God for each individual involved, beginning surely with the leader and presumed exemplar, Br. Ephrem, but extending equally to everyone over whom he was placed in authority. Only a refined and smooth blending of each ingredient would assure Br. Ephrem that he was proceeding correctly and would justify his engaging in a bit of playful bantering and jousting with others along the way. Humor had its place in smoothing over the often abrasive surface of the pathway of life. Br. Ephrem was an apt student and prudent judge in its use.

IV

Laying a Foundation,
Resting on Its Firmness

15

As Simple as One to Three

As noted in an earlier chapter, even before the division of the priests and brothers into autonomous provinces in 1946, Br. Ephrem and others considered as relatively imminent a further subdivision within the societies. Once the brothers were set up homogeneously in one province, they would immediately want to further plans for a geographical partitioning of the single province, perhaps within four years—the time of the next regularly scheduled general chapter, which would have to act on the matter—but surely within ten. In a bulletin dated January 1, 1948, and sent to the province membership by Br. Ephrem, the provincial alluded to the possibility of submitting a proposal for subdividing the province in time for the 1950 chapter to make the request part of its agenda.[1]

The allocation of assets at the 1945 chapter was predicated, as far as the brothers were concerned, on their desire to expand independently and effectively into various corners of the United States and its Holy Cross mission territories. Therefore, in the negotiations preceding the division of assets, the brothers who were members of the special commission or of the general chapter committee had in mind definite types of institutions they felt they must be given charge of, along with cash and scholarship considerations. Realistically Br. Ephrem knew it was highly improbable he could manage to have the single province organized and expanding enough to render further division feasible in time for the 1950 chapter. Still, it was a goal, even a priority. When it became obvious that not all the necessary pieces could be set in place by then, he turned his attention to the 1955 provincial chapter as a more probable time for presenting a proposal for division to the 1956 general chapter, and bent his energies toward founding or procuring the various institutions and recruiting the vocations that would make a proposal possible, even essential. Over the ten-year term in which he served as provincial, he succeeded in developing solid institutional, personnel, and financial bases on which the practical planning for subdivision could be built.

BACKGROUND DATA

As part of the preparation required for the division of the single U.S. brothers' province in 1956, some statistical research was needed in order to arrive, as had been done in 1945 between the priests and brothers, at an equitable distribution of assets and liabilities among the three proposed groups—Midwest, South-West, and East. In the process, membership statistics were gathered. The following figures, therefore, represent the period beginning July 1, 1946, when Br. Ephrem became the first brothers' provincial, until the chapter in the summer of 1955 at which the division of the single province into three was legislated.[2]

The total membership in the single brothers' province in 1946 was 437, of whom 317 were perpetually professed, 86 were temporarily professed, and 32 were novices. At the time of the subdivision in 1956, there were 768 members, of whom 567 were perpetually professed, 139 were temporarily professed, and 62 were novices.

Between 1946 and 1955, 579 novices entered the novitiate. Of them 138 dropped out and 441 were admitted to first profession of vows. The average loss was approximately 24 percent.

During the same time period 24 men died, an average of 2.6 per year. Of the perpetually professed, 39 requested and received dispensations, about 4.3 per year. Ninety-eight temporarily professed left either by dispensation or at the expiration of their vows, an average of 10.8 per year. The total average of deaths and departures, then, was 17.7, a relatively small but nevertheless significant percentage of the membership.

During this time nearly 37 percent of the more than one thousand who entered the postulate left the program before going to the novitiate. But it is interesting to note that, deaths aside, while 24 percent of the novices did not reach profession, after first vows only an average of 15 percent of the perpetually and temporarily professed were leaving, with the weight more naturally inclined toward the temporarily professed.

Thus, while there was sometimes an unusual fluctuation from year to year in the percentage of the increase of the total membership of the province, adequate numbers of men, about thirty-three annually, were being received and were persevering to assure continual growth. Both prudence and statistics dictated the need for separation into smaller and more manageable governmental units.

PRELIMINARY COMMITTEE STUDY

A small committee was set up in mid- to late 1952 to formulate a proposal concerning subdivision. The trio consisted of Br. Bonaventure Foley of the provincial council and Brs. Gerard Fitz and Reginald Justak. On March 1, 1953, they submitted a brief report to Br. Ephrem. They found their work seriously inhibited by having to file their report before they had access to the province financial statement for 1952, which would reveal salary arrangements influencing a potential division of assets. They did, however, make a few general suggestions for the division of assets and aired questions and problems they identified in the process.[3]

Shortly before the provincial chapter of 1955 Br. Ephrem sent a letter to all local superiors asking them to canvass the members of the province within their jurisdiction as to which geographical division each would theoretically choose. The provincial was seeking some statistical information on which to base necessary planning as the chapter approached. The letter read as follows:

As you know, Brother Bonaventure is Chairman of the Committee on Provinces, and he desires to have all possible desirable information for the Provincial Chapter. He has mentioned to me that it would simplify considerations of personnel if he now had Province Preference statistics from our members.

We are therefore sending you a little form on which each member may indicate his preference and asking that this be done within 20 days. The members may either give these filled out forms to the Local Superior for mailing to Brother Bonaventure, or each member may mail his own direct to Brother Bonaventure.

Province (or Vice-Province) boundaries must be officially proposed by the Chapter and approved by the General Council (or General Chapter). All of you have a general idea of what these boundaries may be, the Midwest perhaps being limited to Minnesota, Wisconsin, Iowa, Missouri, Illinois, Indiana, Michigan, Ohio, and Kentucky.

Since all our members are subject to assignment anywhere within the United States it follows that placement may be made irrespective of place of birth or of present location.

Naturally preferences would be given consideration, but no doubt even after choice or selection is determined there will still be need for some members to work outside their official Province.

This canvass is for both perpetually and temporarily professed members, as its main object at this time is to secure an indication of what numerical strength might be considered for each area.

As to area, the South-West is no doubt extensive, and perhaps as time goes on it may be desirable to create a South unit and a West unit.

You should all feel free to write the Chairman any suggestions you may have concerning matters relating to Provinces or Vice-Provinces (more likely).

/s/ Brother Ephrem O'Dwyer, C.S.C.
Provincial[4]

ACTION BY THE 1955 PROVINCIAL CHAPTER

The serious matter of subdivision was brought formally to the 1955 provincial chapter at Notre Dame and a report from the chapter Committee on Province Division was approved, including a recommendation to be forwarded to the superior general for action by the 1956 general chapter.

The issue of dividing the single brothers' province was in the forefront of the chapter agenda. Presuming on continuous growth, Br. Ephrem had actively pursued this objective from the time he became provincial in 1946, and the concept always influenced his setting of goals. With the notable increase in membership during his tenure, numbers alone suggested that any further attempts to govern a single burgeoning province were impractical, even futile.

The chapter committee presented recommendations to the capitulants for action. The committee was chaired by Br. Bonaventure Foley, who had also led the three-man commission that made a preliminary report in early 1953 and who carried the greater part of the burden of responsibility for preparing for the division. The chapter committee consisted of capitulant Brs. Alfonso Comeau, Benedict Gervais, Charles Andersen, Edmund Hunt, Giles Martin, Joachim Reiniche, and Pacificus Halpin.

The committee reported to the chapter as follows:

The members of the Committee on Province Division considered the advisability of dividing the United States Province of the Brothers of the Congregation of Holy Cross. All the members of the committee agreed that a division was in order chiefly for the following reasons:

(a) Since 1946 many new foundations have been established in far-flung places. This has resulted in heavy administrative duties

for the Provincial Administration, making it practically impossible to give close attention to area problems and local development.

(b) Another weakness is the constant necessity to shift personnel from one area to another and to provide for studies and credentials peculiar to certain areas.

These two conditions tend to inefficiency and to considerable increase of costs in certain regions. If the proposed division is carried out, the members feel that the apostolate of the Brothers of Holy Cross will benefit spiritually and materially.

A full analysis of this problem of dividing the Province into three divisions may require further study and may depend on the financial aspects of the Province at the time the proposed division is made. Having made an examination of the finances, the personnel, and the foundations, the Committee on Provinces is of the present opinion that, in principle, it is possible to make these divisions and that the Provincial Administration and the Provincial Accounting Office could work out the financial arrangement by which each division would be solvent. In view of these considerations and in view of the observations submitted in this report on the territorial division, finances, personnel, etc., the Committee on Proposed Provinces suggests that the Chapter present the following recommendation to the Very Reverend Superior General:

The 1955 Provincial Chapter of the United States Brothers' Province respectfully requests the Very Reverend Superior General and his Council to consider the advisability of dividing the present United States Brothers' Province into a Mid-West Province, a South-West Vice-Province, and an East Vice-Province to become effective on or before July 1, 1956.[5]

APPROBATION BY THE 1956 GENERAL CHAPTER

Following the approval of the provincial chapter, work continued on formulating a concrete plan for the subdivision of the single province into three governmental units. The general chapter of 1956, held in Rome at the newly constructed Holy Cross generalate and house of studies on Via Aurelia Antica, approved without objection the proposal as submitted. Between then and November 1, the date eventually targeted for the official implementation of the decree of separation, details were worked out among the three men who would lead the Midwest Province and the South-West and Eastern Vice Provinces. Br. Donatus Schmitz was chosen to continue the administration of the "mother province" with headquarters at Notre Dame as before. The geographical area of this Midwest Province comprised basically those states grouped in the vicinity of the Great Lakes. Br. John Baptist Titzer, who had served Br. Ephrem as assistant provincial between 1950 and 1956, was selected to head the South-West Vice Province, whose geographical area extended from Florida along the gulf coast through Louisiana and Texas and on to cover the entire West coast, including all the mountain states. To no one's surprise, Br. Ephrem himself was chosen to lead the Eastern Province, which comprised essentially the New England states, New York, Pennsylvania, and the Atlantic seaboard from Virginia north, plus the international school in Rome. A brief news release was issued on October 29, 1956, by Br. Bonaventure Foley from the Midwest Province headquarters at Notre Dame.

The United States Brothers' Province of the Congregation of Holy Cross is divided into three new administrative units as of November 1st in accordance with the decree of the General Chapter of the Congregation of Holy Cross which was held at Rome in July this year. As announced by the Very Reverend Christopher J. O'Toole, C.S.C., Superior General, this division is necessitated by the growth of the Brothers of Holy Cross throughout the United States, with present membership of 739 professed Brothers and 93 novices, and the consequent problems of direction and administration. The division will establish a Midwest Province with headquarters at Notre Dame, Indiana, a South-West Vice Province with headquarters at St. Edward's University, Austin, Texas, and an Eastern Vice Province with headquarters at Holy Cross High School, Flushing, New York.

The announcement went on to list the institutions operated by the brothers in the U.S. and to introduce each of the new provincials and the institutions under the supervision of each. A brief biographical sketch of the three provincials followed. The release appeared in the *South Bend Tribune* on November 1, 1956, the date on which the division officially became effective.[6]

A DETAILED AGREEMENT

An agreement had been worked out among the three new provincials as to the specific details surrounding the division of assets and debts. In a formidably titled document they laid out the elements to be observed. The five-page paper was headed, "Agreement Concerning the Dissolution of the United States Brothers' Province and the Establishment of the Midwest Province, the South-West Vice Province, and the Eastern Vice Province As of November 1st, 1956; The Settlement of Inter-Province Loan Balances and Plant Fund Liabilities As of June 30th 1956; and Arrangements for Inter-Province Relations Subsequent Thereto." Apparently the document had been formulated by the Midwest Province council. Paragraph 25 notes that the document had been reviewed by the provincial and the council of the Midwest Province and approved on October 16, 1956. The three provincials were to set their names to the proposal after approving its provisions. It comprised a detailed financial agreement among the three provinces. Paragraph 24 highlighted the spirit in which the mutual agreement was entered into: *Should any Province or Vice Province need assistance in the matter of finances or manpower, it is understood that such assistance will be forthcoming from the other Provinces and Vice Provinces of the Brothers in the United States according to arrangements made by the Provincials in a spirit of Community interest, with the approval of the Superior General.*[7] Concerning the agreement, archivist Br. Laurian LaForest remarked: *A rather unusual stipulation was also written into this agreement: if an opportunity for making a foundation in a particular province arose, and if that province for reasons of finance or manpower could not take advantage of this offer, the opportunity was to be passed on to another province for consideration. If the other province wished to act upon this offer, the foundation could be made with the approval of the Superior General.*[8] Thus, while province boundaries were clearly delineated, the mission spirit of the congregation, not to mention the goodwill persisting among the brothers themselves, demanded that mere structure not supersede charity and that means be available for responding to needs anywhere at any time.

A REVIEW OF PROGRESS IN 1962

Six years after the establishment of the three provinces (both the South-West and Eastern Vice Provinces had been elevated to the status of full provinces in 1958), an undated report was prepared by the Midwest provincial office, most likely for use at the 1962 general chapter, detailing the history of the division of the single U.S. Brothers' Province into three units and their development since their establishment in 1956. An allusion in the text allows the deduction that the report was prepared in 1962. It seems likely that the author of the document was Br. Donatus Schmitz, provincial. The report read as follows:

I. Previous to the Provincial Chapter of 1955, Brother Ephrem O'Dwyer, Provincial Superior of the United States Province of the Brothers of Holy Cross, appointed a committee to study the financial and personnel implications in the possible erection of 3 provinces: Midwest Province, Eastern Vice-Province, and South-West Vice-Province. (The latter is called South-West because it was felt that the Mississippi-Louisiana-Florida-Texas group of states might one day become a Southern Province as opposed to California, etc., or a future Western Province.) Territories were divided by natural working boundaries: areas where houses and schools exist; hence, this problem was not too difficult to solve.

II. Salient factors which motivated territorial division

1. Professional requirements in the various states in which the Brothers of Holy Cross worked from Massachusetts to California encouraged the idea.

2. By Constitutions, the Provincial Superior (or his delegate) must make a visitation once each year to every house in his province. (Exception: houses in foreign countries—for us, South America, Africa, East Pakistan, Italy.) From the point of view of closer supervision both in government and personnel, a division into 3 provinces seemed most desirable.

3. Some areas, particularly the South and West, were weak in recruiting vocations; it was felt that province division would encourage individual religious to be more aggressive in this regard. Before the division Mississippi, Louisiana, Florida, Texas, and California seemed weak recruitment areas, but since the division the number of vocations from these areas has increased. For example, last summer recruitment in the South-West Province surpassed, percentage-wise, both the Midwest and Eastern Provinces.

4. From the point of view of economy, localizing religious personnel meant financial savings both in exchange and in home vacations.

5. It was felt that a division would promote many psychological advantages: solidify expansion in local areas, emphasize recruitment, stabilize economy in both home and foreign mission foundations, and finally, assure religious of working in home territories. This last point, however, can be localized to the south-central section of the United States since it was always felt that it was difficult to get southern recruits to come up north.

6. Frequently religious go on for graduate studies in the areas in which they work. Travel expenses are an important item here.

III. After boundaries were established, two significant points were considered: (1) financial arrangements; (2) distribution of personnel.

A. Financial Considerations

1. Exhaustive study of all financial implications is basic in division into provinces. This has a two-fold aspect, since it concerns (1) an equitable distribution of property houses, with corresponding assets to operate autonomously; (2) income from houses, either community-owned or diocesan-owned, must be sufficient to support the province. (Distinction is made here between the community-owned or property house, such as Mother Guerin High School [sic; likely intended is its neighbor, Holy Cross High School, staffed by the brothers], *and the diocesan-owned house, such as Reitz Memorial High School.)*

2. Province income must be sufficient to sustain all operations within any one province, i.e., formation and training of members, graduate work, facilities for care of aged and infirm, along with expenses of administration, plant and utilities maintenance, general development, support of foreign mission houses and schools, etc.

3. In our case, income from the various proposed provinces was not sufficient to sustain expenses; hence, some legislation was passed to increase the province tax for members working in community-owned schools.

B. Distribution of Personnel

1. By virtue of the fact that religious were working in the East (Connecticut, New York, New Jersey, Massachusetts, Rhode Island, Washington, D.C., and Delaware), the Midwest (Ohio, Indiana, Michigan, Illinois, and Wisconsin), and the South-West (Texas, Mississippi, California, Florida, and Louisiana), this made for a natural division. And when statistics were studied, it was found that the personnel could be distributed into a 50–25–25 ratio: Midwest 50%, East 25%, South-West 25%. Since the United States Province of Brothers was operating with approximately 800 members, the division was based on a 400–200–200 membership. It is interesting to note that six years after the division into provinces, the three provinces now have approximately 1100 members.

2. A delicate question was distributing the personnel. It could be accomplished in one of two ways. (1) We could freeze religious in the area they were in, or (2) offer them a choice. After consultation with the Superior General, it was decided to give the religious his choice of province. A poll of interests was solicited before the 1955 Chapter as follows: 1st choice (MW, SW, E, or NP [no preference]) and 2nd choice (same choices). The survey disclosed an interesting fact: of the 800 members making a choice, 190 members indicated no preference. A second and definitive choice was made a year and a half later, wherein members were requested to be more exact.

3. The matter of choice created some problems. When the final votes were cast, it was found that there was an unequal distribution. Also, where religious who were licensed to teach in a given state chose a province not including this state, other difficulties were raised. For example, the Brothers have four high schools in Indiana. We had close to a hundred religious prepared to teach in Indiana, but after choice of provinces was made, we found that the Midwest province had only 35 religious qualified to teach in Indiana. This, of course, created a hardship, but we found it could be rectified in three or four years. Despite the hardship, we believe that this method was the best course to follow. Interestingly enough, when new dioceses are carved out of old ones, they always seem to <u>freeze</u> the personnel.

When the study was completed, it was presented to the provincial Chapter of 1955. As a province, we could not legislate on such a move because the matter had to go to General Chapter, coming up the next year, 1956. Nevertheless, the members of the 1955 Provincial Chapter reviewed the entire matter in great detail and forwarded the following Recommendation to the Superior General: "The 1955 Provincial Chapter of the United States Brothers' Province respectfully requests the Very Reverend Superior General and his Council to consider the advisability of dividing the present United States Brothers' Province into a Midwest Province, a South-West Vice-Province, and an Eastern Vice-Province, to become effective on or before July 1, 1956."

In the General Chapter of 1956, the following was passed: "The Chapter approves the division of the United States Brothers' Province into a Midwest Province, an Eastern Vice-Province, and a South-West Vice-Province, and requests the Superior General to obtain approval of the Holy See for the erection of the Vice-Provinces into Provinces as soon as possible."[9]

Then a section was added entitled: "Financial Considerations Preliminary to the Division of the United States Province of the Brothers of Holy Cross." Ten major areas were to be determined: (1) analysis of operations, past and present; (2) physical plant and properties; (3) debt; (4) personnel; (5) inter-province exchange of personnel; (6) endowment, burses, trust funds, etc.; (7) settlement of cash working funds, accounts payable, accrued expenses, etc., between the mother province and proposed new provinces; (8) transfer of accounting records, personnel data, other records, and archives; (9) creation of corporate entities for new provinces and legal transfer of properties, etc., thereto; and (10) provision for care of aged and infirm; central infirmary facilities, cemetery, etc.

The outline concluded: *These preliminary considerations eventually evolved into a definitive plan which, after some revisions, was approved by Provincial Chapter and later incorporated into a formal "Inter-Province Agreement" which was accepted by the Provincial and Vice-Provincials concerned.*[10]

A CAPSTONE AND A FOUNDATION

Chronologically the division of the single U.S. Brothers' Province into three subgroupings in July of 1956 signified the termination of Br. Ephrem's ten-year administration as provincial. The setting up of the three governmental units crowned years of planning, organization, building, supervision, and prayer and sacrifice throughout the province. In his ten years as provincial, Br. Ephrem had been responsible for the establishment of fifteen new institutions throughout the United States and abroad: Gilmour Academy, Gates Mills, Ohio (1946); Notre Dame High School, Sherman Oaks, California (1947); St. Francis of Assisi School, Brooklyn, New York (1947); Boysville, Clinton, Michigan (1948); St. Edward High School, Lakewood, Ohio (1949); Mt. Carmel School, Bronx, New York (1949); Vincent Hall Scholasticate, Austin, Texas (1949); Ginasio Dom Amando, Santarém, Para, Brazil (1951); Notre Dame International School, Rome, Italy (1952); Archbishop Hoban High School, Akron, Ohio (1953); Rancho San Antonio, Chatsworth, California (1953); Sacred Heart Military Academy, Watertown, Wisconsin (1955); Holy Cross High School, Flushing, New York (1955); St. Francis High School, Mountain View, California (1955); and the Variety Club Boys Ranch, Bedford, Texas (1956). All that Br. Ephrem and his collaborators had intended and hoped for had in fact come to be—decidedly and irreversibly so. Without ignoring or downplaying the actual and potential imperfections in both planning and implementation, the situation as it existed was an extremely positive development for the Brothers of

Holy Cross in the United States. It served as an affirmation of the vision of Br. Ephrem and his leadership of the brothers, and laid to rest any suspicions that the brothers of and for themselves would be unable to negotiate the demands of autonomy.

At the same time, his being selected to head the newly formed Eastern Vice Province was a sign that his leadership was still effective, still desired, still very much needed. At the age of sixty-eight Br. Ephrem was asked once more to sacrifice for the sake of his beloved Holy Cross. Just when he thought he must surely be beyond the prospect of further direct involvement in the active development of the congregation, he was burdened yet again with the challenging task of guiding one of the fledgling governmental units into the future.

What was in a very real sense the capstone of his administrative life thus became the foundation for his continuing leadership in building the East. But if he had to rely at all on anyone's contribution to assure his success in the new venture, whose better than his own proven guidance and achievements? Another six years as provincial lay before him, and the members of the vice province, all of whom knew him well, set out with their *new* vice provincial toward the achievement of solidity as one of three influential branches of the Brothers of Holy Cross in mission to the Church in the United States.

16

Beyond 1956—A Retrospective
(1956–1978)

On July 26, 1956, Br. Ephrem formally wrote his resignation as president of the Brothers of Holy Cross, Inc., headquartered at Notre Dame, Indiana, and as a member of that corporation. This legal move signified his official transition from provincial of the single brothers' province to vice provincial of the Eastern Vice Province, whose offices were first to be located in the brothers' residence atop Holy Cross High School on the border between the suburbs of Bayside and Flushing, Long Island. When a new provincial residence was constructed in West Haven, Connecticut, in 1959 at 24 Ricardo St., Br. Ephrem moved his administration there.

Br. Ephrem assumed office in the East on November 1 with a council composed at least temporarily of Brs. John William Donoghue (assistant), Maurus O'Malley, Armel Latterel, and Pacificus Halpin. In September of 1957 after brothers serving in other areas were free to join their confreres in the new vice province, a new council was formed of Brs. Elmo Bransby (assistant), Sidney Halligan, Bertram Madden, and John Berchmans Aery. Together with these men Br. Ephrem wasted no time in carrying forward plans he had laid even before the division for the needed expansion of the new governmental unit.

St. Edward's University in Austin almost immediately acknowledged its debt of gratitude to Br. Ephrem for his support in its ongoing development and that of the Brothers of Holy Cross in general by announcing the conferring of an honorary doctor of laws degree on him on May 30, 1957.

The vice provincial of the South-West Vice Province, Br. John Baptist Titzer, knew Br. Ephrem well from his days as assistant provincial and respected him highly. At a testimonial farewell in honor of Br. Ephrem on September 22, 1956, as he prepared to take on his new duties as eastern vice provincial, Br. John Baptist had said: *This testimonial dinner this evening in addition to being an important event is really a necessary one, for Br. Ephrem's Life and Career*

307

as the First Provincial of the Brothers of Holy Cross is deserving of public recognition and gratitude; and not to have this testimonial would be something of an act of ingratitude. In other words, this is not an attempt to honor merely the office of Provincial; it is an attempt to honor the man—Br. Ephrem—who held that office so long and so well.

. . . As a Religious, Br. Ephrem is a man who lives by the Constitutions; as a Superior, he is a man who believes that all members should live by the same Constitutions. To carry out these basic principles has meant a necessary firmness—but a firmness that was always tempered with fairness. This uniform fairness and firmness has strengthened the common religious life of the Community, which fact, I believe, is at the very roots of our expansion and success. For God must be pleased with our life and work, since He has so generously sent us worthy vocations to develop and grow. As Superior, Br. Ephrem has been fatherly and understanding as many of his subjects can testify who found themselves in straits and needed his help.

Likewise, God has used the genius of Br. Ephrem as an Administrator. His vision and leadership in recognizing and seeking opportunities for expansion are excelled only by his ability as a financier and by his faith and courage to act upon his convictions.

What he has done for the Brothers of Holy Cross will be forever remembered and admired by those who come after him.[1]

GROWTH AND DEVELOPMENT

The following year, 1957, he supervised the inauguration of a boys' home in the East—the Pius XII home and services—headquartered near Chester, New York, some fifty miles northwest of New York City. At the same time a large and substantial novitiate building was constructed and opened in April 1958 at Valatie, the site of the aspirancy program, canceling the need for the Eastern Province to share crowded novitiate facilities with the other provinces. The aspirancy remained in operation in the older buildings already used for that purpose, and, during periods candidates were not using those facilities, the Holy Cross Fathers assisted the brothers in providing retreats for laity and religious from the area.

On April 29, 1958, both the Eastern and South-West Vice Provinces evolved into full provinces, a move foreseen at the time of the general chapter of 1956 in its formal authorization of the division of the single brothers' province.

In 1959, besides continuing their mission presence along with several other provinces in East Pakistan, the Eastern brothers turned their attention to new apostolic activity in Africa. Two years before, the Midwest Province had accepted a mission in Ghana, West Africa. Br. Ephrem responded to needs in Uganda, East Africa, and assigned several brothers to teach at St. Augustine's School in Butiti, not far from Fort Portal, the see city of the diocese entrusted to the Holy Cross priests. But expansion in the eastern United States was not ignored. Bishop Hendricken High School in Warwick, Rhode Island, was opened, as was St. Edmond's Academy, an elementary school in Wilmington, Delaware.

1959 also marked the fiftieth anniversary of Br. Ephrem's profession of vows as a Holy Cross religious. At the age of seventy-two and at the time in his career when most men are partially or fully retired, Br. Ephrem was but midway through his productive six-year term as the first provincial of the Eastern Province. A jubilant and well-attended celebration was held on July 6 at Holy Cross High School, Flushing, to mark the special occasion.

Stonehill College, a Holy Cross priests' institution in North Easton, Massachusetts, bestowed on the provincial an honorary doctorate on June 5, 1960, citing, as did St. Edward's, the notable contribution of Br. Ephrem to the growth and development of the Brothers of Holy Cross and Catholic secondary education in the United States.

In 1961 the Ugandan mission was expanded by the extension of the brothers' presence to St. Leo's College in Fort Portal, and another primary school was accepted in the United States, St. John Baptist School in Hillsdale, New Jersey.

A beautiful but practical scholasticate was built on the edge of the campus at Stonehill College to house young brothers doing their university studies. This move in collaboration with the priests completed Br. Ephrem's expansion program for the province.

In accord with his well-designed plan, Br. Ephrem, as his term expired in 1962, had supervised the setting up in the East of two secondary schools, two primary schools, a boys' home, two mission apostolates, a novitiate and a scholasticate for the university training of Holy Cross religious, and a provincial headquarters. He was, at the age of seventy-four, ready and most willing to hand over leadership to his successor, Br. John William Donaghue, the young administrator who under Br. Ephrem's guidance had begun St. Edward High School in Lakewood, Ohio.

According to Br. Laurian LaForest, chronicler of the Eastern Province history, *It could be said that when Br. Ephrem left office*

*in 1962, the Eastern Province of Brothers was on a solid footing
financially; and as far as one can judge such things, in community
living, sufficient apostolates and vocations. The province has prof-
ited greatly from Br. Ephrem's solid faith and clear vision of the
future. His many years of service to the community have assured
him of a place among the stalwarts of Holy Cross.*[2]

RETIRED FROM ADMINISTRATION BUT ACTIVE

From 1962 until 1970 Br. Ephrem did not consider himself fully
retired. He had both the energy and the desire to be of use to the
province in any way he could. For the first time since 1932 he was
not directly involved in some role of authority in the congregation.
Thirty years of administration, not counting his years in the schools
previous to that time, had formed a personality whose strengths and
determination were found in decision making, organization, planning,
and construction. Such activity had become habitual to him. The
already strong character had been further refined over more than
a generation by the constant give and take he encountered, not only
within the congregation but in the wider world of apostolic growth and
expansion. It was, then, impossible for him to lay aside characteristics
which had been an essential part of his personality for so many years
and which had contributed so significantly to the development of the
Brothers of Holy Cross. It is not surprising, therefore, that he moved
rather restlessly from institution to institution during these eight years,
seeking to be useful once more as a teacher, or to assist in the financial
offices of schools, seeming at times more an administrator than an
aide. When asked, he made himself available to his successors in the
provincial's office for advice and counsel and was quietly pleased when
his help was solicited. As an elder statesman in the province, indeed
the *paterfamilias* of all the brothers, he was sought out by many.
During the 1962–1963 school year he functioned as a teacher and
accountant at Moreau Hall, the newly opened scholasticate in North
Easton. The following year he taught and served as the house steward
at St. Edmond's in Wilmington.

It was at this time that Br. John William Donoghue, provincial,
assigned Br. Franciscus Willett the task of writing a biography of
Br. Ephrem, who at first welcomed the news and offered Br. Franciscus his full cooperation saying, *I shall be fully on exhibition. . . .
You are welcome to have here whatever I may have and also
take any papers with you.* The biography was never written, and
the reason is unclear beyond the fact that Br. Ephrem himself had
second thoughts and put obstacles in the way of the biographer. On

February 8, 1964, Br. John William wrote to Br. Franciscus that Br. Ephrem had discarded written answers he had prepared to questions submitted by Br. Franciscus, but that the writer should once more submit the questions in writing for Br. Ephrem to think about and then answer eventually in an interview. On February 14 Br. John William penned another brief note to Br. Franciscus: *The Ephrem book is not really important now—getting all you can in information is. Until Ephrem kicks you out* <u>*three*</u> *times, don't ask to give up interviewing him. Perhaps this summer we can set up some traps where you and himself get together by accident. Perhaps after a cup of Irish coffee!* Later on Br. Ephrem wrote Br. Franciscus that all information would have to come from interviews, not in writing. The project was never carried forward and Br. Franciscus died at fifty-three while engaged in prison ministry in Dannemora, New York, on March 23, 1976.

The 1964–1965 academic year found Br. Ephrem teaching at Holy Cross High School in Flushing. Then for two years he taught at Bishop Hendricken High School in Warwick, and the final three years of his active life he spent as assistant to the treasurer, once more at Holy Cross High School in Flushing. By this time he was eighty-two and fully open to retirement. Still, for two more years he remained in the East, spending one year at Holy Cross High School in Waterbury, Connecticut, and another at Holy Cross in Flushing.

RETURN TO NOTRE DAME

For a man whose health during much of his active life had been precarious at best, it could hardly be surprising that when Br. Ephrem eventually retired and returned to the area he had known and loved for so many years he would need fairly regular medical attention and supervision. So at eighty-four he moved back to Notre Dame, Indiana, and took up residence at Dujarie House, the infirmary facility shared by the three provinces of brothers since its construction as part of the large Holy Cross Brothers Center complex in 1966. His now ailing heart, so long burdened by the strain engendered by his asthmatic condition, had to be bolstered by a pacemaker, which was implanted on December 6, 1972. For the next six years the device enabled him to lead a relatively active and satisfying life in retirement.

One more major honor came to him at the age of eighty-eight. The University of Notre Dame, of which he had been treasurer from 1931–1933 and on whose campus he had lived and taught for many long years, extended an invitation to Br. Ephrem to be the recipient of an honorary doctor of laws degree at the commencement exercises held May 16, 1976. To Fr. Theodore M. Hesburgh, C.S.C., president, he acknowledged that he felt more highly honored by this degree than the other two honorary doctorates he had previously received, because it was at Notre Dame that he had joined Holy Cross, had done his undergraduate and graduate studies, had worked, and had emerged as a significant and effective leader among both brothers and priests in the congregation. Fr. Christopher J. O'Toole, former superior general, wrote to Br. Ephrem on June 9, felicitating the former provincial on his receiving the honorary doctorate. He said, *All along you have been one of the pillars of the Congregation, particularly in the States, and when the autonomous Provinces were formed in 1945, I really don't know what C.S.C. could have done without the help of your experience and organizational ability. It is really a marvel, despite some passing difficulties and problems, how smoothly this reorganization took place. And ninety percent of this at least is due to you.*[3]

While at Dujarie House, Br. Ephrem kept himself occupied with a bit of correspondence and hobbies such as reading. For the residents of Corvilla House, a home for the mentally challenged operated in South Bend by Br. Flavius Ellison, Br. Ephrem delighted in fashioning rosaries made out of a particular type of dried berry he found along the banks of the St. Joseph River flowing just below Dujarie House. He also took pride in crocheting afghans, scarves, and various other useful items for Corvilla residents as well as for others.

The proximity of Dujarie House to the faculty residence at the Brothers Center encouraged association among the members of the two houses. Regularly, especially on Friday evenings, the Center hosted a social gathering, and Br. Ephrem, when he felt up to it, made his way to the Center to participate in the camaraderie and the refreshments. Whether or not he was still relying on some of the stronger beverages to alleviate the ill effects of his earlier asthmatic condition, he regularly prescribed an adequate dosage of the cure for himself, and occasionally found it useful to be assisted in his return to Dujarie House.

During his declining years Br. Ephrem received many letters of respectful gratitude from brothers in the three provinces testifying to his influence and impact on them over the years.[4]

As his ninetieth birthday approached, Br. Ephrem realized that even with the pacemaker, which kept him alive and at least minimally active, the quality of his participation in daily events was diminishing. He told one visiting brother about to return to Ghana in the early fall of 1977 that he did not intend to have the power source renewed in his pacemaker the next time it needed to be, and that ninety years was long enough to live. He declined steadily but slowly, lingering even then beyond most people's expectations, and finally on August 21, 1978, having achieved his goal of ninety years of life and having accomplished a prodigious lifetime of work, he died peacefully at Dujarie House.

The next day a memorial mass was celebrated for the repose of his soul at the Brothers Center; then the body was transported to Valatie, New York, for final services and burial. The wake took place on Friday evening, August 25, and the funeral mass and burial were held on Saturday the 26th with Fr. Thomas Barrosse, superior general, presiding at a service concelebrated by eleven priests and attended by a host of brothers. He was laid to rest in the community cemetery in the beautiful and peaceful rural surroundings of St. Joseph Spiritual Life Center, formerly the novitiate he himself had built twenty years earlier. His sister, Mrs. Peter Quinn of New York, was in attendance, accompanied by several nieces and nephews.

IN RETROSPECT

Long before his death people had been speaking well of Br. Ephrem. He was a man appreciated in his own lifetime, yet one not able to accept praise with aplomb or even indifference, for he better than anyone recognized his shortcomings. Nevertheless he was humble enough to acknowledge he had allowed the Lord to use his gifts and talents effectively in furthering the mission of Holy Cross.

Br. Laurian LaForest noted in "A Brief History of the Brothers of Holy Cross, Eastern Province," that *Brother Ephrem's administration was one of exceptionally strong leadership, leading to unity of purpose. As in the founding of any organization, economics and family spirit dictated strong measures in order to insure success.*[5]

On the occasion of Br. Ephrem's golden anniversary of religious profession in 1959, Fr. Christopher J. O'Toole, unable himself to be present, had written an encomium to be included in the printed program. Among other comments made, the superior general, no doubt recalling the time in 1951 when Br. Ephrem had submitted his resignation as provincial but obediently continued in office at Fr. O'Toole's urging, said, *With the establishment of the homogeneous Provinces, numerous and taxing administrative problems arose for Brother Ephrem. However, his long experience in administration as well as his rich native talents enabled him to meet these problems and to establish policies—religious, academic and financial—which have proved to be sound and successful and which have contributed immensely to the growth of the Brothers of Holy Cross in the United States. . . .*

I mention these facts to indicate the zeal and success with which our Jubilarian has applied himself to the apostolate. These projects and many others which Brother Ephrem undertook before the division of the Brothers' Province, as well as the exceptional increase in candidates for the brotherhood, are a source of legitimate pride for the entire Congregation. As our Jubilarian looks back over fifty years as a Religious of Holy Cross and particularly over the years since 1945, he will find many reasons for gratitude to God, our Blessed Mother and St. Joseph whose instrument he has been in extending the work of Holy Cross. . . . I appreciate most sincerely his loyalty and devotion, his sound religious spirit, his helpfulness and cooperation. His contribution to the success of the Congregation and his own Province has been indeed large; and for this we should all be grateful.[6]

At the same ceremony the provincial councilors had expressed the best wishes of the entire province: *For your faithful services to Holy Cross, for your relentless devotion to your vocation as a Brother of Holy Cross, for your faithfulness to principle, for your ready wit, for your reasonable and zealous efforts, for the numerous graces and blessings God has given you—for these and for so many things, we of Holy Cross are most grateful.*[7]

Several years later, as the Midwest Province forum gathering of 1972 recognized Br. Ephrem's recent return to Notre Dame and his contribution to the development of all of the three brothers' provinces, Br. Columba Curran, a provincial councilor during Br. Ephrem's entire ten-year term in the midwest, read a citation from the membership: *In Brother Ephrem O'Dwyer the Brothers of Holy Cross recognize a strong leader and a lover of men who, in his time and to this very day, serves Holy Cross with clarity of vision and with fidelity, undaunted courage, and strength of purpose.*

As an extremely human person, he knows men through that particular gift of insight that comes from living and working with others. He has a sense of humor and a depth of understanding that sees both limitations and possibilities in a perspective that only a loving man possesses.

His spirituality, not dependent on the exterior, manifests firm religious conviction, a love of Holy Cross, and a knowledge of the gospels that has always been so well reflected in his concerns and his decisions as an administrator.

Brother Ephrem has always been a religious endowed with wisdom and insight which springs from a living faith. The Brothers of Holy Cross thank God for Brother Ephrem in our midst.[8]

The citation proclaimed by the University of Notre Dame on the occasion of its conferring an honorary doctorate on Br. Ephrem began in much the same vein as the above, then continued: *His gift of leadership is based on justice, honesty, and a compassionate understanding of others. His dedication—not dependent on the exterior—manifests a deep conviction which is always his: a love of the Church, the Community to which he belongs, and the principles of the gospel story. Despite the fact that he shouldered responsibility for many of his active years, and because of his deep trust and belief in God, he always remained human and his solicitude never wavered even as school principal, provincial superior, and provincial or general councilor.*

A merry wayfarer, gifted with humor and Irish wit, his convictions strengthened many people on life's journey. He believed in others and himself. During life he always disclosed a living faith and for this reason he was raised many times as the man of the hour. And as a leader, he knew how to share responsibility with others.[9]

The day following Br. Ephrem's death, Br. Francis Englert, assistant provincial of the Midwest Province, notified the province membership in the name of the provincial, Br. Charles Krupp, absent at the time, reflecting: *Our entire Congregation was shaped in a large measure by the vision of Holy Cross which Brother Ephrem helped to bring into being in the midyears of the century. For the Brothers he has been called our second founder. To Brother Ephrem we owe a sharpened sense of our vocation in the Congregation and in the Church.*

All of us have our own memories of him. We will certainly miss Brother Ephrem the man. He never lost that Irish accent and wit which he brought to the United States in 1907.[10]

Fr. Theodore M. Hesburgh, president of the University of Notre Dame, was also away at the time of Br. Ephrem's death, but immediately upon his return from abroad wrote Br. Charles Krupp, *I did want to send you and all of the Brothers my deepest sympathy, since he was such a great leader of the Brothers over so many years since the separation of the Provinces. I had much fun fencing with him at many of our General Chapters and always admired his firmness of purpose and quiet Irish humor underneath the seeming asperity of his judgments at times. He was a model to all of us and I wanted you to know that I am offering Mass for the repose of his good soul, with a prayer that many more like him may join us.*[11]

HOMILY OF BR. ELMO BRANSBY

In a homily at the funeral service at Valatie on August 26, Br. Elmo Bransby, assistant general, traced the impact of Br. Ephrem on the community and quoted some of Br. Ephrem's own words spoken at his fiftieth anniversary of profession nearly twenty years earlier:

"The wise magistrate will be strict with his people, and the government of a prudent man will be well regulated. . . . The government of the earth is in the hands of the Lord; He sets the right man over it at the right time." (Sirach 10:1, 4–5)

Because the government of the earth, including life and death, is in the hands of the Lord, we can today gather in faith to bury the man whom that Lord had set over a portion of the earth at the right time and place. In faith and hope, we can also pray that the government of Brother Ephrem will be judged as both prudent and well regulated.

The psalmist says: "We have spent our years like a sigh. Seventy is the sum of our years, or eighty, if we are strong; and most of them are fruitless toil, for they pass quickly and we drift away." Any person who has spent such a sum of years surely must have gained at least a glimpse of the meaning of life, provided that person has been open to growth and has been brightly aware of the joyful heartbeat as well as the misfortunes of life. In facing these, every person is given the opportunity to grow. And at death, such a person leaves behind an image, noble or ignoble, which is indestructible in its consequences. The quiet touch of enthusiasm which comes from a person searching to become a vibrant Christian can be far-reaching in its influence. To do good where one is, and to do it uniquely and with his special gifts, is the lot provided every man: as it was given Christ who left no person untouched by his presence.

In his own inimitable way, Brother Ephrem caught the imagination of our growing community with his optimism, with his love of life, with his courage, with his belief in the work of the Lord, but most of all, with his deep sense of personal involvement. Few in Holy Cross knew Brother Ephrem well, but those who took to him their personal problems experienced kindness, deep understanding, and an unexpected gentleness. On the other hand, we know also that he could be objective, apparently heedless of the feelings of others, stubborn in a way, because when it came to getting things done or wanting to be understood, when it came to principles he so much believed in, he could be unswerving and dauntless.

In Brother Ephrem the Congregation saw a strong leader, who served Holy Cross with a clarity of vision and fidelity, a man of intrepid courage and strength of purpose. Being an extremely human person himself, Brother Ephrem knew men through that special gift of insight which comes only from living and working with others. He had a sense of humor and a depth of understanding that viewed both limitations and possibilities in a perspective that only a zealous and loving man possesses. His spirituality, which manifested firm religious conviction, a love of Holy Cross, and knowledge of the gospels, was always reflected in his concern and in his decisions, especially as an administrator. He wanted to be honest and just, because the Lord as well as reason demanded it.

Words spoken by Brother Ephrem himself on the occasion of his Golden Jubilee best describe him:

"Today I heard many wonderful things said about me. . . . I am grateful to God for many things, above all my baptism, my vocation to Holy Cross, my years in Holy Cross, and for your presence to help me celebrate this day. . . .

"My only thought in all these years was—and is—to do God's will. My only hope is that I can continue in and finally die in Holy Cross: this is my greatest ambition in life. . . .

"I am convinced that if we are going to be punished for bad example, then we are entitled to reward for good we may have done, and which may not be productive for many, many generations. . . . If in life we get no reward, no adulation, and appear a failure in the eyes of others, so be it. If I work for myself, I have no reward. If you in your words have simply praised me today, your words have been wasted. In my conscience, I know my weaknesses: above all, my pride. I wish I could get rid of my faults, but it's not easy. If you in your charity accept them and make the most of them, the Lord bless you. In my life I have honestly tried not to be partial, and I have tried to follow the advice given me years ago by old Brother Evaristus, who said to me: 'In dealing with people, don't look for a pound of flesh. Don't kill a fellow if he makes a mistake, go easy with him. He may have something yet to give to God. Go slow; be tolerant. Be patient with the fellow who has problems. But hit hard the fellow who is proud, opinionated *and thinks he is somebody. These are the dangerous people in the community. And you can have trouble with the proud.'*

"*I think we get to heaven because of our simplicity and humility, not because of brains, talents, scholarship, but because of humility; this is the lesson we got from the Lord himself, who forgives our faults if we are humble in heart.*

"*How happy I am that God let me live these years in Holy Cross. They have been happy years. Yes, there were trials, worries, troubles, but I wouldn't exchange these years for anything. I love Holy Cross. It is all my love . . . and Holy Cross will be loved only if Holy Cross loves God.*"

These words of Brother Ephrem speak for themselves.

Let us then give thanks to God for Brother's leadership. Although his shortcomings were well known to many of us, none of them were less well known to him, and they were for him, I personally feel, a great cross and humiliation. And despite these faults, he was a religious endowed with wisdom which springs from a living faith.

Years ago, the religious of Holy Cross used to say this prayer as part of night prayer: "O Jesus, who has said, 'Suffer the little children to come to me,' deign to bless my vocation, to assist me in my work and increase within me the spirit of charity and humility, in order that nothing may drag me away from your service; and I may be among the number of those to whom you have promised salvation."

So may it be, Lord, for Brother Ephrem . . . and for all of us![12]

LATER ENCOMIUMS

Some years later Br. Elmo was asked, as a former provincial, to reflect briefly on the impact of Br. Ephrem on the congregation. He wrote in a theme similar to that of his homily: *Those of us who knew him well are much aware of his generous and almost stubborn determination to do what he considered his responsibility as provincial. He was direct, strong in his convictions, a planner, and very objective and unwavering in his relationship with others— with individuals as well as with groups, including his council; yet, no one was better able to show understanding and compassion, especially to the wayward, the misunderstood, and the burdened. This side of him was like the best of wines, hidden in the cellar and saved for those special occasions.*

We, the religious of Holy Cross, certainly owe Ephrem a great debt of gratitude, despite the "rough times" he may have engendered. He saw obedience and fulfillment of responsibility and accountability as the best expression of God's will—and nothing or no one would ever attempt or could sway him to think otherwise. He placed a high premium on reasoning and intelligence—and not on blind obedience. His oft-quoted response to one's statement: "What do you mean," etc., was a trademark of his. It was either a challenge for one to be more explicit with his remarks, or else the pause in one's reply gave him more time to re-think quietly what he wanted to say.

At times, he was a puzzle, quite enigmatic, difficult to understand and frustrating to relate to. At other times, he was humorous and just good to be around. I know I had my difficult times with him, but now I see him somewhat as a catalyzer, trying to draw out the best in one, despite the anguish involved.

I know that much with me is there because I knew, lived and worked with Ephrem when I was assistant provincial. He was truly a father, a blend of tough love and compassion . . . and above all strong in honesty. And although his philosophy and approach to religious government would be fruitless in today's circumstances, nonetheless, his life, his efforts, and his leadership brought us the means, strength and identity to cooperate better with the right man the Lord chooses in many aspects of our life. That surely is a challenge to our faith—but then faith wilts if it is not challenged.[13]

Another successor in the office of provincial of the Eastern Province, Br. Renatus Foldenauer, had this to say about Br. Ephrem: *In Brother Ephrem the Congregation of Holy Cross experienced a strong leader, a religious who served Holy Cross with a clarity of vision and strength of purpose. His courage to deal with problems as an administrator, and his loyalty to the Society of Brothers strike me as being outstanding. Though he often portrayed a stern external appearance of being impersonal, I found that in relating a problem or difficulty to him he would respond with genuine kindness, deep understanding, and with a certain gentleness. And, he had a sense of humor and depth of understanding that viewed both limitations and possibilities in a perspective that only a zealous and loving man possesses.*

In my own provincial visits to Brother Ephrem during his last days in the infirmary at Notre Dame, he would always advise me to "spend my time and energy" serving the province and to give that an absolute priority. He always appeared interested in the growth and development of the membership, and particularly interested in our efforts at furthering and encouraging vocations to Holy Cross. Indeed, Brother Ephrem manifested a firm religious conviction, a love of Holy Cross, a knowledge of the gospel, which was always respected in his decisions as an administrator in the Congregation. He wanted to be honest and just because the Lord and reason demanded it.[14]

MORE OF BR. EPHREM'S OWN WORDS

As he prepared to leave office as provincial of the Eastern Province, completing six years in that position and sixteen years overall as a provincial, Br. Ephrem wrote to the membership on June 8, 1962: *My uppermost thought is one of sincere gratitude to God for granting me the necessary health to carry out the obedience given me; and my deepest feeling is one of relief that my term of office is ending.*

The last six years have not been without trials and burdens, but they have also been years of consolations and gratitude. I owe heartfelt thanks to many in the Congregation, but to none more than our Very Reverend Superior General for his great kindness to me, his confidence in the Province, his encouragement and approval of the many projects undertaken.

He mentioned in several paragraphs the expansion which was made possible by the sacrifice and dedication of the province members under the guidance and blessing of God.

. . . Though material progress is necessary it is but a means to an end—the salvation of our members and the spread of Christ's kingdom by our apostolate of education. The material things are but of time; their proper use is to purchase eternal values. A thorough intellectual and religious formation of our members is the best guarantee that we are fulfilling the purpose for which we were founded by Fathers Dujarié and Moreau.

Prayer, work and sacrifice on the part of each member will keep our Community strong, virile, efficient and holy.[15]

Prayer, work and sacrifice might well be a trio of equally valued words in Br. Ephrem's lexicon of success. Nothing in his life, early or late, ever belied the validity of the concepts suggested by persevering prayer, tireless work, and endless sacrifice. He was a master of each and an exemplar of all.

As Br. Elmo Bransby noted in his reflection on Br. Ephrem, perhaps it is true that the precise philosophy and methodology he employed to lead and to achieve in the forties, fifties, and sixties would simply not be workable, even tolerated, in today's world. That is irrelevant. Were Br. Ephrem among his confreres in Holy Cross today, were he at the prime of his physical and mental powers, were he entrusted once more with a position of authority and responsibility in the congregation, his native acumen would without doubt suggest to him those adaptations appropriate to the accomplishment of today's goals, and circumstances would merely challenge him, as they always did, to rise to the occasion once more.

Br. Ephrem possessed the ability to work through and beyond a variety of personal shortcomings and limitations in collaboration with other gifted and dedicated Holy Cross religious and to do so resolutely seeking the achievement of clearly defined goals which assured the growth, development, and realization of the mission of the Congregation of Holy Cross, especially the brothers. His accomplishments, his example, his leadership are elements of encouragement to his sons in religion and his coworkers in the ongoing apostolates of Holy Cross today. The congregation and its ministries are in no small way indebted to his guidance and perseverance, and the qualities he exemplified serve as stimulants to the continuing efforts of Holy Cross to engage in relevant ministry in the Church and to make available to everyone, most visibly through their institutions, the still very tangible results of his thoroughly dedicated life.

V

Reminiscences of
Brother Ephrem

INTRODUCTION

Conflicting factors exert their unavoidable impact on the writing of a biography of Br. Ephrem O'Dwyer. His life was lived concurrently with the lives of many religious still active in Holy Cross today. The privacy and sensitivities of these men must be observed, and the normal passage of time should be respected in allowing an opportunity for judicious retrospection in order to sift for accuracy some assertions about him. However, profit can be gained from peer reflection on the former provincial: some who knew him personally, who perhaps lived with him or worked with him, who were the beneficiaries of his leadership skills, are able today to recount his influence in their lives and on Holy Cross and to share their memories advantageously with others.

As he aged in retirement, Br. Ephrem stubbornly resisted every effort on the part of many, including superiors, to coax him into writing his personal memoirs, recording on tape reminiscences of his life in the congregation, or preserving via any mode of communication his interpretations of people and events. These, he argued, were likely to be colored by his own possibly biased perceptions. He conversed informally with visitors about the past but was always on his guard and never overstepped the bounds of propriety in discussing the involvement of individuals in the unfolding of events. Apart from two brief written reflections mentioned in an earlier chapter concerning the circumstances leading to the separation of the single U.S. Province into two homogeneous groups in 1946, almost nothing is extant of Br. Ephrem's own interpretation of this or other significant events.

So, the need for prudence acknowledged, the exigencies of historical fact and recent community development permit a freer approach today to Br. Ephrem's own life than he would have allowed only fifteen or twenty years ago and gives us some perspective in which to appraise his impact on events and circumstances.

Of the total current membership of the congregation, perhaps three or four hundred men personally remember Br. Ephrem. Most of these would only recently have entered the congregation as Br. Ephrem completed his terms as provincial at Notre Dame or in the East, and would likely not have had more than a cursory and quite formal, even impersonal, superior-subject relationship with him. We must also bear in mind that, after the 1946 separation of the brothers' and priests' provinces, Br. Ephrem's direct association with the clerics in Holy Cross was by the nature of the new structuring far more limited than it had been before, so very few priests remain who knew him well.

Some fifty Holy Cross religious among these "elders" were invited to participate in a personal interview or to record reminiscences on audiotape or in writing. A few felt that while they had known Br. Ephrem, their direct contact with him had been so restricted as to produce practically nothing memorable. But nearly forty men were subsequently interviewed or submitted tapes or letters with anecdotal recollections of the former provincial.

In these personal reminiscences certain aspects of Br. Ephrem stand out in greater relief than they could from his correspondence or other sources of documentation. It is always possible, of course, that some unintentional distortion of fact has intruded, assisted by the passage of time, to skew the accuracy of some of the less consequential aspects of an anecdote and perhaps to elevate it into the realm of legend. For example, four individuals recalled a particular joke Br. Ephrem used to tell about aging. No two accounts were exactly the same, yet the essence of the content was there. What is important is that absolutely nothing surfaces in the reminiscences in so contradictory a way as to make one wonder if these men could possibly be referring to the same individual. On the contrary, the reminiscences confirm documentable sources and many long-standing assumptions about Br. Ephrem, or they emphasize personal characteristics, habits or methods he employed. The man is portrayed as he truly was experienced; he has not been refashioned through fantasy. The years since his death have not been numerous enough to have honed his craggy character into an airbrushed, preternatural myth. His contemporaries categorically insist on his humanity, whatever his prowess, and rightly so.

What follows, then, are special appendixes dedicated to these reminiscences. Written recollections have been slightly edited only if necessary, and those acquired by tape or by personal interviews have been minimally refashioned, honoring the original intent and rhetoric, with an eye to accuracy, continuity, coherence, and a degree of entertaining nostalgia for those who knew Br. Ephrem, or of revealing honesty for those who did not.

Written Reminiscences

BR. REMIGIUS BULLINGER (MIDWEST PROVINCE)

What can I say about Ephrem? Enabler, curmudgeon, irritating rascal, far-sighted, intensely interested in the brothers' affairs, one to be often talked about, an enigma.

I first knew Ephrem about sixty years ago, I a scholastic at Dujarie, he a math teacher at the Little Sem or on the provincial council; I living on the second floor as housekeeper, he living on the second floor in the end room, south end with two windows just over the south entrance that brothers used to come and go (Ephrem, I'm sure, knowing every voice and nuance).

. . . Now I was busy as the proverbial one-armed paperhanger doing my school work, so I paid little attention to Ephrem, who seemed to be hunched over his desk, pipe in mouth, working out a problem quietly.

His room was austere. His attire, austere. I would venture to state that all his life, or all of his life that I knew of, he could easily fit all his belongings in two suitcases packed loosely.

He was not interested in things. He was interested in ideas, projects, case studies, the brothers' future.

He was always asking questions—the original twenty-question man. In fact, he made me nervous by his questions. As he asked them, I got the feeling he already knew the answers!

. . . Actually, I did not like him. There, now, I've said it. Not my type of guy, it seems. Frankly, I don't know anyone who liked him that much. Easily, that is. Did he have any close friends then? No, none that I can recall. Perhaps people are turned off by one who can see through them. I knew all the time, however, that he was someone special, like him or not.

. . . Skip now to the year we became a separate brothers' province. There is some background info necessary for this horrendous hassle. For eleven years I taught a course at the summer school sessions at Notre Dame, a required Indiana course for future English teachers. . . . For seven or eight of these eleven years I was superior at the brothers' summer residence, usually Walsh Hall. . . . Chapter over, the brothers were declared a province. All is calm, all is bright except when I returned for summer school and was superior again, I walked into Walsh Hall to find no sheets, no pillow cases, no towels— no linen. The Hungarian housekeeper, a darling lady, told me Father had told her that since we were no longer members of the Indiana Province we got no free linens. So I went over to tell Ephrem. He burst into flame in indignation, took me across the hall to Chrysostom Schaefer, a meek, brilliant, quiet soul, and raised holy hell with him, the econome not doing his duty. Then Ephrem phoned a linen company and ordered tons of stuff, just like that. The brothers arrived, and all had linens galore. It was an amazing feat. (I understand that Ephrem apologized to Chris, humbly.)

. . . But back to summer school, Ephrem and I do battle over what to post [on the bulletin board of Walsh Hall]. Each year Ephrem would call me over and read to me summer directives, ten or fifteen, in his terse style. I would listen listlessly, knowing a flare-up was about to take place. When Ephrem finished reading the items, he would ask me what I thought. I'd say boldly, well, I'll put them up but no one will pay any attention to them. He would go into his flare-up act with why? why? why? I'd reply with a reason for each item. For instance, one directive was that the superior was to give out three or four packs of cigarettes a week to anyone who smoked. I told him this was sheer hell for me, since they kept knocking on my door day and night. Hence, I would give out cartons only. And on and on, down the list. Each item I'd change. He was determined; so was I. Then Ephrem would snatch the paper, tell me to sit down while he re-did the whole page my way. And this scenario was repeated each year.

. . . But Ephrem had a humorous side too. In 1958 Br. Stanislaus Rusilowski died suddenly while on vacation in Grand Rapids, his home town. Now I was at Indianapolis early that year since Pedro, the principal, was vacationing. I got a special delivery from Donatus informing me I was appointed principal at Monroe to replace Stan, that I was to come to Notre Dame for the funeral and instructions. At the cemetery after services, at the end, someone poked me in the back. It was Ephrem, who said, after his he-he chuckle, *Well, now you'll find out you're damned if you do and damned if you don't, he-he!*

. . . I don't wish to be judgmental. Ephrem was hard to take. Stern, fiercely picky, a prickly burr at times. He had been superior or on that level as long as I knew him. He knew the Brotherhood through and through; hence, the perfect one to be made provincial. His personality mellowed with age and retirement. But I would say he always had what I call the Dr. Fell syndrome:

> I do not like thee, Doctor Fell,
> For what reason I cannot tell;
> But this I know, and know quite well:
> I do not like thee, Doctor Fell.

. . . Ephrem was the necessary man-of-the-hour, in the right place at the right time, always. This I know for sure. God bless his cantankerous soul, the Irishman who led us, sustained us these many years.

BR. JOHN FEDEROWICZ (MIDWEST PROVINCE)

Canasta was a card game that was Ephrem's favored form of recreation. At times he would bend the rules—in his favor. Most of the players were fearful of challenging the provincial on what looked like cheating. Not Br. Eli Pelchat. As postmaster of Notre Dame, Indiana, Eli was unquestionably the highest salaried brother in the United States. Eli objected to Ephrem's plays, and Ephrem challenged Eli's objections. Eli held fast. *When you are in your office you are provincial, and you can play that game any way you want. Down here in the Community House rec room, you are just another Canasta player, and we are going to play according to Hoyle.* Or words to that effect. And the players gave him several days to ponder this. For the next few days they did not show up in the rec room for a game of Canasta. In time, the nightly games resumed—all according to Hoyle.

BR. EVAN SCHMID (MIDWEST PROVINCE)

The only recollection I have is how upset Br. Ephrem was to find a double-page spread photo of Tudor House [Gilmour Academy] in the Association of St. Joseph magazine, with a caption mentioning something about the brothers' buying "a million dollar estate"—or something on that order. I was the editor of that magazine at the time (circa 1945–46) when Theophane was in the process of founding Gilmour.

. . . I had few personal dealings with Ephrem except for the brief incident mentioned above. Certainly I liked his wit, his "snappy" way of talking, his bustling manner, his quick and efficient handling of things, his success in putting the Brothers of Holy Cross on the map as an autonomous province, and swift founding of a number of schools; his stewardship of province funds. I still think there was always a hint of humor behind some of his brusque remarks, and a smile hiding behind what may have sometimes been a stern-looking face. His pipe smoking was a comfortable touch!

BR. EDWARD SNIATECKI (EASTERN PROVINCE)

When September 1923 came, I found that I was to attend one class at the University with Brother Ephrem—metaphysics—taught by a Belgian, Professor Mercier. The class was a trying experience, mainly because of the teacher's meagre knowledge of English and his impatience with the American boy. But at Dujarie Hall I attended a class in accounting taught by Br. Ephrem.

And if that was not enough for Br. Ephrem, he took on the enormous task of determining the scholastic standings of the brothers teaching and of the scholastics at Dujarie. Fortunately, Fr. Joseph Burke, the director of studies at the University, gave Br. Ephrem access to the records of the brothers and with the help of several scholastics, he was able to discover how near these brothers were to their degrees, and what might be needed to be eligible for graduation. As a result, sixteen brothers received degrees in 1924 and another twenty in the summer of 1925.

Up to this time teachers could qualify for certification by an annual test in their particular fields. But Br. Ephrem could see the system was crude and cumbersome, and would soon be eliminated because several states were already requiring degrees for certification. So now it was an entirely new view of the teaching profession—and the Brothers became much more interested in their fields and more accomplished academically and professionally.

. . . For quite some time Fr. James Donahue, the superior general, was urging Bishop Noll of Fort Wayne to open a high school in South Bend. During the summer of 1934, the bishop approved the idea and arranged to have the school housed in the vacant second floor of the large St. Matthew's parish school on Miami Street in South Bend. The second floor was vacant but completely unfinished—the walls were unplastered, no ceilings, and the floors just bare concrete. In July 1934 Br. Ephrem contacted me to inform me that I was selected as principal of the new school, beginning with just a freshman class. Br. Herman Weltin and I were to be the faculty. When Br. Herman and I visited the building, we were crushed. We were expected to begin classes early in September and pastors were to be notified, grade school graduates were to be notified and prepared for registration, and ready for the opening of school in the second week of September. On registration day, sixteen boys from South Bend and Mishawaka came. Since our only furniture available was card tables and folding chairs, we feared that most of the sixteen boys might not return on the following Monday for class. It is remarkable that not only did they return, but they also remained for the entire four years and graduated in 1938. We began acquiring furniture and supplies, mainly from the warehouse at the University.

. . . The chronicles of St. Joseph Juniorate in Valatie, New York, show that Br. Ephrem, as provincial councilor, visited on March 30, 1936, to learn what might be done to provide better and more ample housing for the candidates for the Brothers of Holy Cross from the East. He returned on September 16 with architectural plans for the two-story building. With a contractor in Kinderhook and the assistance of a few brothers, a new building was constructed.

. . . In 1945, as a member of the general chapter in Washington, D.C., Br. Ephrem was on the committee for the division of assets. Several times in later years he told me how disappointed and hurt he was with the meagre share the brothers received. It was at that chapter too that he was elected the first brother provincial—his area was the entire United States.

In the summer of 1946 the brothers held their first all-brothers provincial chapter and it was held at Dujarie Hall. It was a beautiful experience to see the brothers in a position to control their own affairs. Br. Ephrem made us feel proud of ourselves, and we were pleased to see him there as our leader. I shall always remember a statement he made as things were progressing during the chapter: *Now, don't pass any legislation that you might later find difficult to live with, because I shall be obliged to see that it is observed.* Only genuinely needed decrees or recommendations passed.

During the school year which followed (1946–47), Br. Ephrem visited all the bishops in whose dioceses we served, to present our needs—freedom of operation and necessary financial remuneration—and his assurance of good service in our ministry.

He always managed well with bishops, especially in Cleveland and Providence, Rhode Island. In 1946 when he visited us and Msgr. Geoffrey O'Connell, the superintendent of schools in Biloxi, Br. Ephrem was very strong in his description of the dreams the Monsignor had about future possibilities, dreams rather than the more practical things that could be done with what was presently available. On the day of the visit, the Monsignor told me that he would not have accepted such language except from another Irishman. Br. Ephrem was an exceptionally adept judge of people.

. . . I always found him wonderful in accepting us when we had difficulty, supportive of superiors, a genius in financial matters, very kind to the sick or disabled, challenging to intellectuals, a fine sense of humor, dedicated in his own spiritual life and seeking complete dedication of all religious.

BR. PAUL SCHWOYER (EASTERN PROVINCE)

The parlor at Flushing was a most convenient place for putting things on the table after climbing five stories and while making a visit to the Blessed Sacrament or checking the mail room. The trouble was that this table seems to have been a special piece of furniture for meetings. It had importance, since the provincial and his assistants had moved in on the top floor of Flushing.

On one particular morning I arranged a pile of old newspapers on the table so I could take them with me when I went down to the band room. Old newspapers were very important since they blotted up the saliva and valve oil from the instruments. I went to my room to get my textbooks and test papers and I had more than an armful, but figured that I would be able to stack most of them on top of the newspapers. When I returned to the parlor to pick up the papers, I found "his majesty" standing there with a glare in his eyes. I expected trouble, but not the lashing that was heard all over the top floor. I knew it was useless to make any kind of excuse or explanation, so I just took it on the chin. It surely upset my day. I was glad to get away. I really expected to be called into Br. Ephrem's office later in the day and was surprised that nothing happened. A week later I received a phone call telling me that my Aunt Mary had passed away. They wondered if I could get home for the funeral. At that time one couldn't get permission to attend funerals unless they were of the immediate family. When I spoke to my superior, he suggested that I ask the provincial. After the lashing I had gotten a week earlier, I felt it was useless even to ask. Imagine my surprise when he gave me permission not only for the two days I asked for, but he even suggested I take a whole week. You can draw your own conclusions.

BR. FRANCIS JOHNSON (EASTERN PROVINCE)

Your recent letter brought to focus "our man of the times" who gave the brothers an image to be recognized and respected in Holy Cross. As we know, all of us are better people for being blessed with such a capable leader in our early encounters.

I first came to meet him on Reception Day (February 1, 1949), and his message to the class remained with me. *I wish to congratulate you all on this joyous occasion along the line. If you've come to give, you'll be a long time, but if you've come to receive, you might just as well leave with your family visitors.*

Ephrem never kept bad feelings toward a member, as one would know he was forgiven and back in good graces with the top man when he'd say, *How you doin' on a new day?*

Back in August of 1970 he attended my Dad's wake and returned in the morning to be with the family at the funeral mass.

The enclosed is a communique I cherish from him in his golden years:

Dear Happy Comedian:
It is still nice to know that you are still full of pep and life and are not weigned down with any burdens.

Thanks for the Venerable St. Patrick Day greetings. It is nice to be remembered.

All things are going well here [Dujarie House]. *And thank God I am feeling in very good health. I am even "chesty" though not in Chester. Had big doings here lately when President Ford visited. Spring is at hand, and I am planning on more outdoor life now. But in or out I manage to keep busy and get a few extra prayers in.*

Say hello to anyone who remembers me.

One who appreciates you,
/s/ Br. Ephrem

BR. EDMUND HUNT (SOUTH-WEST PROVINCE)

Br. Ephrem was authoritarian, at times tyrannical, even with his councilors or chapter delegates. I recall at one chapter: *Stop talking and sit down* and *Go ahead and pass it; I'll just have the superior general eliminate it* (which he did twice for me). When I got to write the statutes on authority, I made sure there was some due process in how to reverse a provincial chapter.

Coming to Texas, he claimed I was a one-man show and he would show me how to run a faculty meeting. Simon and Majella made some opening remarks; he cut them off with *I want you all to know that I am in charge here.* Not a single brother said anything thereafter; it was a half speech, hardly a faculty meeting.

Br. Ephrem put up some rather horrible buildings at Sherman Oaks, New Orleans, St. Ed's. . . . Even the Brothers Center at Notre Dame (except the chapel and the provincial house) was a mess of small rooms for the hoi polloi. . . . Somehow on many buildings he got the wrong direction, next to noisy streets, too much glass for hot weather.

He made a blooper on tuition for brothers at Notre Dame, an amount cancelled if not used. He tried six years later to have the chapter change this, but Fr. John Cavanaugh stonewalled him to the end. He was amazed to be given St. Ed's as part of the brothers' settlement. He hated the place. He first told the state that he wanted it changed to a junior college; I changed it right back, and he never reproached me. He wanted it to be a scholasticate only.

. . . Ephrem was a work of art in general chapters where brothers' concerns came up (though he was beaten down in the division of goods when brother-priest provinces were formed). At our first chapter in Rome (at the Canadian College) there was a solemn high mass, and when the priests would genuflect their calves would stick out of knee-length boy scout pants. Ephrem bent to my ear and said: *I think the first step in the reform of the clergy is to put pants on them.*

. . . I've often thought how amazing it was for one brother and two councilors in their Columba Hall quarters to handle so many in formation, multiply schools, fill obediences and at small expense, whereas in recent years we have tripled administrations for far fewer brothers.

BR. GERALD COMEAU (SOUTH-WEST PROVINCE)

Br. Ephrem always liked brothers who were not afraid of him because he felt that this type of religious, the type who spoke up and argued, augured well for the future of the brothers.

Every so often Br. Ephrem would come to New Orleans "to get away from it all." He had a burdensome position as the first provincial. He had to set policies, to establish the brothers as masters of their own destiny.

He had pleasant and unpleasant memories of former general chapters, but felt no possible use could be served by resurrecting the old quarrels between the two societies. As far as I know he refused to do so.

He was, of course, very impatient and curt at times. But I never felt it was personal. He did have health problems. I found him very caring for the older members. I remember giving one of the older brothers some extra summer money. Ephrem brought it up and asked why. I told him why. I believe he really did it to let me know that he knew what was going on and really felt good that the brother received what he needed.

BR. KERIC DEVER (SOUTH-WEST PROVINCE)

My first remote contact with Ephrem was as a young brother at Dujarie Hall, Notre Dame. My roommate, Br. Nelson McMahon, and I came back from the scholastics' summer camp at Bankson Lake in Michigan to find a couple of suitcases and some books in our room, on the top floor of the old Dujarie Scholasticate. So, moving back in and scattering our own personal effects in place, we gathered the intruder's goods and put them out into the corridor. Later, Br. Dominic Elder, the superior, came by and loudly protested: *That's Br. Ephrem's stuff!* Our reaction was just, *So, who's he? This is where we live!* He had come in during the summer on province business—probably the brothers' provincial chapter which was held that year at Dujarie Hall (1946). I can't recall how the problem was solved, but I do recall being impressed by Br. Dominic's reaction: nobody messes with Ephrem!

At Notre Dame during a summer session, Brs. Charles Andersen and Francis Assisi Davis were walking on the campus having one of their typical fun-and-games recreation breaks. In their perambulations they encountered Br. Ephrem, who was accompanied by a visiting religious. When the four met, Ephrem said to the visitor: *These two illustrate that our community is directed by a mighty providence!*

BR. ROMARD BARTHEL (SOUTH-WEST PROVINCE)

In all my life in Holy Cross there was no doubt among the members that Br. Ephrem was the leader of the Brothers of Holy Cross in the United States. He had some trusted co-workers such as Br. William Mang, Br. John Baptist, Br. Donatus, but when Br. Ephrem spoke, that was the final word. He dealt as equals with bishops and civic leaders. His leadership style was imperious, but if you could survive his attack and rigid scrutiny, he would consider what you suggested. He seemed to respect those who respectfully stood up to him, and did not hold grudges.

. . . There was a holy fear of Ephrem throughout the province, but it was more because of reputation than personal experience. I personally shared the fear, but he was always kind to me—and I think the same would be said by most province members. Once in a while he was publicly obstreperous—and I think he did it deliberately to keep up his reputation. Once when he visited St. Edward's University he attended a faculty meeting which Br. Simon Scribner, as dean, was leading. Br. Ephrem took over the meeting and told Br. Simon in no uncertain terms that he didn't need any help.

To get back to the earlier days—when we were scholastics at Dujarie Hall, Notre Dame, Ephrem would occasionally teach us a class in educational administration during the summer. I don't remember much detail. I have the impression that the class was practical, included some attempts at humor, and was rather boring at 1:15 on a summer afternoon. He was noted for his pause-filling expressions: "you know" and "on the plan."

He insisted on economy, personal and institutional. Without this frugality we would probably never have made it through the early days when money was scarce. Budgets were tightly controlled. Vacation travel had to be approved in detail. The institutional buildings he approved and built were usually the most economical possible, ordinarily square boxes—but they were functional.

He had great visions for the future of the Brothers of Holy Cross, and the institutions they operated were major parts of that vision. He was a strong promoter of institutional apostolates.

While provincial his expectations of St. Edward's University were not high. Br. Edmund Hunt often tugged at him to get him to invest even small amounts of money in the university. That's why the early buildings were largely war-surplus barracks. Br. Ephrem saw St. Edward's as a teacher's college for brothers; he didn't seem to see it as a university in its own right.

His health seemed generally good, but toward the end of his time as provincial he had serious asthma attacks when he came to Austin, and he spent a considerable amount of time in the hospital. Toward the end of his life irregularities in his heart beat required the installation of a pacemaker.

Br. Ephrem could be the life (and center) of a party. He liked a nip of Irish whiskey occasionally, and was a great storyteller at a party. Yet, he did not talk about community affairs. In later years he was often urged to write his memoirs, but he always refused.

Br. Ephrem seemed like an iron man, never wearing out. . . . But finally heart difficulties forced him into Dujarie House. I used to visit him frequently there (I was S-W provincial at the time). He seemed at peace, and gentle. He always wanted to know what was going on in the provinces, but he didn't make any effort to interfere. He still loved to talk; he tried to keep busy and he learned to knit to keep his hands occupied. Once when I visited him he gave me a scarf that he had knitted. I still use it.

BR. JACOB EPPLEY (SOUTH-WEST PROVINCE)

On one occasion when a brother died and it was the next move of the superior of the house [Community House at Notre Dame] to examine his trunk, I found two bottles of scotch whiskey. I thought it was right to involve the provincial. So I asked Brother, *What shall we do with the whiskey?* Br. Ephrem replied: *There's only one thing to do: you take one bottle and I'll take the other.*

BR. FRANCIS BORGIA WOEHLER (SOUTH-WEST PROVINCE)

Sometime during my freshman school year (1922–1923), I was a student in Br. Ephrem's general science class [at the Catholic boys' high school, Evansville, Indiana]. On one occasion he had a student come to the front of the class to assist him with an experiment. Through some mishap the student's glasses were broken. As he was returning to his seat I whispered to him, asking if Br. Ephrem would pay to have them repaired. Before he had a chance to answer me, Br. Ephrem called out my name and asked me if I had been talking. At once I answered *No.* Then he called me up to the front of the class. After giving a short bit of advice on lying, he slapped me on both cheeks and sent me back to my seat. That was the first and last time that I had any unpleasant encounter with Br. Ephrem during the two years he was principal in Evansville.

The next time I remember any personal dealings with Br. Ephrem was when I was superior at Sacred Heart College in Watertown, Wisconsin. In the fall of 1951 all superiors of Holy Cross in the U.S. met at the University of Notre Dame to discuss the changes in the contents and format of the Constitutions of the Congregation of Holy Cross. While I was there, I decided to see Br. Ephrem, the first provincial of the Brothers of Holy Cross, concerning the need for one more teacher at Watertown. Previous to this meeting, Br. Charles Andersen had counselled me that the best way to get anything from Br. Ephrem was to fight for it. I took his advice literally. Finally the provincial, who had not been counselled by Br. Charles, thought differently. He literally ejected me by the back of my neck from his office at the Community House. I don't remember whether I wet my pants or not at the time, but I'm sure I felt like it.

Two days later when I was getting ready to return to Watertown I didn't want this incident to hang over my head every time I received a letter from the provincial office, so I decided to see Br. Ephrem before I left. He was all smiles, telling me that he and his council had decided to send another teacher to Watertown.

Later in discussing these two opposite incidents at Notre Dame with Br. John Baptist Titzer, I was told that this happened quite often. On my first visit to Br. Ephrem, I had been the first to see him in his office that morning, whereas on my second visit I had seen him later in the day. During this period Br. Bonaventure Foley and Br. John Baptist were assistants on the provincial council. They had a gentleman's agreement to alternate being the first one to see the provincial each morning. In this way, both would be able to share the brunt of any like happenings.

BR. SIMON SCRIBNER (SOUTH-WEST PROVINCE)

The man was, and remained, not so much a mystery, not so much an enigma, as simply someone outside my normal calculations. Others may have been quite comfortable with him, but I never really was.

. . . One of my recollections finds me as chairman of a meeting of some sort. Typically, I prepared for the meeting with a public agenda, speakers, topics, etc. I opened the meeting, was about to call on our first speaker, when I heard the voice of Br. Ephrem: *Just one minute. Who is in charge of this meeting?* Not one to argue such a minor point, I said, *You are*, and, red-faced, sat down. The meeting proceeded with no assistance from me.

. . . We—St. Edward's University, that is—were sort of a white elephant. I concluded that if we could somehow or other prepare Brothers for high-school teaching, without becoming a full-fledged university, that is what we would do. I think Br. Ephrem was really in favor of secondary education, and would tolerate college education only if it did not interfere with our "mission to the secondary school." I think also that he had to make what could be called unpopular decisions because from one point of view he had to fortify his position as provincial. On the other hand, he was very much *for* the brothers' society and for their mission in Holy Cross. I have heard that he was not averse to "talking turkey" with bishops and archbishops when it came right down to the nitty-gritty.

BR. THEO FLYNN (SOUTH-WEST PROVINCE)

In 1934, when I answered the brothers' vocation ad in *Our Sunday Visitor*, I was working full time in a grocery store. After supper on the day I received the booklet written by Br. Ephrem, I sat down and read the entire booklet. I recall that when I finished the booklet, I thought, "This is what I am going to do." I began to make plans hoping that I might be going to Watertown within the next few months, but that was not to be.

. . . In 1935 Br. Ephrem became the vocation director. As I recall, the vocation director in those days handled everything by correspondence, and I began writing Br. Ephrem explaining my delay in responding to Holy Cross' invitation. A few times I set a date about six months in the future, but when that date arrived, I felt I still needed to stay at home to help a while longer. Br. Ephrem's letters were encouraging, his writing style was very clear and right to the point. I enjoyed his supportive letters and was inspired by them.

This went on for a couple of years, during which I had a few setbacks including a month's stay, sick with scarlet fever, in a hospital. I began to doubt a possible vocation, but finally things worked out and I went to Watertown in the summer of 1937. I have sometimes thought that in a certain sense I owe my vocation to Br. Ephrem, as when I finally went to Watertown I seemed more impelled by a desire not to disappoint him than by the idea of responding to a more religious and spiritual call.

. . . As I recall, the generalate was located in the major seminary building [in Washington, D.C.], and the members of the general council lived there when they gathered for meetings. One afternoon, after meeting all day, Br. Ephrem and another member decided to take an outside walk. Dressed in sweaters or jackets without a Roman collar, they were met at the front door by Fr. William Doheny, the local superior, who had a great devotion to the letter of the law. Despite their rank as general councilors, he sent them back to their rooms to get properly dressed. When I told this story to Br. Romard recently, he recalled that at Msgr. Doheny's funeral [1982 in Rome] someone had remarked that whenever he received a phone call from Msgr. Doheny he would become uneasy if he were not properly dressed!

[At Valatie] Br. Ephrem kept the conversation at the table lively and interesting, and we also played bridge occasionally in the evening. I recall going to his room one day and was pleased to see him reading one of Shakespeare's plays.

. . . I was a patient at the community infirmary, as I had a lung infection and needed almost constant bed rest. A few days before the 1952 chapter, Br. Ephrem also became a patient there with a bad case of asthma. One evening, I looked out the window to see Br. John Baptist helping Br. Ephrem into a car to go to a hospital. The asthma seemed serious, as Br. Ephrem had great difficulty in breathing and seemed very weak. As I recall, he was out of the hospital in a couple of weeks but did take the entire summer off and went away from his office to recuperate. After I was released from the infirmary I went to the Community House to spend several months of recuperation.

Frequently we played bridge at the community evening recreation, and I was often Br. Ephrem's partner. I wasn't as quick and sharp as he was, but he was very very patient with my slower playing and more mistakes than he would have made.

. . . I was always impressed by Br. Ephrem's letters, as they were always very clear, to the point with a simple, easy style. I also recall his friendliness and his kindness. I once heard someone quote Br. Ephrem to the effect that if he ever had a serious argument with anyone, an argument in which tempers may have flared, he always tried to get back to that person that day to have a friendly, if short, conversation.

He was certainly an excellent leader for the brothers in his time.

BR. FISHER IWASKO (SOUTH-WEST PROVINCE)

Br. Ephrem was high in my appreciation and respect. He came to Watertown while I was a postulant. Apparently he had something to do with recruitment at that time. That was in early 1937. He asked me, *What year were you born in?* I told him 1916. *Not so*, he said, *you were born in 1915*. Again, *What date were you born on?* I told him August 27th. *Not so*, he replied, *you were born on June 27th*. Then he asked me what town I was born in. I told him Superior, Wisconsin. *Not so*, he stated, *you were born in Cloquet, Minnesota*. I finally asked: *Br. Ephrem, am I a boy or a girl?* He often reminded me of this conversation. My birth certificate, by the way, was destroyed in a 1918 forest fire.

Br. Alfonso asked me to take Br. Ephrem to Waveland to see the new brothers' house just finished there. I sensed something right away. When we got there, Brother became very upset at the two small wrought iron railings that bordered the five or six steps. Without thinking, I said, *Brother, those were gifts*. Brother looked at the railings thoughtfully and then asked, *Who gave them?* I replied, *The community*. Well, he went into a rage for a few minutes, talking about waste. I felt awful. On the way home, he tapped my leg and said, *I have to admit, it's very nice.*

I remember Br. Ephrem as very fair, keeping to his rules and to the community rules. I know he was a battler for the brothers, and at meetings involving both priests and brothers, everyone listened to him.

I know he was principal and superior here [New Orleans] in the 20s and the first push towards modernizing this place came under his direction—the new steam plant, the tearing down of the ugly fence around the place, the urging on of a better sports program.

BR. RICARDO HELMANN (SOUTH-WEST PROVINCE)

I took a class (education) from Br. Ephrem at the old Dujarié Hall. Ephrem frequently, and I mean frequently, used the expression "on the plan," but he would at times change it to something like "on the situation."

He asked me to walk around the lake with him once, and he told me about the changes that would take place, the things he could talk about, in 1946, when we got our first provincial from the ranks of the brothers.

Before that, I was finishing up my B.A. work at Notre Dame and living in the then Community House, where Ephrem was also living. I had been unable earlier to attend a family reunion, as I was hospitalized because of tuberculosis. And now, since my one brother had gotten out of the service, my family wanted to have me present for the forthcoming family reunion. I was refused permission by Fr. Steiner [provincial], but he was, I think, really concerned about the cost to the community. However, in those days we still had personal accounts and my family could have taken care of the travel expense anyway; but Fr. Steiner did not voice any of that. I guess I just wanted to unload on Br. Ephrem about the thing, not expecting that he could do anything about it; but he did ask me if I wanted him to say anything to Steiner. Ephrem did, and I went home in February for a family reunion. A personal touch!

That [1945–1946] was really some historical time in the community at the Community House. People moving in and out. So-called "working brothers" had to choose between a brother provincial and a priest provincial. Two out of three stayed with the brothers, if I remember correctly. Priests moved to a special dining room off the kitchen except for the chaplain to the brothers who was permitted to be in the big dining room. Council members moved in.

BR. FRANKLIN CULLEN (SOUTH-WEST PROVINCE)

Probably no one knew as much about the history of the brothers as Br. Ephrem, but he always refused to write or even talk about it. I remember at a soiree where he was being plied with drinks and he said, *Oh, I know what you are trying to do! You want me to loosen my tongue and tell about what happened in the community. But I don't want to do that because I would have to make judgments on why people acted the way they did and I don't want to do that.* Too bad that he didn't write up the non-judgmental aspects at least.

BR. FULGENCE DOUGHERTY (SOUTH-WEST PROVINCE)

I remember talking to Br. Ephrem when he was provincial about a problem in the house. I was a very young, very inexperienced brother, but he listened carefully, and reacted with great sympathy and understanding and speed.

I experienced another side of him on a train trip from South Bend to Toledo when I found myself sitting next to him. I had to defend every statement I made. It was like a terribly severe oral examination. I no longer recall clearly the subjects we covered, but they were probably education and the religious life. I recall how glad I was, though, to see the Toledo station.

Br. Ephrem went to Pakistan for the centenary of Holy Cross in Bengal in 1952. He went in spite of the fact that he had been at death's door just a few months before. At the time, there were many points of friction between Archbishop Graner and Br. Jude. The archbishop was a dominant person in body and spirit (a bit of a Prussian), so we were delighted to see him concede on almost all points after only one meeting with Br. Ephrem. One problem was lack of adequate housing for the brothers, but bricks were delivered to the site before Ephrem left Dhaka.

Brother Jude started an English high school on the trade school site in 1954. He wanted to move the school to a location of its own but needed capital in order to do it. He proposed that each of three provincials and the Bengalese give $25,000. With a hundred thousand he would be able to build a good school. The provincials— one of whom was Ephrem—refused repeatedly.

When I became superior, I was faced with the same problem, but now Ephrem was no longer involved with supporting the Bengal missions. He called me aside and said, *Brother, this is the way to get money out of provincials.* Then he explained that no one would give a sum as large as $25,000, but they wouldn't even notice a gift of $5,000. He told me to ask them to pledge $5,000 each for five years, and then to ask the Bengalese to pledge the same and to advance me money as I needed it on the strength of the provincials' pledges. I followed his advice and the provincials all agreed immediately. In fact, Br. Donatus suggested that they up the pledge to $6,000 a year because, as he said, *Buildings always have a way of running over the estimates.* I ended up with $130,000 and a very nice building. I certainly appreciated Ephrem's advice, but why couldn't he have told us that while he was still provincial?

He took advantage of me on two occasions, both in 1956. I went home on leave in December of 1955 and spent Christmas and the month of January at home. I fully expected an assignment for the spring semester as that was the usual practice. When nothing came, I began to get antsy. Finally, I went to Notre Dame and Ephrem told me that he wasn't giving me or Tom More assignments because we would have to return to Dhaka in July to cover for Jude and Andy, who would be at the general chapter of 1956. It was nice to escape teaching that semester, but we lost five months of our sabbatical year too.

When it came time to return to Dhaka, Ephrem asked Tom and me to take Br. Norbert home to France. Now a dozen people who knew Norbert were going to Europe for the chapter that summer, and any one of them could have taken Norbert back, but he asked Tom and me—the only travelers who didn't know Norbert and didn't know how senile he had become. I am afraid Ephrem knowingly took advantage of Tom and me on both scores.

KENNETH AUSTIN (FORMER BR. RANDOLPH)

Don't slight Ephrem's concern for a brother as an individual. He visited with me one afternoon as we discussed my leaving the brotherhood. The man was deeply spiritual, caring, a master at healing. His accomplishments were monumental. His soul was sublime.

Taped Reminiscences and Interviews

BR. JOHN WILLIAM DONOGHUE (EASTERN PROVINCE)

Br. John William Donoghue, first principal of St. Edward High School, Lakewood, Ohio, recalls that there was some problem obtaining the deed for the school after the brothers had submitted their part of the payment to the archbishop of Cleveland, Edward F. Hoban. Br. Ephrem needed the deed in order to use St. Edward as collateral for a loan with which to begin constructing another school in Bayside (Flushing), Long Island. Deadlines were approaching and he was getting uneasy. The lawyer for St. Edward happened one day to be in City Hall in Cleveland and checked to see under whose name the school was registered. It was that of the Brothers of Holy

Cross, though they had never been told the deed was theirs. He notified Br. John William, who immediately telephoned Br. Ephrem. The provincial instructed Br. John to have a copy made at once, then boarded the train for Cleveland, where, the next morning, he took possession of the deed and moved ahead in negotiations for the eastern school.

The archbishop also wanted Holy Cross to conduct a school in Akron, located in the southern part of his diocese. He confided to Br. John William that for some reason Br. Ephrem did not seem receptive to this suggestion. Br. John told the archbishop that the next time the prelate was in the Notre Dame area he should show his sincerity by stopping in to see Br. Ephrem personally and then make his case for the school. The archbishop did so, and Br. Ephrem accepted the proposal.

Br. John Baptist Titzer, assistant provincial, made a visit to St. Edward and noted that there seemed to be disciplinary problems concerning some of the seniors. He urged action before the situation got out of hand, and out of the 125 senior students who had begun as freshmen, eight were identified by the faculty as worthy of suspension. Word of this move reached the diocesan school office and the auxiliary bishop supervising education summoned Br. John William and expressed his disapproval of the action taken. He remarked that he knew Br. Ephrem was stubborn and difficult on such issues; perhaps as a result, he mused, the archbishop might be moved to reconsider the role of the brothers in conducting the school. Br. John William telephoned Br. Ephrem and the provincial told Br. John to forget the matter entirely. Several days later Archbishop Hoban called Br. John to his office where he told him things had been settled, there was no problem at all.

On one occasion Br. Ephrem was visiting St. Edward High School. Near the end of breakfast one brother lit a cigarette. Br. Ephrem arose and snatched the cigarette out of the mouth of the offending brother. A stunned silence settled onto the dining room and everyone left quietly shortly after that. Br. John William went to Br. Ephrem's room and apologized for the breach in regular discipline, saying that perhaps things had gotten a bit loose in the confusion of the early organization of life in the school and house.

Br. John remembers that Br. Ephrem himself seldom apologized when he felt he had made a mistake or had been too severe with a person. Nevertheless, the provincial had a way of demonstrating his desire to set things right. He would often walk up to the individual he had offended, put his arm around the man's shoulders and make some lighthearted remark as an indication that as far as he was concerned, things were right between them once more.

Br. Ephrem frequently repeated the kernel of a lesson he had learned, he said, from Br. Evaristus years earlier: *I never demand a pound of flesh from anyone.* He recognized the circumstances and the individual limitations of the people involved and realistically dealt with the consequences.

Br. John recalls a humorous incident Br. Ephrem told on himself during one visit to St. Edward High School. The previous night Br. Ephrem had gone to bed but could not fall sleep because the room felt too warm and stuffy. He got up and opened the window, returned to bed and slept soundly the entire night. In the morning he arose to find that though he had opened the window, he had not opened the outside storm sash, and in fact there had been no more movement of cool air than before. He laughed and said that it must have been his imagination that provided him with a good night's sleep.

Br. John William likes to remember the biblical admonition: "The fear of God is the beginning of wisdom." He says that many of Br. Ephrem's subjects found over the years that the fear of Br. Ephrem was also the beginning of wisdom.

BR. JOHN FEDEROWICZ (MIDWEST PROVINCE)

Br. John recalls Br. Ephrem as convivial, loving to be among people. He was conversant on almost any topic, though he was not an athlete and did not seem to be current on the sports news. He did not come across as overly profound; he was not an academic or an intellectual as such. When he conversed, he was easy to understand. One time Br. John remarked to Br. Ephrem about the great variety of subjects being studied by the scholastic brothers at Notre Dame. Br. Ephrem replied that education is like food—you can't get along without it, but it makes little difference what types of food are eaten. The provincial was a proponent of a broad-based education as opposed to narrow specialization.

Once a brother who had been sent out to teach long before acquiring his degree requested of Br. Ephrem the opportunity to take time off to complete his academic work. The provincial, always pressed for teachers, asked the man to continue to teach and to pick up his credits bit by bit over time. The brother responded that he would never learn anything that way. Br. Ephrem replied: *Who cares? Just get the credits, y'know!*

Br. Ephrem's spirituality of the religious life was that of the time: keep the rule, be faithful to your exercises, and you will save your soul.

Br. John describes Br. Ephrem's gait as slow, measured, and deliberate, the provincial's apparent approach to daily life. In any case, Br. Ephrem was a prodigious worker and accomplished much. He was his own secretary and typed rapidly and well. His handwriting was beautiful.

As for Br. Ephrem's interpersonal relationships, Br. John believes they were good. The provincial was congenial, always the center of attention in a group. He could quip and joke easily. Yet there somehow remained a reserve which kept him from developing any deep friendships. It was not an era for such in the religious life. He bore no grudges. He could certainly call people vociferously to task, but the next day things would be fine again between him and them. He was an eminently just man. He played no favorites, or if he did, it was not perceptible. He was surely not a sportsman. Br. John remembers no incident of seeing Br. Ephrem exercise in any way other than through his relatively slow-paced walks outdoors. It seemed that every movement was considered.

Br. John does not remember any of Br. Ephrem's undertakings which had to be reversed or redone. The provincial was a thoughtful man, and Br. John recalls that his white hair contributed to his appearance as a wise person. He seemed outwardly to be in generally good health. He had a good ear for the spoken word and had the gift of being able to tell from which part of Ireland a native came just from hearing the person speak.

Br. John recalls that during the summer of either 1942 or 1943 Br. Ephrem was teaching a course in Principles of Secondary Education to the scholastics at Dujarié Hall. Br. Ephrem prepared his own brief but concise textbook for the course—thirty pages with thirty topics. Br. John remembers Br. Ephrem's being a generally satisfying teacher, though he had some speech mannerisms which everyone began to copy and mock, some even keeping track of how often he used particular ones such as "y'know" or "on the plan." Such phrases seemed never to relate naturally to the context in which they were used.

When the Second World War ended and the general chapter of 1945 was preparing to separate the brothers and priests into autonomous provinces, Br. John remembers that Br. Ephrem's name continuously surfaced among the brothers at Notre Dame as the "heir apparent," the logical candidate for first provincial of the brothers' province. At the time, the Community House was in some turmoil over the implications of the change because most of the brothers resident there were non-teaching brothers and during the subsequent year they would have to determine which province to join. Much conversation took place over this issue, sometimes growing loud and argumentative. Br. John, a young religious at the time, grew disturbed by the confusion and went to Br. Ephrem with his concern. By his confidence and self-assuredness the future provincial was able to calm the young man's anxiety.

Br. John remembers Br. Ephrem reading light novels for recreational purposes. This type of literature was seen in the provincial's room regularly. However, Br. Ephrem was not a great collector of books and his motto for the brothers was "one trunk and one suitcase" for holding all one's effects. When Br. John asked him whether this applied also to books, Br. Ephrem said of course it did because you could always find books in the libraries where you were assigned. Br. John, himself a librarian in later years, found that this did not always prove true.

When the first brothers' provincial council was set up, Br. Ephrem made sure to include two non-teaching brothers, a very politic move given the tension which had existed prior to the separation of provinces and the fact that the provincial offices were housed in the Community House, which continued to be the residence for more non-teaching brothers than those who did teach.

Br. John, when stationed at Holy Trinity High School in Chicago, recalls living on the third floor of the old primary school building during the construction of the new brothers' faculty house on the site of the one that had been torn down. The windows in the temporary residence did not in any effective way keep out the cold breezes of the Windy City, and the central heating plant was expected to dole out heat piecemeal to the various sectors of the parish complex. So the brothers experienced extreme cold, especially on weekends when they spent most of their time in their rooms. Br. Reginald Justak, principal and superior, complained to Br. Ephrem, who immediately telephoned the pastor of the parish—a Holy Cross priest—and declared that if the heat did not improve, he would pull the brothers out of Trinity to come get warm at Notre Dame. The heat came on at once.

It was apparently all right for Br. Ephrem to make long distance telephone calls, but once when Br. Reginald telephoned Br. Ephrem at Notre Dame, the provincial scolded the principal for wasting eighty cents on something which could have been handled in a three-cent letter.

In 1957 on the occasion of the centenary of the approval by Rome of the constitutions of the Congregation of Holy Cross, a huge celebration was held in Cleveland, where Br. John was teaching and organizing the library. The archbishop and dozens of others were present, including the former provincial, who had come in for the occasion. Br. John recalls being amazed at the amount of alcohol Br. Ephrem could manage with ease. As a matter of fact, Br. Ephrem and Br. John were the last two to leave the party.

Br. John remembers there being a tremendous spirit of unanimity among the brothers in the mid-fifties. He wonders whether this was something consciously forged by Br. Ephrem or whether the provincial just naturally exemplified those characteristics which of themselves called forth this spirit from among the brothers, many of whom were engaged during those years in pioneering apostolates for the brothers' province.

When Br. Ephrem came to Notre Dame in retirement, Br. John was residing at the Center between assignments and remembers Br. Ephrem visiting the Center nearly every day and fortifying himself at the beverage cabinet from time to time. It was because Br. Ephrem came to the Center so regularly that few of the brothers resident there made special efforts to visit the aging ex-provincial in the infirmary.

Br. John remembers feeling that Br. Ephrem, when provincial, had held too stringent an interpretation on the possession and use of property such as radios, golf clubs, typewriters, photographic equipment, and other professional materials. Such items were not, according to a strict reading of the 1950 constitutions, to be carried by an individual from one house to another when his assignment was changed. Br. John possessed some very fine bookbinding equipment which he had to leave behind and which he knows was never subsequently used by anyone.

Br. John also remembers that Br. Ephrem as provincial had a tendency when in a local house to override the decisions of the local superior if he disagreed with him. On one occasion in Holy Cross High School in Flushing, New York, a brother passed by Br. Ephrem dressed in his street suit, and when Br. Ephrem asked him where he thought he was going, the brother replied that he was going to see *My Fair Lady*. Never having paid much attention to the title of the then-popular musical, Br. Ephrem misinterpreted the reply as a flippant remark and ordered the religious to return to his room. Later the superior, Br. John William Donoghue, came to Br. Ephrem to explain the situation and diplomatically to remind him who was in charge in the house. On the matter of proper attire, Br. Ephrem was a stickler and issued an ordinance to the brothers about the use of the Roman collar, even on walks. When a brother at St. Edward in Lakewood dressed casually for a walk down the railway tracks behind the school toward Rocky River, Br. Ephrem made him change into his suit and collar for the outing.

Br. Ephrem stepped in to resolve an impasse in South Bend when various interest groups connected with the planning of the new Catholic boys' school there were having difficulty agreeing on the best location for the new institution. The provincial offered the diocese a piece of property at the corner of Angela Blvd. and U.S. 31, which the bishop promptly accepted.

BR. JOHN JOSEPH DONNELLY (EASTERN PROVINCE)

Br. John Joseph's first remembrance of Br. Ephrem is of his being director of vocations in the late 1930s while a member of the general administration in New York. Br. John remembers receiving letters from Br. Ephrem which were personal, interesting, and challenging. Sometimes Br. Ephrem would include with the letter an article from a paper or magazine and ask for the young man's response to it, an interesting and constructive way of learning something about the potential candidate.

When Br. Ephrem spent time teaching at the candidate house in Valatie, though a member of the general council headquartered in New York City, he always seemed to have a need to be in control, even at the expense of the local superior.

Br. Ephrem was a builder, a developer. He would have been, Br. John believes, a fine politician or businessman. In the early days of the Eastern Province Br. John feels Br. Ephrem might have sacrificed quality in vocations to the need for the quantity required to staff the quickly opening institutions of the new province. He also seemed not to value learning as such over the mere earning of credits. Scholastic excellence among the brothers was not a priority. At the first vice province chapter Br. Michel Miller, director of the boys' home near Chester, New York, proposed that more brothers be trained in social work. Br. Ephrem, who at that moment had other priorities, exploded that if the chapter voted for more brothers in social ministry he would personally see to it through his influence that the legislation never received approval from the superior general. The chapter ran only three days and Br. Ephrem was perceived to be in total control throughout.

Most brothers look upon Br. Ephrem as something of a saint and a savior. Br. John feels that he would, indeed, have made a great chief executive officer for some major corporation or a very effective Madison Avenue man. The provincial had great respect for Fr. Edward Sorin's capacity to move ahead boldly in the building up of the University of Notre Dame and the Congregation of Holy Cross in the United States. When it was suggested to Br. Ephrem that Fr. Basil Moreau, the congregation's founder, was also a notable figure, Br. Ephrem retorted that Fr. Moreau was a man who did little, who just sat around.

One Christmas at Flushing after midnight mass Br. Ephrem decided he wanted to play bridge before retiring. Br. Bertram Madden, one of his usual partners, was not in the room, so Br. Ephrem sent for him. The messenger returned to say that Br. Bertram's room was dark and there was no reply to the knock, so he must be asleep. Br. Ephrem insisted on his being awakened to play; Br. Bertram eventually arrived to begin the game.

BR. SIDNEY HALLIGAN (EASTERN PROVINCE)

Br. Sidney went to Valatie as a postulant in 1942. Br. Eymard Salzman was the superior, but Br. Ephrem was on the staff, commuting from New York where he was on the general council. It was wartime, and expenses had to be watched scrupulously. Br. Eymard lowered the thermostats. But someone kept nudging them upward. Naturally Br. Eymard blamed the postulants. In fact, it was Br. Ephrem who desired the higher temperature.

When Br. Sidney was local councilor and treasurer for the brothers at New Orleans, Br. Ephrem came as provincial to make a visit. During his stay he held a meeting in one of the classrooms so he could use the blackboard—which he delighted in doing—to draw images of proposed building construction and changes he envisioned for the institution. Br. Sidney remembers Br. Ephrem's quick eye for any new alterations each time he came for a visit, especially material changes which he had not specifically authorized. The provincial would be quick to question faculty members as to whether permission had been obtained for such alterations.

When in 1956 the new vice provincial council moved into the Flushing house, Br. Ephrem insisted that the vice provincial and his councilors eat the same food as the brothers in the house, even though the administration had its own small dining area. The first time the same fare was served, however, Br. Ephrem complained because what had been prepared did not appeal to him.

Br. Ephrem arranged a meeting at Flushing between himself and Fr. Richard Sullivan, the provincial of the Eastern Priests' Province. He invited the priest to come and have lunch before their meeting. Apparently Fr. Sullivan tarried at the table a bit too long for Br. Ephrem's liking, and he urged him, *Hurry up and take your time!*

While Br. Ephrem was in the process of building the novitiate at Valatie, he was borrowing money for the project from the Midwest Province and from a bank. He wrote a note to the Midwest provincial concerning an amount in the neighborhood of a million and a half to two million dollars, then consulted with Br. Sidney, the provincial treasurer, as to whether he ought to send the note by first-class mail or at a cheaper rate to save postage.

Earlier, when the novitiate proper to the Eastern Brothers' Province was being planned, Br. Ephrem at first sought to acquire an already-constructed building in Massachusetts, but the bishop there would not permit it as he felt there were already too many non-profit organizations in his diocese.

Br. Bertram Madden told Br. Sidney that when Br. Ephrem was in a hospital in New York in 1959 for a cataract operation he found it difficult, as was to be expected, to remain as quiet and motionless as the procedure required. At one point, in order to get the attention of the nurses Br. Ephrem thought were ignoring him, he threw the bedpan out into the corridor.

While it may have been politically useful for Br. Ephrem to have non-teaching brothers on his first provincial council at Notre Dame, apparently it was not so important when he became Eastern vice provincial. Nevertheless, he did have one farming brother on the council, Br. John Berchmans Aery. Br. Ephrem did not have much interest in the farm at Valatie, for which Br. John was responsible. Whenever Br. John would bring up an agenda item about the farm, Br. Ephrem became impatient and irritated.

Br. Pierre Schu was also a council member under Br. Ephrem in the East. Br. Pierre had the practice of taking a shower daily after breakfast before beginning his school day. Br. Ephrem felt that a daily shower was unnecessary. He took his on Friday between two of his favorite television programs. As for video entertainment, he was particularly fond of Perry Como, Perry Mason, and Mitch Miller.

Br. Sidney recalls that in the provincial house there was only one desk telephone, the one belonging to Br. Ephrem. All the other councilors had to use a wall phone in the corridor and could not lay papers out in front of them or easily write messages.

Br. Ephrem loved to play bridge. His usual partners at one stage were Brs. Elmo Bransby, Bertram Madden, and Pierre Schu. Br. Ephrem tried to get Br. Sidney to learn bridge so he too could play, saying that it was a game, it was fun, it didn't matter who won. Br. Sidney had enough experience to know that with Br. Ephrem it was usually otherwise.

Br. Ephrem wanted to construct a level pedestrian bridge between the brothers' house, built on an incline, and the school at West Haven, but an architect said it was impossible from an engineering standpoint. Br. Ephrem designed such a passageway and the brothers built it themselves. At the time of the transfer of the structure to a local university the bridge was still standing and in use.

Celebrating his fiftieth anniversary of profession in 1959, Br. Ephrem was seated on the dais. At one moment while laughing heartily at some remark, he inadvertently pushed his chair back a bit and it slipped from the platform, taking the provincial along with it to the floor. He extricated himself, got up and laughed it off as a joke on himself.

Br. Sidney believes that though Br. Ephrem may have caused an ulcer here or there, he was the person needed at the time, and no one else could or would have done the job he did. He was a great leader. With vehemence he more than held his own with the priests whenever issues of the priest-brother relationships arose. Yet he evidenced a sincere kindness to any brother who was experiencing personal difficulties.

One time when discussing a contract for Bishop McNamara High School in Forestville, Maryland, with the archbishop of Washington, Patrick Cardinal O'Boyle, Br. Ephrem made a remark to which the cardinal for some reason took strong exception. The cardinal pointedly stated, *You're talking to the cardinal-archbishop of Washington!* Br. Ephrem retorted, *So what? I'm the brother provincial of the Brothers of Holy Cross!*

When in 1956 Br. Ephrem became vice provincial in the East, he pushed for as rapid a transition as possible to the status of province because, he declared, he would not want to die a vice provincial.

BROTHER ELMO BRANSBY (EASTERN PROVINCE)

Br. Elmo lived at the generalate in New York as a doctoral student at Fordham University when Br. Ephrem was a member of the general council. Had there been another Holy Cross house in the vicinity, the students would have resided there, and in fact when one of the primary schools opened, both Br. Elmo and Br. John Baptist Titzer, the other doctoral candidate, moved to that location. Meanwhile, Br. Elmo was barber for the generalate personnel. He and Br. John did not regularly eat with the generalate staff but did share in their prayer life. Fr. William Doheny was the superior, and, as a result of conflicts of personality between him and Br. Ephrem, the latter sought to employ his spare time outside the generalate when possible. That is why he spent long periods at Valatie teaching the candidates.

As Br. Elmo recalls, the selection of Br. Ephrem as first provincial of the single brothers' autonomous province was formalized through the canvassing of all of the brother local superiors and of the brother provincial councilors and brother general assistants. Br. Ephrem garnered four more votes than did Br. Venard Gorman, the other candidate for the office.

Br. Elmo remembers hearing it told that when Fr. Andrew Morrissey was provincial of the single province of priests and brothers in the early part of the century, Br. Ephrem complained to him about the difference in the amount of orange juice served to the priests as compared with that served to the brothers. Even in such small things Br. Ephrem was an early proponent of equality.

In 1945 when the division of assets was arranged by the general chapter Br. Ephrem would have preferred that the brothers be given the University of Portland rather than St. Edward's in Texas. He expressed some disappointment over this situation. St. Edward's had at the time a reputation for being something of a place of exile for Holy Cross religious. Also, the building up of facilities and programs was needed more in Texas than in Oregon. Br. Ephrem consequently did not exert extraordinary effort in the development of St. Edward's at the outset. Only after nine years did the university manage to construct a much-needed library, and it was not until Br. John Baptist Titzer became vice provincial of the South-West Province that St. Edward's began to blossom into a notable institution. Despite his reservations about the future of the university in Texas, Br. Ephrem sincerely wanted the brothers to succeed there, if for no other reason than as proof to the priests' society that the brothers could do well independently even in higher education. Br. Ephrem respected the priests but held his own among them.

Br. Elmo was president of St. Edward's University from 1952 to 1957. He remembers that during his term Br. Ephrem's principal involvement with the university was in the fiscal area, because of the school's precarious financial situation. The relationship between provincial and president was cordial and supportive, and Br. Ephrem counseled Br. Elmo not to be discouraged, because, as he said, the problem was not too many expenses but not enough enrollment. The university depended heavily on the boarding/day high school attached to the college to make up for its deficit. For Br. Elmo the priority was for the university to become accredited by the Southern Association, and over the years of his presidency this goal was achieved. As part of the process, statutes delineating lines of authority had to be structured. Those set up by Stonehill College in North Easton, Massachusetts, another Holy Cross institution of higher education, were adopted almost verbatim. Under these statutes the brothers had to begin adapting to new forms of authority, which for some meant that for the first time they were directly under lay superiors in their apostolic work.

Br. Ephrem's plans for expansion and building were not always wholeheartedly supported by everyone, but he naturally had the last word and normally things worked out well in the end. Br. Elmo recalls that it was during times of heavy planning and building that Br. Ephrem appeared more vibrant and animated than usual.

Br. Ephrem was sympathetic to his men but continuously challenged them. Br. Elmo believes that occasionally Br. Ephrem would take a contrary stance in a discussion for the express purpose of arousing reactions from a particular religious, forcing him to defend his own position, thereby solidifying his enthusiasm and excitement over what he believed in. The provincial loved argument not for its own sake but as a battlefield on which the opponents could expand their capabilities.

Br. Elmo recalls that even after Br. Ephrem had left office as provincial he still relished being asked advice, as it gave him a sense of pride in what he had accomplished in the past and of still being important in the continuing development of the community.

Early in Br. Ephrem's administrative career, Br. Elmo remembers, the provincial was somewhat shy, but as his experience and success grew, so did his confidence. This personal sense of growth and achievement helped Br. Ephrem to encourage others in a similar way, and over time he assisted many young administrators to develop their own self-confidence and achievements. Br. Ephrem's assurance was in some sense contagious.

Br. Ephrem loved to attend gatherings of all kinds, including parties. He played the role of *paterfamilias* among his religious and enjoyed it. He liked to tell jokes and repeated—many times—stories he had heard that he particularly liked. He loved to have company, especially other provincials, either priests or brothers, or chaplains of the province institutions. He enjoyed repartee between himself and others, and would sometimes prolong enjoyable discussions into the night.

One personal incident Br. Elmo remembers concerned his being exhausted by his role as superior of Dujarie Hall scholasticate at Notre Dame and his seeking some respite by slipping away to the community infirmary occasionally to take a room there for some hours of undisturbed rest. Once Br. Ephrem dropped in at Dujarie Hall without being announced. Searching for Br. Elmo, he learned where the superior had gone and telephoned for him to return to Dujarie at once. On Br. Elmo's arrival, the provincial immediately demanded that Br. Elmo pack a bag and get away from Notre Dame for a while by going to Chicago to take several days' rest and relaxation.

BR. EDWIN MATTINGLY (MIDWEST PROVINCE)

The most outstanding recollection Br. Edwin has of Br. Ephrem concerns the provincial's health in the early 1950s. In the spring of 1952 Br. Ephrem suffered what Br. Edwin came to understand as a nervous breakdown. Br. Edwin does not remember whether Br. John Baptist, at that time assistant provincial, actually used the term "nervous breakdown," or whether Br. Edwin drew his own conclusion, but the symptoms were to him appropriate. Because of Br. Edwin's circumspection in guarding information he might have overheard from Br. Ephrem while acting as his driver on occasion, there was a fundamental respect between the two men. Thus, Br. Edwin was immediately notified when Br. Ephrem was taken to St. Joseph's Hospital, Mishawaka, Indiana, for rest and possible treatment of the symptoms he was experiencing. The choice of hospital was in itself unusual because the brothers were normally admitted to the medical facility bearing the same name in South Bend. Br. Edwin made several visits to Br. Ephrem during the next two weeks and always found the provincial reading and in good spirits. Their conversations were on general topics, not community business. The reason for the hospitalization was never referred to in the Community House, where both Br. Ephrem and Br. Edwin lived, and because the religious were accustomed to Br. Ephrem's frequent and sometimes sudden absences, there was little curiosity expressed as to where he was or how long he would be away.

Br. Edwin, at that time principal of Central Catholic High School in South Bend, was a frequent bridge partner of Br. Ephrem at the Community House. Brs. Quentin Hegarty and Columba Curran also joined in the bridge games regularly. Br. Edwin recalls Br. Ephrem as an excellent bridge player and a fierce competitor.

As Br. Ephrem's driver on frequent occasions, Br. Edwin remembers that the provincial liked just to get away from the Community House and Notre Dame for a time and would usually invite one or two others to ride along. During the outing the subjects of conversation were not normally focused on community issues or other business.

Br. Edwin was not intimidated by Br. Ephrem's sometimes gruff exterior and brusque behavior. One time during a bridge game Br. Edwin criticized the way Br. Ephrem had bid a hand. The irate Irishman exploded that Br. Edwin had no right to talk to his provincial that way and that he should go to his room at once. Br. Edwin obeyed, then shortly after that went to chapel for the regularly scheduled night prayer. After prayer, Br. Ephrem stopped by Br. Edwin's room to apologize for having overreacted in the recreation room.

Citing Br. Ephrem's concern for his men, Br. Edwin relates an incident that occurred while he was on vacation with his family. He was out hunting with one of his brothers, and in the course of their taking a rest break somehow Br. Edwin's rifle, a .22 caliber, fell and discharged. The bullet struck his brother and wounded him seriously though not critically. While his brother was still in the hospital, Br. Edwin returned to Notre Dame and duly reported the incident to Br. Ephrem. The provincial, unasked, gratuitously provided the money to pay the hospital bill, giving the sum to Br. Edwin to take personally to Indianapolis.

While Br. Edwin was principal of Central Catholic High School in South Bend, plans were initiated in the diocese for the construction of a new Catholic high school that would merge the several smaller Catholic secondary units already in existence, including Central Catholic. In the course of the planning the brothers on the faculty had several opportunities to review and critique architectural drawings of the proposed new structure. Because Br. Reginald Justak, then in Chicago at Holy Trinity High School, was to be named the principal of the new school in the fall, he, along with Br. Ephrem, represented the brothers at any diocesan meetings relating to the school. Br. Edwin recalls that during the process the brothers were perceived by the pastors of various parishes somewhat as obstacles for being too critical of the plans. The brothers had in fact seen many practical problems in the layout of the proposed structure, and Brs. Ephrem and Reginald held out for the necessary alterations.

Br. Ephrem was normally lighthearted and liked to be with people. He was able to scrutinize personalities and had the capacity to find the humorous side of a person's idiosyncrasies, even at times poking some fun at the individual. But he found it difficult to countenance the same when directed at him.

Br. Edwin remembers that in the time immediately preceding the division of the priests and brothers into autonomous provinces members of the brothers' society perceived Br. Ephrem as being the champion of the brothers and their interests, particularly where the University of Notre Dame was concerned. Br. Ephrem was seen as a highly capable administrator and the brothers trusted his judgment in making arrangements for the distribution of assets at the time of the division into homogeneous provinces.

BR. WALTER FOKEN (MIDWEST PROVINCE)

Br. Walter was stationed in Texas on the faculty of St. Edward's University beginning in the late 1940s. On one occasion Br. Ephrem came to visit the campus and to investigate sites in Texas for a possible high school apart from the boarding/day school already attached to the university. Responding to an invitation, he traveled to Amarillo to investigate Price College, a secondary school despite its name. Br. Ephrem looked into the possibilities, then returned to Austin where he revealed that while in Amarillo he had experienced one of the region's famous dust storms. He proclaimed unambiguously that under no circumstances would Holy Cross ever go to Amarillo!

Before his assignment to Texas, Br. Walter was at Notre Dame pursuing studies as a scholastic. Vocations immediately following the war were numerous, but so were departures. When a brother left the congregation, Br. Walter remembers that Br. Ephrem would shrug and say, *We don't need him in our organization.*

Br. Walter, along with most of the other student brothers, took education courses taught in Dujarie Hall by various brothers. Br.

Ephrem gave such a course on the teaching of social studies. The scholastics noted Br. Ephrem's frequent use of certain phrases: "y'know," "on the plan," and "on the situation." Br. Walter remembers one particular occasion when Br. Ephrem described the circumstances in a tropical country and said, *Y'know, they don't wear many clothes there on the situation.*

Br. Ephrem was often the life of the party. People were attracted to him and, recounting humorous stories for them, he made them feel at ease.

In Br. Ephrem's presence young religious felt that his leadership qualities and his ability to make decisions stood out. Without question he was in charge, highly respected by the brothers.

During the official provincial visit to the scholasticate at Notre Dame, Br. Ephrem observed formalities and followed the rubrics of the visit exactly as outlined in the community Directory. He listed the problems he judged to be present in the house, then gave concrete suggestions as to what he expected would be done to resolve them.

Br. Walter recalls that Br. Marius Wittner, at one time assigned to Gibault Home for Boys in Terre Haute, Indiana, mentioned an occasion on which Br. Ephrem was visiting the brothers in Terre Haute and noticed that they were wearing variously colored cast-off trousers left by the boys. The provincial immediately reminded the brothers that black was the basic color for religious and instructed them to *change back now!*

Concerning St. Edward's University one big question that surfaced when the brothers assumed its control was whether it would remain a university or would instead have its status altered to that of a junior college. Br. Ephrem preferred that it become a junior college and cater primarily to the needs of student brothers, and that the focus should be placed rather on the attached high school program, which was fiscally sound.

The faculty brothers at St. Edward's never had much luck convincing Br. Ephrem of certain needs at the university because of his reluctance to devote any serious money to the institution. On one occasion, however, he visited during a particularly rainy period and experienced the extremely muddy paths which ran from one war-surplus structure to another. Br. Ephrem exclaimed at one point, *You have got to have sidewalks!* The brothers were secretly delighted that the weather had cooperated in illustrating the situation in a way that no words could have done.

BR. LAWRENCE MILLER (MIDWEST PROVINCE)

Br. Lawrence, longtime director of St. Charles Boys' Home in Milwaukee, remembers that he got along with Br. Ephrem because, as he says, he could not operate *without* getting along with him. Br. Lawrence was at St. Charles all ten years of Br. Ephrem's term as provincial of the single brothers' province.

Br. Lawrence recalls three categories of brothers stationed at St. Charles from which he had to make up his staff: those assigned there because of their fitness for or interest in the work; those who could not be placed elsewhere by Br. Ephrem for a variety of reasons; and those awaiting dispensations from their vows. While the total number of brothers was quite adequate to staff the program, the aptness of several sometimes left Br. Lawrence with problems. Nevertheless, Br. Ephrem confided to the director that he allowed this situation to prevail because he knew Br. Lawrence had the capacity to handle things positively—which in fact he did. Br. Ephrem was straightforward and honest in all his dealings with Br. Lawrence.

In order to help Br. Ephrem assign men to St. Charles who might eventually become certified in social work, Br. Lawrence arranged for scholarships to be offered either through Catholic Charities or another similar organization. The agreement was that such men, on completing their degrees, would devote at least two years to working at St. Charles. Br. Ephrem cooperated by sending good men to study in Milwaukee while living at St. Charles. These men did their fieldwork in institutions other than St. Charles to gain a broader experience. The first two men to benefit from the scholarships completed their studies but eventually left the congregation, one after having been director of St. Charles for some years. It is said, though Br. Lawrence cannot document it, that when these men left, Br. Ephrem saw to it that the amount of each scholarship was reimbursed.

Much earlier in Br. Ephrem's career, at the time he was principal in Evansville, Br. Lawrence's hometown, a new certification law was passed governing teachers in Indiana. In 1923 Br. Ephrem returned to Notre Dame to begin graduate studies and to ascertain for the province the academic status of all the brothers then teaching. The result of this study was the certification of many brothers and the establishment of a summer school program for the brothers to continue working toward licensing. As Br. Lawrence remembers it, though the summer school was primarily for brothers, it was open to others, and this was the official beginning of the summer programs catering to teachers that the University of Notre Dame conducted for many summers thereafter.

Br. Lawrence recalls that Holy Cross was one of the first congregations to take an avid interest in the proper certification of its teaching members. Br. Ephrem saw this move as a way to advance the quality, reputation, and effectiveness of the brothers. When properly licensed, brothers were usually sent to salary schools belonging to dioceses rather than to property schools owned by the brothers, as the latter were entirely the responsibility of the brothers and could better absorb the uncertified teachers until such a time as everyone could be properly qualified.

BR. FLAVIUS ELLISON (MIDWEST PROVINCE)

Br. Flavius, who lived with Br. Ephrem at the Community House for many years, remembers him as a man of deep faith. Br. Ephrem believed that God would provide the necessary resources to permit the brothers to expand apostolically. He used to say it was God's work and that the money would somehow be there when needed.

Br. Ephrem could be blunt and to the point, but with him you knew where you stood, and he was fair if you were honest in your dealings with him. He was, as Br. Flavius recalls, "a man's man." He was also compassionate. While Br. Flavius was still in temporary vows, his parents died, one within five days of the other, and he went home for the funerals. He was permitted of course to stay on for some time afterward—he remembers forty days—to help settle the estate, and during that time his vows were to expire. He telephoned Br. Ephrem to ask what he ought to do. The provincial told him to stay there, and authorized the local pastor and his assistant to witness the renewal of vows in the parish church. Upon returning to Notre Dame, Br. Flavius was met by Br. Ephrem, who told him that being home during those weeks was surely not to be considered a vacation and if Br. Flavius felt the need for one now he ought to take it immediately.

Br. Ephrem enjoyed good-natured teasing and jokes, sometimes even when directed at himself. One time Br. Flavius was a waiter at the table where Br. Ephrem was sitting in the dining room and he brought Br. Ephrem a dessert which the provincial did not recognize. He asked Br. Flavius, *What is it?* The young religious playfully retorted, *Dessert!* and walked away. When he returned some minutes later, Br. Ephrem laughed, *You got me that time!* He had a good sense of humor. On another occasion, one August 15, Br. Flavius was in the process of cleaning the provincial's sitting room. On the feast of the Assumption Br. Ephrem made a practice of traveling the twenty miles west to Rolling Prairie to attend the ceremony for the reception of the habit by incoming novices, and Br. Flavius presumed that is where Br. Ephrem was on this particular day. So the young religious, who had not yet seen the newspaper from the night before, made himself comfortable in Br. Ephrem's chair with his feet up, reading the comics. He had turned on the vacuum cleaner to convince the casual passerby that he was at work. Without warning Br. Ephrem appeared from behind and shouted, *Ha! I caught you! You thought I'd be out on the prairie, didn't you?* But he laughed at the incident, enjoying the irony of it.

There were bound to be occasions on which the provincial administration and the local administration, both housed in the same building, would come into some conflict over procedures, especially as the provincial and his council ate, prayed, and recreated with the other men residing in the Community House. One evening during supper Br. Ephrem was anxious for the meal to be over so he could get back to work. He leaned over and told Br. Jacob Eppley, superior, to ring the bell to signal the end of the meal. Br. Jacob paid no heed and in fact moved the bell closer to himself. Br. Ephrem repeated his request a bit more forcefully. Br. Jacob, somewhat irritated, replied, *I am the superior of this house!* Br. Ephrem respected a superior when he stood up for his rights even if they conflicted with the provincial's own interests.

Br. Flavius was not particularly conscious of the health problems Br. Ephrem experienced, though he does remember the provincial's being in the hospital on one occasion and one of the young brothers from the Community House was asked to sit with him regularly. Br. Ephrem did not as a rule have any special diet requirements. If Br. Ephrem did in fact suffer from a nervous breakdown, there was no talk of it in the house at the time. Curiously, at one time Br. Ephrem, knowing Br. Flavius had some eye problems, told the young religious that he himself used only one eye at a time. When Br. Flavius required eye surgery later, Br. Ephrem granted the permission at once and was sympathetic to his needs.

Br. Flavius remembers Br. Ephrem enjoying rides in a car off campus, sometimes out to St. Joseph Farm, some seven miles from the campus, to visit the brothers there informally. Sometimes Br. Ephrem would ask Br. Maynard Rabidoux to accompany him.

The priests on the campus of the University of Notre Dame, Br. Flavius recalls, had a very good opinion of Br. Ephrem and respected him highly.

Br. Flavius believes that the only administrative mistake Br. Ephrem made was in the settlement on scholarships for the University of Notre Dame when the assets were divided and allotted to the two provinces in 1946. The scholarships were based on amount rather than number. As inflation rose, the value of each scholarship decreased and it became necessary for more and more brothers to be sent to St. Edward's University in Texas for their undergraduate work.

Some older brothers remarked in Br. Flavius's hearing that at the time of the first meeting of the brothers on the Notre Dame campus following the division into autonomous provinces, July 1, 1946, Br. Ephrem arose as their new provincial and spokesman and stated boldly, *I don't feel second to anyone!*

BR. CHRISTIAN STINNET (EASTERN PROVINCE)

Br. Christian recalls taking a trip by train to New York from Notre Dame. Unexpectedly he met Br. Ephrem on the train. The provincial knew that Br. Christian did not have permission for the trip and reprimanded him then and there, leaving Br. Christian feeling uneasy and spoiling the journey for him. Br. Ephrem always knew what was going on and was, Br. Christian remembers, fully in control.

Under Br. Ephrem the province experienced one-man rule, Br. Christian recalls, but no one begrudged Br. Ephrem the technique because he did an excellent job of leading the province.

BR. CHARLES HILL (MIDWEST PROVINCE)

Br. Charles remembers one story Br. Ephrem used to tell about losing one's memory: *First, you begin to forget names, y'know. Then you begin to forget faces. Then, y'know, you begin to forget to close your fly. Finally you begin to forget to open it!*

ALVIN GLOMBOWSKI (FORMER BR. ALOYSIUS)

When Al was a member of the community in the early 1950s he was on the staff at the novitiate at Rolling Prairie and was in charge of bringing the laundry in each week to the facility at Notre Dame. On one such occasion he chanced to encounter Br. Ephrem on campus. As it was summer time, Al was dressed in khaki trousers and a sport shirt. The provincial, always a stickler for proper dress, said nothing, but the two passed the time of day. At one point Br. Ephrem inquired whether Al would be interested in resuming university studies soon at St. Edward's in Texas. Al said he believed he would like to do that, and Br. Ephrem wrote out a note for Al to pass on to Br. Dominic Elder, his superior at the novitiate. Al presumed the content had to do with notifying Br. Dominic that Al would be leaving the novitiate for Texas in the near future. He was astonished, therefore, when Br. Dominic summoned him to his office not to discuss his departure for Texas, but to relate Br. Ephrem's displeasure at the manner in which Al had been dressed on campus and the provincial's demand that on subsequent trips Al wear black trousers, white shirt, and black tie.

BR. REX HENNEL (MIDWEST PROVINCE)

Br. Rex recalls a story told about Br. Ephrem when the provincial was in his early years of administration at the boys' Catholic high school in Evansville, Rex's hometown. The Ku Klux Klan made an appearance in the city, and Br. Ephrem organized some students from the school to protest and hopefully to drive the KKK out of town. Some hours later the police arrived at the school to investigate claims that students from Memorial had been involved in whatever unruliness had erupted during the demonstration. Br. Ephrem dutifully called in students one by one to talk with the police, but chose only boys he knew had not been part of the protest so that in good conscience they could deny knowing anything about it.

Br. Rex was never fearful of Br. Ephrem, and in fact was conscious of being well liked by the provincial. Br. Ephrem was one to push a person to his limits, especially one with potential, but it was a challenge productive of growth, not a demonstration of meanness.

Br. Ephrem loved witty exchanges and was willing to take as good as he gave if he sensed strength in his opponent.

Br. Ephrem enjoyed a fine reputation among other brothers' communities in the United States, particularly the Sacred Heart Brothers, who had many men in the South when Br. Rex was principal of Notre Dame High School in Biloxi, Mississippi. Br. Ephrem was a highly regarded figure who had done much in those days to uplift the image of lay religious.

On one occasion Br. Ephrem had an appointment to see the bishop of Fall River, Massachusetts. The provincial arrived at the chancery office only to discover the bishop's absence. Instead of sitting down to wait, Br. Ephrem informed the secretary that if when he returned the bishop still wanted to see him, he could find him at the brothers' house. Br. Ephrem had no intention of wasting time waiting.

When Br. Ephrem became provincial in 1946 there was in the province a keen sense of expectancy. The brothers looked forward through his leadership to an upsurge of growth and maturity as lay religious. There was in those days a universally positive attitude; what was happening was creative, and new apostolates were being established. Enthusiasm prevailed. Br. Rex believes Br. Ephrem was largely responsible for this spirit in the province.

Br. Ephrem invested in the younger men of the province as the hope of the future. Several of these young religious were appointed superiors and principals, including Br. Rex himself and Brs. Alfonso Comeau and John William Donoghue.

On one visit to Biloxi, Br. Ephrem was invited by Br. Rex to relax and have a drink before bedtime and discuss confidential issues of concern. This environment was Br. Ephrem's forte, and before the conversation ended, well into the night, the freshly opened bottle was empty.

Br. Rex was not conscious of Br. Ephrem's health problems apart from realizing he had some difficulty with asthma and had missed the provincial chapter of 1952, which Br. Rex attended.

BR. EDUARDO MICHALIK (MIDWEST PROVINCE)

The first time Br. Eduardo met Br. Ephrem, the young man was a novice at North Dartmouth, Massachusetts, and Br. Ephrem was visiting the house as assistant general. Br. Ephrem passed along the line of novices to be introduced, and when he came to Br. Eduardo the novice completely forgot Br. Ephrem's name and felt utterly embarrassed by the lapse of memory.

At Holy Trinity High School sometime between 1947 and 1949 Br. Eduardo was seriously considering leaving the community to study for the priesthood. He had gone so far as to request a dispensation from his vows in view of ordination and in fact the request had been processed. All that remained was for him to sign the letter accepting the release. Meanwhile, Br. Ephrem came to Chicago for a visit and found that Br. Eduardo was beginning to have second thoughts about his decision. The young religious approached Br. Ephrem, intending to let the provincial make the final decision in the matter and then to act accordingly. But Br. Ephrem flatly refused, placing the burden for such a decision on Br. Eduardo, where it properly belonged. Br. Eduardo decided to remain in Holy Cross as a brother.

On one occasion as Br. Eduardo, a missionary to Africa, was passing through New York on his way to Ghana, he stayed for several days at Holy Cross High School in Flushing, where Br. Ephrem maintained his offices as vice provincial of the Eastern Province. One day Br. Ephrem invited Br. Eduardo to ride with him on business to Valatie, some three hours to the north. Br. Eduardo accepted the invitation and his primary recollection of the journey is of Br. Ephrem's pipe and its very noticeable effects in the car.

Many years later, after Br. Ephrem had retired to Dujarie House at Notre Dame, the former provincial used to come to the Brothers Center for a drink or two fairly regularly. What struck Br. Eduardo on such occasions was Br. Ephrem's ability to blend so well into the community after having been so many years in positions of authority. This was more impressive than Br. Ephrem's many concrete accomplishments.

BR. BARRY LAMBOUR (MIDWEST PROVINCE)

Br. Barry remembers Br. Ephrem to have been a formidable man to run afoul of. Whatever his strengths, he must also be acknowledged for his weaknesses. Br. Barry recognized that Br. Ephrem had some difficult decisions to make for which he had to take responsibility, and he probably felt he had to operate more out of the model of military officer than that of older brother. Such methods may have been criticized, but Br. Ephrem could neither wait for nor feel at ease with a more democratic process.

Br. Barry recalls a meeting of brothers at St. Edward's University when Br. Ephrem was making a visit there. The gathering was something of an open forum. At one point Br. Simon Scribner, dean, spoke up about needing some policies set at the university. Br. Ephrem jumped up and said that all policies were made at Notre Dame and to forget making them locally.

Though there were times Br. Ephrem gave the impression he did not value the opinions of others, it is clear that he in fact did.

Br. Barry knew that Br. Ephrem was stringent on financial matters and those affecting regular discipline in the religious life, but it seems there were circumstances for which the provincial could relax his strictness. One time, Br. Barry recalls, the engineering department of St. Edward's University, of which Br. Barry was a member, had raised some money on its own for some much-needed equipment for the laboratory. The president of the university, however, let it be known that any money which came in would go directly into the general coffers of the school and the department should simply budget for its equipment. Br. Ephrem happened to be on the campus and heard about the reallocation of funds by the president. He came to Br. Barry and said that the next time he had a vacation coming he ought to ask for some extra money. The clear message was that, as Br. Ephrem controlled from the provincial office the amount given for vacations, he wanted Br. Barry to take a little extra time and do something special to compensate for his disappointment in not having money available for lab equipment.

Br. Barry became superior of Vincent Hall, the brothers' scholasticate at St. Edward's University. At one point the sanitary facilities had to be improved. Br. Barry solicited the help of local authorities in the city in planning how this could best be done, and a scheme was drawn up. Br. Barry took photographs of the extensive piece of campus property through which the necessary piping would have to be extended, and along with a written report sent the photos special delivery to Br. Ephrem for approval of the project. The only reply he received was a testy letter asking who had authorized the taking of *all those photographs*, and the provincial also questioned the use of special delivery mail. He said, *Once mail reaches Notre Dame, it's all special delivery to me!*

When he wanted to remain aloof from something Br. Ephrem could be difficult if not impossible to contact. While superior of the scholasticate in Texas, Br. Barry went through the experience of having an only recently arrived young brother come to him requesting permission to leave the congregation at once. Despite arguments the scholastic would brook no delays. So that very evening Br. Barry asked the young man to sit down and type out a letter to Br. Ephrem while Br. Barry did the same. The letters went out—actually posted by the young scholastic—that same night. Days, even weeks, went by and there was no reply. The curious and impatient scholastic continued to inquire of Br. Barry the status of his request. Eventually the young man left after a few months without a reply. Br. Barry felt that Br. Ephrem had a way of ignoring a person or a situation if he did not agree with the manner in which it was being handled or when he did not have a large stake in the results. On another occasion Br. Barry and his staff at the scholasticate wanted to send away a young brother in whose room had been found objectionable printed material that had arrived by mail. Br. Barry wrote to Br. Ephrem, and the provincial's response was that the scholasticate staff ought not overreact to this peccadillo, that it was just a passing phase in the young man's life. The brother remained at the scholasticate. During the following summer, however, he was stationed at the brothers' summer camp at Lawton, Michigan, and events transpired that made it apparent his behavior was clearly unacceptable, and he left the community at once. Br. Barry remembers this as being one instance in which Br. Ephrem's judgment was not borne out, but usually when the provincial made a judgment call, it was the right one.

Even if they did not see eye to eye on all occasions, Br. Barry is happy to have worked with Br. Ephrem. His recollection is that you could get bruised working with the man, but the provincial was fundamentally a good man and was without doubt the right man for his time.

Br. Barry remembers Br. Ephrem in his later years as being an outstanding man of faith and one who mixed freely with his confreres.

Br. Barry feels that Br. Ephrem taught him through word and example how to deal with the hierarchy. The lessons, Br. Barry believes, were equally applicable for dealing with Br. Ephrem himself. Br. Ephrem was a respected and knowledgeable man who could hold his own at any time.

When Br. Donatus Schmitz became the first Midwest Province provincial in 1956 and Br. Ephrem went East as vice provincial there, Br. Donatus requested the outgoing provincial to return for a brief time to help him with the transition. Br. Ephrem apparently refused, and only the intervention of the superior general prodded Br. Ephrem to come back to Notre Dame to help his successor for a time.

While at Vincent Hall in Texas, Br. Barry had a special telephone line installed to bypass the all-too-regular difficulty of getting a free outside line on the university switchboard. When Br. Ephrem came for the visit, he heard of this unbudgeted expense and immediately ordered the phone removed, because permission had not been received for this unusual outlay. Shortly afterward, Br. Theo Flynn took over Br. Barry's position and installed the phone again at once, couching the expense in some more general category in the house books.

BR. JOHN CHRYSOSTOM RYAN (EASTERN PROVINCE)

When in high school, Br. John was attracted to the life of the brothers, but did not want to teach, as did the Christian Brothers who conducted the school he attended. So when an ad prepared by Br. Ephrem appeared in the Troy, New York, Catholic newspaper, Br. John answered it. Br. Ephrem replied immediately with a personal letter plus several pamphlets. Br. John went to Valatie to visit and found Br. Ephrem to be the ideal vocation director. He was also impressed favorably by Br. Eymard Salzman, superior. A week later Br. John agreed to join Holy Cross.

Though it is fairly generally known that Br. Ephrem and Fr. William Doheny, superior of the generalate house in New York, did not get along well and that because of this circumstance Br. Ephrem went up to Valatie to teach the aspirants each semester, something less well known is that one reason Br. Ephrem made his periodic escape was to avoid being named the steam man—the person in charge of firing the boiler in the generalate house—a task which Fr. Doheny apparently wished to assign to Br. Ephrem.

On one occasion when relations between the priests and brothers were strained at North Dartmouth, Massachusetts, where the novitiate in the East was located, the superior general sent Br. Ephrem to mediate the situation and restore harmony.

In 1946, the first year of autonomy as a single brothers' province, Br. Ephrem was very supportive of his men, encouraging them to move forward boldly on their own. He was tough on superiors, because they needed to be models showing that the brothers could stand on their own feet.

Br. Ephrem maintained a good relationship with the non-teaching brothers, and in Br. John's case the provincial used on occasion to slip the young man some extra money for vacation.

Br. Ephrem was proud of the 24 Ricardo St. house in West Haven, because it was the first house of the brothers specifically designed to be a provincial residence and office. In the house Br. Ephrem was a stickler for religious discipline, but on the wearing of the habit he had relaxed his expectations during the warmer weather. Br. Theophane Schmitt, assistant general, came to the house for an official visit. After his return to New York a letter arrived from Fr. Christopher J. O'Toole, superior general, requesting that the habit be worn at all times in the house. Br. Ephrem did not take kindly to having been reported to the superior general for laxity in the observance of the rule.

Br. Ephrem was a close friend of Br. John Chrysostom, even after the provincial had left office. Br. Ephrem was universally respected, even venerated. He liked a drink now and then, especially on Saturday evenings when he would take his weekly shower, then return to the recreation room to watch Lawrence Welk on television. Br. John remembers Br. Ephrem criticizing those who took showers more than once a week.

Br. Ephrem did not ordinarily like to show his feelings, but in various ways he let his sensitivity to persons be known. He was very strict on matters of regular discipline in the house, especially when the province was getting underway in 1946 and then in the East in 1956, but he could relax his stringent supervision of such matters when there was a good reason to do so, and he had ways of showing his compassion and understanding.

There is no question in Br. John's mind that Br. Ephrem was the right man for the job at the time.

Br. Ephrem liked to have a clear desk at the end of the day. Whenever death was discussed, he would say that his desk was clear and he was ready to go.

BR. LIGUORI DENIER (MIDWEST PROVINCE)

On his first home leave from Bengal in 1948 Br. Liguori chanced to meet Br. Ephrem in the eastern United States, where the provincial was traveling on business. Br. Ephrem, happy to see the missionary and solicitous that he take adequate rest, said: *Go home. Stay as long as you want.* Five months later, Br. Liguori turned up at Br. Ephrem's office at Notre Dame and found the provincial scarcely able to contain his irritation that he had been taken literally by the young missionary. Two to three months at home was the maximum stay allowed under ordinary circumstances. But Br. Ephrem could say nothing.

Br. Liguori recalls the first occasion on which Br. Bede Stadler returned from Bengal on home leave. His health was seriously impaired after spending the war years in India. Br. Ephrem met him at Notre Dame, took one look at him, and insisted that Br. Bede remain there until his health had improved and a few pounds had found their way back onto his frame. The provincial did not want Br. Bede's family to see him in such a condition.

CONCLUSION

Indeed, as Br. John Chrysostom remembers, Br. Ephrem's desk was clear and he was ready to go. And there were probably those who were ready for him to go. In all his ninety years he did not cease being Br. Ephrem. When one reflects on Br. Ephrem's life, the personality traits and talents which brought him to prominence in Holy Cross and were exercised and sharpened over a period of forty-three years of nearly uninterrupted responsibility and then another sixteen in partial or full retirement, both his stunning accomplishments and the unique reality of the person leap out at even the casual observer.

These reminiscences could no doubt be embellished further by the tellers. Still others could also contribute an interesting detail here and there concerning one or another anecdote about Br. Ephrem not represented in this volume.

Whatever the expectations, it is hoped that something of the very effective generativity of the tough little Irishman from County Tipperary who answered the call of the Lord as he heard it and committed himself irreversibly and energetically to follow it will remain in the heart and mind of the reader. Perhaps it may stimulate a similar response to the equally valid and exciting call of God today to participate appropriately in his mission in the Church.

Though not a priest or parent, Br. Ephrem can with reason be called "father." Though far from canonization, he is claimed as venerable by many. Though not strictly a *founder,* he can be validly acknowledged in some manner as such by the Brothers of Holy Cross in the United States. Responsible for nearly superhuman apostolic achievements over half a century and more, he nevertheless retains the marks of simple humility and humanity. No one's sole model, he is still an exemplar, even a paradigm. Recognized as the man for his time and place, he responded habitually with graceful panache to the expectations placed on him. The product of a small farm family and minimal education in rural Ireland, he became through principle and determination the image of keen intelligence, indomitable wit, practical morality, unfailing perseverance, religious commitment, and pastoral compassion.

These virtues are needed in every generation, and it is a fortunate one which recognizes it has been blessed with someone possessing them all. Indeed, Br. Ephrem O'Dwyer was, always, the right man in the right place at the right time.

Notes

(GA refers to the archives of the General Administration, Rome, Italy; MW to the archives of the Midwest Province, Notre Dame, Indiana; SW to the South-West Province archives, Austin, Texas; EB to the Eastern Province of Brothers archives, Valatie, New York; and IP to the Indiana Province archives, Notre Dame, Indiana.)

1. THE EARLY YEARS (1888–1931)

1. MW archives, letter of Br. Maurus O'Malley to Br. Edward Sniatecki, May 17, 1983.

2. EB archives, Box 7, Br. Ephrem O'Dwyer, letter of February 12, 1964.

3. Ibid., letter of February 22, 1964.

4. Ibid., letter of February 9, 1964.

5. Ibid., letter of February 4, 1964.

6. EB archives, notes for Br. Franciscus Willet, presumed to be from Br. Ephrem. See letter of Br. Laurian LaForest, archivist, to Br. Philip Armstrong, March 4, 1993.

7. In 1910 Holy Trinity High School in Chicago opened, followed in 1912 by Holy Cross High School in New Orleans and Sacred Heart College in Watertown WI, in 1919 by Boys Catholic High School (later Reitz Memorial) in Evansville IN, and by Cathedral High School in Indianapolis in 1923.

8. Brief of Col. Hoynes, U.N.D. Press, undated, MW archives, Br. Ephrem deceased file #1.

9. EB archives, Box 7.

10. Br. Maurus O'Malley, "The Portrait of a Builder," paper given at the Sixth Annual Holy Cross History Conference, Manchester NH, June 1987, p. 6.

11. MW archives, *N.D. Bulletin*, Brothers listed in, 1850–1950, p. 39.

12. MW archives, Br. Ephrem to Fr. William Cunningham, undated.

13. Br. Maurus O'Malley, p. 6.

14. EB archives, Br. Ephrem to Br. Maurus O'Malley, April 1963.

15. MW archives, *N.D. Bulletin*, 1924/25, v. 20, #4, p. 24.

16. Ibid., #3, p. 14.

17. IP archives, Finnigan & Burns collection, Cathedral High School, 1970/7, Box 1, file #26.

18. Br. Edward Sniatecki, monograph, dated April 29, 1983; see also Br. Maurus O'Malley, "The Portrait of a Builder," p. 7.

19. EB archives, Box 7.

2. AT NOTRE DAME (1931–1938)

1. MW archives, Minutes of Provincial Council meetings, Fr. James A. Burns, 1927–1938.

2. IP archives, George Finnigan and James Burns provincial administration, 1970/8, Box 8/49, file 3:30, October 3, 1931.

3. IP archives, Finnigan and Burns administration, 1970/8, Box 11/49, file 4:23.

4. EB archives, Br. Ephrem, correspondence, letter of April 11, 1965, to Br. Franciscus Willett.

5. James E. Armstrong, class of 1925, N.D. Alumni Director 1926–1967, personal recollections of Br. Ephrem as related to the author.

6. IP archives, memo of Br. Ephrem to Fr. Burns, James A. Burns, Provincial, Papers, University of Notre Dame, 1933, 1970/8, Box 13/49, file 5:11.

7. MW archives, Minutes of the Burns administration.

8. IP archives, position paper of Fr. Hagerty, p. 17, November 20, 1930, Burns papers, files 16:16 and 16:17.

9. MW archives, Minutes of Burns administration, July 29, 1932.

10. MW archives, Minutes of Burns administration.

11. IP archives, memo to Fr. Burns, April 7, 1933, 1970/8, Box 13/49.

12. MW archives, Minutes of Burns administration, April 11, 1933.

13. IP archives, memo of Br. Ephrem to Fr. Burns, Province 1932–1933, 1970/8, Box 13/49, file 5:14.

14. MW archives, Minutes of Burns administration, November 25, 1933.

15. Ibid., June 10, July 3, 1934.

16. Ibid., July 12, 1934.

17. Ibid., August 26, 1935.

18. IP archives, Br. Ephrem to Fr. Burns, July 30, 1936, Vincentian Institute, Albany NY, 1936–1937, 1970/8, Box 23/49, file 8:37.

19. IP archives, Br. Ephrem to Fr. Burns, October 1938, 1970/8, Box 20/49, file 7:42.

20. IP archives, Burns papers, Br. Ephrem to Fr. Burns, April 1936, Valatie 1935–36, 1970/8, Box 20/49, file 7:28.

21. MW archives, Minutes of Burns administration, July 20, 1937.

22. IP archives, Burns papers, Br. Ephrem to Fr. Burns, Dujarie Institute 1936–37, 1970/8, Box 20/49, file 7:42.

23. IP archives, 1970/8, Box 25/49, files 9:54/55.

24. IP archives, Br. Ephrem to Fr. Burns, August 20, 1937, 1970/8, Box 24/49, file 8:65.

25. MW archives, Minutes, Burns Administration, May, 1938.

26. IP archives, Burns papers, Fr. Burns to Br. Ephrem, March 1938, Sacred Heart College 1937–38, 1970/8, Box 25/49, file 9:20.

3. THE O'HARA LETTER (1933)

1. *N.D. Bulletin*, 1931/32, v. 27, #3, pp. 5–6; and 1932/1933, v. 28, #3, pp. 5–6.

2. MW archives, O'Dwyer, deceased file, letter of Br. Ephrem to Fr. John F. O'Hara, December 3, 1933.

4. TOWARD AUTONOMY (1938–1945)

1. Br. Maurus O'Malley, "Portrait of a Builder," p. 8.

2. MW archives, file 9-3/38, letter to Br. Justin, May 16, 1941.

3. Ralph E. Weber, *Notre Dame's John Zahm* (Univ. of Notre Dame Press, 1961), p. 156.

4. Ibid.

5. Ralph E. Weber, "The Life of Reverend John A. Zahm, C.S.C., American Catholic Apologist and Educator," doctoral thesis, Notre Dame, IN, 1956, Special Collection, BX4705.Z13 W375, pp. 371–373.

6. Weber, *Notre Dame's John Zahm*, p. 140.

7. Weber, "Life of Rev. John A. Zahm," p. 319.

8. Ibid., p. 366n.

9. Weber, *Notre Dame's John Zahm*, p. 140.

10. Weber, "Life of Rev. John A. Zahm," p. 319, quoting from Fr. Burns' diary for January 23, 1898.

11. Weber, *Notre Dame's John Zahm*, p. 140.

12. Weber, "Life of Rev. John A. Zahm," p. 375.

13. Ibid., p. 376, letter of Fr. Zahm to Fr. Français, January 12, 1906.

14. Ibid., p. 379.

15. File 9-3/38, MW archives, letter to Fr. Steiner, May 23, 1944.

16. SW Province, William Mang papers, Br. Ephrem to Br. William, May 23, 1944.

17. IP archives, Superior General Correspondence, administration of Fr. Thomas A. Steiner, March-July 1944, file 31/47.

18. MW archives, "Brothers of Holy Cross in the U.S.," p. 24.

19. From the late eighteen hundreds until the end of the first decade of the twentieth century, the brothers in the U.S. outnumbered the priests by approximately three to one. Community lists for those years show 161 brothers and 46 priests (1883), 157 brothers and 60 priests (1900), and 153 brothers and 90 priests (1910). But the tide was beginning to change. In 1915 there were 138 brothers and 119 priests; in 1920, 134 brothers and 131 priests, and in 1925, 145 brothers and 162 priests. Yet in 1945 when the decision was made to divide into autonomous provinces, the priests and brothers were virtually equal, with 368 in the lay society and 367 in the clerical. (Data from community lists is found in the Midwest Province archives and from research done by Br. Thomas Moser.)

20. O'Dwyer, "Brothers of Holy Cross in the U.S.," pp. 62–63.

21. Ibid, p. 170.

22. Ibid., pp. 170–171.

23. Ibid., p. 174.

24. EB archives, letter to Br. Elmo Bransby, October 15, 1976.

25. EB archives, letter to Br. Maurus O'Malley, April 1963.

26. Fr. Donahue had died at the relatively young age of fifty-seven on June 30, 1943, and was buried on July 3, with Frs. Cousineau, Steiner, and Deguire presiding at the solemn high requiem mass.

27. MW archives, Br. Bonaventure Foley, letter to Br. Elmo Bransby, October 19, 1976, file Correspondence Re: Proposed Autonomy, 18/3-4.

28. SW archives, Mang Papers.

29. MW archives, file 18/3-3, Br. Léopold to Br. Ephrem, January 21, 1945.

30. Ibid., Br. Ephrem to Br. Léopold, March 31, 1945.

31. Ibid., Br. Léopold to Br. Ephrem, April 6, 1945.

32. Ibid., letter of Br. Ephrem to Br. Léopold Taillon, April 17, 1945.

33. SW archives, Br. Ephrem to Br. William from Valatie NY, March 9, 1942.

34. Ibid., June 1, 1943.

35. Ibid., February 2, 1945.

36. Ibid., December 3, 1943.

37. Ibid., January 13, 1945.

38. Ibid., December 19, 1944.

39. MW archives, Division of Property and Assets between Societies, 1945, file 18/3-5.

40. Ibid.

41. Ibid.

42. SW archives, Br. Ephrem to Br. William, May 21, 1945.

43. Ibid., May 23, 1945.

44. MW archives, Proposed Autonomy, file 18/3-4, Br. Ephrem to Br. Bonaventure, January 21, 1945.

45. Ibid., Br. Bonaventure to Br. Ephrem, February 6, 1945.

46. Ibid., Br. Ephrem to Br. Bonaventure, February 9, 1945.

47. Ibid., Br. Bonaventure to Br. Ephrem, March 7, 1945.

48. Ibid., May 8, 1945.

49. Ibid., Br. Ephrem to Br. Bonaventure, May 9, 1945.

50. IP archives, Report of the priest members of the committee, Thomas A. Steiner, provincial administration papers, 1945 General Chapter, Homogeneous Provinces, Box 12/12, file 31/75.

51. MW archives, file 18/3-4, undated memo of Br. Ephrem to Br. Bonaventure, possibly a companion document to the May 11 letter.

52. Ibid., May 11, 1945.

5. THE GENERAL CHAPTER OF 1945

1. SW archives, Br. Ephrem to Br. William from New York, June 12, 1944.

2. File 18/3-4, MW archives, Correspondence re: Proposal for Autonomy, letter of February 28, 1945, from Br. William to Br. Ephrem.

3. File 18/3-6, MW archives, letter of Br. Ephrem to Br. William Mang, May 26, 1945.

4. Ibid., letter of Br. William to Br. Ephrem, May 29, 1945.

5. SW archives, Br. Ephrem to Br. William, June 1, 1945.

6. Ibid., May 11, 1943.

7. Ibid., November 8, 1943.

8. Ibid., December 3, 1943.

9. MW archives, Division of Property and Assets between Societies, 1945, Concerning Union of Two Societies, Fathers and Brothers in the Congregation of Holy Cross, file 18/3-5.

10. *Directory,* Congregation of Holy Cross, Ave Maria Press, Notre Dame IN, 1946, p. 376.

11. MW archives, file 18/3-5.

12. MW archives, file 18/3-3.

13. MW archives, file 18/3-5.

14. GA archives, Rome, serial #22, Minutes, 1943–1950, Cousineau administration, meeting of November 29, 1943, pp. 9–11.

15. MW archives, file 18/3-5.

16. Ibid.

17. Ibid.

18. IP archives, Report of the Superior General, Steiner papers, 12/12, file 31/75, 1945 General Chapter, Homogeneous Provinces.

19. IP archives, Steiner papers, Box 4/12, file 27/15, and Box 13, file 31/49, correspondence with the superior general. Curiously the letter appointing the committee is dated March 6, 1945, the exact day on which the report submitted by the priest members of the committee is dated. It is probable that the date was May 6, as the opening paragraphs refer to the first meeting of the committee as having taken place on March 22.

20. Br. Maurus O'Malley, p. 8.

21. MW archives, Preparation for Autonomy, 1944, files 18/3-3, 18/3-4, and 18/3-5, consisting of letters, reports, minutes and other documents.

22. This paragraph seems incomplete.

23. MW archives, Correspondence re: Proposed Autonomy, file 18/3-4, October 19, 1976, letter to Br. Elmo Bransby, assistant general.

24. IP archives, Steiner papers, Box 12/12, file 31/75, 1945 General Chapter, Homogeneous Provinces, dated April 6, 1945, Ottawa, Canada.

25. GA archives, Rome, file 011, "Union and Distinction of Societies," folder 1, Fr. Thomas Barrosse, "History of the Union of the Two Societies—Longer Study," p. 14.

26. MW archives, CL No. 21 of Fr. Cousineau, file 18/3-5.

6. A BUSY INTERIM (1945–1946)

1. MW archives, Minutes of Steiner administration, August 3 and September 29, 1945.

2. South Bend Tribune, July 7, 1946.

3. MW archives, letter of Br. Ephrem to Br. Maurus O'Malley, April 1963.

4. Ibid.

5. GA archives, Rome, file 083.11, Homogeneous Provinces, letter in French of Fr. Cousineau to Archbishop Cicognani, December 8, 1945.

6. Ibid., letter of Fr. Cousineau to Archbishop Cicognani, January 2, 1946.

7. MW archives, Br. Ephrem to Br. Maurus O'Malley, April 1963.

8. MW archives, file 18/3-6, letter of Br. Venard to Br. Ephrem, October 3, 1945. Three subsequent letters from Br. Venard to Br. Ephrem (December 14, 1945 and January 1 and 5, 1946) can be found in the same file.

9. GA archives, Rome, file 083.11, Homogeneous Provinces, letter of Fr. Cousineau to Fr. Georges Sauvage, December 11, 1945.

10. Ibid., letter of Archbishop Cicognani to Fr. Cousineau, December 4, 1945.

11. MW archives, Report to the Apostolic Delegate, Dec. 9, 1945, by Brothers mentioned.

12. See GA archives, Rome, file 083.11, Homogeneous Provinces, letters of Fr. Cousineau to Fr. Georges Sauvage dated December 24, 1945, to Archbishop Cicognani dated January 2, 1946, another to Fr. Sauvage dated January 11, 1946, and one to Fr. Pierre Poisson dated December 31, 1945.

13. GA archives, Rome, file 083.11, Homogeneous Provinces, Fr. Cousineau to Fr. Sauvage, December 24, 1945.

14. Ibid., letter of Fr. Cousineau to Archbishop Cicognani, December 20, 1945, and to Fr. Georges Sauvage, December 24, 1945.

15. Ibid., letter of Fr. Cousineau to Archbishop Cicognani, December 20, 1945.

16. Ibid., letter of Fr. Cousineau to Msgr. Pasetto, N. 2857/45 F. 24, January 6, 1946.

17. Ibid., letter of Fr. Cousineau to Archbishop Cicognani, January 7, 1946.

18. Ibid., letter of Fr. Cousineau to Fr. Sauvage, January 11, 1946.

19. MW archives, file 18/3-6.

20. MW archives, letter of Fr. Heston to Br. Gervais, January 13, 1945.

21. MW archives, file 18/3-6.

22. EB archives, letter of Br. Ephrem to Br. Elmo Bransby, October 15, 1976.

23. EB archives, 255, A9.1, Item 17.

24. MW archives, file: General Chapter—1968, "The Coadjutor Brother Problem."

25. MW archives, file 18/3-21, CL No. 1, August 30, 1946.

26. EB archives, 255, A9.1, Item 16, letter of Br. Ephrem to Br. Renatus, December 17, 1976.

27. IP archives, Steiner papers, Brothers of Holy Cross, Early Incorporation, Box 4/12, file 27/13.

28. MW archives, Provincial council minutes, June 29, 1946.

7. A MAN FOR HIS TIME (1946–1956)

1. *South Bend Tribune*, July 7, 1946.
2. MW archives, a characterization of Br. Ephrem as quoted in a typed copy of an unsigned manuscript, chapter 2, Administration of Br. Ephrem (1956–1962), pp. 4–5.
3. SW archives, Br. Ephrem to Br. William Mang, March 28, 1945.
4. This alternate form is noted on an undated, unsigned memo in the SW archives in the William Mang papers and refers to a request from the superior general to consider the question of provinces at the chapter *next summer.*
5. MW archives, file 9/4-10, House Schedules, 1953.
6. MW archives, "Br. Ephrem O'Dwyer, C.S.C.: The Years 1946–1956," Br. Columba Curran, May 1977, O'Dwyer, deceased file.
7. MW archives, *The Brothers of Holy Cross*, vol. 2, no. 5, February 1950, p.1, O'Dwyer, deceased file.

8. AN ASTUTE ADMINISTRATOR

1. SW archives, Br. Ephrem to Br. William, February 14, 1952.
2. Ibid., October 8, 1952.
3. General Archives, Rome, Italy, Kelley papers, letter from Fr. Kelley to Fr. Cousineau, February 23, 1947.
4. Ibid., letter of Fr. Kelley to Fr. Sauvage, February 17, 1947.
5. SW archives, Br. Ephrem to Br. William, May 28, 1947.
6. MW archives, file 9-1/3, letter to Br. Alcuin Nuss, April 3, 1950.
7. MW archives, file 9-1/5, letter to Br. Sabinus, March 31, 1954.
8. MW archives, file 9-1/35, letter to Br. Jude, May 14, 1951.
9. MW archives, file 9-2/11, letter to Br. Lawrence Miller, May 19, 1956.
10. MW archives, file 9-2/27, letter to Br. Marcellinus Fahey, postmaster, September 24, 1955.
11. MW archives, file 9-2/33, letter to Fr. Charles Delaney, September 1, 1954.
12. MW archives, file 9-3/8, letter to Br. Eymard, November 17, 1947.
13. Ibid., letter to Br. Eymard Salzman, February 4, 1948.
14. MW archives, file 9-3/32, letter to Fr. Fitzpatrick, February 4, 1956.
15. MW archives, file 9-3/37, memo to Br. John Baptist, November 3, 1950.

16. MW archives, file 9-4/16, letter to Mrs. Mary C. Martin, mother of Brothers John and Raymond Martin, July 1, 1953.

17. MW archives, file 9-4/17, memo titled "Concerning the Meeting of the Local Superiors at N.D., July 15, 1946," dated August 15, 1946.

18. Ibid., MW archives, directives approved by Br. Ephrem, no date given, but the directives were in response to recommendations of superiors of houses of formation made on August 13 and 14, 1953.

19. MW archives, file 9-1/3, letter to Br. Ernest Ryan, August 18, 1949.

20. MW archives, file 9-1/5, letter to Br. Sabinus, April 23, 1955.

21. MW archives, file 9-1/26, letter to Br. Theophane Schmitt, September 9, 1950.

22. MW archives, file 9-1/31, letter to Br. Laurian LaForest, April 26, 1955.

23. MW archives, file 9-1/36, letter to Br. Jude Costello, March 10, 1950.

24. Ibid., letter from Br. Jude Costello to Br. Ephrem, March 20, 1950.

25. MW archives, file 9-1/37, letter to Br. Jude Costello, November 28, 1951.

26. MW archives, file 9-2/3, letter to Br. John William Donoghue, May 2, 1952.

27. Ibid., letter to Br. John William Donoghue, November 18, 1952.

28. MW archives, file 9-1/3, letter to Brothers Jacob Eppley and Alcuin Nuss, Aug. 14, 1946.

29. Ibid., letter to Fr. Theodore Mehling, June 13, 1953.

30. MW archives, file 9-1/4, letter to Br. Alcuin Nuss, January 19, 1952.

31. Ibid., letter to Fr. Theodore Mehling, April 17, 1952.

32. MW archives, file 9-1/5, letter to Fr. Duffey, February 9, 1953.

33. MW archives, file 9-1/36, letter to Br. Jude Costello, July 4, 1947.

34. MW archives, file 9-2/20, letter of Br. Nicholas to Br. Ephrem, March 29, 1950; and from Br. Ephrem to Br. Nicholas, March 31, 1950.

35. Ibid., letter to Brs. Dominic and Nicholas, August 4, 1949.

36. MW archives, file 9-2/24, letter of Fr. Cavanaugh to Br. Ephrem, July 28, 1949.

37. MW archives, file 9-2/45, letter to Br. Bonaventure, June 5, 1946, nearly a month prior to the official establishment of the Brothers' Province.

38. MW archives, file 9-3/19, letter of Fr. Cousineau to Br. Ephrem, June 7, 1946.

39. General Archives, Congregation of Holy Cross, Rome, Italy, Steiner papers, letter of Fr. Cousineau to Fr. Steiner, June 7, 1946.

40. General Archives, Rome, Italy, O'Toole papers, letter of Fr. Cousineau to Fr. O'Toole, June 7, 1946.

41. MW archives, file 9-3/19, letter to Fr. Cousineau, June 7, 1946.

42. General Archives, Rome, Italy, O'Dwyer papers, letter from Fr. Cousineau to Br. Ephrem, June 11, 1946.

43. General Archives, Rome, Italy, O'Toole papers, letter of Fr. O'Toole to Fr. Cousineau, June 11, 1946.

44. IP, Steiner papers, Superior General Correspondence, Fr. Steiner to Fr. Cousineau, September 13, 1946.

45. MW archives, file 9-3/19, letter to Fr. Cousineau, April 28, 1947.

46. Ibid., letter to Fr. Albert Cousineau, superior general, July 9, 1947.

47. Ibid., letter to Br. Venard Gorman, June 7, 1946, the day he had also written to Fr. Cousineau on the same matters.

48. MW archives, file 9-3/25, letter to Fr. O'Toole, March 25, 1954.

49. MW archives, file 9-3/23, letter to Fr. O'Toole, April 14, 1952.

50. SW archives, Br. Ephrem to Br. William, June 2, 1942.

51. MW archives, file 9-3/25.

52. MW archives, files 9-3/2 and 9-3/3, letters to Msgr. Olen A. Broussard, Opelousas LA, June 19, 1951; Rev. Joseph Somes, Columbus IN, March 6, 1953; Rev. A. W. Steinhauser, Louisville KY, May 8, 1954; Msgr. Bernard Dolan, Long Beach CA, February 2, 1955; Bishop Charles Buddy, San Diego CA, November 16, 1951; Archbishop Egidio Vagnozzi, Manila, Philippines, January 8, 1954 (see also letters of Fr. Christopher J. O'Toole, superior general, November 11 and December 12, 1953 in file 9-3/25, MW archives); Bishop Wendelin Nold, Galveston TX, January 22, 1954; and Msgr. D. F. Cunningham, superintendent of schools in Chicago IL, January 6, 1956.

53. Cf. MW archives, file 9-3/26.

54. MW archives, file 9-1/16, letter of Br. Ephrem to Fr. O'Toole, mid–1954.

55. MW archives, file 9-2/31, letter to Br. Barry, September 19, 1952.

56. MW archives, file 9-3/25, letter to Fr. O'Toole, September 23, 1953.

57. MW archives, file 9-3/38, letter to Br. Ephrem, May 9, 1955.

58. Ibid., letter to Br. Ephrem, August 11, 1928.

9. EDUCATIONAL SUPERVISION

1. SW archives, Br. William to Br. Ephrem, November 20, 1951.

2. SW archives, Br. Ephrem to Br. William, April 11, 1951. Bishop McEntegart of the Diocese of Ogdensburg, NY, offered the brothers a small college, Clarkson College in upstate New York. It was a tempting offer, but Br. Ephrem was interested only if a tie-in could be made with the training of the scholastics. Br. Ephrem was familiar with the area because relatives lived close by.

3. MW archives, file 9-1/6, letter to Msgr. Deady, March 22, 1948.

4. Ibid., letters to and from Msgr. Deady, December 9, 13, 15, 1948.

5. Ibid., letters of Msgr. Deady and Br. Ephrem of June 12 and 17, 1949, and July 12 and 14, 1949.

6. MW archives, file 9-1/29, letter to Br. Laurian LaForest, headmaster of Gilmour Academy, December 3, 1953.

7. MW archives, file 9-1/14, letter to Rev. William Shaw, December 5, 1953.

8. MW archives, file 9-3/20, letter to Fr. Louis Kelley, vice superior general, May 16, 1948.

9. Ibid., letter to Fr. Cousineau, February 22, 1949.

10. MW archives, file 9-2/1, letter to Br. John William Donoghue, January 17, 1951.

11. MW archives, file 9-2/3, letter to Br. John William Donoghue, April 12, 1952.

12. MW archives, Lakewood drawer, Correspondence—Personal, 1945–1954, letter to Br. John William Donoghue, October 11, 1949.

13. Ibid., letter to Br. John William, June 9, 1953.

14. MW archives, Lakewood file, Diocese of Cleveland, 1949–1970, letter of Br. Ephrem to Archbishop Hoban, February 7, 1956, and letter of Archbishop Hoban to Br. Ephrem, February 10, 1956. It is curious to note that on December 3 of that very same year, Msgr. Edward Seward, Chancellor for the archdiocese, wrote to Br. Donatus Schmitz, provincial of the newly established Midwest Province, that permission was given in accord with Br. Donatus's request to raise the tuition at St. Edward High School from $120 to $135 per student.

15. MW archives, file 9-2/36, letter of Br. Ephrem to Fr. Albert Cousineau, April 5, 1948.

16. MW archives, file 9-1/8b, letter to Br. Reginald Justak, March 2, 1948.

17. Ibid., letter to Br. Reginald Justak, March 24, 1948.

18. MW archives, file 9-1/31, letter to Br. Alfonso Comeau, November 23, 1955.

19. MW archives, file 9-1/31, letter of Br. Alfonso to Br. Ephrem, November 28, 1955.

20. Ibid., letter to Br. Alfonso Comeau, November 27, 1955. The date of this letter does not correspond to the chronology found in the previous two letters of November 23 and 28.

21. MW archives, file 9-2/5, letter to Br. John William Donoghue.

22. MW archives, file 9-1/22, letter to Br. Ambrose Nowak, January 15, 1954.

23. MW archives, file 9-2/4, letter to Br. John William Donoghue, principal of St. Edward High School, Lakewood OH, March 24 and 25, 1953.

24. MW archives, file 9-1/2, letter to Br. Noel Romanek.

25. MW archives, file 9-1/6, letter to Br. Hilarion Brezik, September 14, 1949.

26. MW archives, file 9-1/9, letter to Br. Norbert Henske, January 13, 1948.

27. MW archives, file 9-1/21, letter to Br. Isaac Jogues Motz, October 24, 1952.

28. Ibid., letter to Br. Isaac Jogues Motz, March 2, 1953.

29. Ibid., letters to Rev. Robert A. Deig, superintendent, June 8 and 19, 1953.

30. MW archives, file 9-1/28, letter to Br. Laurian LaForest, headmaster at Gilmour Academy, April 12, 1952.

31. MW archives, file 9-1/31, letter to Brs. Laurian, Noel and John William, October 8, 1954.

32. MW archives, file 9-1/41, letter to Br. Pedro Haering, principal of Cathedral High School, Indianapolis, October 10, 1955.

33. MW archives, file 9-1/22, letter to Br. Ambrose Nowak, September 21, 1953.

34. MW archives, file 9-1/24, letter to Br. Theophane Schmitt, July 31, 1946.

35. Ibid., letter to Br. Theophane Schmitt, August 1, 1946.

36. Ibid., letter of Br. Theophane to Br. Ephrem, August 5, 1946.

37. Ibid., letter to Br. Theophane Schmitt, October 23, 1946.

38. MW archives, file 9-1/26, letter to Br. Theophane Schmitt, November 22, 1950.

39. Ibid., letter of Br. Theophane Schmitt to Br. Ephrem, November 24, 1950.

40. MW archives, file 9-1/29, letter to Br. Laurian LaForest, headmaster at Gilmour, August 22, 1953.

41. MW archives, file 9-1/39, letter to Br. Regis Regensberger, April 30, 1949.

42. MW archives, file 9-2/1, letter to Br. John William Donoghue, September 15, 1949.

43. MW archives, file 9-3/5, letter to Br. Ambrose Nowak, Reitz Memorial High School, Evansville, IN, June 20, 1954.

44. MW archives, Lakewood drawer, Correspondence—Personal, 1945–1954, letter to Br. John William concerning Brothers Paul Schwoyer and Regius Gendron, October 11, 1949.

45. Ibid., letter to Br. John William, March 11, 1953.

46. Ibid., letter to Br. John William Donoghue.

47. MW archives, file 9-1/2, letter to Archbishop Hoban.

48. MW archives, file 9-2/6, letter to Br. Barry Lambour, St. Edward High School, Lakewood OH.

49. MW archives, file 9-1/2, letter to superiors of property schools.

50. MW archives, file 9-1/22, letter to Br. Ambrose Nowak, February 6, 1956.

51. MW archives, file 9-1/31, letter to Br. Laurian, April 6, 1955.

52. MW archives, file 9-3/41, letter to Fr. Heston, August 14, 1947.

53. Ibid., Summary to Fr. Heston re: Sisters, August 13, 1947.

54. Ibid., letters from Fr. Heston to Br. Ephrem, January 31, 1948, and May 20, 1953.

55. MW archives, file 9-1/18, a group of letters within the file categorized "Brother Elmo, 1947–1954."

56. MW archives, file 9-3/40, undated memo on Br. Ephrem's personal memo pad paper, presumed to allude to the August 2, 1954, meeting of the Committee on Studies.

10. PERSONNEL ISSUES

1. SW archives, Br. Ephrem to Br. William, October 17, 1950.

2. Ibid., December 4, 1954.

3. MW archives, file 9-2/6, letter to Br. Barry Lambour, May 10, 1956.

4. MW archives, file 9-1/16, letter to Br. Joseph Kerr, April 24, 1952.

5. MW archives, file 9-2/8, letter to Br. Lawrence Miller, April 11, 1950, regarding a Br. Sylvester.

6. MW archives, file 9-2/9, letter to Br. Lawrence Miller, April 17, 1951.

7. MW archives, file 9-2/14, letter to Br. Cyprian, June 8, 1954.

8. MW archives, file 9-3/37, letter to Br. John Baptist, November 18, 1950.

9. Ibid., letter to Br. John Baptist, December 13, 1950.

10. Ibid., letter to Br. John Baptist, November 18, 1950.

11. SW archives, Br. Ephrem to Mr. Cherry, January 28, 1956.

12. MW archives, file 9-1/7, letter to Br. Hilarion Brezik, January 14, 1951.

13. MW archives, file 9-1/11, letter to Br. Roman Witowski, February 19, 1954.

14. MW archives, file 9-1/39, letter to Br. Kerran Dugan, April 29, 1949.

15. MW archives, file 9-2/30, letter to Br. Raphael Wilson, December 27, 1950.

16. MW archives, file 9-3/10, letter to Daniel M. Lynch, Pullman, Washington, March 8, 1951.

17. MW archives, file 9-3/33, letters of Br. Ephrem to Br. Meloche, March 25, 1949, and from Br. Meloche to Br. Ephrem, March 29, 1949. Also, letter to Br. Meloche from Br. Ephrem, July 29, 1949, and from Br. Meloche to Br. Ephrem, August 23, 1949; Br. Ephrem to Br. Meloche, April 13, 1950; Br. Meloche to Br. Ephrem, April 15, 1950, and Br. Crête to Br. Ephrem, August 29, 1950; and Br. Ephrem to Br. Crête, September 1, 1950. Information concerning the courses completed in Montreal provided on November 16, 1992, by Br. Raymond Dufresne, who did three summers of work at the university. The other was Br. François Gibault, who subsequently left the congregation.

18. MW archives, file 9-1/8b, letter to Br. Reginald Justak, February 20, 1951.

19. MW archives, file 9-2/27, letter to Br. Eli Pelchat, November 25, 1954.

20. MW archives, file 9-3/10b, letter to Br. Eymard, September 23, 1953.

21. MW archives, file 9-1/3, letter of Br. John Baptist Titzer to Rev. Theodore Mehling.

22. MW archives, file 9-1/5, letters of Br. Ephrem and Fr. Reedy.

23. MW archives, file 9-3/31, letter to Fr. McCauley, April 24, 1952.

24. MW archives, file 9-1/9, letter to Br. Sigismund Danielski, June 9, 1948.

25. MW archives, file 9-1/29, letter to Br. Martin Stuck, May 15, 1953.

26. MW archives, file 9-1/33, letters to and from Br. Julian Beaudry, June 6, 1949 to January 18, 1951.

27. MW archives, file 9-1/39, letter to Br. Regis, January 27, 1950.

28. Ibid., letter to Br. Paul of the Cross Bozek, November 5, 1947.

29. MW archives, file 9-2/40, letter to Br. Dacian Renner referring to Br. Ignatius Boyd, local superior of Gibault Home for Boys, Terre Haute IN, August 10, 1948.

30. MW archives, file 9-2/45, letter to Br. Martin Stuck, November 18, 1947.

31. MW archives, file 9-3/35, circular letter to the membership, August 15, 1948.

32. Ibid., August 22, 1954.

33. MW archives, file 9-4/4, cover letter for visit report to Fr. Cousineau, October 1, 1949.

34. MW archives, file 18-3/21 bulletin from the Provincial Office dated August 22, 1954.

35. MW archives, file 9-4/14, letter to Br. Donatus, May 10, 1948.

36. Ibid., *Vacations* policy dated June 1, 1948. This memo may have been specifically directed to the Community House membership.

37. Ibid., letter to Br. Octavius, May 28, 1947.

38. Ibid., letter to Br. Maurus O'Malley, May 21, 1951, concerning Brothers William Babbitt and Theodore LaTour.

39. Ibid., letter to Br. Rex, May 21, 1951.

40. Ibid., letter to Br. Christian, May 21, 1951.

41. Ibid., letter to Br. Ellis, May 22, 1951.

42. Ibid., letter to Br. Francis Assisi, May 22, 1951.

43. Ibid., letter to Br. Theophane, May 23, 1951.

44. SW archives, Br. Ephrem to Br. Alfonso, June 10, 1953.

45. MW archives, file 9-2/6, letter of November 19, 1955.

46. MW archives, file 9-1/12, letter to Br. Joseph Walter Olszowka, Holy Trinity H.S., Chicago, about a brother who had left. Letter written November 8, 1955.

47. MW archives, file 9-2/22, letter to Br. Gerontius, April 14, 1956.

48. MW archives, file 9-2/46, letter to Br. Eymard, December 13, 1948.

49. MW archives, file 9-3/19, letter to Fr. Cousineau, May 16, 1947.

50. MW archives, file 9-3/35, circular letter to the membership, December 1, 1952.

51. MW archives, file 9-4/5, letter to Br. John Baptist, November 22, 1950.

52. MW archives, file 18-3/21 bulletin of Br. Ephrem to superiors, November 1, 1947.

53. Ibid., bulletin of Br. Ephrem, May 13, 1948.

54. MW archives, file 9-1/2, letter to Br. William Babbitt and to Dr. Theodore Gerlinger, M.D.

55. MW archives, file 9-1/7, letter to Br. Alexander Buckley, April 4, 1953.

56. MW archives, file 9-1/8b, letter to Br. Reginald Justak, April 28, 1948.

57. MW archives, file 9-1/33, letter to Br. Columbanus Murphy, November 30, 1950.

58. MW archives, file 9-1/34, letter to Mr. and Mrs. William Redmond about their son, Br. William Redmond, August 24, 1955.

59. MW archives, file 9-2/2, letter to Br. John William Donoghue regarding Br. Regius Gendron's request, November 1, 1951.

60. MW archives, file 9-2/9, letter to Br. Lawrence Miller, November 29, 1951.

61. MW archives, file 9-2/40, letter to Br. Ignatius Boyd, June 16, 1948.

62. MW archives, file 9-1/29, letter to Br. Thomas Cousineau, June 27, 1953.

63. MW archives, file 9-1/31, letter of June 13, 1955..

64. MW archives, file 9-3/20, letter to Fr. Cousineau, April 21, 1948.

65. MW archives, file 9-3/37, letter to Br. John Baptist, January 24, 1952.

66. MW archives, file 9-2/11, letter to Br. Joseph Buersmeyer, C.S.C., January 19, 1955.

67. MW archives, file 9-2/31, letter to Br. Elmo Bransby, Vincent Hall Scholasticate, Austin TX, March 9, 1951.

68. Ibid., letter to Br. Elmo Bransby, December 26, 1951.

69. Ibid., letter to Brother Nicholas Lyddane, January 16, 1951.

70. MW archives, file 9-2/46, letter to Br. Donald Shirey, Sacred Heart Juniorate, Watertown WI, April 5, 1949.

11. SOCIETAL IMAGE AND IDENTITY

1. IP archives, B-2, Burns Papers, Acc. No. 1970/8, Box 13/49, Province 1932–1933, file 5:14.

2. IP archives, B-2 Burns Papers, Acc. No. 1970/8, Box 25/49, Papers 1937–38, File 9:18, Province 1936–1938, letter of Br. Ephrem to Fr. Burns, July 10, 1937.

3. MW archives, file 9-1/18, located within a group of letters entitled C.S.C.'s 1947–1954.

4. MW archives, file 9-3/38, letter to Fr. Cousineau, April 21, 1941.

5. MW archives, file 9-2/19, letter to Fr. Duffey, October 14, 1946.

6. MW archives, file 9-3/20, letter to Fr. Cousineau, March 29, 1948.

7. MW archives, file 9-3/35, circular letter to the province, May 13, 1948.

8. MW archives, file 9-2/46, letter to Br. Donatus Schmitz, Sacred Heart Juniorate, Watertown WI, March 6, 1949.

9. MW archives, file 9-1/36, letter to Br. Jude Costello, April 9, 1949.

10. MW archives, file 9-1/3, letter to Fr. Theodore Mehling of June 10, 1953.

11. MW archives, file 9-1/22, letter to Br. Ambrose Nowak, December 30, 1953.

12. MW archives, file 9-2/49, letter to Br. Lambert, June 23, 1954.

13. MW archives, file 9-1/5, letters of Br. Ephrem and Fr. Reedy.

12. THE SPIRITUAL UNDERPINNING

1. MW archives, file 18-3/21, Circular Letter #1, Br. Ephrem O'Dwyer, August 30, 1946, pp. 1, 11, 13, 14.

2. Ibid., bulletin of Br. Ephrem, May 13, 1948.

3. Ibid., May 18, 1948.

4. IP archives, Steiner papers, Box 4/12, file 27/17, letter of Br. Ephrem to Fr. Steiner, April 29, 1949.

5. MW archives, file 9-3/37, letter to Br. John Baptist, November 22, 1950.

6. MW archives, file 9-3/27, letter to Fr. O'Toole, April 25, 1955.

7. SW archives, Br. Ephrem to Br. William, June 2, 1942.

8. MW archives, file 9-3/29, letter to Brothers Hobart, Martinian, Fulgence, and Ivan, undated carbon copy, but surely in 1947.

9. Ibid., letter to Br. Emilian Maniaci, November 19, 1948.

10. MW archives, file 9-2/46, letter of June 6, 1949.

11. MW archives, file 9-1/9, letter to Br. Jerome Feldman, December 9, 1950.

12. MW archives, file 9-2/9, letter to Br. Lawrence Miller, St. Charles Boys Home, Milwaukee WI, March 30, 1951.

13. MW archives, file 9-2/48, letter to Br. Francis Borgia Woehler, superior of Sacred Heart Juniorate, Watertown WI, March 20, 1953.

14. MW archives, file 9-4/1, circular letter to membership, August 15, 1948.

15. MW archives, file 9-2/2, letter to Br. John William Donoghue, November 5, 1951.

16. MW archives, file 9-1/16, letters to and from Br. Gerard Fitz, October 8, 1952.

17. Ibid., letter to Br. Gerard Fitz, February 20, 1954.

18. MW archives, file 9-2/4, letter to Br. John William Donoghue, principal of St. Edward High School, Lakewood OH, September 15, 1953.

19. MW archives, file 9-2/22, letter to Br. Dominic Elder, June 10, 1953.

20. MW archives, file 9-1/8, letter to Br. Hilarion Brezik, March 12, 1955.

21. EB archives, 255, B1.1b, July 6, 1959.

22. Ibid., January 15, 1959.

23. Br. Maurus O'Malley, "The Portrait of a Builder," pp. 18–19.

13. A MAN LIKE US

1. SW archives, Br. Ephrem to Br. William, June 2, 1942.

2. Ibid., December 3, 1943.

3. MW archives, file 9-3/20, letter to Fr. Kelley, January 28, 1948.

4. Ibid., letter to Fr. Louis Kelley, vice superior general, May 10, 1948.

5. MW archives, file 9-2/24, letter to Fr. Gartland, March 17, 1949.

6. MW archives, file 9-1/6, letter to Br. Patrick Cain of April 30, 1949.

7. MW archives, file 9-2/8, letter to Br. Lawrence Miller, September 19, 1950.

8. MW archives, file 9-3/30, letter to Br. Ephrem, October 24, 1950.

9. MW archives, file 9-1/14, letter to Br. Charles Andersen, December 14, 1950.

10. MW archives, Lakewood drawer, Correspondence—Personal, 1945–1954, letters to Br. John William, January 12, 1951 and January 17, 1951.

11. SW archives, Br. Ephrem to Br. William, March 28, 1954.

12. MW archives, file 9-3/32, letter to Fr. Fitzpatrick, February 18, 1956.

13. MW archives, file 18-3/4 Correspondence re: Proposal for Autonomy, letter of February 9, 1945, to Br. William Mang.

14. IP archives, Steiner papers, 30/75, St. Joseph Novitiate #5.

15. SW archives, William Mang papers.

16. SW archives, Br. Ephrem to Br. William, July 18, 1947.

17. SW archives, William Mang papers.

18. MW archives, file 9-3/41, letter to Fr. Heston, August 14, 1947.

19. MW archives, file 9-3/37, letter to Br. John Baptist, February 15, 1951.

20. MW archives, file 9-3/33, letter to Br. Dominique, July 25, 1951.

21. MW archives, file 9-3/37, letter to Br. John Baptist, September 9, 1951.

22. Ibid., letter to Br. John Baptist, September 11, 1951.

23. MW archives, file 9-3/37, September 1951.

24. MW archives, O'Dwyer, "Deceased" drawer (1).

25. MW archives, file 9-3/35, documents as dated in brackets.

26. Ibid., circular of Br. John Baptist to the province, October 17, 1951.

27. MW archives, file 9-3/22, letter to Fr. O'Toole, October 22, 1951.

28. MW archives, file 9-3/38, letter of Fr. O'Toole to Br. Ephrem, October 25, 1951.

29. MW archives, file 9-1/7, letter to Br. Ephrem, October 26, 1951.

30. MW archives, file 9-3/39, letter of Br. William to Br. Bonaventure, November 2, 1951.

31. MW archives, file 9-1/37, letter to Br. Jude, November 9, 1951.

32. MW archives, file 9-3/33, letter to Br. Leopold, December 13, 1951.

33. MW archives, file 9-3/39, letter of Br. Bonaventure to Br. William, June 10, 1952.

34. SW archives, Br. Ephrem to Br. William, December 24, 1952.

35. MW archives, file 9-1/38, letter to Br. John Baptist Titzer from Br. Ephrem, January 14, 1953.

36. MW archives, file 9-3/25, letter to Fr. O'Toole, March 21, 1953.

37. MW archives, file 9-1/34, letter to Br. Kieran Ryan, August 4, 1954.

38. SW archives, Br. Ephrem to Br. William, October 12, 1954.

39. MW archives, file 9-3/37.

40. SW archives, Br. Ephrem to Br. William, February 15, 1955.

41. MW archives, file 9-3/38, letter to Br. Ephrem, January 26, 1943 (my numbering of an unnumbered file found between files 9-3/37 and 9-3/39).

42. MW archives, file 18-3/4, Correspondence re: Proposal for Autonomy, letter of February 28, 1945, from Br. William to Br. Ephrem.

43. IP archives, Steiner papers, Box 4/12, file 27/15, letter of Fr. Cousineau to Fr. Steiner, June 7, 1946.

44. MW archives, file 9-1/18, found in a small group of letters identified as "Bro. Dominic Elder, 1946–1948."

45. MW archives, file 9-3/19, letter to Fr. Cousineau, June 21, 1947.

46. MW archives, file 9-2/46, letter to Br. Donatus Schmitz, superior of Sacred Heart Juniorate, Watertown WI, March 6, 1949.

47. MW archives, file 9-2/31, letter of Br. John Baptist to Br. Elmo Bransby, superior of the scholasticate at St. Edward's University, February 8, 1951.

48. MW archives, file 9-3/37, letter to Br. John Baptist, April 26, 1951.

49. MW archives, file 9-3/25, letter to Fr. O'Toole, April 4, 1953.

50. MW archives, file 9-2/5, letter to Br. John William Donoghue.

14. THE LIGHTER SIDE

1. IP archives, Finnigan-Burns file, High School, Indianapolis (Cathedral), Coll. No. 1970–7, Box 1, Folder 26, Br. Ephrem to Fr. Finnigan, April 1, 1927. Interestingly, Fr. James Burns unexpectedly succeeded Fr. Finningan as provincial one month later and finished out Fr. Finnigan's term. Fr. Finnigan had been made bishop of Helena MT and had left Notre Dame to assume his role in the diocese.

2. MW archives, file 9-1/8b, letter to Br. Reginald Justak, October 19, 1947.

3. MW archives, file 9-2/46, letter to Br. Francis Borgia Woehler, Sacred Heart Juniorate, Watertown WI, April 6, 1948.

4. MW archives, file 9-1/8b, letter to Br. Reginald Justak, April 7, 1948.

5. MW archives, file 9-3/20, letter to Fr. Kelley, June 18, 1948.

6. MW archives, file 9-2/20, letter to Br. Nicholas, December 21, 1949.

7. Ibid.

8. Ibid., February 9, 1950.

9. MW archives, file 9-3/37, letter to Br. John Baptist, November 18, 1950.

10. MW archives, file 9-1/8b, letter to Br. Reginald Justak, January 14, 1951.

11. MW archives, Lakewood drawer, Correspondence—Personal, 1945–1954, letter to Br. John William Donoghue, Lakewood OH, November 19, 1952.

12. MW archives, file 9-1/29, letter to Br. Laurian LaForest, August 22, 1953.

13. MW archives, file 9-1/22, letter to Br. Ambrose Nowak, April 8, 1954.

14. Ibid., incident from a much earlier time recounted by Br. Ephrem in a letter to Br. Ambrose Nowak, October 12, 1954.

15. MW archives, file 9-1/8, letter to Br. Hilarion Brezik, December 26, 1954.

16. MW archives, file 9-1/32, letter to Br. Alfonso, April 14, 1956.

15. AS SIMPLE AS ONE TO THREE

1. MW archives, file 18-3/21.

2. Data taken from material found in MW archives, file 18/3-12, Tentative Province Division U.S. Brothers 1950–1956; file 18/3-12, Establishment of the Three Provinces of Brothers, November 1, 1956; and file 18/3-14, Observations to Proposed Provinces Prior to 1956.

3. MW archives, files 18-3/12, 18-3/14.

4. MW archives, file 18-3/14.

5. MW archives, file 18-3/12.

6. Ibid.

7. MW archives, file 18-3/13.

8. EB archives, Br. Laurian LaForest, "A Brief History of the Brothers of Holy Cross, Eastern Province," p. 3.

9. MW archives, undated report by anonymous author, file 18-3/12.

10. MW archives, file 18-3/12.

16. BEYOND 1956—A RETROSPECTIVE

1. EB archives, 255, B1.1b.

2. EB archives, Br. Laurian LaForest, "A Brief History," p. 12.

3. EB archives, Box 8, Item 7.

4. EB archives, Box 7.

5. Br. Laurian, A Brief History, p. 5.

6. MW archives, O'Dwyer, deceased file (1).

7. Ibid.

8. Ibid.

9. Ibid.

10. Ibid.

11. Ibid., letter of Fr. Hesburgh to Br. Charles, September 26, 1978.

12. MW archives, O'Dywer, deceased file (1).

13. Cited in Br. Maurus O'Malley, "Portrait of a Builder," p. 16.

14. Ibid., p. 17.

15. MW archives, O'Dwyer, deceased file (1).

Index